Data Contracts
Developing Production-Grade Pipelines at Scale

Chad Sanderson, Mark Freeman, and B.E. Schmidt

O'REILLY®

Data Contracts

by Chad Sanderson, Mark Freeman, and B.E. Schmidt

Published by O'Reilly Media, Inc., 141 Stony Circle, Suite 195, Santa Rosa, CA 95401.

O'Reilly books may be purchased for educational, business, or sales promotional use. Online editions are also available for most titles (*http://oreilly.com*). For more information, contact our corporate/institutional sales department: 800-998-9938 or *corporate@oreilly.com*.

Acquisitions Editor: Aaron Black	**Interior Designer:** David Futato
Development Editor: Melissa Potter	**Cover Designer:** Karen Montgomery
Production Editor: Katherine Tozer	**Cover Illustrator:** Karen Montgomery
Copyeditor: J.M. Olejarz	**Interior Designer:** David Futato
Proofreader: Sonia Saruba	**Interior Illustrator:** Kate Dullea
Indexer: nSight, Inc.	

November 2025:   First Edition

Revision History for the First Edition
2025-11-04:   First Release

See *http://oreilly.com/catalog/errata.csp?isbn=9781098157630* for release details.

978-1-098-15763-0

[LSI]

Table of Contents

Part II. Implementation of the Data Contract Architecture

Part III.   Getting Leadership Buy-in for the Data Contract Architecture

Foreword

I still remember when Chad Sanderson first started writing about data contracts, back when the concept was brand new and the data world was still figuring out ideas like "shift left" and data quality.

Around that time, I was also friends with Mark Freeman, an up-and-coming, brilliant data engineer who was also mentoring part-time. When Chad and Mark became friends, I knew something great was going to happen.

When I first heard that Chad and Mark were writing a book on data contracts, I was both curious and a bit envious. Curious, because the topic sits right at the intersection of everything we wrestle with daily as data professionals, namely trust, communication, and accountability. Envious, because I knew they'd articulate what so many of us have felt for years but struggled to put into words: that the biggest challenges in data aren't purely technical, but mostly human.

For too long, we've treated data quality as a downstream problem to be fixed by "the data team." Data teams have built monitoring systems, observability dashboards, and clever duct tape patches that help us react more quickly when something breaks. Data debt keeps piling up. However, as this book demonstrates, none of that addresses the underlying issue. At its core, data quality relies on how effectively people communicate across teams. We nerds forget this. This communication depends on how clearly expectations are defined, how change is managed, and how responsibility is shared. In other words, it's about relationships.

What I love most about this book is that it bridges the gap between theory and practice. The authors don't just argue for a new paradigm; they show you how to build it, step by step, in the same pragmatic language that data engineers use every day. Through their real-world case studies and hands-on guidance, they make an idea that once felt abstract, "data contracts," feel both attainable and deeply necessary.

Reading this, you'll see why data contracts represent more than a technical framework. They're a cultural shift, a way for us to rebuild trust in our pipelines, our teams, and ultimately, our data itself. I'm proud of my friends for writing this book, and even more proud that it's now in your hands.

— Joe Reis
Data engineer, data contracts fan, author
October 2025

Preface

If you have picked up this book, it's likely that you've deeply felt the pain of managing data while lacking control of your data's ingestion and generation. Though at one point our industry centered around well-thought-out on-prem implementations with robust data models, the rise of cloud computing and the explosion of data products within organizations, via AI, have incentivized speed to market at the cost of turning the data layer into chaos. Many data teams within this situation find themselves constantly being reactive, repeatedly fixing the next data-related fire within the company.

At its core, we believe this challenge in our industry stems from the difficulty of change management between historically siloed teams of data producers and consumers. Specifically, there is a disconnect between upstream application code, which defines how data is captured within a software system, and the downstream data products that leverage this data. We argue that data contracts serve as a mechanism for aligning data producers and consumers through automation and defining expectations as code.

What Are Data Contracts?

Data contracts are an architecture pattern that enables an agreement between data producers and consumers that is established, updated, and enforced via an API. They're part of a larger movement called *shift left*, where you use automation to enable upstream software developers to account for required enforcement pertinent to their domain—this approach was first validated within DevOps and DevSecOps.

Data contracts consist of four key components:

- Data assets that need protection via change management
- A contract specification file that codifies expectations of data assets as version-controlled code

- Detection via an ability to extract, analyze, and take action on changes to metadata related to data assets under contract

- Prevention by automating data contract enforcement within the developer workflow, typically during CI/CD pipelines

We argue that the data industry is having its shift left moment, and that data contracts are critical for this change.

How to Use This Book

One of the main drivers of us writing this book stemmed from early pushback that the concept of data contracts was too theoretical. This viewpoint is understandable, as many implementations were not public at the time, yet we knew that data contracts were gaining adoption. We've interviewed hundreds of companies and supported numerous teams with their own data contract adoption.

Thus, our aim for this book is to serve as a practical guide for 1) framing the problems in our industry that create the need for data contracts, 2) implementing data contracts (including by using a public GitHub repository with a sandbox environment (*https://github.com/data-contract-book*)), and 3) building buy-in among executive leadership and scaling adoption organization-wide.

We've organized the chapters as three distinct parts, so that you can come back and reference this book along your data contract implementation journey.

Part I: Introduction to the Data Contract Architecture

Chapters 1 to 4 provide historical and market context as to why the challenges of managing data still persist today, while also providing a foundational understanding of data quality, data infrastructure, and the workflow of data contracts for enforcement of expectations. Here's the breakdown:

- Chapter 1: Why the Industry Now Needs Data Contracts
- Chapter 2: Data Quality Isn't About Pristine Data
- Chapter 3: The Challenges of Scaling Data Infrastructure
- Chapter 4: An Introduction to Data Contracts

Part II: Implementation of the Data Contract Architecture

Chapters 5 to 8 detail the technical components of the data contract architecture and provide a walkthrough for implementing data contracts via an accompanying GitHub repository (*https://github.com/data-contract-book*). In addition, we highlight multiple real-world case studies of data contracts in production, ranging from startups to enterprises. This part includes the following:

- Chapter 5: The Data Contract Components: Data Assets and Contract Definition
- Chapter 6: The Data Contract Components: Detection and Prevention
- Chapter 7: Implementing Data Contracts
- Chapter 8: Real-World Case Studies of Data Contracts in Production

Part III: Getting Leadership Buy-in for the Data Contract Architecture

Chapters 9 to 12 underscore how data contracts solve sociotechnical problems that stem from the difficulty of change management within organizations. Solving such problems requires having tremendous influence to align multiple teams that historically have been siloed from one another. These chapters are the result of the lessons we learned helping organizations adopt data contracts, grow their adoption, and measure their impact. Chapters in this part are as follows:

- Chapter 9: Shift Left: The Cultural Change Needed for Data Contracts
- Chapter 10: Change Management: The Crux of People, Process, and Technology
- Chapter 11: Creating Your First Wins with Data Contracts
- Chapter 12: Measuring the Impact of Data Contracts

Conventions Used in This Book

The following typographical conventions are used in this book:

Italic
> Indicates new terms, URLs, email addresses, filenames, and file extensions.

`Constant width`
> Used for program listings, as well as within paragraphs to refer to program elements such as variable or function names, databases, data types, environment variables, statements, and keywords.

`<Constant width in angled brackets>`
> Shows text that should be replaced with user-supplied values or by values determined by context.

> This element signifies a general note.

This element indicates a warning or caution.

Using Code Examples

Supplemental material (code examples, exercises, etc.) is available for download at *https://github.com/data-contract-book*. That includes a sandbox environment, which you can run locally or within the browser, that walks you through how to implement data contracts and the data contract violation workflow.

If you have a technical question or a problem using the code examples, please email *support@oreilly.com*.

In addition, the book has an accompanying website (*http://data-contract-book.com*) that provides additional articles from the authors, as well as corresponding videos to guide your reading throughout the chapters.

This book is here to help you get your job done. In general, if example code is offered with this book, you may use it in your programs and documentation. You do not need to contact us for permission unless you're reproducing a significant portion of the code. For example, writing a program that uses several chunks of code from this book does not require permission. Selling or distributing examples from O'Reilly books does require permission. Answering a question by citing this book and quoting example code does not require permission. Incorporating a significant amount of example code from this book into your product's documentation does require permission.

We appreciate, but generally do not require, attribution. An attribution usually includes the title, author, publisher, and ISBN. For example: "*Data Contracts* by Chad Sanderson, Mark Freeman, and B.E. Schmidt (O'Reilly). Copyright 2026 Manifest Data Labs, Inc., and Benjamin Schmidt, 978-1-098-15763-0."

If you feel your use of code examples falls outside fair use or the permission given above, feel free to contact us at *permissions@oreilly.com*.

O'Reilly Online Learning

O'REILLY®

For more than 40 years, *O'Reilly Media* has provided technology and business training, knowledge, and insight to help companies succeed.

Our unique network of experts and innovators share their knowledge and expertise through books, articles, and our online learning platform. O'Reilly's online learning platform gives you on-demand access to live training courses, in-depth learning paths, interactive coding environments, and a vast collection of text and video from O'Reilly and 200+ other publishers. For more information, visit *https://oreilly.com*.

How to Contact Us

Please address comments and questions concerning this book to the publisher:

O'Reilly Media, Inc.
141 Stony Circle, Suite 195
Santa Rosa, CA 95401
800-889-8969 (in the United States or Canada)
707-827-7019 (international or local)
707-829-0104 (fax)
support@oreilly.com
https://oreilly.com/about/contact.html

We have a web page for this book, where we list errata and any additional information. You can access this page at *https://oreil.ly/DataContracts*.

For news and information about our books and courses, visit *https://oreilly.com*.

Find us on LinkedIn: *https://linkedin.com/company/oreilly-media*.

Watch us on YouTube: *https://youtube.com/oreillymedia*.

Acknowledgments

While our names are on the cover, this book would not be possible without the support of our colleagues and community. We would like to thank our colleagues at Gable who have been with us throughout the whole process of diving deep into understanding data contracts and making implementations a reality: Aaron Phillips, Adrian Kreuziger, Adrian Kuepker, Alex DeMeo, Andrew Oliver, Chayanne Aranda, Daniel Dicker, Daniil Tiganov, Demetrios Brinkmann, Geoffrey Wukelic, Hana Um, James Frost, Jasmine Simpelo, Jazmia Henry, Jon Shaiman, Karan Banwasi, Kidanekal Hailu, Leonie Jean Parojinog, Maks Sydorenko, Max Zunti, Mike Perrone, Mindaugas Rukas, Nazar Repak, Rachel Rosefigura, Ran Liu, Ravi Vooda, Rebecca Swords, Russell Rivera, Sara La Torre, Suzanne Wen, Tom Erwin, Tommy Guy, and Yuhang An. We would also like to thank Gable's investors, who were some of the first people to not only believe but also back the idea of data contracts: Apoorva Pandhi (Zetta Venture Partners), Scott Sage (Crane Venture Partners), Nick Giometti (B Capital), and our other various angel and follow-on investors.

In addition, we would like to thank our amazing editors at O'Reilly Media with whom we worked directly throughout our time writing the book: Aaron Black, Melissa Potter (and Evie the cat), and Katherine Tozer. We thank our friends at Omniscient Digital, who also supported our book-writing efforts: Alex Birkett and Megan Otto.

Finally, we would like to thank the members of the Shift Left Data community who provided feedback on the book and many of the ideas around data contracts: Aishvarya Verma, Ali Khalid, Amanda Manley, Ashraf Mohammad, Ben Heron, Bill Coulam, Christian van Eeden, Cristóbal Carvajal Benavides, Eddy Zulkifly, Eric Callahan, Eric Dressler, Erik Dahlberg, Gene Vestel, Ignatius Soputro, Joel Anderson, Jon Yeo, Jonathan Bergenblom, Jose Santos, Kiran S., Lars Nielsen, Luka Stepinac, Mahesh Kumar, Matt Nylin, Michael Day, Mohamed Mansour, Nachiket Mehta, Narayanan V., Nidhi Vichare, Oliver Rudolph, Pawel Stradowski, Perry Philipp, Prashant Verma, Rafael Socorro, Raghu Mundru, Rubén Arévalo, Rukmani All, Saqib Ali, Satya Vandrangi, Sharon Sokoloff, Tanya Mackinnon, Thanh Khong, Tony McCray, Wei Hao, Yesh Kaushik, and Zakariah Siyaji.

Chad Sanderson

This book has been a journey. It wouldn't have been possible without the support of some incredible people both professionally and personally. My cofounders—Adrian, James, and Daniel—for building in the trenches when data contracts were nothing but an idea. The entire team at Gable for bringing data contracts to life. Our investors—Apoorva, Scott, Nick, and so many others—for believing in the power of data contracts when no one else saw the vision.

Personally, I'd like to dedicate this book to my amazing wife, Laila, who has been a perfect angel through it all, as well my sisters, Cat, Izzy, and Taylor, my wonderful mother, and my dad, who first encouraged me to start writing. Love you all.

Mark Freeman

I stand firmly in the belief that it takes a village to reach various milestones in your life. Thus, I would like to thank my amazing wife for her unending support, patience, and encouragement over the course of writing this book (as well as our beloved dog, Albus). I would also like to thank my mom, dad, Justin, Charene, and additional family and friends who have shared similar support.

Furthermore, I would like to thank all of my mentors who have invested their time in supporting my career in data. The list includes, though it's not exhaustive, the Stanford Prevention Research Center (Dr. Michael Baiocchi, Dr. Janine Bruce, my Community Health and Prevention Research advisers, my WELL for Life research colleagues), Lisa Tealer, Dr. Joe Orsini, Omead Arami, Dr. Stefanie Tignor, Joe Reis, and Vin Vashishta.

Finally, a huge thank-you to my coauthors, Chad and Ben, as it was truly a team effort and I've learned so much from both of you.

B. E. Schmidt

Thank you to my two coauthors for graciously inviting me along for this most excellent adventure, and to the smart and kind folks at Omniscient Digital for the opportunity to work with Chad and Mark in the first place.

Thanks more generally to good editors and good friends, and the vital give-and-take they enable with writers in their lives.

And, finally, thanks and all my love to my patient wife, our two children, and most of our three dogs.

(Ignore all the haters, Gus. You are a good boy.)

## PART I

Introduction to the Data Contract Architecture

## CHAPTER 1

Why the Industry Now Needs Data Contracts

Unfortunately, data quality and its foundations, such as data modeling, have been severely deprioritized with the rise of big data, cloud computing, and the Modern Data Stack. Though these advancements enabled the prolific use of data within organizations and codified professions such as data science and data engineering, data's ease of use also came with a lack of constraints, leading many organizations to take on substantial data debt. With pressure for data teams to move from doing R&D to actually driving revenue, as well as the shift from model-centric to data-centric AI, organizations are once again accepting the merits of data quality being a must-have instead of a nice-to-have. Driving this even further is the tight coupling between data produced or ingested upstream, typically by software engineers, and downstream data teams that have historically been siloed from each other.

While these all sound like explicitly technical problems, at their root they come down to issues with change management within complex systems. Thus, we believe that data contracts—agreements between data producers and consumers that are established, updated, and enforced via an API—are necessary for scaling and maintaining data-related change management within an organization. Before going in depth about what data contracts are and how to implement them, this chapter highlights why our industry has forgone data quality best practices, why we're prioritizing data quality again, and the unique conditions of the data industry post-2020 that warrant the need of data contracts to drive data quality.

Garbage-In, Garbage-Out Cycle

Talk to any data professional, and they will fervently state the mantra of "garbage-in, garbage-out" as the root cause of most data mishaps and/or limitations. Despite us all agreeing on what the problem is within the data lifecycle, we still struggle to produce and utilize quality data. In large part, this issue stems from the fact that most data teams don't control the source of the data they receive and that this data often has a separate primary purpose (e.g., CRUD events for a software application). While the data might be aligned for its primary purpose, it often requires data teams to massage it for its secondary purpose, such as being used for analytics or machine learning models. Under these constraints, even the most diligent data teams are limited to the quality of the data they receive.

Modern Data Management

From the outside looking in, data management seems relatively simple—data is collected from a source system, moved through a series of storage technologies to form what we call a pipeline, and ultimately ends up in a dashboard that is used to make a business decision or a data product, such as a user-facing machine learning model. This impression could be easily forgiven. The consumers of data, such as analysts, product managers, and business executives, rarely see the mass of infrastructure responsible for transporting data, cleaning and validating it, discovering it, transforming it, and creating data models. Like an indescribably large logistics operation, the cost and scale of the infrastructure required to control the flow of data to the right parts of the organization is virtually invisible, working silently in the background.

At least, that should be the case. With the rise of machine learning (ML) and artificial intelligence, data is increasingly taking the spotlight—yet organizations still struggle to extract value from it. Among companies that struggle, the pipelines used to manage their dataflows are breaking down, the data scientists hired to build ML models and deploy them can't move forward until data quality issues are resolved, and executives make million-dollar "data-driven" decisions that turn out to be wrong. As the world continues its transition to the cloud, our silent data infrastructure is not so silent anymore. Instead, it's groaning under the weight of scale, in terms of both volume and organizational complexity. Exactly at the point in time when data is poised to become the most operationally valuable it's ever been, our infrastructure is in the worst position to deliver on that goal.

The data team is in disarray. Data engineering organizations are flooded with tickets (*https://oreil.ly/V99Ie*) as pipelines actively fail across the company. Even worse, silent failures result in data changing in backward-incompatible ways with no one noticing, resulting in multimillion dollar outages (*https://oreil.ly/I8h5g*) and, worse, a loss of trust in the data from employees and customers alike. This doesn't even account for the high cost of rerunning pipelines and backfilling the data, or the labor costs for expensive technical staff. Data engineers are often caught in the crossfire of downstream teams that don't understand why their important data suddenly looks different today than it did yesterday, and data producers who ultimately are responsible for these changes have no insight into who is leveraging their data and for what reason. The business is often confused about the role data engineers are meant to play. Are they responsible for fixing any data quality issue, even those they didn't cause? Are they accountable for rapidly rising cloud compute spend in an analytical database? If not, who is? Again, the problems of change management and enforceable expectations show up among technical teams.

This state of the world is a result of *data debt*. Data debt refers to the outcome of incremental technology choices made to expedite the delivery of a data asset like a pipeline, a dashboard, or a training set for machine learning models. Data debt is the primary villain of this book. It inhibits our ability to deploy data assets when we need them, destroys trust in the data, and makes iterative data governance almost impossible. The pain of data engineering teams is caused by data debt—either managing it directly or managing its secondary impacts on other teams. Over the subsequent chapters you will learn what causes data debt, why it is more difficult to handle than software debt, and how it can ultimately cripple the data functions of an organization.

What Is Data Debt?

If you have worked in any form of engineering organization at scale, you have likely heard the words "tech debt" repeated dozens of times from concerned engineers who wipe sweat from their brow, discussing a future with 100x the request volume to their service.

Simply put, tech debt is a result of short-term decisions made to deploy code faster at the expense of long-term stability. Imagine a software development team working on a web application for an enterprise. They have a tight deadline to release a new feature, so they decide to take a shortcut and implement the feature quickly without refactoring some existing code. The quick implementation works, and they meet their deadline, but it's not a very efficient or maintainable solution.

Over time, the team starts encountering issues with the implementation. The new feature's code is tightly coupled with the existing codebase, which makes it challenging to add or modify other features without causing unintended side effects. Bugs related to the new feature keep popping up, and every time developers try to make changes, it takes longer than expected due to the lack of proper documentation. The cost incurred to fix the initial implementation with something more scalable is *debt*.

At some point, this debt has to be paid, or the engineering team will suffer, slowing development velocity to a crawl.

If you are reading this book, you have probably experienced similar situations of data debt, such as:

- A key metric relying on a misinterpreted data value, such as conflating `custom ers` and `active_customers` for calculating revenue
- Logs meant for testing being pushed to a database used for ML model training and thus creating incorrect predictions
- Hardcoded transformation logic (e.g., `CASE WHEN` in SQL) that initially solved a data quality issue but no longer aligns with the data's assumptions

Like tech debt, data debt is a result of short-term decisions made for the benefit of speed. However, data debt is *much worse* than software-oriented tech debt for a few reasons.

First, in software the typical trade-off that results in tech debt is speed in favor of maintainability and scale. In other words, how easy is it for engineers to work within this codebase, and how many customers/requests can we service? The operational function of the application is still being delivered, which is intended to solve a core customer problem. In data, however, the primary value proposition is trustworthiness. If the data that appears in our dashboards, machine learning models, and customer-facing applications can't be trusted, then it is worthless. The less trust we have in our data, the less valuable it will be. Data debt directly affects *trustworthiness*. By building data pipelines quickly without the core components of a high-quality infrastructure, such as data modeling, documentation, and semantic validity, we are directly impacting the core value of the data itself. As data debt piles up, the data becomes more untrustworthy over time.

Going back to our enterprise web application example, imagine that not only did the shortcut implementation make the code difficult to maintain, but every additional feature layered on top actually made the product increasingly difficult to use until there were no customers left. That would be the equivalent of data debt.

Second, data debt is far harder to unwind than technical debt. In most modern software engineering organizations, teams have moved or are currently moving to microservices. Microservices are an architectural pattern that changes how applications are structured by decomposing them into a collection of loosely connected services that communicate through lightweight protocols. A key objective of this approach is to enable the development and deployment of services by individual teams, free from dependencies on others. By minimizing interdependencies within the code base, developers can evolve their services with minimal constraints.

As a result, organizations scale easily, integrate with off-the-shelf tooling as and when it's needed, and organize their engineering teams around service ownership. The structure of microservices allows for tech debt to be self-contained and locally addressed. Tech debt that affects one service does not necessarily affect other services to the same degree, and this allows each team to manage their own backlog without having to consider scaling challenges for the entire monolith.

The data ecosystem is based on a set of entities that represent common business objects. These business objects correspond to important real-world or conceptual domains within a business. As an example, a freight technology company might leverage entities such as shipments, shippers, carriers, trucks, customers, invoices, contracts, accidents, and facilities. Entities are nouns—they are the building blocks of questions that can ultimately be answered by queries.

However, most useful data in an organization goes through a set of transformations built by data engineers, analysts, or analytics engineers. Transformations combine real-world domain-level data into logical aggregates called facts, which are leveraged in metrics used to judge the health of a business. A "customer churn" metric, for example, could combine data from the customer entity and the payment entity. "Completed shipments per facility" would combine data from the shipment entity and the facility entity. Because constructing metrics can be time-consuming, most queries written in a company depend on both core business objects and aggregations. That means data teams are tightly coupled to each other and to the artifacts they produce—a distinct difference from microservices.

This tight coupling means that data debt that builds up in a data environment can't be easily changed in isolation. Even a small adjustment to a single query can have huge downstream implications, radically altering reports and even customer-facing data initiatives. It's almost impossible to know where data is being used, how it's being used, and the level of importance the data asset in question has to the business. The more data debt piles up between producers and consumers, the more challenging it is to untangle the web of queries, filters, and poorly constructed data models, which limits visibility downstream.

To summarize: data debt is a vicious cycle. It depreciates trust in the data, which attacks the core value of what data is meant to provide. Because data teams are tightly coupled to each other, data debt cannot be easily fixed without causing ripple effects through the entire organization. As data debt grows, the lack of trustworthiness compounds exponentially, eventually infecting nearly every data domain and resulting in organizational chaos. The spiral of data debt is the biggest problem to solve in data, and it's not even close.

How Garbage-In, Garbage-Out Compounds

Data debt is prominent across virtually all industry verticals. At first glance, it appears as though managing debt is simply the default state of data teams: a fate which every data organization is doomed to follow even when data is taken seriously at a company. However, there is one company category that rarely experiences data debt, and for a reason you might not expect: startups.

When we say startup, we are referring to an early-stage company in the truest sense of the word: around 20 software engineers or less, a lean but functioning data team (though it may be only one or two data engineers and a few analysts), and a product that has either found product-market fit or is well on its way. We have spoken to dozens of companies that fit this profile in our research for this book, and nearly all of them report not only having minimal data debt but also having virtually no data quality issues at all. The reason this occurs is simple: the smaller the engineering organization, the easier it is to communicate when things change.

Most large companies have complex management hierarchies with many engineers and data teams that rarely interact with each other. For example, Convoy's engineering teams were split into "pods," a term taken from Spotify's product organizational model. Pods are small teams built around core customer problems or business domains that maximize for agility, independent decision making, and flexibility. One pod focused on supporting our operations team by building machine learning models to prioritize the most important issues filed by customers. Another worked on Convoy's core pricing model, while a third might focus on supplying real-time analytics on shipment ETA to our largest partners.

While each team rolled up to a larger organization, the roadmaps were primarily driven by product managers in individual contributor roles. The product managers rarely spoke to other pods unless they needed something from them directly. This resulted in some significant problems arising for data teams when new features were ultimately shipped. A software engineer managing a database may decide to change a column name, remove a column name, change the business logic, stop emitting an event, or any other number of issues that are problematic for downstream consumers. Data consumers would often be the first to notice the change because something looked off in their dashboard, or the machine learning began to produce incorrect predictions.

At smaller startups, data engineers and other data developers have not yet split into multiple siloed teams with differing strategies. Everyone is part of the same team, with the same strategy. Data developers are aware of virtually every change that is deployed, and can easily raise their hand in a meeting or pull the lead engineer aside to explain the problem. In a fast-moving organization with dozens, hundreds, or thousands of engineers this is no longer possible to accomplish. This breakdown in communication results in the most often referenced phenomena in data quality: garbage in, garbage out (GIGO).

GIGO occurs when data that does not meet a stakeholder's expectations enters a data pipeline. GIGO is problematic because it can *only be dealt with retrospectively*, meaning there will always be some cost to resolve the problem. In some cases, that cost could be severe, such as lost revenue from an executive making a poor decision off a low-quality dashboard whose results changed meaningfully (e.g., being incorrect but looking plausible) overnight, or a machine learning model making incorrect predictions about a customer's buying behavior. In other cases, the cost could be less severe—a dashboard shows wrong numbers that can be easily fixed before the next presentation with a simple CASE statement. However, even straightforward hotfixes underlie a more serious issue brewing beneath the surface: the growth of data debt.

As the amount of retroactive fixes grows over time, institutional knowledge hotspots begin to build up in critical areas within the data ecosystem. Massive SQL files, with line after line of business logic, are completely indecipherable to everyone besides the first data professionals in the company. It is not clear what the data means, who owns it, where it comes from, or why a data asset value is providing unexpected results without any explanation in the documentation.

Over time, data debt caused by GIGO starts to increase exponentially as the ratio of software to data developers grows larger. The number of deployments increases from a few per week to hundreds or thousands per day. Breaking changes become a common occurrence, while many data quality issues that impact the contents of the data itself (business logic) can go unnoticed for days, weeks, or even months. When the problem has grown enough that it is noticeably slowing down analysts and data scientists from doing their work, you have already reached a tipping point: without drastic action, there is essentially no way out. The data debt will continue to mount and create an increasingly broken user experience. Data engineers and data scientists will quit the business for a less painful working environment, and the business value of a company's most meaningful data asset will degrade.

While GIGO is the most prominent cause of data debt, challenges around data are also rooted in the common architectures we adopt.

The Death of Data Warehouses

Beginning in the late 1980s and extending through today, the data warehouse has remained a core component of nearly every data ecosystem, and the foundation of virtually all analytical environments.

The data warehouse is one of the most cited concepts in all of data, and is an essential concept to understand at a root level as we dive into the causes of the explosion of data debt. Bill Inmon is known as the "father of the data warehouse," and for good reason: he created the concept. In Inmon's own words: "A data warehouse is a subject-oriented, integrated, time-variant, and nonvolatile collection of data in support of management's decision-making process."

According to Inmon, the data warehouse is more than just a repository; it's a subject-oriented structure that aligns with the way an organization thinks about its data from a semantic perspective. This structure provides a holistic view of the business, allowing decision makers to gain a deep understanding of trends and patterns, ultimately leveraging data for visualizations, machine learning, and operational use cases.

In order for a data structure to be a warehouse, it must fulfill three core capabilities:

- The data warehouse is designed around the key subjects of an organization, such as customers, products, sales, and other domain-specific aspects.
- Data in a warehouse is sourced from a variety of upstream systems across the organization. The data is unified into a single common format, resolving inconsistencies and redundancies. This integration is what creates a *single source of truth* and allows data consumers to take reliable upstream dependencies without worrying about replication.
- Data in a warehouse is collected and stored over time, enabling historical analysis. This is essential for time-bounded analytics, such as understanding how many customers purchased a product over a 30-day window, or observing trends in the data that can be leveraged in machine learning or other forms of predictive analytics. Unlike operational databases that constantly change as new transactions occur, a data warehouse is nonvolatile. Once data is loaded into the warehouse, it remains unchanged, providing a stable environment for analysis.

The creation of a data warehouse usually begins with an entity relationship diagram (ERD), as illustrated in Figure 1-1. An ERD represents the logical and semantic structure of a business's core operations and is meant to provide a map that can be used to guide the development of the warehouse. An *entity* is a business subject that can be expressed in a tabular format, with each row corresponding to a unique subject unit. Each entity is paired with a set of dimensions that contain specific details about the entity in the form of columns. For example, a *customer* entity (not related to the following ERD example) might contain dimensions such as:

- Customer_id
- Birthday
- FirstName
- LastName

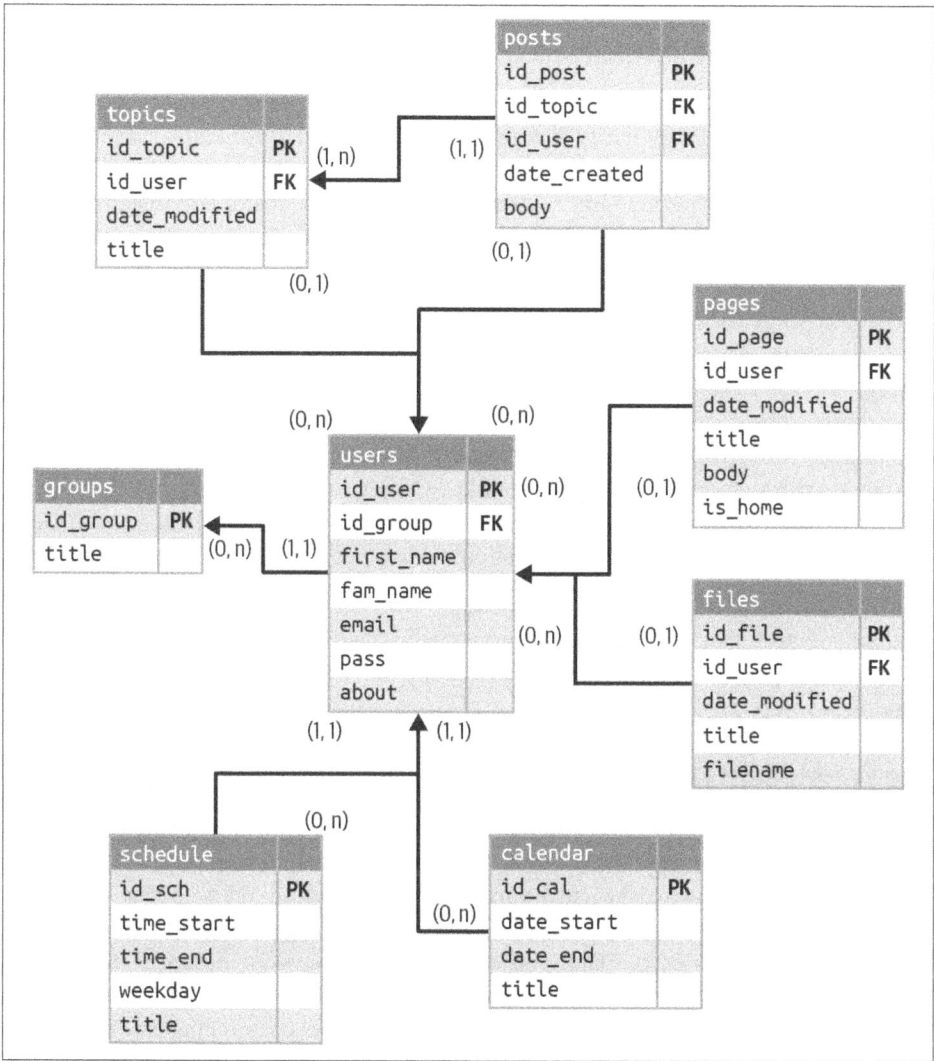

Figure 1-1. Example of an entity relationship diagram (https://oreil.ly/3-SAp)

Foreign keys are an important dimension in ERD design. They are unique identifiers that allow analysts to combine data across multiple entities in a single query. As an example, the customers_table might contain the following relevant foreign keys:

- Address_id
- Account_id

By leveraging foreign keys, it is possible for a data scientist to easily derive the number of logins per user, or count the number of website registrations by city or state.

The relationship that any entity has to another is called *cardinality*. Cardinality is what allows analysts to understand the nature of the relationship between entities, which is essential to performing trustworthy analytics at scale. For instance, if the customer entity has a 1-to-1 relationship with the accounts entity, then we would never expect to see more than one account tied to a user or an email address.

These mappings can't be done through intuition alone. At the highest abstraction level, domains of data and their purpose within a business are represented as a *conceptual data model*. Then the process of determining the ideal set of entities and their dimensions, foreign keys, and cardinality is called a *logical data model*, while the outcome of converting this semantic map into tables, columns, and indices that can be queried through analytical languages like SQL is the *physical data model*. All three practices taken together represent the process of data modeling. It is only through rigorous data modeling that a data warehouse can be created.

The original meaning of data warehousing and data modeling are both essential components to understand in order to grasp why the data ecosystem today is in such disrepair. But before we get to the modern era, let's understand a bit more about how warehouses were used in their heyday.

The Pre-Modern Era

Data warehouses predate the popularity of the cloud, the rise of software, and even the proliferation of the internet. During the pre-internet era, setting up a data warehouse involved a specialized implementation within an organization's internal network. Companies needed dedicated hardware and storage systems due to the substantial volumes of data that data warehouses were designed to handle. High-performance servers were deployed to host the data warehouse environment, wherein the data itself was managed using relational database management systems (RDBMSs) like Oracle, IBM DB2, or Microsoft SQL Server.

The use cases that drove the need for data warehouses were typically operational in nature. Retailers could examine customer buying behavior, seasonal foot traffic patterns, and buying preferences between franchises in order to create more robust inventory management. Manufacturers could identify bottlenecks in their supply chain and track production schedules. Ford famously saved over $1 billion by leveraging a data warehouse along with *Kaizen*-based process improvements to streamline operations with better data. Airlines leveraged data warehouses to plan their optimal flight routes, departure times, and crew staffing sizes.

However, creating data warehouses was not a cheap process. Specialists needed to be hired to design, construct, and manage the implementations of ERDs, data models, and ultimately the warehouse itself. Software engineering teams needed to work in tight coordination with data leadership in order to coordinate between transactional and analytical systems (i.e., OLTP and OLAP, respectively). Expensive ETL tools like Informatica, Microsoft SQL Server Integration Services (SSIS), Talend, and more required experts to implement and operate. All in all, the transition to a functioning warehouse could take several years, millions of dollars in technology spends, and dozens of specialized employees.

The supervisors of this process were called data architects, multidisciplinary engineers with computer science backgrounds and a specialty in data management. The architect would design the initial data model, build the implementation roadmap, buy and onboard the tooling, communicate the roadmap to stakeholders, and manage the governance and continuous improvement of the warehouse over time. They served as stewards of the data, ensuring their stakeholders and business users were always receiving timely, reliable data that was mapped to a clear business need. This was a best-in-class model for a while, but then things started to change….

Software Eats the World

In 2011 Marc Andreessen, venture capitalist and cofounder of the legendary venture capital firm Andreessen Horowitz, wrote an essay titled "Why Software Is Eating the World" in *The Wall Street Journal*. In the essay, Andreessen explained the rapid and transformative impact that software and technology were having across various industries:

> Software programming tools and Internet-based services make it easy to launch new global software-powered start-ups in many industries—without the need to invest in new infrastructure and train new employees. In 2000, when my partner Ben Horowitz was CEO of the first cloud computing company, Loudcloud, the cost of a customer running a basic Internet application was approximately $150,000 a month. Running that same application today in Amazon's cloud costs about $1,500 a month.

The 2000s marked a period of incredible change in the business sector. After the dot-com bubble of the late '90s, new global superpowers had emerged in the form of high-margin, low-cost internet startups with a mind-boggling pace of technology innovation and growth. Sergey Brin and Larry Page had grown Google from a search engine operating out of a Stanford dorm room in 1998, to a global advertising behemoth with a market capitalization of over $23 billion by the late 2000s. Amazon had all but replaced Walmart as the dominant force in commerce, Netflix had killed Blockbuster, and Facebook had grown from a college people-search app to a company with $153 million a year in revenue (*https://oreil.ly/xsCeu*) in only three years.

One of the most important internal changes caused by the rise of software companies was the propagation of Agile, a software development methodology popularized by the consultancy Thoughtworks. Up until this point, software releases were managed sequentially, and typically required teams to design, build, test, and deploy entire products end-to-end. The waterfall model was similar to movie releases, where the customer gets a complete product that has been thoroughly validated and has gone through rigorous quality assurance. However, Agile was different. Instead of waiting for an entire product to be ready to ship, companies managed releases far more iteratively, with a heavy focus on rapid change management and short customer feedback loops.

Companies like Google, Facebook, and Amazon were all early adopters of Agile. Mark Zuckerberg once famously said that Facebook's development philosophy was to "move fast and break things." This speed of deployment allowed Agile companies to rapidly pivot their companies closer and closer to what customers were most likely to pay for. The alignment of customer needs and product features achieved a sort of nirvana referred to by venture capitalists as product-market fit. What traditional businesses took decades to achieve, internet companies could achieve in only a few years.

With Agile as the focal point of software-oriented businesses, the common organizational structure began to evolve. The software engineer became the focus of the R&D department, which was renamed product for the sake of brevity and accuracy. New roles began to emerge that displayed support for the software engineer: UX designers who specialized in web and application design. Product managers who combined project management with product strategy and business positioning to help create the roadmap. Analysts and data scientists who collected logs emitted by applications to determine core business metrics like sign-up rates, churn, and product usage. Teams became smaller and more specialized, which allowed engineers to ship code even faster than before.

With the technical divide growing, traditional offline businesses were beginning to feel pressure from the market and investors to make the transition into becoming Agile tech companies. The speed at which software-based businesses were growing was alarming (see Figure 1-2), and there was a deep-seated concern that companies that adopted this mode of company building could emerge as competitors with too much of an advantage to catch. Around 2015, the term *digital transformation* began to explode in popularity as top management consultant firms such as McKinsey, Deloitte, and Accenture pushed offerings to modernize the technical infrastructure of many traditionally offline companies by building apps and websites and, most importantly for these authors, driving a move from on-premise databases to the cloud.

We originally wrote the first draft of this section in 2023 before the massive spike you see in the graph in 2025. While cloud played a major role in the sharp increase from 2013 to 2025, we would be remiss to not call out the heavy correlation of the near-vertical line and 2025's AI boom.

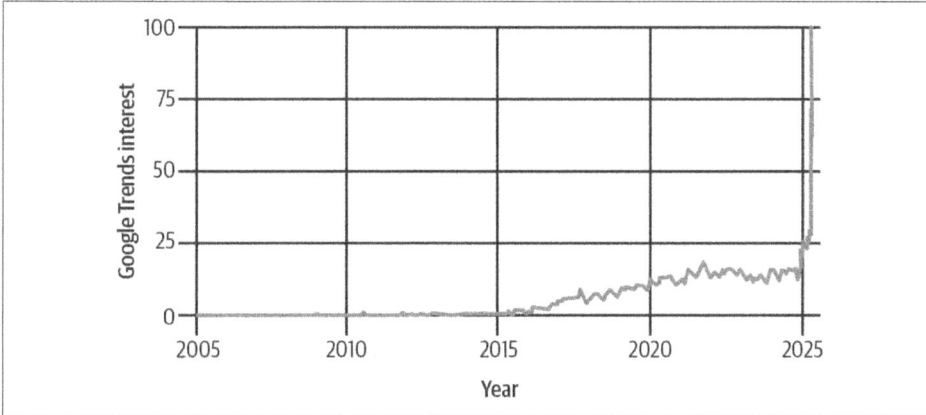

Figure 1-2. Google Trends for "digital transformation"

The biggest promise of the cloud was one of cost savings and speed. Companies like Amazon (AWS), Microsoft (Azure), and Google (GCP) removed the need to maintain physical servers, which eliminated millions of dollars in infrastructure and human capital overhead. This fit within the Agile paradigm, which allowed companies to move far faster by offloading complexity to a service provider. Companies like McDonald's, Coca-Cola, Unilever, General Electric, Capital One, Disney, and Delta Airlines are all examples of entrenched *Fortune* 500 businesses that made massive investments in order to digitally transform and ultimately transition to the cloud.

A Move Toward Microservices

In the early 2000s, by far the most common software architectural style was a monolith. A *monolithic architecture* is a traditional software design approach where an application is built as a single, interconnected unit, with tightly integrated components and a unified database. All modules are part of the same codebase, and the application is deployed as a whole. Due to the highly coupled nature of the codebase, it is challenging for developers to maintain monoliths as they become larger, leading to a significant slowdown in shipping velocity. In 2011 (the same year as Marc Andreessen's iconic *The Wall Street Journal* article) a new paradigm was introduced called microservices.

Microservices are an architectural pattern that changes how applications are structured by decomposing them into a collection of loosely connected services that communicate through lightweight protocols. A key objective of this approach is to enable the development and deployment of services by individual teams, free from dependencies on others. By minimizing interdependencies within the codebase, developers can evolve their services with minimal constraints. As a result, organizations scale easily, integrate with off-the-shelf tooling as needed, and organize their engineering teams around service ownership. The term *microservice* was first introduced by Thoughtworks consultants and gained prominence through Martin Fowler's influential blog (*https://martinfowler.com*).

Software companies excitedly transitioned to microservices in order to further decouple their infrastructure and increase development velocity. Companies like Amazon, Netflix, Twitter, and Uber were some of the fastest-growing businesses leveraging the architectural pattern, and the impact on scalability was immediate. As Werner Vogels, CTO of Amazon, put it:

> Our services are built around microservices. A microservices-based architecture, where software components are decoupled and independently deployable, is highly adaptable to changes, highly scalable, and fault-tolerant. It enables continuous deployment and frequent experimentation.

Data Architecture in Disrepair

In the exciting world of microservices, the cloud, and Agile, there was one silent victim—the data architect. Data architects' original role was to be stewards, designing ERDs, controlling access to the flow of data, designing OLTP and OLAP systems, and acting as a vendor for a centralized source of truth. In the new world of decentralization, siloed software engineering teams, and high development velocity, the data architect was perceived as (rightly) a barrier to speed.

The years it took to implement a functional data architecture were far too long. Spending months creating the perfect ERD was too slow. The data architects lost control—they could no longer dictate to software engineers how to design their databases, and without a central data model from which to operate, the upstream conceptual and physical data models fell out of sync. Data needed to move fast, and product teams didn't want a third party providing well-curated data on a silver platter. Product teams were more interested in building minimum viable products, experimenting, and iterating until they found the most useful answer. The data didn't need to be perfect, at least not to begin with.

In order to facilitate more rapid data access from day one, the *data lake* architecture pattern emerged. Data lakes are centralized repos where structured, unstructured, and semistructured data can be stored at any scale for little cost. Data lakes are typically hosted in hyperscalable storage systems, such as Amazon S3, Azure Data Lake Storage, and Google Cloud Storage. Analytics and data science teams can either extract data from the lake or analyze/query it directly with frameworks like Apache Spark or SaaS vendors such as Looker or Tableau.

While data lakes were effective in the short term, their lack of governance resulted in major data quality issues due to the absence of defined schemas required by OLAP databases. Ultimately, this prevented the data from being used in a more structured way by the broader organizations. Analytical databases emerged like Redshift, Big-Query, and Snowflake, where data teams could begin to do more complex analysis over longer periods of time. Data was pulled from source systems into the data lake and analytical environments so that data teams had access to fresh data when and where it was needed.

Businesses felt they needed *data engineers* who built pipelines that moved data between OLTP systems, data lakes, and analytical environments more than they needed data architects and their more rigid, inflexible design structures.

The elimination of the data architect resulted in the gradual phasing out of the data warehouse. In many businesses, data warehouses exist in name only. There is no cohesive data model, no clearly defined entities, and what does exist certainly does not act as a comprehensive integration layer that is a near 1:1 of business units reflected in code. Data engineers do their best these days to define common business units in their analytical environment, but they are pressured from both sides—data consumers and data producers. The former are always pushing to go faster and "break things," and the latter operate in silos, rarely aware of where the data they produce is going or how it is being used.

There is likely no way to put the genie back in the bottle. Agile, software-oriented businesses, and microservices add real value, and these methods allow businesses to experiment faster and more effectively than their slower counterparts. What is required now is an evolution of both the data architecture role and the data ware-house itself. We need a solution built for modern times, delivering incremental value where it matters.

Rise of the Modern Data Stack

The term Modern Data Stack (MDS) refers to a suite of tools that are designed for cloud-based data architectures. These tools have overlap with their offline counter-parts but in most cases are more componentized and expand to a variety of additional use cases. The MDS is a hugely important tool in a startup's toolkit. Because new companies are cloud-native—meaning they were designed in the cloud from day one—performing analytics or machine learning at any scale will require an eventual adoption of some or all of the MDS.

The Big Players

Snowflake is the largest and most popular of the MDS options, often cited as the company that first established the term. A cloud-oriented analytical database, Snowflake went public on September 16, 2020. During its initial public offering (IPO), the company was valued at around $33.3 billion, making it one of the largest software IPOs in history. Its cloud-native architecture, which separates compute from storage, offers significant scalability, eliminating hardware limitations and manual tuning. This ensures high performance even under heavy workloads, with dynamic resource allocation for each query. Snowflake could save compute-heavy companies hundreds of thousands to millions of dollars, providing a slew of integrations with other data products.

There are other popular alternatives to Snowflake, like Google BigQuery, Amazon Redshift, and Databricks. While Snowflake has effectively cornered the market on cloud-based SQL transformations, Databricks provides the most complete environment for unified analytics, built on top of the world's most popular open source large-scale distributed data-processing framework—Spark. With Databricks, data scientists and analysts can easily manage their Spark clusters, generate visualizations using languages like Python or Scale, train and deploy ML models, and much more. Snowflake and Databricks have entered a certifiable data arms race, their competition for supremacy ushering in a new wave of data-oriented startups over the course of the late 2010s and early 2020s.

The analytical databases however, are not alone in the modern data infrastructure. The Extract, Load, and Transform (ELT) tool Fivetran has gained widespread recognition as well. While not publicly traded at the time of writing this book, Fivetran's impact on the modern data landscape remains notable. Thanks to a collection of user-friendly interfaces and prebuilt connectors, Fivetran allows data engineers to connect directly to data sources and destinations, which organizations can quickly leverage to extract and load data from databases, applications, and APIs. Fivetran has become the de facto mechanism for early-stage companies to move data between sources and destinations.

Short for data build tool, dbt is one of the fastest-growing open source components for the Modern Data Stack. With modular transformations driven by Yet Another Markdown Language (YAML), dbt provides a CLI that allows data and analytics engineers to create transformations while leveraging a software engineering–oriented workflow. The hosted version of dbt extends the product from just transformations to a YAML-based metrics layer that allows data teams to define and store facts and their metadata that can be leveraged in experimentation and analysis downstream.

This is only a sample of the tooling within the MDS. Dozens of companies and categories have emerged over the past decade, ranging from orchestrations systems such as Airflow and Dagster, to data observability tooling such as Monte Carlo and Anomalo, to cloud-native data catalogs like Atlan and Select Star, to metrics repositories, feature stores, and experimentation platforms, and on and on.

The reason the velocity of data tooling has accelerated in recent years is primarily the simplicity of integrations most tools have with the most dominant analytical databases in the space: Snowflake, BigQuery, Redshift, and Databricks. These tools all provide developer-friendly APIs and expose well-structured metadata that can be accessed and leveraged to perform analyses, write transformations, or otherwise be queried.

Rapid Growth

The Modern Data Stack grew rapidly in the years between 2012 and 2022. This was the time teams began transitioning from on-prem-only applications to the cloud, and it was sensible for their data environments to follow shortly after. After adopting the core tooling like S3 for data lakes and an analytical data environment such as Snowflake or Redshift, businesses realized they lacked core functionality in data movement, data transformation, data governance, and data quality. Companies needed to replicate their old workflows in a new environment, which led data teams to rapidly acquire a suite of tools in order to make all the pieces work smoothly.

Other internal factors contributed to the acquisition of new tools as well. IT teams which were most commonly responsible for procurement began to become supplanted with the rise of product-led growth. The main mode of selling software for the previous decade was top-down sales. Salespeople would get into rooms with important business executives, walk through a lengthy slide deck that laid out the value proposition of their platform and pricing, and then work on a proof of concept over a period of many months in order to prove the value of the software. This process was slow, required significant signoff from multiple stakeholders across the organization, and ultimately led to much more expensive day-one platform fees. Product-led growth changed that.

Product-led growth is a sales process that allows the product to do the talking. SaaS vendors would make their products free to try or low-cost enough that teams could independently manage a signoff without looping in an IT team. This allowed them to get hands-on with the product, integrate it with their day-to-day workflows, and see if the tool solved the problems they had without a big initial investment. Furthermore, these solutions' pay-per-use model and easy cloud setup meant that contract sizes scaled with the business—a boon for the vendors as well.

Data infrastructure companies were often funded by venture capital firms due to the high up-front R&D required. In the early days of a startup, venture capitalists tend to put more weight on customer growth over revenue. This is because high usage implies product-market fit, and getting a great set of "logos" (customers) implies that if advanced, well-known businesses were willing to take a risk on an early, unknown product then many other companies would be willing to do the same. By making it far easier for individual teams to use the tool for free or cheaply, vendors could radically increase the number of early adopters and take credit for onboarding well-known businesses.

In addition to changing procurement methodologies and sales processes, the resource allocation for data organizations grew substantially over the last decade (*https:// oreil.ly/BrB4y*). As data science evolved from a fledgling discipline into a multibillion-dollar-per-year category, businesses began to invest more than ever into headcount for scientists, researchers, data engineers, analytics engineers, analysts, managers, and chief data officers (CDOs).

Finally, early- and growth-stage data companies were suddenly venture capital darlings after the massive Snowflake initial public offering. Data went from an interesting nice-to-have to an indisputable long-term opportunity. Thanks to the low interest rates and a massive economic boost to tech companies during COVID, billions of dollars were poured into data startups, resulting in an explosion of vendors across all angles of the stack. Data technology was so in demand that it wasn't unheard of to invest in multiple companies that might be in competition with one another!

Problems in Paradise

Despite all the excitement for the Modern Data Stack, there were noticeable cracks that began to emerge over time. Teams that were beginning to reach scale were complaining: the amount of tech debt was growing rapidly, pipelines were breaking, data teams weren't able to find the data they needed, and analysts were spending the majority of their time searching for and validating data instead of putting it to good use on ROI-generating data products. So what happened?

First, software engineering teams were no longer engaging in proper business-wide data modeling or entity relationship design development. This meant that there was no single source of truth for the business. Data was replicated across the cloud in many different microservices. Without data architects serving as the stewards of the data, there was nothing to prevent unique implementations of the same concept repeated dozens of times, with data perhaps providing varying results!

Second, data producers had no relationship to data consumers. Because it was easier and faster to dump data into a data lake than to build explicit interfaces for specific consumers and use cases, software engineers threw their data over the fence to data engineers whose job it was to rapidly construct pipelines with tools like Airflow, dbt, and Fivetran. While these tools completed the job quickly, they also created significant distance between the production and analytical environments. Making a change in a production database had no guardrails. There was no information provided about who was using that data (if it was being used at all), where the data was flowing, why it was important, and what expectations of the data were essential to its function.

Third, data consumers began to lose trust in the data. When a data asset changed upstream, downstream consumers were forced to bear the cost of that change on their own. Generally that meant adding a filter on top of their existing SQL query in order to account for the issue.

For example, if an analyst wrote a query intended to answer the question "How many active customers does the company have this month?" the definition of *active* may be defined from the visits table, which records information every time a user opens the application. Additionally, the BI team may decide that a single visit is not enough to justify the intention behind the word "active." They may be checking notifications but not using the platform, which results in the minimum visit count being set to 3, as this code example shows:

```
WITH visit_counts AS (
    SELECT
        customer_id,
        COUNT(*) AS visit_count
    FROM
        visits
    WHERE
        DATE_FORMAT(visit_date, '%Y-%m') =
        DATE_FORMAT(CURDATE(), '%Y-%m')
    GROUP BY
        customer_id
)

SELECT
    COUNT(DISTINCT customers.customer_id) AS active_customers
FROM
    customers
LEFT JOIN
    visit_counts ON
    visit_counts.customer_id = customers.customer_id
WHERE
    COALESCE(visit_counts.visit_count, 0) >= 3;
```

However, over time, changes upstream and downstream impact the evolution of this query in subtle ways. Say the software engineering team decides to distinguish between visits and impressions. An impression is *any* application open to any new or previous screen, whereas a visit is defined as a period of activity lasting for more than 10 seconds. Before, all visits were counted toward the active customer count. Now, some percentage of those visits would be logged as impressions. To account for this, the analyst creates a CASE WHEN statement that defines the new impression logic, then sums the total number of impressions and visits to effectively get the same answer as their previous query using the updated data:

```
WITH impressions_counts AS (
    SELECT
        customer_id,
        SUM(CASE WHEN duration_seconds >= 10 THEN 1 ELSE 0 END)
            AS visit_count,
        SUM(CASE WHEN duration_seconds < 10 THEN 1 ELSE 0 END)
            AS impression_count
    FROM
        impressions
    WHERE
        DATE_FORMAT(impression_date, '%Y-%m') =
        DATE_FORMAT(CURDATE(), '%Y-%m')
    GROUP BY
        customer_id
    HAVING
        (visit_count + impression_count) >= 3
)

SELECT
    COUNT(DISTINCT customers.customer_id) AS active_customers
FROM
    customers
LEFT JOIN
    impressions_counts ON
    impressions_counts.customer_id = customers.customer_id
WHERE
    COALESCE(impressions_counts.visit_count, 0) >= 3;
```

The more the upstream changes, the longer these queries become. All the context about why CASE statements or WHERE clauses exist is lost. When new data developers join the company and go looking for existing definitions of common business concepts, they are often shocked at the complexity of the queries being written and cannot interpret the layers of tech debt that have crusted over in the analytical environment. Since these queries are not easily parsed or understood, data teams review directly with software engineers to understand what data coming from source systems meant, why it was designed a particular way, and how to JOIN it with other core entities. Teams would then "re-create the wheel" for their own purposes, leading to duplication and growing complexity, beginning the cycle anew.

Fourth, the costs of data tools began to spiral out of control. Many of the MDS vendors have usage-based pricing. Essentially that means "pay for what you use." Usage-based pricing is a great model when you can reasonably control and scale your usage of a product over time. However, the model becomes venomous when growth of a service snowballs outside the control of its primary managers. As queries in the analytical environment became increasingly complex, the cloud bill grew exponentially to match. The increased data volumes resulted in higher bills from all types of MDS tools—which were now individually gouging on usage-based rates that continued to skyrocket. In addition, many MDS tools that relied on venture capital had to rapidly raise prices as the post-pandemic funding frenzy dried up.

Almost overnight, the data team was larger than it had ever been, more expensive than it had ever been, more complicated than it had ever been, and delivering less business value than it ever had.

Data-Centric AI and the Rise of Shift Left Data Practices

While there are earlier papers on arXiv mentioning "data-centric AI," the term's widespread acceptance was pushed by Dr. Andrew Ng and DeepLearningAI's 2021 campaign (*https://oreil.ly/FDyX5*) that advocated for the approach. In short, data-centric AI is the process of increasing machine learning model performance via systematically improving the quality of training data either in the collection or in the preprocessing phase. This is in comparison to model-centric AI, which relies on further tuning an ML model, increasing the cloud computing power, or utilizing an updated model to increase performance. Through the work of his AI lab and conversations with his industry peers, Ng noticed a pattern where data-centric approaches vastly outperformed model-centric approaches. We highly encourage you to watch his referenced webinar, linked in the further resources section, but two key examples from him best encapsulate why the data industry is shifting toward a data-centric AI approach.

First, Ng highlights how underlying data impacts the fitting of ML models for the following conditions, represented in Figure 1-3:

Small data, high noise
> Results in poor-performing models, as numerous best-fit lines could be applied to the data and thus diminish the ability for the model to predict values. This often requires ML practitioners to go back and collect more data or remediate the data collection process to have more-consistent data.

Big data, high noise
> Results in an ML model being able to find the general pattern, where practitioners use a model-centric approach that can realize gains by tuning the ML model to account for the noise. Though ML practitioners can reach an acceptable prediction level via model-centric approaches, Ng argues that for many use cases there is better ROI in taking the time to understand why training data is so noisy.

Small data, small noise
> Represents the data-centric approach where high-quality and curated data results in ML models being able to easily find patterns for prediction. Such methods require an iterative approach to improving the systems in which data is collected, labeled, and preprocessed before model training.

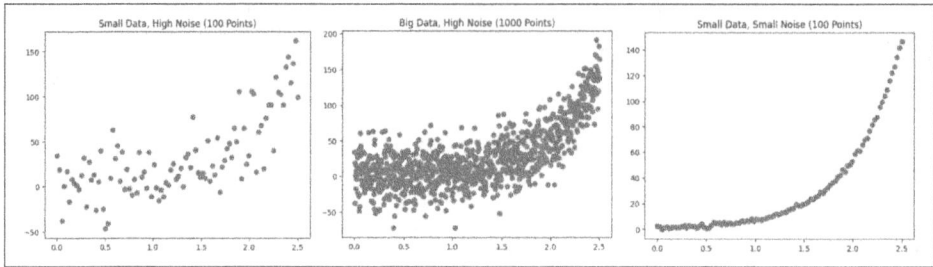

Figure 1-3. The impact of the varying levels of data volume and noise on predictability

We encourage you to try out this accompanying Python code to get an intuitive understanding of how noise (i.e., data quality issues) can impact an ML model's ability to identify patterns:

```python
import numpy as np
import matplotlib.pyplot as plt

def generate_exponential_data(min_X, max_x, num_points, noise):
    x_data = np.linspace(min_X, max_x, num_points)
    y_data = np.exp(x_data * 2)
    y_noise = np.random.normal(loc=0.0, scale=noise, size=x_data.shape)
    y_data_with_noise = y_data + y_noise

    return x_data, y_data_with_noise

def plot_curved_line_example(min_X, max_x, num_points, noise, plot_title):
    np.random.seed(10)
    x_data, y_data = generate_exponential_data(min_X, max_x, num_points, noise)
    plt.scatter(x_data, y_data)
    plt.title(plot_title)
    plt.show()

example_params = {
    'small_data_high_noise': {
        'num_points':100,
        'noise':25.0,
        'plot_title': 'Small Data, High Noise (100 Points)'
    },
    'big_data_high_noise': {
        'num_points':1000,
        'noise':25.0,
        'plot_title': 'Big Data, High Noise (1000 Points)'
    },
    'small_data_low_noise': {
        'num_points':100,
        'noise':1.0,
        'plot_title': 'Small Data, Small Noise (100 Points)'
    },
    # 'UPDATE_THIS_EXAMPLE': {
    #     'num_points':1,
```

```
    #       'noise':1.0,
    #       'plot_title': 'Your Example'
    # }
}

for persona in example_params.keys():
    persona_dict = example_params[persona]
    plot_curved_line_example(
        min_X=0,
        max_x=2.5,
        num_points=persona_dict['num_points'],
        noise=persona_dict['noise'],
        plot_title=persona_dict['plot_title']
    )
```

Second, Ng provided the analogy of comparing an ML engineer to a chef. The colloquial understanding among ML practitioners is that 80% of your time is spent preparing and cleaning data, while the remaining 20% is spent actually training your ML model. This is similar to a chef, who spends 80% of their time sourcing and preparing ingredients for mise en place, while the remaining 20% is spent actually cooking the food. Though a chef can improve the food substantially by improving cooking techniques, the chef can also improve the food by sourcing better ingredients—which is arguably easier than mastering cooking techniques. The same holds true for ML practitioners, as they can improve their models via tuning (model-centric AI approach) or improving the underlying data during the collection, labeling, and preprocessing stages (data-centric AI approach). Furthermore, Ng found that for the same amount of effort, teams that leveraged data-centric approaches had better-performing models than teams using model-centric approaches.

Diminishing ROI of Improving ML Models

Incrementally improving machine learning models follows the Pareto Principle, shown in Figure 1-4, where 80% of the gains are achieved through 20% of the effort. In a model-centric approach, we reach a point where every improvement grows exponentially harder, such as going from 93% to 95% accuracy.

Furthermore, taking a model-centric approach to AI often requires a substantial amount of data, hence why big tech SaaS companies have been the first successful adopters of machine learning at scale, given their access to massive amounts of weblogs. Ng argues that as AI branches outside of these big tech domains, into areas such as health care and manufacturing, ML practitioners are going to need to adopt methods that account for having access to substantially less data. For example, on average a single person generates around 80 MB of health care imaging and medical record data a year (*https://oreil.ly/qbAcH*), as compared to the around 50 GB of data a single user generates a month on average via their browsing activity (*https://oreil.ly/lkvxj*).

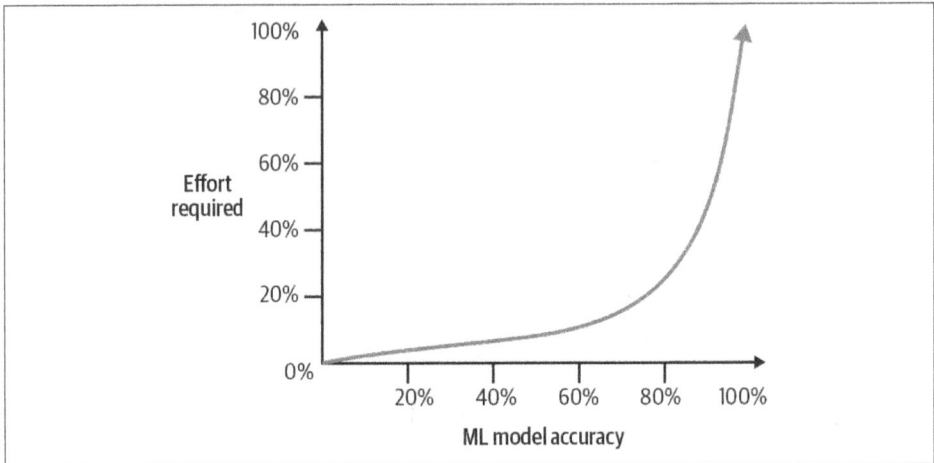

Figure 1-4. The Pareto Principle when tuning ML models

In addition, Ng argues that even with big data use cases, ML practitioners still need to wrestle with the challenges of small data. Specifically, after ML models are tuned on large datasets, gains come from accounting for the long tail of use cases, which is ultimately a small-data problem as well. Taking a data-centric AI approach to these long-tail problems within big data can provide more gains with substantially less effort than optimizing the ML model.

Commoditization of Data Science Workflows

While machine learning and AI have been developed for decades, it wasn't until around 2010 that they gained widespread utilization within industry. This is apparent in the number of ML vendors growing from around five companies in 2014 (*https://oreil.ly/VQt0k*) to over two hundred in 2024 (*https://oreil.ly/Ono3v*), as illustrated in Matt Turck's yearly data vendor landscapes.

Furthermore, as the data industry matured, less emphasis has been placed on developing ML models, and instead the focus has turned to putting ML models into production. Early data science teams could get by with a few STEM PhDs toiling away in Jupyter notebooks for R&D purposes, or sticking to traditional statistical learning methods such as regression or random forest algorithms. Fast-forward to today, and data scientists have a plethora of advanced models they can quickly download from GitHub, or they can leverage automated ML via dedicated vendors or products within their cloud provider. Also, there are entire open source ecosystems, such as scikit-learn and TensorFlow, that have made developing ML models easier than ever before. It's simply not enough for a data team to create ML models to drive value within an organization—the value is generated in their ability to reliably deploy machine learning models in production.

Finally, the rise of generative AI has further entrenched this trend of the commoditization of data science workflows. In a matter of an API call that costs fractions of a cent, anyone can leverage the most powerful deep learning models to ever exist. For context, in 2020 Mark AI put a natural language processing (NLP) model into production for an HR tech startup looking to summarize free text responses from employee surveys, utilizing the spaCy library. At the time, spaCy abstracted away the need to fine-tune an NLP model, hence why it was chosen for a quick feature development cycle. If tasked with the same project today, it would be sound to strongly consider using a large language model (LLM) for the same task, as no amount of tuning spaCy NLP models could compete with the power of LLMs. In other words, the process of developing and deploying an NLP model has been commoditized to a simple API call to OpenAI.

Data's Rise Over ML in Creating a Competitive Advantage

In parallel with the commoditization of data science workflows, the competitive advantage of ML models themselves is decreasing. The amount of specialized knowledge, resources, and effort necessary to train and deploy an ML model in production is significantly lower than what it was even five years ago. This lower barrier to entry means that the realized gains of machine learning are no longer relegated to big tech and advanced startups. Especially among traditional businesses outside of tech, the implementation of advanced ML models is not only possible but expected. Thus, the competitive advantage of ML models themselves has diminished.

The best representation of this reduced competitive advantage is once again the emergence of generative AI. The development of ChatGPT, and other generative AI models from big tech, was the culmination of decades of research, model training on expensive GPUs, and an unfathomable amount of web-based data. The requirements to develop these models were cost-prohibitive for most companies, and thus the models themselves maintained a competitive advantage up until recently. At the time of writing, open source and academic communities have been able to replicate and release similarly powerful generative AI models (*https://oreil.ly/DoEtu*) in a matter of months within the releases of their closed source counterparts.

Therefore, the ways in which companies can maintain their competitive advantage, in a market where machine learning is heavily commoditized, is through their underlying data itself. Using a data-centric AI approach, taking the time to generate and/or curate high-quality data assets unique to a business will extract the most value out of these powerful but commoditized AI models. Furthermore, the data generated or processed by businesses is unique to the businesses themselves and is hard, if not impossible, to replicate. The winners of this new shift in our data industry won't be the ones who can implement AI technology, but rather the ones who can control the quality of the data they leverage with AI.

The Rise of Shift Left Data Practices

To us, these trends—the validation of machine learning in driving outsize gains with data, these advanced models becoming commoditized so any company can leverage them (via generative AI and LLMs), and the increasing importance of the data itself in extracting value from these machine learning and AI systems—represent a key inflection point in the data industry. Specifically, they represent the derivatives of data (e.g., models, insights, analytics) moving further upstream into the application layer and requiring the same rigor as products with respect to testing and maintenance. While these application software systems already use data extensively for operations (e.g., CRUD events, APIs), what's different today is that applications now surface data derivatives rather than just capture the raw data for logs and managing statefulness. This also means that upstream software engineers have a higher incentive for their involvement in data practices, as well as exposure to their pitfalls.

What we are describing is a rising movement called *shift left data*, where the management of data is moved further upstream to the domains where it is generated and/or sourced. We argue that the data contracts architecture is a mechanism in which to enable shift left practices in data. Furthermore, there is precedent in other technical domains, such as DevOps and security, which have faced similar challenges that warranted upstream software engineer teams taking further ownership of ops and security best practices within their workflow. Data is following a similar pattern today. We'll discuss this more in Chapter 9, which is devoted to detailing the implications of shift left data and what it means to have more involvement from upstream software engineers in the data lifecycle.

Conclusion

In this chapter we provided an overview of historical and market context as to why data quality has been deprioritized in the data industry for the past two decades. In addition, we highlighted how data quality is again being deemed integral as we evolve from the Modern Data Stack era and shift toward data-centric AI. In summary, this chapter covered:

- What data debt is and how it applies to garbage-in, garbage-out
- The death of the data warehouse and the subsequent rise of the Modern Data Stack
- The shift from model-centric to data-centric AI

While this chapter provides historical and market context to the challenges we face in data today, it also highlights that we strongly believe there is a pervasive change management problem. There will always be a "new era" of technology where our previously established "best practices" are seen as blockers or antiquated. Likewise, new market contexts may again give rise to the need for previously forgone "best practices."

In Chapter 2, we will define data quality and how it fits within the current state of the data industry, as well as highlight how current data architecture best practices create an environment that leads to data quality issues.

## CHAPTER 2

Data Quality Isn't About Pristine Data

One of the early mistakes Mark made in his data career was trying to internally sell the concept of data quality on the merits of what pristine data could provide the organization. The harsh reality is that, beyond data practitioners, very few people in the business care about data—they instead care what they can do with data. Coupled with data being an abstract concept (especially among nontechnical stakeholders), screaming into the corporate void about data quality won't get one far. It's challenging to connect quality to business value, and thus it is relegated to being a nice-to-have investment. This dynamic changed dramatically for Mark when he stopped trying to internally sell pristine data and instead focused on the risk to important business workflows (often revenue-driving ones) due to poor quality. In this chapter, we expand on this lesson by defining data quality, highlighting how our current architecture best practices create an environment for data quality issues, and what the cost of poor data quality is for the business.

Defining Data Quality

"What is data quality?" is a simple question that's deceptively hard to answer, given the vast reach of the concept, but its definition is core to why data contracts are needed. The first historically recorded form of data (*https://oreil.ly/uTm8c*) goes all the way back to 19,000 BCE, with data quality being an important factor for every century thereafter in areas ranging from agriculture, manufacturing, to computer systems. For this book, our emphasis is on data quality in relation to database systems. Around 1970 is this book's cutoff, given that's when Edgar F. Codd's seminal paper "A Relational Model of Data for Large Shared Data Banks" (*https://oreil.ly/XrH3Q*) kicked off the discipline of relational databases. Figure 2-1 briefly illustrates this timeline and this book's emphasis.

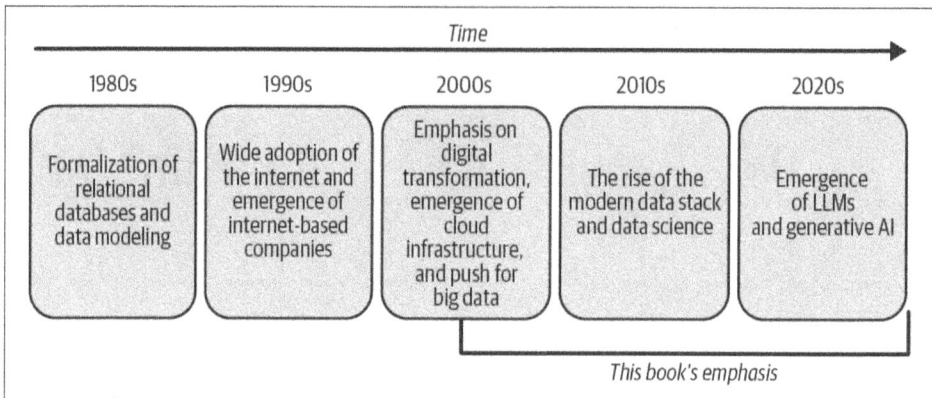

Figure 2-1. Timeline of data industry phases and where this book focuses

During this time, the field of data quality management emerged with prominent voices, such as Richard Y. Wang from MIT's Total Data Quality Management program, formalizing the discipline. In Dr. Wang's and Dr. Diane Strong's most cited research article (*https://oreil.ly/_TUvh*), they define data quality in 1996 as "data that are fit for use by data consumers" among the following four dimensions: 1) conformity to the true values the data represents, 2) pertinence to the data user's task, 3) clarity in the presentation of the data, and 4) availability of the data.

> References to these early works defining data quality can be found in the Appendix.

Throughout the academic works of Wang and colleagues, there is a massive emphasis on the ways in which the field is interdisciplinary (*https://oreil.ly/T3V69*) and is greatly impacted by "new challenges that arise from ever-changing business environments...increasing varieties of data forms/media, and Internet technologies that fundamentally impact how information is generated, stored, manipulated, and consumed." Thus, this is where this book's definition of data quality diverges from the 1996 definition. Specifically, our viewpoint of data quality is greatly shaped by the rise of cloud infrastructure, big data for data science workflows, and the emergence of the Modern Data Stack between the 2010s and the present day.

We define data quality as "an organization's ability to understand the *degree of correctness* of its data assets, and the trade-offs of operationalizing such data at various degrees of correctness throughout the data lifecycle, as it pertains to being fit for use by the data consumer."

We especially want to emphasize the phrase "trade-offs of operationalizing such data at various degrees of correctness," as it's key to a major shift in the data industry. Specifically, NoSQL was coined in 1998 by Carlo Strozzi and popularized again in 2009 by Johan Oskarsson (*https://oreil.ly/Ibpg8*). Since then, there has been a proliferation of ways that data is stored beyond a relational database, leading to increased complexities and trade-offs for data infrastructure. As noted earlier, one popular trade-off was the rise of the Modern Data Stack that opted for ELT and data lakes. Among this use case, many data teams have forgone the merits of proper data modeling to instead have vast amounts of data that can be quickly iterated on for data science workflows. Though it would be easier to have a standard way of approaching data quality for all data use cases, we must remember that data quality is as much of a people and process problem as a technical problem. Being cognizant of the trade-offs being made by data teams, for better or worse, is key to changing the behavior of individuals operating within the data lifecycle.

In addition, we also want to emphasize the phrase "ability to understand the degree of correctness" within our definition. A common pitfall is the belief that *perfect data* is required for data quality, resulting in unrealistic expectations among stakeholders. The unfortunate reality is that data is in a constant state of decay and requires consistent monitoring and iteration that will never be complete.

For example, take the health vitals measurement data that's collected when you visit a primary care doctor (weight, blood pressure, etc.). Within hours your body's vitals have changed, which is not captured in the data used by every data processor in health care—yet this is some of the most valuable data available. (Hackers on the black market value this data at $250 per record, as compared to payment data that's next highest in value at around $5 (*https://oreil.ly/1dXzz*).)

By shifting the language from a "desired state of correctness" for data assets to instead a "desired process for understanding correctness" among data assets, data teams account for the ever-shifting nature of data and thus its quality. In conjunction, with the ability to understand the *degree* of correctness among a data asset, a data team can make properly informed *trade-offs* that balance the needs of the business and the effort of maintaining a level of data quality that supports their respective data consumers. But what's the cost of poor data quality when an organization gets this trade-off wrong?

OLTP Versus OLAP and Its Implications for Data Quality

One of the most common data architecture patterns in our industry is the use of OLTP (online transaction processing) and OLAP (online analytical processing) databases as a way to separate the workloads of data access for transactions and analytics. Surprisingly, many professionals involved in the data lifecycle deeply understand their specific areas of the data architecture but lack knowledge about other parts of the system. Specifically, those who work in OLTP databases often primarily work only in such systems, and the same is true among those who work in OLAP databases. With the exception of roles such as data engineers or architects, few individuals within the data lifecycle of a respective company have an all-encompassing view of the entire data system through their work. We argue that the silos of OLTP and OLAP systems are the catalyst for many data quality issues among organizations, while also maintaining the notion that this data architecture design is valuable and has withstood the test of time.

A Brief Summary of OLTP and OLAP

As the names imply, OLTP databases are optimized for quick data transactions, which maintains the current state of a software application, while OLAP databases are optimized for scanning and calculating statistics on large swaths of data for analytics workflows. In the early stages of a company's data infrastructure, OLTP databases alone often meet the needs of the business, as there isn't enough data even to consider analytics. Furthermore, while the data is small, using SQL on top of these databases to answer simple questions about the logs doesn't cause enough strain to warrant concerns. This changes when the business begins to ask historical questions about the transaction data stored within the OLTP database, as analytical queries often require vast amounts of scanning that can bring the production database to a grinding halt. Thus, we have the need to replicate the transactional data into another database to prevent the production database from going down. Figure 2-2 illustrates at a high level the dataflow of a data-driven organization utilizing OLTP and OLAP databases.

A company's move from using only an OLTP database to the addition of an OLAP database marks an important inflection point in its data maturity. This replication of data from OLTP to OLAP provides substantial gains in understanding organizational data with the trade-off of increased complexity. The replication also creates silos in the respective OLTP and OLAP "data worldviews," which leads to miscommunications. Note that there are other database formats, such as NoSQL or data lakes, but we've placed our emphasis here on relational OLTP and OLAP databases for simplicity.

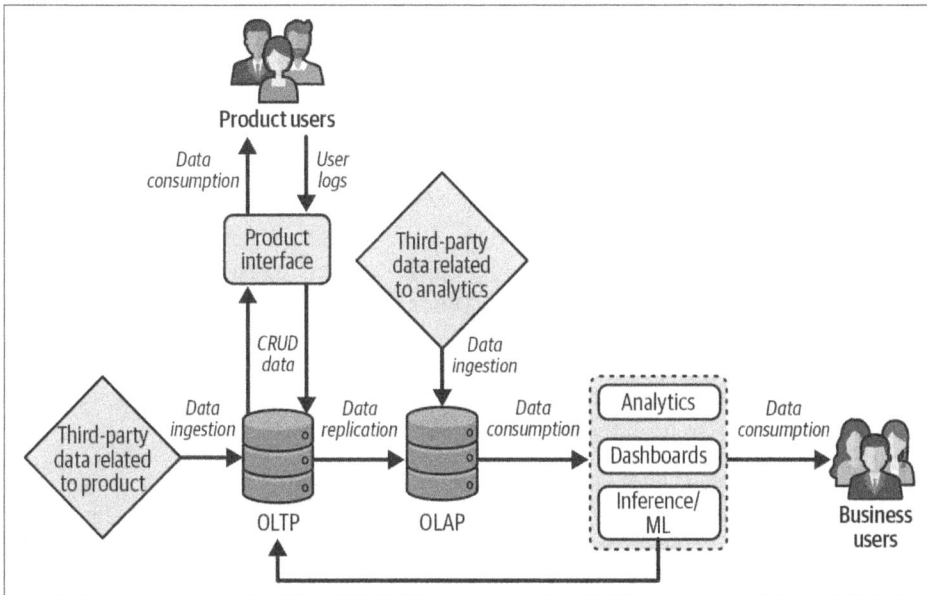

Figure 2-2. High-level dataflow of an organization utilizing OLTP and OLAP databases

Under the OLTP worldview, databases focus heavily on the speed of transactions of user logs, with emphasis on three main attributes:

- Create, read, update, and delete tasks (CRUD).
- Upholding compliance for atomicity, consistency, isolation, and durability (ACID).
- Modeled data should be in the third-normalized form (3NF).

These three components enable low latency of data retrieval, allowing user interfaces to quickly and reliably show correct data to a user in subseconds rather than minutes.

On the OLTP side of the dataflow, illustrated in Figure 2-2, you will see software engineers as the main persona utilizing these databases, and they are often the individuals implementing such databases before a data engineer is hired. This persona's role heavily emphasizes the maintainability, scalability, and reliability of the OLTP database and the related product software—data itself is a means to an end and not their main focus. Furthermore, while product implementations will vary, requirements and scoping are often clear with tangible outcomes.

Under the OLAP worldview, databases focus heavily on the ability to answer historical questions about this business via large scans of data where the data consumers care about the following:

- Using denormalized data to find unique relationships
- Validating and/or improving the nuances of business logic being applied to upstream data
- The ability to work iteratively on complex business questions that don't have clear requirements or may lead to dead ends

Though this additional database increases the complexity of the data system, the trade-off is that this increased flexibility enables the business to discover new opportunities not fully apparent in the product's CRUD data format.

On the OLAP side of the dataflow, illustrated in Figure 2-2, you will see data analysts, data scientists, and ML engineers as primary roles working solely within OLAP data systems. Key to these roles is the iterative nature of analytics and ML workflows, hence the flexibility in the resulting data models compared to OLTP's third-normalized form data.

Translation Issues Between OLTP and OLAP Data Worldviews

To illustrate the different data worldviews of the OLTP and OLAP silos and how this leads to translation issues, we have a mock example of an aquarium business review website called Kelp. In this use case, the Kelp engineering team has recently enabled users to submit updated reviews, and the data analysts want to understand if this added feature increases user session duration. Yet, the data analyst must determine an important nuance with the business logic: "How are average review stars calculated?"

In Figure 2-3, we have Kelp's review data for an aquarium in Monterey, with three reviews represented in third-normalized form within an OLTP database. Note that the engineering team used the average of all reviews for simplicity within the V1 feature release.

```
-- Kelp's Aquarium Review Data Organized in 3NF

-- Aquarium Table
+-----------+----------------+------------------+--------------+---------------------+
|aquarium_id|aquarium_name   |aquarium_location |aquarium_size |adult_admission_price|
+-----------+----------------+------------------+--------------+---------------------+
|123456     |'Monterey...'   |'Monterey, CA'    |'Large'       |25.99                |
+-----------+----------------+------------------+--------------+---------------------+

-- User Table
+-------+----------+--------------+
|user_id|user_name |demographic_n |
+-------+----------+--------------+
|1234   |Mark      |'<user info>' |
|5678   |Chad      |'<user info>' |
+-------+----------+--------------+

-- Reviews Table
+-----------+----------+-------+------------+---------------------+------------+
|aquarium_id|review_id |user_id|number_stars|review_timestamp     |review_text |
+-----------+----------+-------+------------+---------------------+------------+
|123456     |00001     |1234   |1           |2019-05-24 07...     |'Fish we..' |
|123456     |00002     |1234   |5           |2019-05-25 07...     |'I revi...' |
|123456     |00003     |5678   |5           |2019-05-29 05...     |'Amazin...' |
+-----------+----------+-------+------------+---------------------+------------+

-- Average Stars Table
+-----------+--------------+
|aquarium_id|average_stars |
+-----------+--------------+
|123456     |3.67          |
+-----------+--------------+

-- User Activity Table
+-------+------------------------+------------------------+
|user_id|session_start_timestamp |session_end_timestamp   |
+-------+------------------------+------------------------+
|1234   |2019-05-24 T07:46:02Z   |2019-05-24 T07:59:01Z   |
|1234   |2019-05-25 T07:31:01Z   |2019-05-25 T07:48:03Z   |
|5678   |2019-05-29 T05:14:08Z   |2019-05-29 T05:21:12Z   |
+-------+------------------------+------------------------+
```

Figure 2-3. Kelp's aquarium review data organized in 3NF

Figure 2-4 shows Kelp's review data represented as a denormalized wide table created by the data analyst in the OLAP database, along with an ad hoc table of various ways that average stars can be represented. Beyond questions around average stars calculations, the data analyst would consider nuances of the business logic, such as:

- How do we calculate website session duration where multiple sessions are near each other?

- Are there instances of single users with multiple Kelp accounts?

- What session duration change is relevant to the business?
- Is it the user reviews directly or a combination of attributes that lead to changes in session duration?

These questions represent a decoupling of business logic from the data represented in the OLTP worldview—resulting in a multitude of understandings that can lead to downstream data quality issues and data debt.

```
-- Denormalized Wide Table Used by Data Analyst

-- Reviews Wide Table
+-----------+----------+--------+--------------+---------------------+---+
|aquarium_id|review_id |user_id |number_stars  |review_timestamp     |...|
+-----------+----------+--------+--------------+---------------------+---+
|123456     |00001     |1234    |1             |2019-05-24 07...     |...|
|123456     |00002     |1234    |5             |2019-05-25 07...     |...|
|123456     |00003     |5678    |5             |2019-05-29 05...     |...|
+-----------+----------+--------+--------------+---------------------+---+


-- Reviews Wide Table Continued...
+---+------------+-----------------+-----------------+-------------+---+
|...|review_text |aquarium_name    |aquarium_location|aquarium_size|...|
+---+------------+-----------------+-----------------+-------------+---+
|...|'Fish we..' |'Monteray...'    |'Monteray, CA'   |'Large'      |...|
|...|'I revi...' |'Monteray...'    |'Monteray, CA'   |'Large'      |...|
|...|'Amazin...' |'Monteray...'    |'Monteray, CA'   |'Large'      |...|
+---+------------+-----------------+-----------------+-------------+---+


-- Reviews Wide Table Continued...
+---+---------------------+-----------------------+-----------------------+
|...|adult_admission_price|session_start_timestamp|session_end_timestamp  |
+---+---------------------+-----------------------+-----------------------+
|...|25.99                |2019-05-24 T07:46:02Z  |2019-05-24 T07:59:01Z  |
|...|25.99                |2019-05-25 T07:31:01Z  |2019-05-25 T07:48:03Z  |
|...|25.99                |2019-05-29 T05:14:08Z  |2019-05-29 T05:21:12Z  |
+---+---------------------+-----------------------+-----------------------+


-- Adhoc Table: Average Stars
+-----------+---------+-----------+-----------+
|aquarium_id|avg_all  |avg_first  |avg_latest |
+-----------+---------+-----------+-----------+
|123456     |3.67     |3          |5          |
+-----------+---------+-----------+-----------+
```

Figure 2-4. Example of Kelp's denormalized wide table used by data analyst

Given these differences in data worldviews, how can a data team determine which perspective for calculating average stars is correct? In reality, both data worldviews are correct and dependent on the constraints the individual, and ultimately the business, cares about. On the OLTP side, Kelp's software engineers cared about the simplicity of the feature implementation and wanted to avoid any additional complexity unless deemed necessary; hence the default to averaging all the star reviews rather than applying business logic—in other words, it's a product decision rather than a data decision. On the OLAP side, the data analyst is privy to unique combinations of data that don't make sense in an OLTP format but inform ways to improve the existing business logic. The data analyst may make suggestions that are sound from an analytics perspective but difficult to implement upstream in the OLTP database.

This difference in constraints and goals between data producers and consumers gets to the crux of why we believe data contracts are important. This book will go into great depth about data contracts, but in short, a data contract is an agreement between data producers and consumers that is established, updated, and enforced via an API. The process of defining data contracts codifies the trade-offs that both data producers and consumers are willing to make with respect to a data asset and why such configuration is important to the business.

Though this example highlights the OLTP and OLAP data architecture, this same pattern of miscommunication between different databases persists. All of this was exacerbated by the shift from on-prem data warehouses to cloud analytics databases that were inexpensive and easy to scale.

The Cost of Poor Data Quality

The foundational requirement of any software is that it is functional. In essence, does the program behave in the way it was intended to? A software bug is a defect in the expected operating behavior of the codebase. Because the software does not function as expected, there is some business-facing risk that has now been introduced. The risk might be transactional: the system might crash a customer's app in the middle of a purchase, causing the business to lose much-needed revenue. The risk might be experience-degrading: perhaps the app loads too slowly, which causes a customer to drop off the page and potentially use a competitor instead. Or, the risk might relate to internal scalability: a tremendous amount of server load could be put onto cloud infrastructure, causing costs to spiral out of control. And so on and so forth.

Work within data is not the same as software, despite the tooling having substantial overlap. At its core, data is not functional the further downstream it moves in the data lifecycle—it is descriptive. Data is a signal that is meant to effectively describe the state of the world around us. It can then be leveraged for an operational purpose, such as optimizing a process with artificial intelligence, or an analytical one, such as creating a dashboard. However, its foundational requirement is that it accurately reflects the real world and can be trusted by other members of the business. Without this core truth, data means nothing. To put it simply, there is no operational value in incorrect data. A violation of data quality, then, has as much impact on data products as bugs do on customer-facing software.

In software, there are a variety of mechanisms to measure the impact of bugs or scalability issues on production systems. Error rates, downtime, latency, and incident rates are all examples of *trailing indicators,* which measure an outcome, either positive or negative. In an ecommerce shop, a trailing indicator might be revenue. Revenue (money in the bank) is the last step in a long process that begins with a customer registering on a website, browsing the website, adding items to their cart, and checking out. In data quality management, trailing metrics indicate that the damage is done and we are measuring the blast radius. Reactive quality is extremely effective for diagnosing issues, prescribing next steps, and uncovering gaps in operational processes.

For example, a high number of errors being returned from a JavaScript application typically means some aspect of the customer experience has regressed from a previous release. A software engineer may attempt to root-cause the problem by first tracking the error history: at what time did the errors start? What was the error code being returned? Were there commonalities between each error that could narrow down where the problem was occurring? From there, the engineer might check logging or clickstream events to understand where unexpected behavior began to arise: if the number of page loads for a particular screen has dropped to zero, or the purchase of a particular item has been cut in half, these would be great places to start an investigation.

The second mechanism of measurement tracks *leading indicators,* an input to a success metric that precedes the metric itself. In the ecommerce world, a leading indicator might be customer registrations. The act of registration itself yields no value for the business, but if there is a quantifiable relationship between registrations and purchases, an increase in the former will eventually lead to more of the latter. In quality, too, there are leading indicators that can be used to predict the future increase or decrease of a trailing indicator. An example is code coverage, a common mechanism used by software engineering teams to measure how well services follow best practices in terms of security, scalability, and usability. Low code coverage means greater risk!

Measuring Data Quality

Data follows a similar measurement pattern as software when it comes to quality. There are leading indicators, such as trust, ownership, and the existence of expectations and testing. There are also lagging indicators, such as the number of data incidents, data downtime, latency requirements, replication, and more. Let's dig into each one, starting with leading indicators.

Data debt

Data debt is a measure of how complex your data environment is and what its capacity to scale is. While the debt itself doesn't represent a breaking change, there is a direct correlation among the amount of data debt and the development velocity of data teams, the cost of the data environment as a whole, and its ultimate scalability.

There are a few heuristics for measuring data debt:

- How many data assets have documentation (and how much is serviceable)
- The median number of dependencies per dataset in the data environment
- The number of backfilling jobs performed in the past year
- The average number of filters per query

Trustworthiness

The trustworthiness of the data is an excellent leading indicator because it correlates strongly with an increase in replication and (as a result) rising data costs. The less trust data consumers have in the data they are using, the more likely they will spend additional time scrutinizing a result, or not use it all, even if the data is correct.

Trustworthiness can be measured through both qualitative and quantitative methodologies. A quarterly survey to the data team with the following question is a strong temperature check, as seen in this example:

How much do you agree or disagree with the following statements?

- I trust our company's data.
- I am confident the data I use in my own work represents the real-world truth.
- I am confident the data I use will not change unexpectedly.
- I trust that when I use data from someone else, it means exactly what they say it means.
- I am not concerned that my stakeholders will receive incorrect data.

Additionally, the amount of replicated data assets is a fuzzy metric that is correlated with trust. The more trustworthy a dataset is, the less likely it is to be rebuilt using slightly different logic to answer the same question. When this scenario does occur, it usually means that one of the following is true:

- The logic of the dataset was not transparent to data developers, which prompted a lengthy amount of discovery that ultimately ended in replication.
- There is sensitive data the downstream teams won't have access to, and thus they need to rebuild the logic around these constraints.

- The data asset was simply not discoverable, meaning that it likely would have been reused if only the data asset in question had been easier to find.

In our personal experience, it is more rarely the latter case than data teams might assume. A motivated data developer will find the data they need, but no matter how motivated they are, they won't take a dependency on it for a business outcome if they can't trust it!

Ownership

Ownership is a predictive metric, as it measures the likelihood and speed of resolving errors upstream of the quality issue when they happen. Ownership can be measured at the individual table level, but we recommend measuring the ownership as a percentage of the data upstream of a specific data asset with explicit ownership in place. This requires first cataloging data sources, identifying the owners or lack of owners, and aggregating the total number of owned sources divided by the total number of registered sources.

Ownership metrics are great to bring up during Ops meetings. Even better is when the lack of ownership can be tied to a specific outage or data quality issue, and even better still is when a lack of ownership can be framed with the risk of outages for important downstream data products. As an example, imagine that a CFO's executive dashboard takes dependencies on 10 data sources. If only 3 of these data sources have clearly defined ownership, it is fair to say that the CFO has a 70% chance of extended time to mitigation in the event of data outage. The more important the data product, the more critical ownership becomes.

Data downtime

Data downtime is becoming one of the most popular metrics for data engineering teams attempting to quantify data quality. Downtime refers to the amount of time critical business data can't be accessed due to quality, reliability, or accessibility issues. We recommend a three-step process for tracking and actioning on data downtime:

1. *Track and analyze downtime incidents*
   Keep a log of all data incidents, including their duration, cause, and resolution process. This data is crucial for understanding how often downtime occurs, what its common causes are, and how quickly your team can resolve issues.

2. *Calculate downtime metrics*
   Use the collected data to calculate specific metrics, such as the average downtime duration, frequency of downtime incidents, mean time to detect (MTTD) a data issue, and mean time to resolve (MTTR) the issue. These metrics provide a quantitative measure of your data's reliability and the effectiveness of your response strategies.

---

3. Assess impact

Beyond just measuring the downtime itself, assess the impact on business operations. This can include the cost of lost opportunities, decreased productivity, or any financial losses associated with the downtime.

Once completed, data engineering teams should have a comprehensive view of not only how their critical metrics are changing over time but also the impact on the business from downtime. This impact can be used to persuade executives to implement additional tooling for managing quality, bringing in additional headcount, or driving greater upstream ownership to prevent problems before they occur.

Violated expectations

Expectations refers to what data consumers expect from their upstream data systems. Here, upstream can mean a table used as direct input for a query, or a transactional database maintained by production engineers supporting production applications. Depending on the team and use case, the specific expectations of the consumer might differ. A data engineer responsible for orchestrating a series of Airflow pipelines may have expectations of a PostgreSQL database in cloud storage, while an analyst who relies on a set of well-defined business entities to construct their dashboard view would have expectations of a set of analytical database tables in Snowflake SQL.

Expectations can take a variety of forms:

Schema
This is the structure of the data, data types, and column names. For example, we always expect the primary key `customer_ID` to be a six-character string.

Semantics
This is the underlying business logic of the data and the entity itself. For example, we always use the email field to include an "@" symbol.

Service-level agreements (SLAs)
These are the latency and volume requirements of the data. For example, we might expect a minimum of 1,000 events from data sources per hour.

Personally identifiable information (PII)
This is information that can be used, individually or in a combination of data values, to identify a person and/or entity. For example, we might expect a `customer_name` field to be PII, so it will be masked to all consumers.

Ideally, all violated expectations should be centrally logged. Teams can record when these violations occurred, who was responsible, what the data source in question was, and any downstream impacted assets. The success of both the data engineering and data producer teams can be measured against the total number of violations, which represent a range of data quality and governance issues. If this number gradually decreases quarter over quarter, it is an indication that the business is becoming more holistically aware of data quality and responsive to issues.

Quarterly incident count

While not substantially dissimilar from certain data downtime metrics, a quarterly incident count is a great way for business and technical leaders to gain a robust understanding of the impact of data quality on the company and its data products. A data incident technically refers to any event that compromises the integrity, availability, or confidentiality of data. This could include unauthorized access to data (a security breach), loss of data due to system failures or human error, corruption of data because of software bugs or hardware malfunctions, or any situation where data is rendered inaccurate, incomplete, or inaccessible.

The most meaningful types of data incidents have some type of real-world impact. In software, incidents often cause a steep drop-off in revenue, lose valuable customers, or even incur legal and or political blowback. Therefore, not every outage should necessarily be treated as an incident. If an impact to data quality only causes a few noncritical dashboards to show incorrect numbers, it's difficult to argue this had a tangible impact on the business. However, if a decision was made that led to a negative outcome based on those incorrect numbers, that's a very different story.

Here are some common examples of data incidents worth reporting:

Incorrectly allocating marketing spend
> During the COVID pandemic, the marketing team of one popular tech startup was on edge, concerned that users may spike or decline due to the unpredictability of the virus and surrounding legislation. During a monthly report, an analyst noticed that new user sign-ups were down by over 25%, marking a massive decrease in potential revenue. To get ahead of the issue, marketing received approval to significantly increase its budget for email campaigns and public outreach. A few months later, however, it was determined that the cause of the issue was not user behavior at all, but an improper change to how the product engineering team was recording the user sign-up event. Whoops!

Real-world recalls
> A consumer goods company that manufactured expensive home utilities used the `item_id` in its primary transactional database as the serialization number printed on the bar code for each of its products. One day, production engineers tested adding a character to the `item_id`, not realizing how it would affect teams downstream. By the time they realized their mistake, hundreds of incorrect barcodes had been printed, put onto a myriad of different household items, and shipped to homes, hotels, and restaurants. The company had to pay delivery drivers to revisit each drop-off and exchange the barcodes, which was both time-consuming and expensive for such a seemingly small change!

While often less impressive in terms of raw quantifiable data, these stories demonstrate the incredible importance of data quality and what has the highest success rate in driving investment. Even with the best measures, we must remember that data quality is not only about *what* is impacted but also *who* is impacted within these data workflows.

Who Is Impacted

Data quality issues impact stakeholders in a variety of ways depending on the persona of the user. Each persona has a different relationship with data, and therefore feels the pain in a related but unique way when things go wrong.

Data engineers

Data engineers often pull the shortest end of the stick. Because the word data is in their title, business teams make the assumption that any data issue can be dumped on their plate and promptly resolved. This is anything but true! Most data engineers do not have a deep understanding of the business logic leveraged by product and marketing organizations for analytics and ML. When requests to resolve data quality issues arise on the data engineers' backlogs, it takes them days or even weeks to track down the offending issue through root cause analysis and do something about it.

The time it takes to resolve issues leads to an enormous on-call backlog, and tensions with the analytics and AI teams are frequently high due to a litany of unresolved or partially resolved outages. This is increasingly troublesome for data engineers, because when things are running smoothly they are rarely acknowledged at all by the wider business! Data engineers unfortunately fall into the rare category of workers whose skills are essential to the business, but because they can't claim quick wins in the same way a data scientist, software engineer, or product manager might, their visibility in the organization is comparatively diminished. Life is not good when the only time people hear about you is when something is failing.

Data scientists

Data scientists are scrappy builders who often come from academic backgrounds. In academia, the emphasis is more on ensuring that research is properly conducted, interesting, and ethically validated. The business world represents a sudden shift from this approach—focusing instead on doing money-making exercises, executing quickly, and tackling the low-hanging fruits (see: boring problems) first and foremost. While data scientists all know how to perform validation, they are much less used to data suddenly changing, not being able to trust data, or data losing its quality over time.

This makes the data scientist particularly susceptible to the impacts of data quality. Machine learning models frequently make poor or incorrect predictions. Datasets developed to support model training and other rigorous analysis are not maintained for long periods of time until they suddenly fail. Expected to deliver tangible business value, data scientists may find themselves in a bind when it emerges that the model they have been reporting on, which was making the business millions of dollars, was actually off by an order of magnitude, and they just recently found out.

Analysts

Analysts is a broad term. It could refer to financial analysts who make decisions on revenue data, or product analysts who review web logs and clickstream events and measure the impact of new features on user experiences. Most analysts use the same set of tools: third-party visualization software like Looker, Tableau, Mixpanel, Amplitude, or, of course, the trusted Microsoft Excel. Analysts need to have more than a passing familiarity with the underlying data. It is essential they understand how the customers table is JOINed to the items_purchased table, why a long SQL file seems to be filtering out users who haven't visited the website in the last 45 days, and exactly what a purchase_order event refers to. More than any other job function, analysts are the most connected to the business logic of each company.

Data quality impacts analysts by throwing their understanding of the business logic into disarray. If a column in a production database refers to kilometers today but miles tomorrow, it will effectively double the values of any downstream user leveraging that table. Analysts are also in the unfortunate position of being blamed for changes that they can't control. Their worst nightmare is getting an email at 4:45 p.m. on Friday titled: "Why is this data wrong?"

Software engineers

Software engineers are impacted by data quality in a more roundabout way, in the sense that their changes are usually the root cause of most problems since their role often intersects with source data creation and ingestion. So while they may not be impacted in the same way a data engineer, analyst, or data scientist might be, they often find themselves being shouted at by data consumers if an incompatible change is made upstream that causes issues downstream.

This isn't (usually) for lack of trying. Software engineers will often announce potentially breaking changes on more public channels, hoping that any current or would-be users will notice and prepare for the migration accordingly. Inevitably, though, after they receive very little feedback and make the change, data teams immediately start screaming and asking to roll it back.

Business teams

Business teams refer to (typically) nontechnical end customers of the data. This might include a marketing lead using a dashboard on SEO attribution to measure the impact of their content marketing strategy, or a product manager reviewing the clickthrough funnels for a new feature they launched on the website.

Business teams have very little agency when it comes to resolving or identifying data quality issues. When something is noticeably wrong, all they can do is message analysts and ask them to look into it. Worse, it is very challenging for a business user to differentiate between a legitimate unexpected change and a data quality problem.

At a previous company Chad worked at, an application team was using a common third-party vendor for event instrumentation. When COVID happened, the analytics in the application began reporting an incremental but noticeable drop in active customer sessions. This drop continued day by day, until it stabilized at around a 25% decrease from the pre-COVID peak. The product managers and marketers were beside themselves. Convinced the pandemic had permanently impacted churn rates, they funneled money into marketing to rebalance the numbers. It turned out to be a false alarm. An analyst who had been looking into a totally separate issue discovered there was a similar drop in average time on page. It was oddly coincidental that two seemingly unrelated metrics experienced the exact same decrease! After looking into the issue and contacting the vendor, the team discovered the initial drop was due to an implementation mistake that ultimately resulted in a bug. All that marketing spend, wasted. Oops.

Conclusion

In this chapter, we defined data quality and contextualized it to the current state of the data industry, including data architecture implications and the cost of poor data quality. In summary, this chapter covered:

- Defining data quality in a way that looks back to established practices but accounts for recent changes in the data industry
- How OLTP and OLAP data architecture patterns create silos that lead to data miscommunications
- The cost of poor data quality in terms of a loss of trust in one of the business's most important assets

Central to this chapter is the idea that data quality is not about data being pristine, but instead being "fit for use" for your stakeholders. A common mistake we see data professionals make when trying to get buy-in for improving data quality is placing too much emphasis on the best practices associated with high-quality data. At the end of the day, technical and data debt should ideally be a strategic trade-off where you are balancing effort and robustness with ROI. Thus, it's imperative that data professionals anchor their positioning around the business impact associated with engaging with better data quality practices and, more importantly, why solving their particular business problem around data is more urgent than other problems throughout the organization.

In Chapter 3, we will discuss the challenges of scaling data infrastructure within the era of the Modern Data Stack, how scaling data is not like scaling software, and why data contracts are necessary to enable the scalability of data.

## CHAPTER 3

The Challenges of Scaling Data Infrastructure

In this chapter we'll dive further into the challenges of the everyday workflows of data producers and consumers in building and maintaining complex software and data systems. Furthermore, we'll elaborate on how data development is different from software development, and the implications of these differences on our ability to drive value with data in an organization. Being aware of these challenges will equip you to understand how data contracts fit within the workflows of developers, what problems they mitigate, and how you can help developers understand their role within a data contract architecture.

How Data Development Is Not Like Software Development

As mentioned in Chapter 1, data development best practices preceded software development by decades. Previously, a set of best practices, design philosophies, and management methodologies existed wholly separate from the software engineering workflows that came after. Naturally, there are unique differences between data development and software development that prevent one from being a carbon copy of the other in terms of tools or processes. It is useful to walk through these flows to better understand why data requires a similar but unique paradigm for managing scale.

Perhaps the largest of these differences can be found when comparing pre-development patterns. Pre-development refers to engineering time spent on a project outside of writing code. In software engineering, the most important pre-development steps are gathering requirements and designing architecture. However, for data developers, the most essential pre-development steps are formulating the right hypothesis and exploring/understanding the data.

How Software Engineers Build Products

Good software engineering always begins the same way: with a requirements document. A requirements document is a set of customer needs created by the software engineer or someone else on the product team responsible for user research. Most commonly this role belongs to UX designers or product managers. The requirements document focuses on a particular problem that, if solved, would hypothetically result in delivering value for the customer and meaningfully increasing a target success metric.

Software engineers review requirement documents and then, after performing a feasibility analysis, convert the user stories into architectural specifications. If the requirement document defines the why, the spec defines the how. Here, engineers decide which technologies to use, explain why those technologies make the most sense for their application, list assumptions, and make decisions on whether to buy tooling or build it in-house.

The technical spec is usually subject to the most scrutiny by other engineers. During the review phase, they will challenge the primary architect on why they made certain decisions and potentially bring up issues that hadn't yet been considered. Is it necessary to have a real-time data feed? Is this going to require an extensive security review? How will users authenticate? How will we keep latency low on the frontend? These are all common questions during the architecture design meetings.

At this point, engineers begin building. While the actual act of writing code certainly requires a level of expertise and speed, what separates great engineers from the not-so-great is how much thought and planning they put into the initial architecture (even more true with the rise of AI-assisted coding). If the technical spec was well built, there isn't much work to do after the code has been deployed and QA'd in a developer environment. The feature goes live, the team announces their work, and the company cheers. With the exception of bugs, it's rare that the deployed feature would ever need to significantly change if it was well designed.

How Data Developers Build Products

While there certainly are similarities between data development and software development, the workflows have a significant amount of disparity.

For one, most data development *begins with understanding a question* rather than immediately building an application around a known user experience. These questions could come from the data developer themselves, but more often they come from a business partner. Here are a few examples:

Operations lead
"How many resources do we need to deal with the Christmas buying surge?"

Chief revenue officer
"How is our new pricing strategy going? Do customers like it?"

Marketing manager
"How many people are downloading our ebook, and does it lead to sales?"

Sales lead
"Did our team make their quotas? Which region performed the best?"

Product manager
"What was the impact on revenue for the new feature we launched?"

Head of HR
"What is our employee churn rate? What are the most common causes of attrition?"

Before beginning to understand what operational data products we can build on top of these queries, however, data developers must understand if the question can even be answered with the data that exists. This involves data discovery. Data discovery is the process of searching for data in an attempt to answer a question. There are multiple components a data developer must keep in mind when beginning the journey toward discovery:

- Does this data exist?
- Where is the data located?
- Who is the owner of the data?
- Can the owner explain what it means?
- How do I use the data?
- Do I have permission to access the data?

Each of these discovery-oriented questions may take hours, or more realistically days, to answer.

See Chapter 5, where we discuss in detail the various types of data assets one can discover and the various tools to do so, including data catalogs and lineage.

Depending on the answers to the previous questions, the next step could look radically different. For instance, if the data doesn't exist, the data developer must decide if they would rather go down the path of trying to have a data producer generate the data on their behalf or report back on the failed project to the team lead. Similarly, if data doesn't have any owner, they must decide whether to push through with a prototype even though no one is around to take care of quality, or whether to let the asking team know that no answer provided to them would be trustworthy.

Next, the data developer needs to construct the query to answer the question. But here, yet another difference arises. Just because someone has provided an answer does not yet mean it is useful on its own. As an example, a product designer may ask the questions, "How are people interacting with the new chatbot we shipped? Is it leading to more sales?"

To answer that question, first the data developer needs to find the user behavior data that shows the number of times a chatbot was shown to a user, and the number of clickstream events recorded when they interacted with it.

Next, they need to understand the nature of those interactions. Asking the chatbot a question is different from closing out the chatbot window, after all. The analyst would then need to understand more details about the user's session. How long did they interact with the chatbot? Did they add anything to their cart afterward? Did they purchase what was in their cart?

Finally, the developer would need to do a comparative exercise to understand if the current number of purchases was significantly different from the state before the chatbot shipped. Things get even more complicated when you factor in that some percentage of users who saw the chatbot probably would have purchased anyway! How do we deal with those individuals in our research, and how can we identify them?

During this phase the data developer is typically not looking for extreme accuracy. They are simply attempting to discover the data as fast as they can, understand it as best they can, and query it as efficiently as they can en route to an answer. Things like data quality checks, testing, monitoring, and semantic validity are furthest from their mind. Once all these queries are developed and the final report is handed to the designer, it's possible that the signal is simply not strong enough to warrant a deeper dive or follow-up steps. The data may show that there are many more customer interactions but the overall purchase rate seems relatively flat. This type of outcome would yield more questions rather than a tangible operational application: "Why is it that the purchase rate is flat even though chatbot interactions are up? Is the chatbot not helpful, or is there no change in purchases for another reason?"

All of this means the data developer is in a constant state of flux and change. They are responding to new questions being asked, conducting discovery, and providing analysis—which is significantly different from the more structured and rigid workflow of software engineering.

However, when answered questions are useful, other teams and users begin to take a dependency. Answers to common questions like "How many active customers does the business have over the past month?" are useful for almost anyone to know, and the output would likely be leveraged in a large variety of other queries. Once an answered question has been proven to be valuable, there comes with it an expectation of trust (to a certain degree). At this point the quality checks become much more meaningful!

It should be clear from these examples that software developers and data developers have unique workflows and thus different needs in the tools and processes they use. In addition, each group requires a specific environment suited to their needs.

Software engineers need an environment that allows them to seamlessly write code, test for errors, and easily push to production. Data developers need an environment that facilitates prototyping and experimentation—discovering the data that exists, identifying what is trustworthy and what is not, selecting the useful answers, and then creating data quality checks on what is expected to generate value.

Core Challenges for Modern Data Engineering Teams

Change management has existed in the world of software engineering as a discipline for many years. In the early 2010s, version control frameworks and the platforms that supported them, such as GitHub and GitLab, went mainstream. In addition to being user-friendly platforms to host code, they provided agile, iterative mechanisms of conducting code review through a feature called pull requests (PRs).

A PR is a request to merge a development branch back into the main branch, effectively productionizing a code change. Specifically, PRs allow for engineers to register themselves as reviewers for any change within a code repository, as code changes can have negative impacts if not thought through. This in turn allows code review to be managed without long meetings and painful scheduling conflicts. A developer could file a PR and then work on other projects during the code review, as demonstrated in Figure 3-1.

Version control platforms have become code change management systems, and the features they possess are built to reflect the range of use cases where change management is essential. Such features include:

- Version control, to undo changes
- Pull requests, to directly review changes
- Code diff, to visually review changes
- Views and reviewers, to be alerted when changes happen

These systems allow the right people to be in the loop when the code evolves. However, there is no such system for data! It is incredibly difficult, sometimes impossible, to understand how changes to an application codebase will impact data teams. There is no good way for those who would be impacted by changes to advocate for themselves in the way a PR reviewer might, nor is there any indication for the engineer of what is going to happen to their dependents once a change is made. This lack of context makes change management an extremely difficult endeavor in the data space. But why?

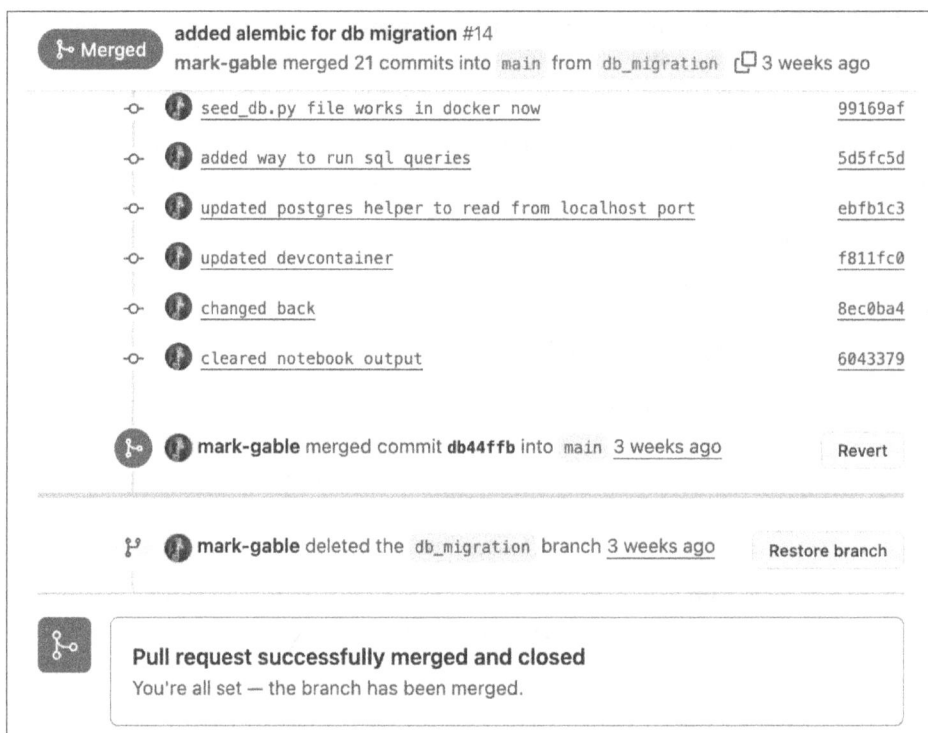

Figure 3-1. GitHub's UI for a pull request

A core reason for this has to do with the organizational structure of most tech-inclined businesses. Generally, software engineering teams want their code to be reviewed by other members on the same team. This is because your teammates are the ones who understand your services the best. It wouldn't make much sense to ask the owner of an unrelated backend service to review a change to the frontend settings page of your application. The two engineers would likely not be speaking the same language, would be missing context, and would not have a grasp on the gotchas, potential security issues, and other best practices within the organization.

For that reason, change review is easy to maintain. Every time a software engineer joins a new team, they immediately subscribe to the repos their team owns. Many engineering teams have Slack channels through which they push new PRs from GitHub so teammates are actively kept in the loop. While this system may not completely cover their bases, it is good enough to catch most major quality issues and allow teams to be functionally self-sufficient.

However, in data this within-team-oriented system does not work (as illustrated in Figure 3-2). Downstream data teams do not produce data themselves and are therefore dependent on upstream teams that maintain transactional systems to provide them with data, or on third-party applications operated by business users or even the customers themselves. Changes to those systems are invisible to the data teams.

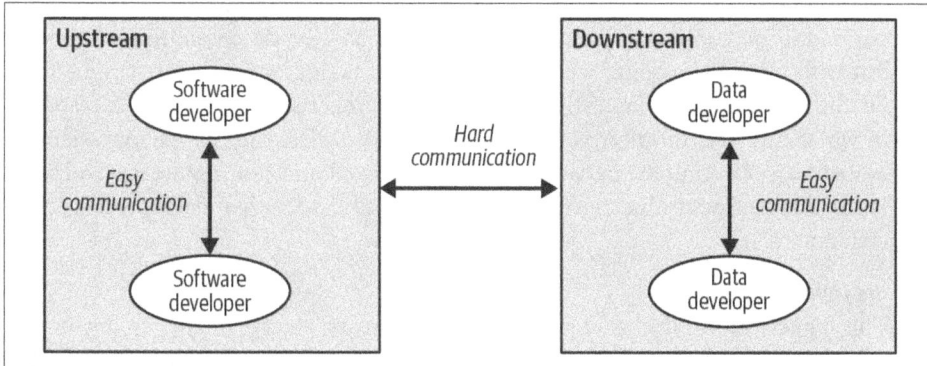

Figure 3-2. Communication patterns between data and software developers

The biggest challenge in creating effective data change management is that it must operate *between teams,* effectively forming a link between the data producer and the data consumer. What increases the challenge is that different teams may have different requirements for their data. A team leveraging customer order information for a weekly report to the chief marketing officer only needs the data refreshed from production every seven days, while a data science team leveraging order information for a real-time recommendation system may need the training data refreshed daily to avoid drift.

The challenges with creating a data change management system are both cultural and technical. These include:

No visibility

Data producers and data consumers both lack visibility of each other in different ways. Data producers do not understand who is using their data, why it's being used, how it's being transformed, and what its tier of importance is. Data consumers, on the other hand, don't understand where their data is coming from, why it's changing, who is changing it, and when changes are coming. Because there is nothing linking the producers and consumers together, it is challenging for this awareness to ever develop organically.

Not everything needs visibility

As we covered earlier, data developers may go through many rounds of prototyping and discovery before settling on a use case that requires production-grade data quality. In some organizations these production use cases may represent 10% of the total data assets or less. Making *all* data visible could lead to an overwhelming amount of information. This causes alert fatigue.

Alert fatigue

Alert fatigue is the result of teams creating too many monitors that either do not communicate enough information to be actionable or do communicate enough but without anyone being willing or capable of taking action. Alert fatigue is by far the best way to make testing a useless exercise, creating a Pavlovian response in which any data monitor is ignored by default. Unless the change management system can discriminate between what is important and not important, and what is actionable versus inactionable, it is not useful to either data producers or consumers.

Not the right time

The biggest cultural challenge with between-team change management is prioritization. Typically, product teams define their roadmap at the start of each quarter, after which it is usually set in stone. Asking another team to consider data quality as a priority at the expense of their own features is unlikely to happen. Simply asking others to be good citizens will not work. Data teams must be empowered to initiate a resolution on their own.

"Hands off my stuff"

Some teams are highly territorial and (unfortunately) inconsiderate. These organizations or individuals also may have very good reasons to be standoffish. The service they maintain might be critically important to the business, and the data may pale in importance by comparison.

If you're reading this from the perspective of a company, it may seem as though there's no light at the end of the tunnel. The sheer scale and scope of the data quality problem you are facing feels inescapable—at every turn there is a new mess to clean up and a different (but related) problem to solve. If you're a growth-stage company it may not be any better! You likely joined a tech company expecting the data to be high quality, easily accessed, and highly usable, only to find the exact opposite—a disjointed, jumbled mess that is constantly breaking. Would you be interested to know, then, that there is a unique class of company that has almost no data quality issues at all?

Early-stage startups. To be even more specific, startups with around 20 engineers or fewer.

We've spoken to dozens of early-stage startups, and in almost all cases data quality issues were minimal if not nonexistent. The reason why is clear: as highlighted in Chapter 1, the smaller the engineering team, the easier it is for the data team to be represented when new features are launched. (We will provide more detail as to why later in the chapter when we discuss Conway's Law and Dunbar's Number.)

Opposite to what some data teams might feel, data producers are actually not out to get you. They are intelligent, thoughtful people who have a rabid appetite for risk mitigation. Breaking things due to a code deployment they introduced is one of their greatest fears. When data engineers are able to clearly explain why and how a new feature can cause problems *before* a deployment occurs, it is extremely unusual for data producers to not be receptive toward that.

So if that approach works at small companies, then what's the problem for the rest of us? Well, companies don't stay small. They grow. And these days the greatest growth lever for tech-oriented businesses is software engineers. According to Mikkel Dengsøe, the median data-developer-to-software-developer ratio is 1:4 among the top 50 European tech companies (*https://oreil.ly/hH_yY*). At Chad's previous companies, he had an engineer team of over 200 with a data engineering team of only 5! There's a few reasons for this:

- Data engineers work on infra, software engineers work on product. It's always easier to get more resources when you're making the company money than if you're running pipelines.

- C-level executives don't know what data engineers do. They know they are important, but due to a lack of visibility their team is rarely staffed properly.

- It's hard to hire data engineers. The sad truth is that there just aren't enough data engineers compared to software engineers. The good ones have options!

- It's hard to retain data engineers. The more data quality becomes a problem, the harder it is to keep them around.

- No one knows quite where they fit. We've seen data engineers as part of the data platform team, part of the data science team, and even (shockingly) part of the product team. Most organizations don't seem to have a great handle on how to manage data engineers, which leads to them leaving for greener pastures.

And even if a reasonable number of data engineers was hired, it would require a multiple order of magnitude improvement for data engineers to be present in every single meeting for every feature. Data teams can't move as fast as software teams—we have a giant source-of-truth monolith to think about, after all.

But there's good news: data teams don't need to be everywhere. We only need to be where it matters, when it matters—in other words, the right place at the right time. If data teams can inject themselves into the development lifecycle at the point where data producers are likely to be the most receptive to their feedback, we can replicate what small startups are doing at tremendous scale. The trick is how to do it programmatically.

Why Data Development Needs a Design Surface

We'll be frank—any system that requires production-quality data must be preceded by some form of change management framework. The purpose of data change management is to ensure that the right teams are looped into the review at the right time. The outcome of such a system is to prevent the garbage in, garbage out problem, increasing the amount of trust in data by creating visibility across data producers and data consumers.

With theoretical alignment in place, we can discuss the practical requirements of data change management and how we might leverage technology to achieve these outcomes, which we'll do over the following chapters:

Prevention first
> The majority of data solutions today rely on reactive measures. These include monitoring, testing, and anomaly detection. Preventative systems are designed to catch breaking changes before they occur. From an implementation perspective, this means integration with a data producer's continuous integration/continuous deployment (CI/CD) pipeline.

Communicative
> The best way to prevent breaking changes is to connect people, namely data developers who understand their own data and the pipelines supporting them, with the data producers, who are familiar with how their upstream sources will change. Bridging the gap between data consumers and data producers is at its core an exercise in communication efficiency.

Contextual
> Simply providing alerts is not enough. Data producers must understand more details about how the data will change in order for it to be truly actionable. This includes information such as:
>
> - What is the data expected to look like versus what does it actually look like?
> - What is the schema of the data?
> - What are the semantics of the data?
> - Does the data contain PII or not?
> - How is the data actually utilized downstream—a dashboard, a training set for a machine learning model, or something else?

The more information that someone can provide, the easier it is for consumers to be able to act accordingly.

At the right time

The right time of communicating changes is right before something breaks, not significantly before or after. If someone approaches a producer about changes too far in advance, it will be ignored and placed into the backlog for later. If it happens after the change has been made, then usually the engineer has already moved on and is working on more interesting projects. The best time to communicate a breaking change is before it is deployed, not after it's detected—often by others such as downstream data consumers within the business. This allows you to interject at the moment the data producer is most likely to listen.

Including the right people

It is critical that the right people be in the change management process. The right people refers to the consumers of data who are going to be impacted by an upstream change. These consumers range from highly technical data engineers and data scientists, to nontechnical product managers, designers, and other business-level personnel. These individuals need to be able to interact with data producers in a background-agnostic interface, in an abstraction layer outside of products that nontechnical teams may not have access to (see Figure 3-3).

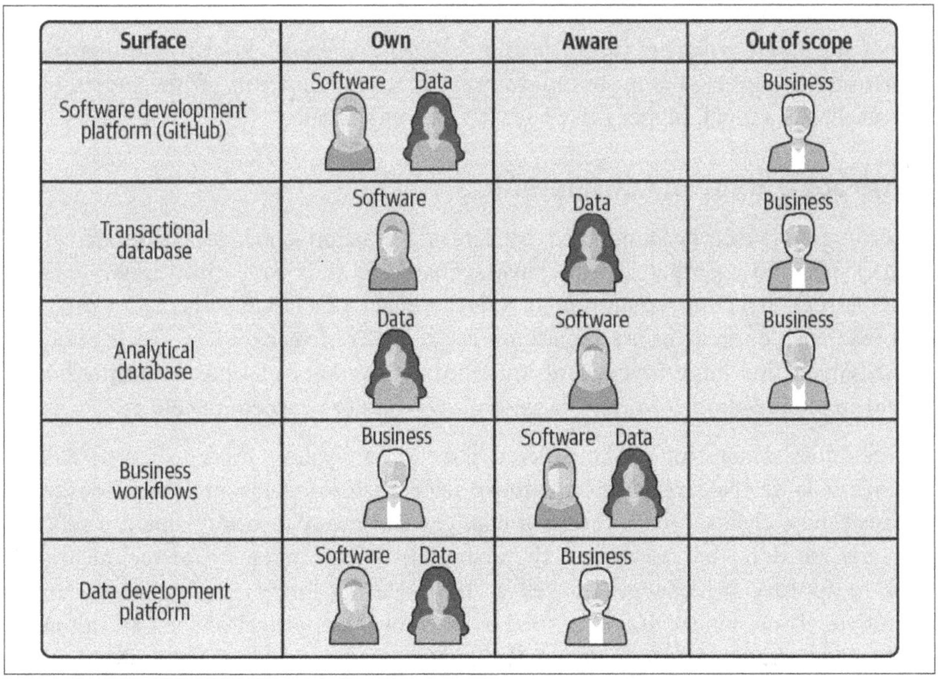

Surface	Own	Aware	Out of scope
Software development platform (GitHub)	Software Data		Business
Transactional database	Software	Data	Business
Analytical database	Data	Software	Business
Business workflows	Business	Software Data	
Data development platform	Software Data	Business	

Figure 3-3. Scope of stakeholders across surfaces within the data lifecycle

In the next sections, we will cover one of the processes where change management and collaboration is essential: large-scale refactors.

The Cost of Large-Scale Refactors

Refactoring is an expected step within the software lifecycle to continually improve a codebase. Martin Fowler, one of the leading voices on refactoring practices, defines refactoring in *Refactoring: Improving the Design of Existing Code* (Addison-Wesley) as "a change made to the internal structure of software to make it easier to understand and cheaper to modify without changing its observable behavior." Typically, these refactors are opportunistic in that small changes happen within the development workflow, as such changes make it easier to implement new features within the codebase. Yet sometimes refactors require massive effort if an organization finds itself in too much technical debt.

Refactors that are on the opportunistic side are considered "floss refactoring" as they are small efforts over time to maintain cleanliness and prevent issues in the long term. On the opposite spectrum are "root canal refactors," which are extensive procedures to deal with a rotting section of the codebase. These root canal refactors are often large-scale efforts to unblock the codebase's ability to implement new features or make the developer experience less painful. Emerson Murphy-Hill and Andrew Black utilized this metaphor of oral hygiene, as it best represented the behaviors of software developers (*https://oreil.ly/_rXOu*), where it's known that flossing or refactoring is a practice one should do every day, yet many put off the practice and ultimately pay a much higher price later to resolve the issue.

Large-Scale Refactor Considerations

According to a survey conducted by James Ivers and colleagues (*https://oreil.ly/Z7IaK*), responding organizations have spent 1,500 staff days on average working on large-scale refactors. Assuming an average salary of $115,000 and 260 work days in a year, such companies are spending over $650,000 a year on large-scale refactors alone. Given this large investment and months to years of time committed, why would an organization consider a large-scale refactor to be worth the effort?

Where "floss refactoring" is considered good code hygiene that's expected among engineers, large-scale refactors are more of a business decision than a desire to improve the codebase. As the scale of changes and the cost to implement a refactor increases, so does the purview of the change in which more senior technical staff need to approve the change, as well as the need for buy-in among nontechnical executives. Thus, a clear ROI is needed to warrant the approval of such an initiative. In the same survey, respondents noted that the top three reasons for going through with a large-scale refactor were the following:

- Reducing the cost of implementing a change to the codebase
- Increasing the speed at which engineers can deliver code
- Migrating to a new architecture that is often driven by an external business decision

One of the survey respondents best captured the pain that pushes organizations to make such a hefty investment in the following quote: "Modernization cycle was held back by 4 years…. Maintenance cost stayed high…cost to implement, deploy, and validate continue to increase."

All of this leads to a poor developer experience that makes it harder both to ship meaningful products for the business and to retain top engineering talent.

Use Case: Alan's Large-Scale Refactor

Finally, the survey was able to surface seven distinct steps for a large-scale refactor among responding organizations:

- Determining where changes are needed
- Choosing what changes to make
- Implementing the changes
- Generating new tests and migrating existing tests
- Validating refactored code (inspection, executing tests, etc.)
- Recertifying refactored code
- Updating documentation

We will apply these steps to Alan, a health insurance company founded in 2016 that needed to conduct a large-scale refactor in 2021 (*https://oreil.ly/3Wbmr*) to account for a major shift in its product's assumptions and ultimately its underlying data. These major changes often unearth data quality issues from the previous system, or embed hidden assumptions in the new infrastructure that will potentially become new data quality issues.

For Alan's use case, the company made a major assumption that there is a one-to-one relationship between a company and its contracts (not data contracts) and that a company will only have one contract at a time. This assumption permeated the codebase, documentation, and beyond in nontechnical roles. Hindsight is 20/20, but such assumptions are part of the startup journey where business hypotheses are made with the goal of trying to disprove them as quickly as possible to iterate to the correct assumption. Let's look at the seven steps from the survey.

Determining where changes are needed

As a startup grows, the population of available customers increases, and thus more assumptions are broken. In the case of Alan, 2019 was when it first started seeing customers break the one-contract assumption, but not enough customers to warrant a large-scale refactor. Thus, Alan strategically took on technical debt by creating multiple company entities for companies that needed multiple contracts. By 2021, the number of companies breaking the one-contract assumption increased enough to warrant a large-scale refactor for anywhere that assumed a one-contract relationship for companies.

Choosing what changes to make

Alan's engineering team was able to determine that the most important change that would enable multiple company contracts was to update its data model. Before, the data model relationship was company-contract and was limited to a one-to-one relationship. The refactor aimed to have the relationship changed to company-contract population and contract population-contract, which enabled one-to-many relationships.

Implementing the changes

Key to Alan's success was getting its large-scale refactor prioritized on the product roadmap and creating a team to conduct the refactor. With the decision to update the data model, it now became clear what pieces of code needed to be deprecated, though it was not easy to do. In one instance, Alan noted how one property was called over five hundred times and subsequently inherited by numerous other properties. Due to this complexity, having a single team to manage the learned domain knowledge and changes was essential.

Generating new tests and migrating existing tests

While testing is unfortunately viewed as a nice-to-have within data, it's a requirement within engineering workflows. Many engineering teams ascribe to test-driven development, where unit tests are written in conjunction with new code being implemented. The same applies to large-scale refactors. In addition to creating new tests, teams also have to account for how their refactor will break existing tests. Though a painful and iterative process, initially creating these unit tests is what enables engineers to confidently implement updates, such as a major refactor.

Validating refactored code (inspection, executing tests, etc.)

With the complexity of a large-scale refactor, it would be wise to also leverage tools to monitor the progress of the refactor, the utilization of the newly refactored components, and new bugs potentially introduced. Alan specifically used an application observability tool and created monitors for each use case it was refactoring. In addition, Alan ran both the old and new implementations to ensure that the refactor did not introduce a deviation from the original code's output.

Recertifying refactored code

Though this is not discussed by Alan, I can speak to this from my own experience working in a health-tech startup in the insurance space: health insurance data is highly regulated, as it's at the intersection of medical and HR data. Going from a one-to-one to a one-to-many assumption meant that the Alan team had to be extremely mindful of the risk of data leakage, or of data being exposed in areas it doesn't belong. I would assume that this refactor was a major point of discussion for the company's yearly SOC 2 security compliance review.

Updating documentation

Once again, large-scale refactors are not a technical problem but a business problem that expands well beyond the codebase. For five years, the notion of "one active contract per customer" was embedded in the culture, training, and documentation of Alan. Thus, in addition to refactoring the codebase, the company also needed to "refactor" the company culture by including nonengineering roles in the process. Alan updated documentation for every impacted party and communicated these changes repeatedly to ensure they were adopted outside the codebase as well.

We highly recommend reading Chaïmaa Kadaoui's article on Alan's large-scale refactor (*https://oreil.ly/ADNTq*) to learn more. In the next section we move away from an engineering perspective experienced with large-scale refactors, and instead focus on the type of codebase change often experienced by data professionals: database migrations.

The Dangers of Database Migrations

While software developers focus on building software systems that are maintainable and easy to scale, data developers unfortunately struggle to do so given the amount of unknowns in our workflows with respect to data. Even with tooling that enables transformation logic as code (e.g., dbt) or table versioning in cloud databases (e.g., Snowflake and Databricks), what the data represents is constantly changing. Thus, data infrastructure focuses on the ability to not only maintain the codebase but also provide consistent and trustworthy data that can be iterated on. When one's data is unable to do this, we call it data debt, and therefore consider the possibility of a database migration. Even with the benefit of reducing data debt, potential pitfalls of database migrations include:

Data loss
> When moving data from database A to database B, there is a risk of data loss if an error occurs during runtime or because of faulty logic. For example, we've

experienced instances where data was missing for some of our earlier customers as that specific data's date was greater than the implemented date filter, and thus never made it into the new database. Fast-forward a year after the migration, and as a data consumer I'm confused as to why I can't answer historical questions for particular organizations.

Introduction of data quality issues

We live by the mantra that data degrades every time you move it. While it's a conservative notion, this skepticism is crucial for being cognizant of the fragile nature of data. In the case of a database migration, you are often moving data in sizes where it's infeasible to determine a 1:1 match between tables and thus have to rely on aggregate metrics such as row counts. Depending on the data, a level of error may be acceptable, but this cutoff must be determined by the business need.

Massive amounts of change management

As stated in the large-scale refactor section, changes at this scale are a business decision more than a technical decision. Thus, change management needs to go beyond the technical staff implementing the change to impacted stakeholders (e.g., a business user reviewing dashboards). Ideally a database migration is an improvement, but regardless, change is happening and will require extensive and repeated communication.

Staff pulled away from main roles

As stated earlier, it's much easier to get budget allocation for revenue-driving workflows than infrastructure. This lack of prioritization is often why data debt can build for so long before a database migration is put on the roadmap—resulting in many data teams spending too much time being reactive rather than focusing on their main roles. This pitfall is less about the migration than about shining a light on how database migrations can grow into a major problem to solve.

Untangling business logic is painful

As noted in the Alan refactor use case, it was five years before a refactor was implemented. In that time, team members leave, assumptions about the business change, and earlier processes are less mature. What results is an attempt to piece together complex business logic that expands for years and ensure it's still maintained in the new database. Doing so perfectly is unlikely, and thus data developers need to be aware of this limitation.

Much like a large-scale refactor, a database migration is a complex and challenging experience for developers.

Despite these pitfalls, organizations still engage with database migrations on a regular basis. Again, such large changes to software and data systems are a business decision rather than a technical decision, and thus the ROI warrants such initiatives. Such considerations include:

Data debt pain

While infrastructure projects are overlooked for revenue-driving projects, it becomes much easier to sell infrastructure projects when the pain of data debt is higher than the pain of migrating. Specifically, as data debt increases, trust in the data decreases, which limits an organization's ability to extract value from data. An example of this is a database approaching its memory limit and thus risking data pipelines going down for key executive dashboards.

Changing business models

The business model changed, thus there are new requirements for revenue-driving work. For example, a company's product may move from batch reporting to real-time analytics as its main product feature. This completely changes the underlying assumptions of the business, and thus the technology and databases need to be migrated to meet technical requirements.

Regulatory changes

Many companies are experiencing the impact of the European Union's General Data Protection Regulation (GDPR) (*https://gdpr.eu*) on data processing and storage, resulting in major database migrations to adhere to regulations and avoid fees. As the United States catches up to Europe for data privacy laws, such as with the California Consumer Privacy Act (CCPA) (*https://oreil.ly/Hdhpp*), we see database migrations becoming more prominent.

Skyrocketing cloud costs

One of the earliest wins a new data team can reach is doing an audit of its cloud spend. With uncertainty in the wider market, chief financial officers are looking at budgets across the organization and seeing the obscene prices of cloud spend. Database migrations can help teams slash cloud spend by migrating to cheaper storage.

Opportunities with new technologies

Finally, as new technologies emerge, so do new use cases in which data can be used. In 2023 the emergence of large language models in production has spurred companies to start looking at vector databases to manage their own LLMs in production, and thus another database migration is needed.

Again, the preceding points must be viewed within the context of business needs. Therefore, it's essential for data teams to translate how these technical considerations apply to the business as means of change management.

The Role of Change Management in Data Quality

In Chapter 2 we defined data quality as "an organization's ability to understand the degree of correctness of its data assets, and the trade-offs of operationalizing such data at various degrees of correctness throughout the data lifecycle, as it pertains to being fit for use by the data consumer." A simplified way to view this definition is "an organization's ability to handle change management for processes related to data." Specifically, poor data quality is the symptom of the data, representing a technology and/or a process, diverging from the real-world truth.

Thus, data teams need to be vigilant of both 1) externally driven changes that impact their workflows (e.g., a new product feature), and 2) the impact of changes implemented by their team (e.g., new data transformation logic). While change management is necessary within software engineering as well, it is amplified for data-related processes given its management needs to be handled around both code and data; unfortunately, data is also significantly less stable than code as it's in a constant state of decay. This decaying of data is what makes it difficult to work with as compared to the stability of software systems.

The Entropic Behavior of Data

Much like entropy, data is in a constant state of change and decay from the moment it's recorded. While some data's decay rate is relatively slow, such as a Social Security number, other forms of data, such as telemetry data, will decay rapidly. Understanding where one's data falls on this spectrum of entropy is integral to understanding the required change management for your data system. With that said, the decay rate of data does not imply a level of value but rather the constraints of the data for its utilization. As an analogy, chemical elements experience entropy, also known as half-lives, which results in valuable quirks for industry use. For example, as illustrated in Figure 3-4, the slow decay of carbon 14 enables scientists to date artifacts and fossils thousands of years old, while the fast decay of technetium-99m enables its use for medical imaging (*https://oreil.ly/2T3Oq*).

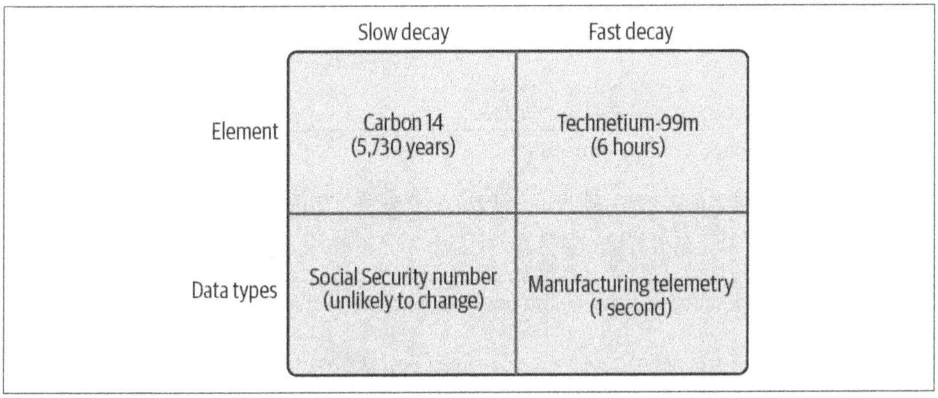

	Slow decay	Fast decay
Element	Carbon 14 (5,730 years)	Technetium-99m (6 hours)
Data types	Social Security number (unlikely to change)	Manufacturing telemetry (1 second)

Figure 3-4. Analogy: entropy of elements compared to data types

Similarly, a Social Security number always being unique and unlikely to change for an individual makes it a great unique identifier (PII aside). At the same time, the quick decay of telemetry data enables it to be extremely useful for real-time streaming.

How Data Drifts from Established Business Logic

Given that data experiences entropy, resulting in organizations needing to manage these changes to continually extract value from data, what type of patterns of change can organizations expect? We once again defer to the field of machine learning, which has established the concept of *data drift* to describe how changes in data and/or understandings of data can impact model performance. While there are multiple types of data drift, the subset of *concept drift* best aligns with the lens of data quality and change management.

In the highly cited paper "Learning Under Concept Drift: A Review," Jie Lu and colleagues define concept drift as "unforeseeable changes in the underlying distribution of…data over time." As illustrated in Figure 3-5, sourced from their research paper (*https://oreil.ly/cwNmi*), concept drift can come in the form of sudden drift, gradual drift, incremental drift, or recurring concepts.

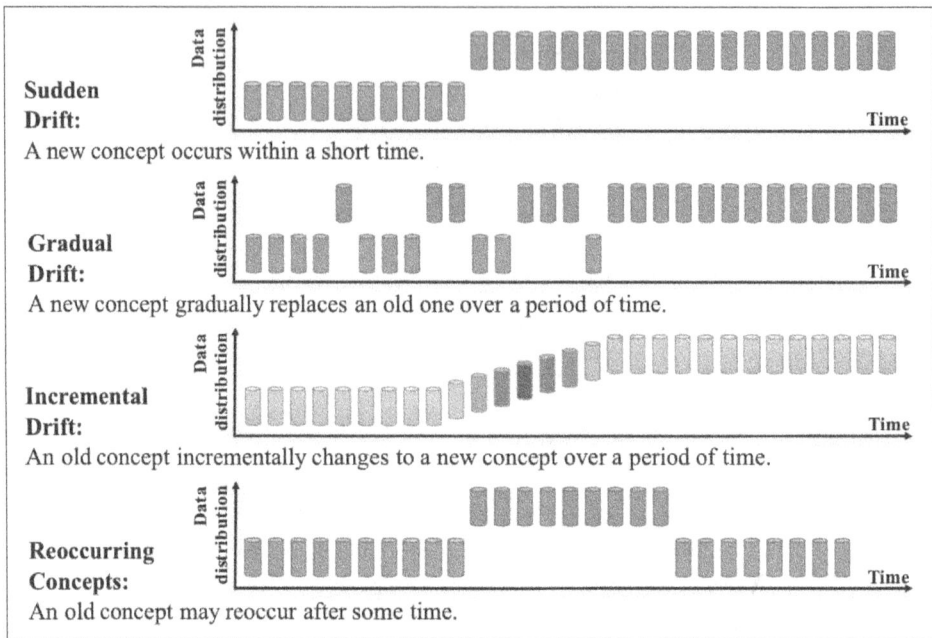

Figure 3-5. An example of concept drift types[1]

Examples of applying the four forms of concept drift to a data quality lens include the following:

Sudden drift

To become GDPR compliant, user data must be removed or changed to meet privacy requirements. On the extreme side, some US news outlets block EU countries from accessing their websites to avoid the regulation (*https://oreil.ly/IqCbj*), and thus completely remove a demographic.

Gradual drift

Over time, a product's target customer changes as a company achieves product-market fit. For example, Netflix moved from DVD sales to streaming and eventually no longer offered DVDs (*https://oreil.ly/RQkpJ*).

Incremental drift

A userbase's median age gradually changes, such as the gaming company Roblox, whose initial demographic was young children. As the same children grew up

---

1 A huge thank-you to Dr. Jie Lu for allowing us to use the image from this research paper: Jie Lu et al., "Learning Under Concept Drift: A Review," *IEEE Transactions on Knowledge and Data Engineering* 31, no. 12 (2019): 2346–2363.

with the platform, their median age is now over 13, and open source projects on the platform reflect that (*https://oreil.ly/984AB*).

Recurring concepts

Recessions in the economy are expected to recur while being impossible to predict precisely. A significant marker of a recession is the drop in discretionary consumer spending (*https://oreil.ly/HlmNQ*); thus, consumer organizations that have existed for decades will have recurring concepts present within their data.

While these four examples are legit changes to data, they can potentially lead to data quality issues if the data teams are not aligned with the business in their change management.

Change Management Needs to Align with the Needs of the Business

The four forms of data concept drift may be clear to a technical team, but it is unlikely that nontechnical business stakeholders will pick up on these nuances until after they are directly impacted. Specifically, stakeholders outside of data struggle with the abstract nature of data and thus struggle to connect data infrastructure to value. For example, ask a stakeholder about a row in an Excel spreadsheet, and they can quickly provide the specific data about the record. Ask the same stakeholder about one hundred thousand rows in the same Excel spreadsheet, and they will likely struggle. This same level of scale required for data infrastructure is similarly abstract and far removed from the workflows of the business stakeholder. Thus, data professionals need to clearly map data infrastructure needs to business outcomes as part of their change management processes.

For example, diving deeper into the "sudden drift" GDPR use case, why would US news outlets block EU countries from accessing their websites to avoid the regulation? According to the GDPR regulatory body (*https://gdpr.eu/fines*), "less severe infringements could result in a fine of up to €10 million, or 2% of the firm's worldwide annual revenue from the preceding financial year, whichever amount is higher." In the case of US news outlets whose primary revenue-providing audience is in the US, making the business case for data quality practices that align with GDPR would fall flat, as the data quality initiative doesn't align with their business model. In comparison, for a major US news outlet with a worldwide audience that drives revenue, making the necessary data quality investments is a substantially easier sell.

These efforts are not about data quality for data quality's sake; they're about data quality to drive business value. As an additional example, data quality is similar to surveys. While an exhaustive survey of every possible person in a population would ideally get the most accurate results, most surveys don't pursue such methods, given how infeasible or cost-prohibitive it is. The same is true for data quality and its associated change management, in that perfect data is theoretically ideal, but achieving it is both improbable and not worth the ROI to the business.

Thus, data teams need to work with the business to align data quality practices with the needs of the business. Specifically, data quality infrastructure needs to enable organizations to scale change management via:

- Codifying domain knowledge of business stakeholders with respect to valuable data use cases and disseminating such knowledge across the organization
- Creating meaningful constraints on the data systems to uphold data standards to the expected domain knowledge
- Identifying when data drift occurs, what type of drift occurs, and its impact on the business
- Alerting key stakeholders when drift impacts an agreed-upon threshold to data quality
- Rectifying data quality or updating the business logic to better match real-world truth after data drift

These five requirements are why we strongly believe in data contracts as a needed mechanism to enable data quality at scale.

How Infrastructure Needs Change at Scale

When considering the scale of technical systems, developers often primarily emphasize the system's technical capacity over the need to scale people and processes through technology. While technical capacity is essential for meeting established requirements, technical teams need to also account for how new technology will change interpersonal relationships and processes, both among their respective team and other internal stakeholders. Two patterns that best reflect the impact of people and processes on technical scale are Dunbar's Number and Conway's Law. Technical teams that account for these two patterns are best equipped to not only successfully implement scaling projects, but also ensure such projects align with the business.

Dunbar's Number and Conway's Law

Anthropologist Robin Dunbar posited that respective species have (*https://oreil.ly/ VigDc*):

> [an] information-processing capacity and that this then limits the number of relationships that an individual can monitor simultaneously. When a group's size exceeds this limit, it becomes unstable and begins to fragment. This then places an upper limit on the size of groups which any given species can maintain as cohesive social units through time.

For humans, Dunbar determined that this number of relationships is around 150 people, on average (*https://oreil.ly/VigDc*), as this number has been observed among businesses, military units, and referenced in popular culture such as Malcolm Gladwell's book *The Tipping Point* (Back Bay Books). Chris Cox, chief product officer at Meta, called it "one of the magic numbers in group sizes" in a 2016 interview (*https://oreil.ly/uoJko*), adding "I've talked to so many startup CEOs that after they pass this number, weird stuff starts to happen.... The weird stuff means the company needs more structure for communications and decision-making."

Key to understanding this phenomena is that the number of potential relationships within an organization grows exponentially, while the number of employees grows linearly—as seen in Figure 3-6. At 150 employees, there are 11,175 potential relationships within an organization, and simply adding 10 employees increases the number of potential relationships by around 1,500. This is roughly 10 times more than the increase in potential connections going from 10 to 20 employees. To reiterate, this is why technical teams need to also account for how new technology will change interpersonal relationships, especially as they pass Dunbar's Number.

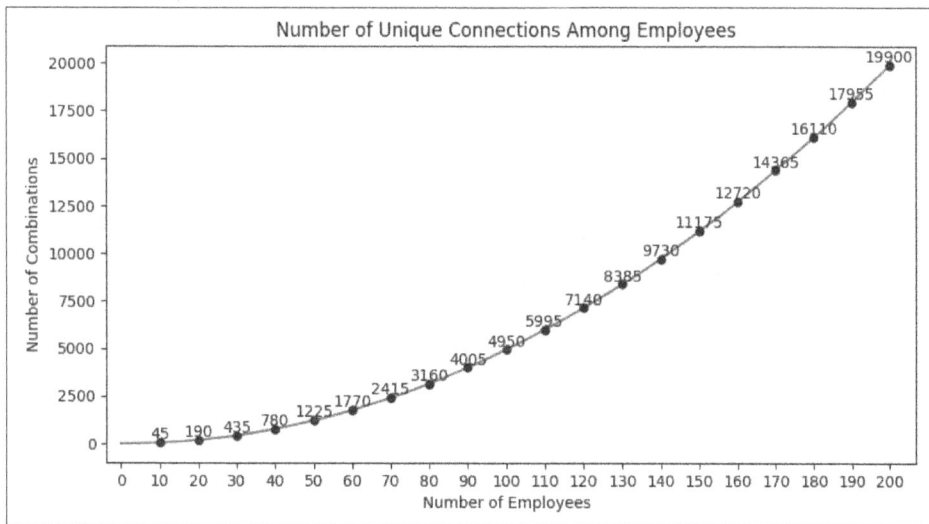

Figure 3-6. Exponential rise in connections as employee count increases

In addition to the number of connections, how organizations communicate among these connections is also important. As Melvin Conway stated in his 1968 paper, "How Do Committees Invent?" (*https://oreil.ly/lha9P*), "Any organization that designs a system...will inevitably produce a design whose structure is a copy of the organization's communication structure." Even Martin Fowler, whom we referenced earlier regarding refactoring, noted how even skeptical engineers accept the power of Conway's Law (*https://oreil.ly/DABd_*) and that it's "[important] enough to affect every system [he's] come across, and powerful enough that you're doomed to defeat if you try to fight it." Ultimately, these two laws reflect the challenges of maintaining complex technical systems within organizations as they scale—and why change management among software and data developers is so important. A great example of this at play is the organization Atlassian, which confronted both laws while scaling its engineering.

Case Study: Atlassian Engineering Team

Even engineering teams at vendors that specialize in software development collaboration and communication are still bound to the impacts of Dunbar's Number and Conway's Law. Atlassian, the company behind the widely used issue tracking product Jira, had to account for these phenomena when it scaled its engineering team.

When Atlassian moved its Confluence Cloud team, one of the first things leadership accounted for was Dunbar's Number by scaling down the team into a manageable number. By scaling the team down, engineers were able to build stronger rapport and collaboration practices. During this phase, Atlassian's Confluence Cloud team focused on relationship building and work sharing across teams, ensuring managers had less than five direct reports, and that direct teammates were colocated. Before the team even considered scaling the team back up, it ensured that its tools, systems, and processes could handle the increased complexity of adding more people.

While Atlassian had success with overcoming Dunbar's Number, it initially struggled with the power of Conway's Law. Specifically, Atlassian tried a "squads and tribes" model but quickly learned that such a team organization was ineffective for managing complex software systems. The individual groups from the squads and tribes model didn't reflect the system they were trying to build, and engineers struggled to ramp up and be effective when they moved to a different group within the organization. From this hard lesson, Atlassian instead focused on being able to pick up signals that a team's organization didn't match up with the system it was trying to build, or that there were duplicative efforts. In instances where such signals were picked up, emphasis was placed on having a single team work on duplicative systems as a catalyst to have the two systems converge and reduce complexity.

Atlassian's use case expands beyond these two examples, and we highly encourage you to learn more via this blog post by Stephen Deasy (*https://oreil.ly/icM62*).

How Data Contracts Enable Change Management at Scale

In summary, Dunbar's Number implies that communication and relationships start to break down as an organization reaches 150 employees. This level of scale requires new processes and team structures to enable effective communication while scaling, especially when building complex technical systems such as those that rely on data. Furthermore, Conway's Law emphasizes the impact of an organization's communication and team structure on the output of its produced system.

Together, Dunbar's Number and Conway's Law highlight that scaling complex data systems cannot be achieved via technical requirements alone. Furthermore, simply scaling a team or process only adds further complexity and thus results in a breakdown of systems. We argue that data teams need to first scale their ability to communicate and collaborate among a growing team before they focus on scaling their technical requirements. Specifically, data contracts enable organizations to scale collaboration and change management within data systems.

Figure 3-7 illustrates this with an example of an organization network where the nodes represent individuals, and the lines represent a connection between two individuals. When an issue is identified by a specific node, it doesn't happen in a vacuum but is instead tied to the contingencies of their respective network—such as an upstream data producer changing the schema of a data asset and thus breaking downstream dashboards. Without data contracts, this individual has a plethora of first- and second-degree connections that the issue needs to be coordinated with. This often looks like widespread messages to teams either informing them of an issue or requesting help. Data contracts significantly limit the problem scope by programmatically monitoring changes for known constraints, keeping track of the data asset owners, and only notifying relevant parties. Thus, data contracts enable organizations to overcome the limitations of Dunbar's Number by limiting the number of relationships an individual needs to keep track of. In addition, data contracts leverage the power of Conway's Law to optimize communication among relevant parties within complex systems.

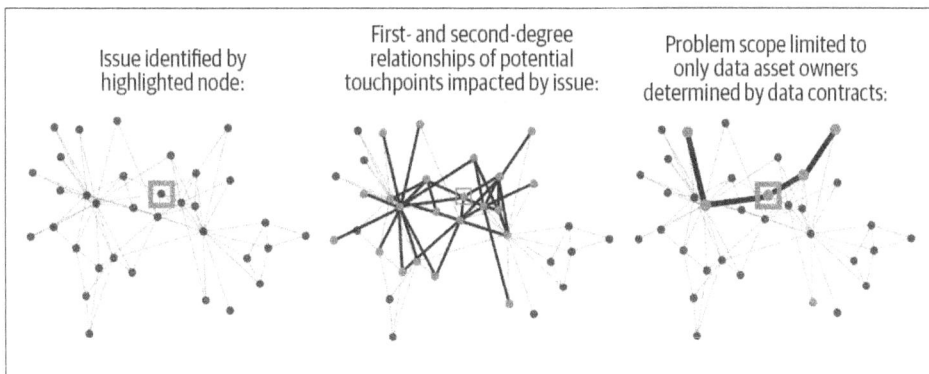

Figure 3-7. The degrees of relationships in resolving issues

Going back to Martin Fowler, he also noted that (*https://oreil.ly/DABd_*):

> if I can talk easily to the author of some code, then it is easier for me to build up a rich understanding of that code. This makes it easier for my code to interact, and thus be coupled, to that code. Not just in terms of explicit function calls, but also in the implicit shared assumptions and way of thinking about the problem domain.

This gets to the crux of the problem that data contracts are aiming to solve. With respect to data change management, data contracts are the glue that holds people and processes together among increasingly complex technical systems.

Conclusion

In this chapter, we discussed the challenges of the everyday workflows of data producers and consumers in building and maintaining complex software and data systems. In summary, this chapter covered:

- How data development is different from software development
- The implications of these differences on our ability to drive value with data in an organization
- How businesses approach large-scale refactors such as for managing technical debt and database migrations
- Why scaling makes managing incredibly difficult, and how Dunbar's Number and Conway's Law give insight as to why it's so challenging

Among all of these challenges, we argue that data contracts are necessary for scaling these workflows among technical teams and managing the necessary change management of data workflows.

With that said, we also want to highlight how focusing on change management is less an emphasis on the changing of data, but rather on the changing of assumptions around data. These assumptions are critical, as they frame how we interpret the underlying data and whether it's trustworthy and fit for purpose for the task it's being utilized for. In the next chapter, we begin to go in depth as to what data contracts are and their various components.

An Introduction to Data Contracts

The previous three chapters focused heavily on the *why* of data contracts and the problem statement that data contracts aims to solve. Starting in Chapter 4, we shift to defining what exactly the data contract architecture is and what its workflow looks like. This chapter will serve as the theoretical foundation before transitioning into discussing real-world implementations in Chapter 5 and implementing it yourself in Chapters 6 and 7. In addition to the theoretical foundation, we will also discuss the key stakeholders and workflows when utilizing data contracts.

Collaboration Is Different in Data

Depending on who you ask, "collaboration" could be either a nebulous executive buzzword or a vague and lofty promise about improving the relationships between team members who already have quite a bit of work to do.

For the purposes of this book, our definition of technical collaboration is the following: "Collaboration refers to a form of distributed development where multiple individuals and teams, regardless of their location, can contribute to a project efficiently and effectively."

Teams may collaborate online or offline, and with comprehensive working models or not. The goal of collaboration is to increase the quality of software development through human-in-the-loop review and continuous improvement.

In the modern technology ecosystem, there are many components to collaboration that have become part of the standard developer lifecycle and release process, with the two most prominent being:

Version control
> Allows multiple contributors to work on a project without interfering with each other's changes. Version control is a fundamental component of collaboration facilitated through source code management systems like Git.

Pull requests
> Another common collaborative feature that has become an essential component of DevOps. Contributors can make changes in the code branches they maintain, then propose these changes to the main codebase using PRs. PRs are then reviewed by software engineers on the same team in order to ensure high code quality and consistency.

With automation, collaboration around the codebase can provide short feedback loops between developers that ensure bugs are mitigated prior to release. The team has a general understanding of which changes are being merged to production and how they impact the codebase, ensuring greater accountability for releases, which are now often made multiple times per day.

All of this is ultimately done to improve code quality. If you are an engineer, imagine what would life be like if your company wasn't using software like GitHub, GitLab, Azure DevOps, or BitBucket. Teams would need to make manual backups of their codebase and leverage centralized locking systems to ensure only one developer was working on a particular file at a time. Teams would also have to consistently check in with each other to plan which aspects of the codebase would be worked on by whom, and all updates would be shared through email or FTP systems. With space for human error, a significant amount of time would be spent dealing with bugs and software conflicts, as illustrated in Figure 4-1.

However, effective collaboration is not only about implementing core underlying technology—it ultimately hinges on the interaction patterns between changemakers and change approvers. These interaction patterns will differ depending on the change being made, the significance of the change, and the organizational design of the company.

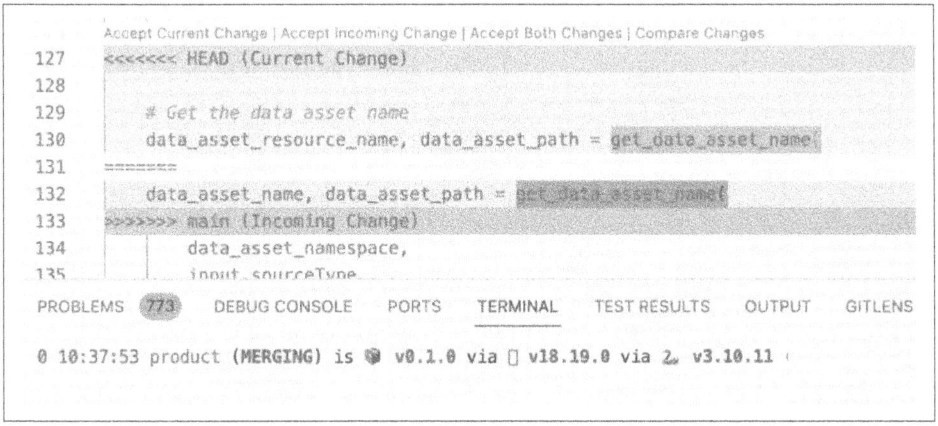

```
Accept Current Change | Accept Incoming Change | Accept Both Changes | Compare Changes
127    <<<<<<< HEAD (Current Change)
128
129        # Get the data asset name
130        data_asset_resource_name, data_asset_path = get_data_asset_name
131    =======
132        data_asset_name, data_asset_path = get_data_asset_name
133    >>>>>>> main (Incoming Change)
134            data_asset_namespace,
135            input_sourceType,
```

PROBLEMS 773   DEBUG CONSOLE   PORTS   **TERMINAL**   TEST RESULTS   OUTPUT   GITLENS

0 10:37:53 product (**MERGING**) is 🌱 v0.1.0 via ▯ v18.19.0 via 🐍 v3.10.11

Figure 4-1. Example of a merge conflict with a version control tool

GitHub, the world's most popular version control system, was launched in 2008 by Tom Preston-Werner, Chris Wanstrath, and PJ Hyett. By 2011, GitHub was home to over one million code repositories, and grew tenfold over the following two years. GitHub not only solved a significant technical challenge by creating a simple-to-use interface for Git and providing a host of collaboration-oriented functionality, but it also allowed leadership teams that were excited by the principles of Agile software development to meaningfully switch to new organizational structures that were better in line with rapid, iterative release schedules and federation.

These organizational structures placed software engineers at the center of product teams. Product teams were composed of a core engineering team, reinforced by a variety of other roles such as product and program managers, designers, data scientists, and data engineers. Each product team acted as a unique microorganism within the company, pursuing distinct goals and objectives that, while being in line with the company's top-level initiatives, were tailored to specific application components. GitHub allowed developers on these teams to further subdivide their tasks, many of which overlapped, without consequence.

Despite federated collaboration becoming a core component of a product development team's workflow, this same cycle of review and release is not present for data organizations, or for software engineers who maintain data sources such as production databases, APIs, or event streams. This is primarily because software engineers operate within teams, while data flows *between* teams, as illustrated in Figure 4-2.

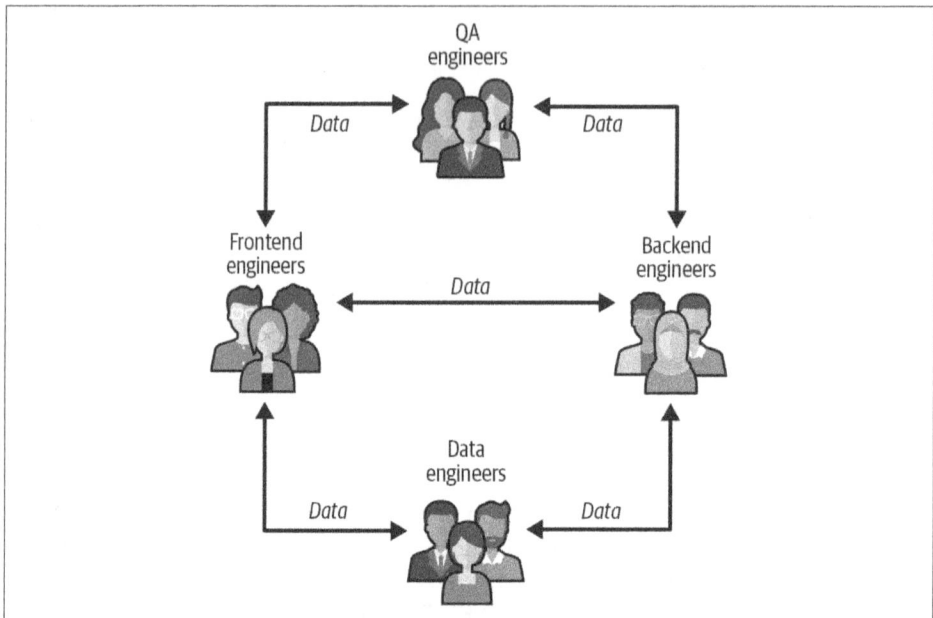

Figure 4-2. Interoperability of data among engineering silos

Each member of a product team has a built-in incentive to take collaboration seriously. Bad code shipped by an engineer could cause a loss of revenue or delays to the feature roadmap. Because product teams are judged according to their component-level goals, each engineer is equally accountable for changes in their codebase.

However, data is a very different story. In most cases, data is stored in source systems owned by product teams, which flow downstream to data developers in finance, marketing, or product. Upstream and downstream teams have unique goals and timelines. Due to the highly iterative and experimental nature of constructing a query (or asking/answering a question), it is often unclear at the moment the query is created whether or not it will be useful. This leads to a split in the way data is being used and a divergence of responsibilities and ownership.

When upstream software engineers make changes to their database, these changes are reviewed by their own team but *not* the downstream teams that leverage this data for a set of totally different use cases. Thanks to the isolated nature of product teams, upstream engineers are kept in the dark about how these changes affect others in the company, and downstream teams are given no time to collaborate and provide feedback to their data providers upstream. By the time data teams detect something has changed, it is already too late—pipelines have been broken, dashboards display incorrect results, and the product team that made the change has already moved on.

The primary goal of data contracts is to solve this problem. Contracts are *a mechanism for expanding software-oriented collaboration to data teams, bringing quality to data through human-in-the-loop review, just as the same systems facilitated code quality for product teams.* The next section goes into more detail about who these stakeholders are and how they collaborate.

The Stakeholders You Will Work With

As stated in the previous section, data contracts center around collaboration in managing complex systems that leverage software and data. To best collaborate, you must first understand who you are working with. The following section details the various stakeholders and their role in the data lifecycle with respect to data contracts.

The Role of Data Producers

Thus far we have been talking quite a bit about the gaps between data producers and data consumers that culminate in data quality issues. But before we go further into the *why* of data contracts as a solution, it is essential to understand the responsibilities of all those who are involved with collecting, transforming, and using data. By understanding the incentive structures of key players in this complex value chain of data movement, we can better identify how technology helps us address and overcome challenges with communication between each party.

Data does not materialize from thin air. It must be explicitly collected by software engineers building applications leveraged by customers or other services. *Data producers* is what we call engineers responsible for collecting and storing this data. While unique roles like data engineers can be both producers and consumers, or nontechnical teams such as salespeople or even customers themselves can be responsible for data entry, for now we will focus primarily on the role of software engineers, who almost exclusively take on the work of most data producers in a company.

Most structured data can be broken down into a collection of *events* that correspond to actions undertaken either by some customer leveraging the application or by the system itself. In general, there are two types of events that are useful to downstream consumers:

Transactional events
> Transactional events refer to individual transaction records logged when a customer or technology takes some explicit behavior that typically (but not always) results in a change in state. An example of a transactional event might be a customer making an order, a backend service processing and validating that order, or the order being released and delivered to a customer's address. Transactional events are either stored in relational database management systems (RDBMSs) or emitted using stream processing frameworks such as Apache Kafka.

Clickstream events

Clickstream events are built to capture a user's interactions with a web or mobile application for the purpose of tracking engagement with features. An example of a clickstream event might be a user starting a new web session, a customer adding an item to their cart, or a shopper conducting a web search. There are many tools available to capture clickstream events, such as Amplitude, Google Analytics, or Segment.

Clickstream events are typically limited in their shape and contents by software development kits provided by third-party companies to emit, collect, and analyze behavioral data. These events are often stored in the vendor's cloud storage environment, where product managers and data scientists can conduct funnel analysis, perform A/B tests, and segment users into cohorts to see behavioral trends across groups. Clickstream data can then be loaded from these third-party providers into first-party analytical databases such as Snowflake, Redshift, or BigQuery.

Transactional events depend entirely on the role of the applications and can vary wildly in terms of their schema, data contents, and complexity. For example, in some banks, transactional events may contain hundreds or even thousands of columns with detailed information about the transaction itself, the account, the payer, the payee, the branch, the transaction channel, security information (which is highly leveraged for fraud detection models), any fees or changes, and much more. In many cases, there is so much data recorded in transactional events that much of a schema goes unused or is simply not leveraged in a meaningful way by the service.

Because transactional events record data that is seen as only being relevant to the functioning of the application owned by the engineering team (as opposed to clickstream events, which are designed specifically for product analytics), it is often said that transactional data is a *by-product* of the application. Data producers treat their relational databases as an extension of their applications, and will generally modify them using CI/CD processes similar to their typical software release process.

In the modern data environment, the data producers' role stops once the data has been collected, processed, and stored in an accessible format. In the past, the responsibility of the data producer was also heavily influenced by design and *data architecture*. However, in federated product environments this function is becoming increasingly rare and is seen as unneeded. It is easier and faster for the data producer to collect whatever data they would like from the application, store it all in their database in the most beneficial format for their application, and then make the data accessible to data consumers so that they might leverage the data for analysis.

To be clear, this is not a statement on what we think is right or wrong, but simply a description of how a significant amount of data producers in technologically advanced organizations actually behave.

The Role of Data Consumers

A data consumer is a company employee who has access to data provided by a data producer, and leverages that data to construct pipelines, answer questions, or build machine learning models. Data consumers are split into two categories, technical and nontechnical.

Technical data consumers are what you might call data developers. Data developers are engineers or analysts who leverage data-oriented programming languages like SQL, Spark, Python, R, and others to either analyze data in large volumes in order to discover trends and insights, or construct pipelines that allow data to flow through a series of transformations on a schedule before being leveraged for decision making. Technical data consumers deal with the nitty-gritty of data management, from data discovery, query generation, documentation, data cleaning, data validation, and much more.

Nontechnical data consumers are often business users or product managers who lack the technical ability to construct queries themselves (or can only do so on pre-cleaned and validated data). This category of users typically are the ones asking the questions, and ultimately they hold the decision-making power for which outcome should be taken, depending on the directionality of the data.

For the remainder of this chapter, we'll be focusing on the technical data consumer, though we'll get back to the role nontechnical teams play later. There are many different types of technical data consumers and where they fit into the data lifecycle, as illustrated in Table 4-1:

Data engineers
> Data engineers are most commonly known as *software engineers with a data specialty*. They focus on extracting data from source systems, moving data into cheap file storage (such as data lakes or delta lakes), then eventually moving it to analytical databases, cleaning and formatting the incoming data for proper use, and ensuring pipelines have been orchestrated properly. Data engineers form the backbones of most data teams and are responsible for ensuring the entire business gets up-to-date, high-quality data on a schedule.

Data scientists
> Once one of the sexiest jobs in the world, data scientists are computer engineers with a higher focus placed on statistics and machine learning. Data scientists are most frequently associated with creating features to be leveraged by ML models, conducting and evaluating hypothesis tests, and developing predictive models to better forecast the success of key business objectives.

Data analyst

Data analysts are SQL specialists. They primarily leverage SQL to construct queries in order to answer business questions. Analysts are on the front lines of query composition—it is their responsibility to understand where data is flowing from, if it's trustworthy, and what it means.

Analytics engineers

Analytics engineering is a relatively new discipline that revolves around applying software development best practices to analytics. Analytics engineers or BI engineers leverage data modeling techniques and tooling like dbt to construct well-defined data models that can be leveraged by analysts and data scientists.

Data platform engineer

Even newer than analytics engineers, platform engineers are responsible for the implementation, adoption, and ongoing growth of the data infrastructure and core datasets. Platform engineers often have data engineering or software engineering backgrounds, and are mainly concerned with selecting the right analytical databases, streaming solutions, data catalogs, and orchestration systems for a company's needs.

Table 4-1. Data consumers and their data lifecycle touchpoints

Data consumer role	Data infra-management	Data ingestion	Transaction data operations	Data replication	Analytical data operations	Analytics, insights, and dashboards	ML model building	Actioning on insights and predictions
Data platform engineer	X	X	X	X	X			
Data engineer		X	X	X	X			
Analytics engineer				X	X			
Data analyst						X		
Data scientist						X	X	
Internal business stakeholder								X
External user of data product								X

Most technical data consumers follow a similar workflow when beginning a new project:

1. Define or receive requirements from nontechnical consumers.
2. Attempt to understand what data is available and where it comes from.
3. Investigate if data is clearly understood and trustworthy.
4. If not, try to locate the source of the data and work with data producers to better understand what the data means and how it is being instrumented in the app.
5. Validate the data.
6. Create a query (and potentially a more comprehensive pipeline) that leverages valuable data assets.

Data consumers access data through a variety of different channels, depending on their skill set and background. Data engineers extract data in batches from multiple sources using open source ELT technologies like Airbyte, or closed source tooling such as Fivetran. Data engineers can also build infrastructure that moves data in real time. The more common example of this is change data capture (CDC). CDC captures record-level transformations in upstream source systems before pushing each record into an analytical environment, most commonly using streaming technologies such as Apache Kafka or Redpanda. Once data arrives in an analytical environment, data engineers then clean, structure, and transform the data into key business objects that can be leveraged by other consumers downstream.

Data scientists, analytics engineers, and analysts typically deal with data after it has already been processed by data engineers. Depending on the use case, their most common activities might include dimensional modeling and creating data marts, building machine learning models, or constructing views that can then be used to power dashboards or reporting.

The output of most data consumers' work is *queries*. Queries are code written in a language designed for either analytical or transactional databases—most commonly SQL, though Python is also a popular data science alternative. Depending on the complexity of the operation, queries can range from simple 5-to-10-line code blocks to incredibly complex files with hundreds or even thousands of lines full of CASE WHEN statements. As these queries are leveraged to answer business questions, they might be extended, replicated, or modified in a variety of ways.

The Impact of Producers and Consumers

As you might imagine, data producers play a large role in the day-to-day work of data consumers. Data producers control the creation of and access to source data. Source data represents information as close to the ground truth as possible, given that it is collected directly from applications. Data consumers often prefer to use upstream data because releveraging queries built by other data consumers can be challenging. The meaning of queries is ultimately subjective—a data scientist may have an opinion on what makes an active customer "active" or a lost order "lost." These opinions are often baked into the query code with very little explanation or documentation provided. Depending on the length and complexity of the query, it might be almost impossible for other data scientists to fully understand what one of their fellow data team members meant.

> This problem of lost context is exacerbated with time. Data consumers regularly leave their place of employment and often take the knowledge of their code along with them. This is called *institutional knowledge*.

For these reasons, data consumers love going to the source. In the same way, it's always easier to get information about a particular person directly from that individual than to rely on rumors and hearsay. However, going to the source can be challenging. It can require understanding the lineage of your data ecosystem. Lineage refers to the spider web of connections that tie data assets to each other within an analytical environment. The older and denser the environment, the more challenging it can be to track lineage across nodes in the graph. The lineage graph creates an additional problem: change management.

As data producers update their application, they regularly make changes to the code of their software. Software changes may or may not affect data structures, such as schema or the contents of data-generating objects like transactional events, logs, or analytical events. Because there is no baseline that sets the expected state of these data objects, data producers make their changes effectively in the dark, as illustrated in Figure 4-3. While integration testing can help check integration errors with the code itself, and production management software like LaunchDarkly (feature management) or Datadog (observability) can detect issues or prevent them from degrading a customer experience, this quality assurance only applies to the application layer, not the data layer where data consumers do their work. The data layer is hidden behind the lineage graph. Such convoluted and tangled data environments make it very difficult for application developers to understand how and where their data is being used.

One option for data producers might be to treat *any* impact to the data layer as part of CI/CD. Unfortunately, this rarely works out well. At most large-scale businesses the amount of data in a data lake is so large that it is rare for even 25% of the data to have meaningful utilization within the company. Slowing down your engineering team to ensure integration testing for data that isn't even relevant or useful for data consumers is a waste of time. Producers must be free to iterate so long as they have limited dependencies.

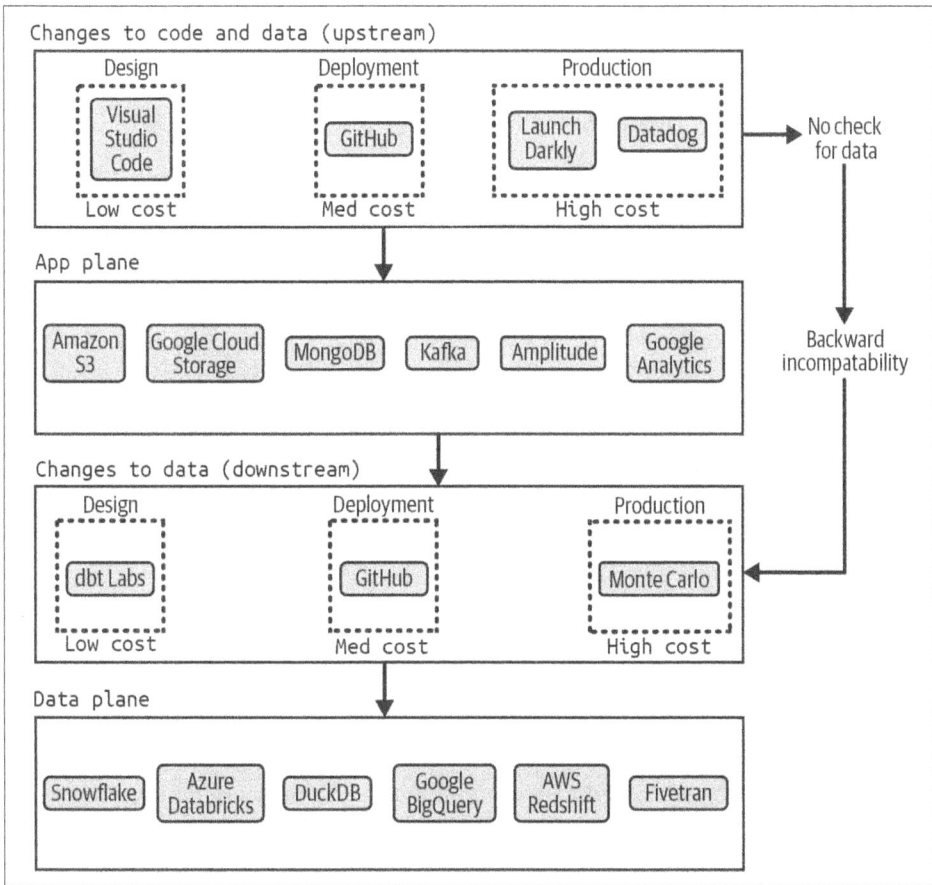

Figure 4-3. How visibility of data use is obstructed

Second, oftentimes backward-incompatible changes are hard requirements. Product teams regularly ship new features, refactor old code, and modify events according to a grander architectural design that has buy-in from across the organization. While these changes may catch downstream consumers unaware, they often have too much momentum to be stopped. Data producers might attempt to communicate migrations to data consumers by sending emails, announcing their intentions during design reviews, or posting plans in Slack channels. Unfortunately, this feedback loop rarely reaches data consumers, who (again, due to complex lineage) rarely realize they will be impacted by an upstream change even if they knew the context.

When change does happen, it is rarely detected in advance. More often than not, downstream consumers (and in the worst-case scenario, nontechnical business stakeholders) are the first to notice a problem exists, which sets them on a long-winded goose chase of identifying and resolving errors caused by an upstream team that barely knows they even exist.

The Trials and Tribulations of Data Consumers Managing Data Quality

Most data practitioners will have a chill run down their spine when they hear the phrase, "These numbers look off." Such statements often lead to hours or days of digging into data and their respective systems to unearth and fix data quality issues. Often, data teams are the "face of failure" for these data quality issues within the business, despite many issues arising from upstream changes outside of their control. In Mark's time in startups as a data scientist and data engineer, he came up with a repeatable pattern for solving these data quality issues in organizations where data maturity was relatively early. While this process is relatively manual, many organizations find themselves in similar positions. The data quality resolution process consisted of the following steps, which we have written about in more detail previously (*https://oreil.ly/NmiRw*):

1. Stakeholder surfaces issue
2. Issue triage
3. Requirements scoping
4. Issue replication
5. Data profiling
6. Downstream pipeline investigation
7. Upstream pipeline investigation
8. Consult technical stakeholders
9. Pre-deploy—implement DQ fix
10. Deploy—implement DQ fix
11. Stakeholder communication

Note that a majority of these steps are not technical but rather center around communication across the business to triage breaks within the data lifecycle and coordinate a solution among multiple teams. In more detail, each step consists of the following from the perspective of the analytical database:

1. Stakeholder surfaces issue

The best-case scenario is that a data consumer, such as a data analyst, surfaces a data quality issue before downstream business stakeholders notice. Getting ahead of the data quality issue is less about avoiding the downstream users noticing than about making sure your stakeholders are confident that you are handling issues in a timely manner. How you respond to such requests shapes the data culture among your stakeholders.

2. Issue triage

While it's important to respond quickly, data teams should not try to solve the data issue until they properly triage the issue as an urgent fix, assign it for later, or decide to not work on it. Key to this is having managers on the data team serve as a buffer and set expectations. In addition, requests should never be accepted within individual chat channels (e.g., direct Slack message) but rather should be directed toward a shared channel with visibility, such as Jira.

3. Requirements scoping

Mark's early-career mistakes in data often stemmed from jumping straight into solving the problem without properly scoping the issue. Often there are trade-offs between the effort and the impact of the fix, and thus you need to consult with the downstream stakeholder to understand why this data is important and how it impacts their workflows. In addition, this step further fosters trust with your stakeholder as it shows the due diligence you are taking as well as includes them in the resolution process.

4. Issue replication

Once the problem is scoped, problem replication provides the first clues as to where the data quality issue is stemming from. In addition, it prevents you from pursuing a data quality issue that is the result of a human error—which instead implies a communication or process issue. Typically, issue replication can be done by either using the data product in question or pulling data from the source table via SQL.

5. Data profiling

At this stage you can do a series of aggregates and cuts of the tables in question. While not exhaustive, the following are great starting points:

- Data timelines
- Null patterns
- Data count spikes or drops
- Counts by aggregate (e.g., org ID)
- Reviews of the data lineage of impacted tables

The goal isn't to find the issue, but rather to reduce the scope of the issue surface so you can do a deep dive in a targeted fashion. These quick data searches become the hypotheses to test out.

6. Downstream pipeline investigation

With the hypotheses created from data profiling, test assumptions via downstream investigation in the analytical databases and data products. While the issue may be caused by an upstream change, its visibility is often most present downstream. Again, emphasis is on building a complete picture of the data quality issue and potentially discovering other surfaces impacted by the issue that were not in the original problem. Two common issues that surface in this stage are the following:

- A bug was introduced in the SQL transformation code, such as a misuse of a JOIN, a WHERE clause missing an edge case, or data pulled from the wrong table (e.g., `user_table` versus `user_information_table`).

- The SQL code no longer aligns with evolving business logic, and thus transformations need to be updated accordingly.

7. Upstream pipeline investigation

After exploring downstream impacts, the next step is to trace the data lineage upstream to the transactional database. Specifically, go beyond the database and review the underlying code generating data, conduct the CRUD operations, and capture logs. In this step, lineage moves from tables and databases to instead also reviewing function calls and the inheritance of these functions. For example, the `product_table` in the database is updated by the `product_sold_count()` function within the `ProductSold` class within the *product_operations.py* file, as seen in this example:

```
# product_operations.py example code

import db_helper_functions as db_helper

class ProductSold:
    def __init__(self) -> None:
        # Connect to the database
        self.db_connection = db_helper.connect_to_database()
        pass

    def product_sold_count(self, product_id, sold_count):
        # Update the product_table in the database with new count
        <python code implementing logic>

        # Update database
        db_connection.commit()
        db_connection.close()
```

Often the most "hidden" data quality issues lurk within the codebases outside the scope of the data team. Without this step, data teams often create additional transformations downstream to deal with it quickly.

8. Consult technical stakeholders

With the facts collected, you may think the solution is apparent, but knowing the solution is only half the battle if the source issue is outside your technical jurisdiction (e.g., limited read-write access to the transactional database). The other half is convincing upstream teams that the proposed solution is correct and that it's worth prioritizing over their current work. Thus, the emphasis is on *consulting* (rather than *requesting*) with stakeholders to make them a stakeholder in the solution and help them understand where it fits within their priorities. Furthermore, there may be some nuances that only those who often work in the upstream system would be aware of.

9. Pre-deploy—implement DQ fix

Once a solution is determined, take the results from the data profiling stage for a baseline reference and identify which values should be changing or staying the same. This is key in both ensuring that your solution does not introduce further data quality issues and documenting the due diligence of resolving the issue for your impacted stakeholders.

For downstream data quality issues, this typically looks like changing the underlying SQL code making the transformations until you are satisfied with the expected behavior of the data. Ideally these SQL files are version controlled via a tool like dbt, and thus will go under code review before changing the database. For upstream data quality issues, changes will certainly go through code review, but the challenge is instead getting a separate team to implement the fix. This will hopefully not be an issue if the consult technical stakeholders stage goes well, but you do need to account for a timeline outside of your control.

10. Deploy—implement DQ fix

Once changes are confirmed and pushed into the main branch of the code repository, the solution needs to be deployed into production and then monitored to ensure changes work as expected. Once the change for the underlying code has been deployed, backfilling the impacted data should be considered and implemented if warranted.

11. Stakeholder communication

One area many technical teams forget to consider is the role of communication among stakeholders, especially business leaders impacted by data quality. Resolving data quality issues in a timely manner is mainly an effort in mitigating lost trust in the data organization; thus simply resolving the issue silently is not enough. Key stakeholders need to be continually informed of the status of the data quality issue, its timeline to being resolved, and its ultimate resolution. The way in which a data quality issue is handled is just as important for maintaining trust in the data organization as resolving the issue.

Though this process is tremendously useful in handling data quality issues, it is still quite manual and reactive. While there are numerous alternatives to automating and scaling data quality (e.g., data observability), we believe that data contracts are the ideal choice for implementing a solution that involves multiple teams along the same data lifecycle within an organization.

An Alternative: The Data Contract Workflow

The current state of resolving data quality issues revolves around reactive processes that require considerable iteration during breaking changes. Furthermore, the largest bottleneck in this process is coordinating various parties to resolve a breaking change —especially among parties where data quality is not their focus.

The data contract workflow moves the data quality resolution process from reactive to proactive, where constraints, owners, and resolution protocols are established well before a breaking change. In addition, while data contracts ideally prevent a breaking change, in the case where a contract violation is unavoidable, the relevant parties are automatically made aware to resolve it accordingly and prevent the stakeholder coordination bottleneck.

Steps of the Data Contract Workflow

As highlighted in Figure 4-4, the data contract workflow consists of the following steps:

1. Data constraint identified by data consumer.
2. Data consumer requests data contract for asset.
3. Data producer confirms data contract is viable.
4. Data contract confirmed as code.
5. Data producer creates a pull request to change a data asset.
6. Automatically check if requested change violates a data contract.
7. Depending on whether the CI/CD check passes or fails:
   a. Data asset owners are notified of data contract violation, and change follows failure protocol.
   b. Data asset updated for downstream processes.

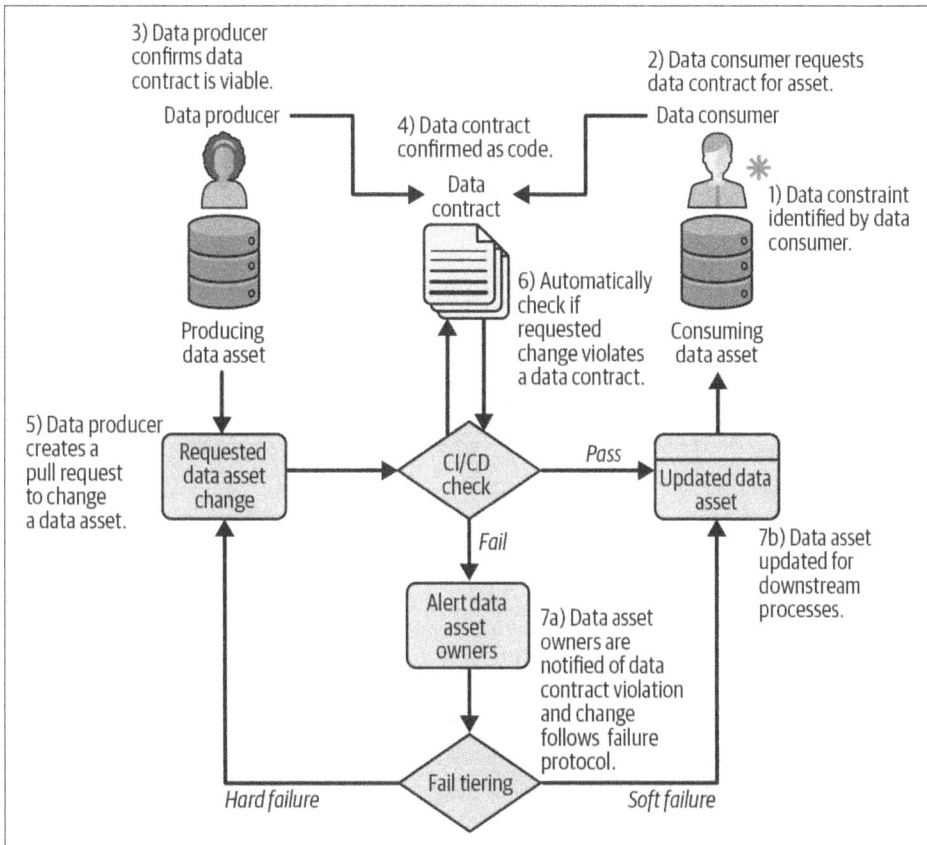

Figure 4-4. *The data contract workflow*

Let's look at each step in detail:

1. Data constraint identified by data consumer.

As mentioned in Chapter 1, the needs of data consumers inform what data is captured, and thus data quality requirements. This is because the data consumer is the interface between available data assets and the operationalization of such assets to drive value for the business. Though it's possible for a data producer to be aware of such business nuances, their work is often far removed from the business stakeholders and their needs. A great example of this divide is comparing the business knowledge of a data analyst and a software engineer. While both can be business savvy, the data analyst's job revolves around answering questions for the business with data and thus will likely be more abreast of pertinent requirements of the business in real time.

2. Data consumer requests data contract for asset.

One of the most important roles of a data consumer is to translate business requirements into technical requirements with respect to data, as highlighted in Figure 4-5. This is reflected in the fact that business stakeholders are often relegated to interfacing with data via dashboards rather than by accessing raw data directly. Therefore, we need to differentiate between technical data consumers and business data consumers when thinking of the data contract workflow. Thus, technical data consumers will use their knowledge of business and data requirements to request a data contract for data producers to abide by.

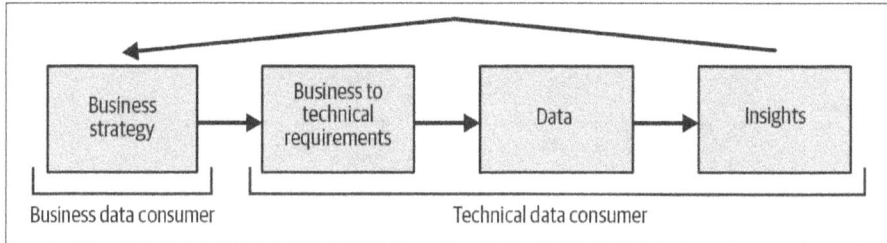

Figure 4-5. The data utilization flywheel

3. Data producer confirms data contract is viable.

While technical data consumers are skilled in matching business requirements to technical requirements, their limitation is understanding how technical requirements align with the entire software system. Thus, the data producer will be the one to determine the viability of a request and make necessary adjustments of the proposed data contract.

For example, a data consumer may be aware that the degree of data freshness required by the business is one day for a specific business need. The need can be a simple update to a data pipeline schedule, or a massive refactor to scale capabilities of the data pipeline. The data producer can support the data consumer in becoming aware of these constraints and communicating such limitations to the business.

4. Data contract confirmed as code.

Data contracts have a heavy emphasis on the automatic prevention of and alerting about data quality violations, but the step of creating the data contract is actually the most important. Specifically, this step serves as a forcing function for data teams to communicate their needs, inform producers of the business implications of data assets, and establish owners and workflows when a violation is encountered. As noted in the previous step, it's not a one-way request but rather a negotiation among stakeholders to align on how to best serve the business with data.

Furthermore, since the data contract is stored as version-controlled code (typically YAML files), the evolution of historical business to technical requirements mappings is saved. This historical information is gold for technical data consumers, who often work with data spanning across timelines of various product and/or business changes.

5. *Data producer creates a pull request to change a data asset.*
This step is self-explanatory, as version-controlled code and code reviews are a minimum requirement for any software system. With that said, changes to data assets to meet changing software requirements may seem innocuous, but these changes are the fuel for major technical fires that start off as silent failures. This is because data producers are often not privy to downstream business implications and are removed from the fallout of such failures until after a root cause analysis is conducted. Data contracts move these requirements from being downstream and obscured to being readily available for any technical stakeholder to review.

6. *Automatically check if requested change violates a data contract.*
Once the data contracts are in place for the relevant data assets, data quality prevention can happen in the developer workflow rather than being a reactionary response. Specifically, CI/CD requires new pull requests for code changes to pass a set of tests, and data contract checks fit within this workflow.

7a. *Data asset owners are notified of data contract violation, and change follows failure protocol.*
As stated earlier in this chapter, it's not enough to just be aware of data quality issues. Instead, the relevant stakeholders need to be notified and given the context to motivate them to take action to resolve the issue. While data quality is a requirement for data consumers, the state of data has limited impact on the constraints of data producers, who primarily focus on software. As illustrated in Table 4-2, data contracts realign the impact of data quality with the motivations of data producers via alerts on their pull request.

Table 4-2. Differences between data producers and consumers

	Data producer	Data consumer
Problem	Need to update the underlying software system to align with changing technical requirements.	Need to ensure underlying data is trustworthy to drive meaningful insights for the business.
Motivations	Need to pass CI/CD checks to merge pull requests. Don't want to have a business-critical failure point back to a code change where they were notified of the risk.	Ensure proper due diligence surrounding the data has been conducted to know limitations of a data asset. Have insights accepted by the business, especially executives.
Outcome	Robust software that accounts not only for technical trade-offs but also for critical business logic tied to data.	Reduced time spent investigating and resolving data quality issues for critical business workflows.

Note that a data contract violation does not equate to an automatic full block of the change. Again, the role of data contracts is to serve the needs of the business with respect to data. It may be the case that the contract itself needs to be changed or that there is a technical trade-off being made where the data quality is a lower priority. For example, there are times where major outages require urgent hot fixes by engineers and code to be deployed quickly. These changes can't wait for approvals beyond the "war room," and other teams won't be informed until after the root cause analysis report. A hard failure would not be ideal in this scenario, but a soft failure that only alerts impacted downstream teams would automate the communication (one less thing to worry about during an already stressful time). Regardless, the contract spec itself ideally specifies if the violation results in a hard or soft failure and under what contexts exceptions should occur.

7b. Data asset updated for downstream processes.
After data contract CI/CD checks have passed, the code with the requested change to the data asset will be merged into the main branch and eventually deployed to production. Ideally this workflow will happen with minimal intervention, but in the case of a data contract violation, the resolution process will be documented on the pull request itself, given that relevant stakeholders have been notified to engage.

What makes this workflow powerful is that it's not relegated to a single section of the data lifecycle (e.g., tools that only focus on the data warehouse), but rather works anywhere there is movement of data from a source to a target. In the next section, we'll discuss where you can implement data contracts and their various trade-offs throughout the data lifecycle.

Where to Implement Data Contracts

Note that the data contract workflow is abstracting away the business logic, data quality rules, and surrounding data asset information as an API. By creating this abstraction, stakeholders no longer need to interact with a multitude of touchpoints to understand data and resolve quality issues. Instead, they now only need to interact with the contract itself and only engage when alerted by a contract violation.

Data contract architecture can be bundled into four distinct components:

- Data assets
- Contract definition
- Detection
- Prevention

We will do a deep dive into each component in Chapter 5 from a conceptual level, Chapter 6 will provide the open source tools we recommend to build data contracts, and Chapter 7 will provide an end-to-end implementation.

In addition to the numerous components, there are also multiple stages in the data lifecycle in which you can implement data contracts, as illustrated in Figure 4-6.

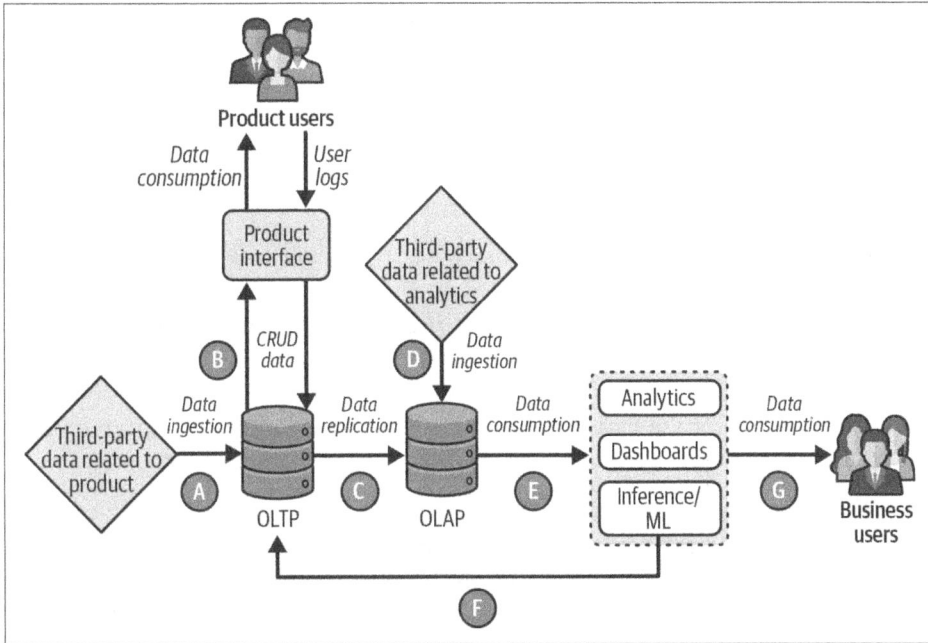

Figure 4-6. The various locations to implement data contracts within the data lifecycle

Here are the considerations for each stage of the data lifecycle:

A. *Third-party data → Transactional database (OLTP)*
    While we recommend going as upstream as possible for data contracts, one of the most challenging areas to enforce data contracts is third-party data. While possible, it is unlikely that a third party would agree to additional restrictions without your organization having leverage. With that said, while you can't control the third-party data, data contracts can be utilized between ingestion and your transactional database as a way to triage data that violates a contract and provides early alerting. (Chapter 5 provides a more in-depth illustration of this scenario.)

B. *Product interface → Transactional database*
    Changes to the underlying schema and semantics for CRUD operations are often the root of data quality issues, and would be an ideal location for the first implementation of data contracts. One huge consideration, though, is whether

your team oversees the transactional database; often software engineering teams control this database, which means this would not be an ideal location for a first implementation if you are a data team.

C. Transactional database → Analytical database (OLAP)

The data pipeline between transactional databases and analytical databases is where we recommend most organizations start implementing data contracts. Specifically, both software engineering and data teams are active stakeholders in this stage of the data lifecycle, with data teams often having considerably more autonomy for implementing changes. In addition, this lifecycle stage is often the most upstream source of data for analytical and ML workflows, and thus has the highest probability of preventing major data quality issues.

D. Third-party data → Analytical database

Similar to third-party data entering transactional databases, putting contracts between third-party data and an analytical database is often not feasible. One major exception is cloud-based customer relationship management (CRM) platforms (e.g., Salesforce and HubSpot), which are often synced with an analytical database with data connectors. While the data is third-party, CRMs still allow customizability of the underlying data models and columns, which can be controlled with data contracts. This is especially true given these data sources.

E. Analytical database → Data products

From our conversations with organizations interested in data contracts, many data teams strongly consider first placing data contracts on their analytical database to control data transformations used for analytics, machine learning, and dashboards. While valuable, we strongly encourage teams to focus on the stage between transactional and analytical databases and then work downstream. Specifically, starting too far downstream will diminish your ability to prevent data quality issues before they are stored in the analytical database. With that said, this is an excellent location *after* placing the upstream data contracts.

F. Analytical database → Transactional database

While it's possible to place data contracts for "reverse ETL" workflows, it's less common as data contracts on the analytical database are ideally preventing data transformations from having data quality issues. Furthermore, unless the engineering team is spearheading the implementation of data contracts, upstream developers will unlikely request data contracts as it often falls in the purview of the data team.

G. Data products → Business users

Placing data contracts between analytical databases and downstream consumers serves as a way to ensure trust and consistency for the data being served via data products. While too downstream to prevent data quality issues, it enables data teams to tier the data they serve and set expectations. For example, would you want to make key business decisions that rely on a dashboard that was or wasn't using data under contract?

The key deciding factor of where to implement data contracts is the relationship between upstream and downstream producers. While ideally this will always be on good terms, realistically it's more nuanced and challenging. In Chapters 9 to 12, we will detail how to navigate these nuances in team dynamics within the business and build buy-in.

The Maturity Curve of Data Contracts: Awareness, Ownership, and Governance

While data contracts are a technical mechanism for identifying and resolving data quality and governance issues upstream, cultural change is as important to address as technology. Culture change here refers to the shifts in behavior required by data producers, data consumers, and leadership teams in order to help their company implement data contracts and successfully roll out federated governance at scale. While this section briefly touches on culture change, we devote Chapters 9 to 12 to detailing exactly how to get data contracts adopted throughout an organization.

It's important to acknowledge that not all companies are equally ready for data contracts from day one. Some businesses are already data-driven: these companies understand and appreciate the value of data for its capacity to add operational and analytical functions from the top of the organization to the bottom. Others are simply data aware: they understand data is used at their company, but outside the data organization there isn't much recognition of the need to invest in infrastructure, tooling, and process. Others are data ignorant: their journey in data has barely started!

To make matters more complex, these differences in maturity and communication may differ not only between organizations but *within* organizations across teams. For example, a machine learning team may have a sophisticated appreciation for the value of data that the sales team may not. In our experience, it is important to acknowledge these differences. Companies cannot be treated as monolithic! To succeed with the implementation of data contracts, data heroes must take a pragmatic approach that relies on rolling out contracts across a maturity curve, depending on organization- and team-based readiness.

The data contract maturity curve has three steps: 1) awareness, 2) collaboration, and 3) ownership. We'll outline each step, as well as their corresponding goals.

Awareness

Goal: Create visibility into how downstream teams use upstream data.

The goal of the awareness phase is to help both data producers and data consumers become aware of their responsibilities as active stakeholders in the data supply chain. As mentioned previously, data contract requirements must start with the consumers, who are the only ones with an explicit understanding of their own use cases and data expectations. In order to limit the surface over which data teams must begin implementing contracts, it is advisable to select a subset of useful downstream data assets, known as tier-one data products.

Data product is a term that has many different definitions. We prefer to look to our software engineering counterparts for directional guidance. A software product is the sum of many engineering systems organized to serve an explicit business need. Products have interfaces (APIs, user interfaces) and backends. In the same way, a data product is the sum of data components that are organized to serve a business need, as illustrated in Figure 4-7.

A dashboard is a data product. It is the sum of many components, such as visualizations, queries, and a data pipeline. The interface: a drag-and-drop editor, charts, and data tables. The backend: a data pipeline and data sources. This framing rings true for a model's training set, embedded data products, or other data applications. *The data contract should be built in service of these products*, not the other way around.

In the awareness phase, data producers must understand that changes they make to data will harm consumers. In our work helping other companies adopt data contracts, we found numerous instances of software engineering teams that had no idea a downstream team was taking dependencies on their data. Unfortunately, most data producers are operating in a black box regarding the data they emit. They don't *want* to cause outages, but without any context provided pre-deployment, it is incredibly challenging to do so.

Even without the implementation of a producer-defined data contract, producers should still be aware of when they are making code changes that will affect data, exactly what those changes will impact, and who they should speak to before shipping. This pre-deployment awareness drives accountability and, most importantly, conversation.

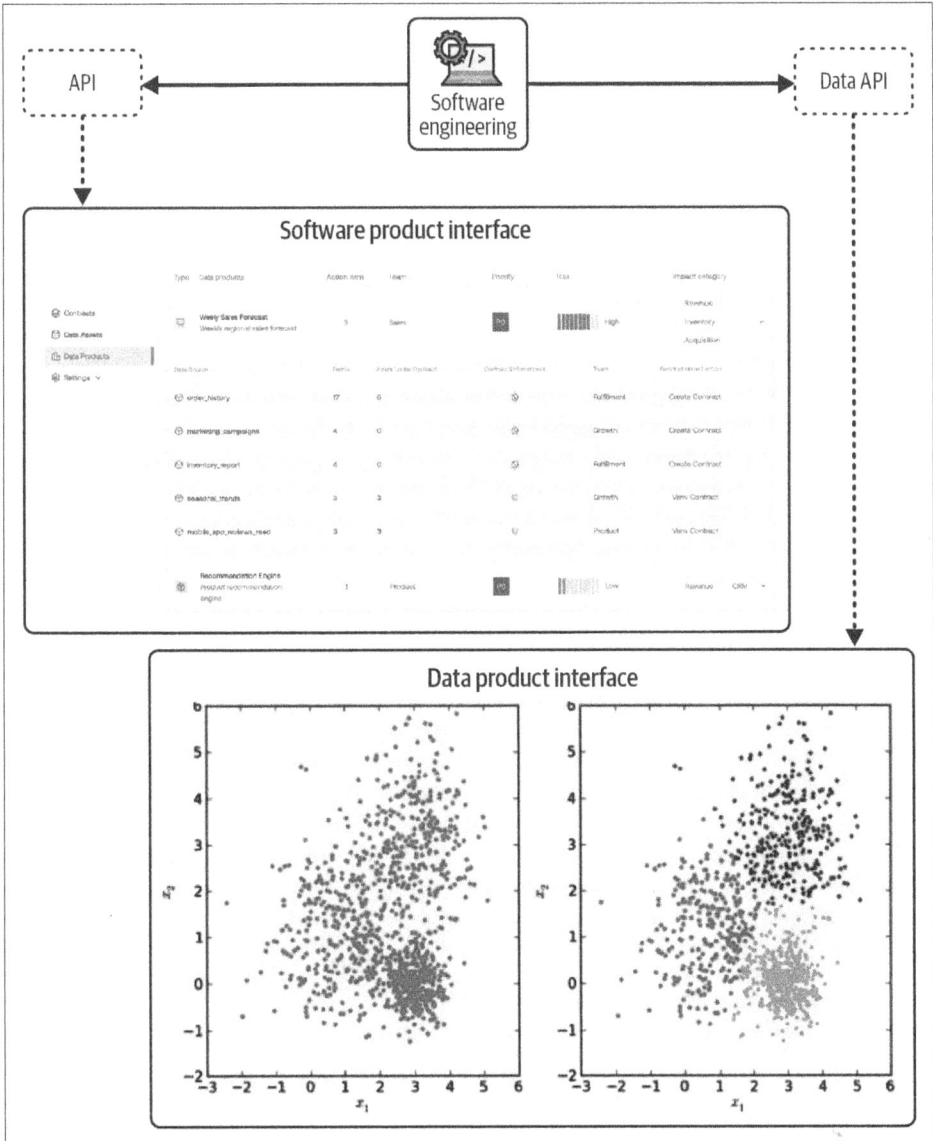

Figure 4-7. Software versus data product interfaces

Collaboration

Goal: Ensure data is protected at the source through contracts.

Once a data producer has some understanding of how their changes will impact others in the organization, they are faced with a set of choices: 1) make the breaking change and knowingly cause an outage or 2) communicate with the data consumers that the change is coming. The second option is better for a wide variety of reasons that should be obvious!

Communication resolves most problems for data consumers. They are informed in advance before breaking changes are made, have plenty of time to prepare, and can potentially delay or deter software engineers' deployment by advocating for their own use cases of the data. This sort of change management functions in a similar way to pull requests. Just as an engineer asks for feedback about their code change, with a consumer-driven contract they may also "ask" for feedback about their change to data.

> The importance of this collaboration happening pre-deployment, driven by context, can't be stressed enough. Once code has been merged, it is no longer the responsibility of the engineer. You can't be accountable for a change you were never informed about.

Ownership

This shift left toward data accountability resolves problems but also creates new challenges. Imagine you are a software engineer who regularly ships code changes that affect your database. Every time you do so, you see that there are dozens of downstream consumers, each with critical dependencies on your data. It's not impossible to simply communicate with them about which changes are coming, but doing that for *each* consumer is incredibly time-consuming! Not only that, but it turns out certain consumers have taken dependencies on data that they shouldn't, or are misusing data that you provide.

At this point, it is beneficial for producers to define a data contract, for the following reasons:

- Producers now understand the use cases and consumers/customers.
- Producers can explicitly define which fields to make accessible to the broader organization.
- Producers have clear processes in place for change management, contract versioning, and contract evolution.

Data producers clearly understand how changes to their data impact others, have a clear sense of accountability for their data, and can apply data contracts where they matter most to the business. In short, consumer-defined contracts create problem visibility, and *visibility creates culture change*. The next section details the outcomes of enabling this change.

Outcomes of Implementing Data Contracts

There are several extremely important outcomes that occur as a result of data contracts being implemented across your organization. Some of them are obvious and can be measured quantitatively, while others are softer but nevertheless have some of the greatest impact on culture change and working conditions as a data developer. The three core metrics are the following:

Faster data science and analytics iteration
> When Mark was a data scientist, a majority of his time for any project was spent on sourcing data that was of high enough quality to use within a data lake, and spending considerable time understanding the quirks of the data in question and validating it. Specifically, in his previous role at an HR tech company, one of the most important data assets was "manager status of an employee." Despite this being a critical data asset for an HR company, it was constantly changing as new customers created various edge cases or the product evolved. For example, an enterprise customer would change employee management systems, and thus ingested employee data would change from a daily batch job to a monthly one—unfortunately, management status doesn't align with a monthly cadence. Thus, the same exploration and validation stage was present on every new project with the same data asset.
>
> By implementing data contracts, the outcome would considerably cut this exploration and validation stage. First, having data assets under contract creates a shortlist of data to use for data science projects and ensures that proper due diligence has already taken place. Second, the data contract itself documents the quirks of the data one needs to be aware of and its expectations. Third, since data contracts are version controlled, data teams also have a log of past changes in constraints and assumptions, as well as a mechanism to document and enforce new ones that arise and or evolve. In short, data contracts provide a mechanism to handle the discovery and validation of data assets at scale while also disseminating this information across teams in a manner that's version controlled.

Developer and data team communication
> In Chapter 3, we referenced Dunbar's Number and Conway's Law as two powerful phenomena within businesses that shape how technical teams communicate (or don't) with each other. Specifically, we reviewed how an increase in employee count corresponds with an exponential rise of potential connections

that ultimately breaks down communications—which is reflected in the technical systems built by the organization. Data contracts aim to overcome this challenge via automation and embedding itself within existing CI/CD workflows.

Data contracts increase the visibility of dependencies related to data assets that are generated and/or transformed by upstream producers (e.g., application engineers) in the three following ways:

- For a data contract to be enforceable, both the consumer and the producer parties need to agree to the data contract spec before implementing it within the CI/CD pipeline—serving as a forcing function for communication between both parties.

- Since an enforceable contract is within the CI/CD process, violations generate failed test notifications within pull requests and notify data asset owners, thus supporting code reviews with relevant information and the people who can help resolve issues.

- There may be cases where a contract violation is no longer relevant due to evolving needs, implying that a new constraint is needed. Thus changes to the contract specs inform downstream data asset owners rather than them finding out reactively with the data itself.

Mitigation of data quality issues

Ultimately, the reason for going through the effort of implementing data contracts and coordination among technical teams is to reduce business-critical data quality issues. But to reiterate, data quality is not about pristine data, it's about fitness of use by the consumer and their relevant trade-offs. Furthermore, poor data quality is a people and process problem masquerading as a technical problem. Data contracts serve as a mechanism to improve the way in which people (i.e., data producers and consumers) communicate about the captured process of the business (i.e., data). Resolving data quality issues then shifts from being a reactive problem to instead being a change management problem in which teams can iterate, as in the consumer use cases that become clearer over time.

While this section highlights high-level outcomes of data contracts, we encourage you to review Chapter 11, where we go into the specific metrics used to measure the success of a data contract implementation.

Data Contracts Versus Data Observability

Through our hundreds of conversations with companies about data contracts, one question was often asked: "How are data contracts different from data observability, and when would I need data contracts or observability?" This section aims to answer this question.

According to Gartner, data observability is defined as the following:

> [The] ability of an organization to have a broad visibility of its data landscape and multi-layer data dependencies (like data pipelines, data infrastructure, data applications) at all times with an objective to identify, control, prevent, escalate, and remediate data outages rapidly within acceptable data SLAs.[1]

Key here is the term *data outages*, which means that data either is not accessible or is available but shouldn't be trusted. The only caveat we will make to this definition is that data observability can't be preventative in itself, as an event needs to happen for it to be observable, but observability can definitely inform preventive workflows such as data contracts themselves. Table 4-3 provides further information on the comparison of the two.

Table 4-3. Data contracts versus data observability

Data contracts	Data observability
Prevents specific data quality issues. Data contracts emphasize preventing changes to metadata that would result in breaking changes in related data assets.	**Highlights data quality trends.** The main value proposition of data observability is that it gives you visibility of your data system and how that system is changing in real time.
Included in CI/CD workflow. Data contract checks are embedded within the developer workflow, specifically CI/CD, so that breaking changes can be addressed before a pull request is merged.	**Complements CI/CD workflow.** Observability serves as a measurement of your data processes, and thus is not within the developer workflow; but the output of observability will inform which additional tests you need to have within your CI/CD workflow.
Informed by business logic. Data contracts are technology to scale communication among data producers and consumers. One of the most important data consumers are business stakeholders, who provide domain knowledge that enables value generation from data.	**Reflects how data captures business logic.** While business logic is an input into data contracts, observability instead measures the output of business logic within data systems and how well they align with reality (e.g., capturing data drift).
Targeted visibility. Data contracts should not be on every data asset and pipeline, but rather only on the most important ones (e.g., those generating revenue or utilized by executives). This prevents alert fatigue, as the goal of data contracts is not only to alert, but also to encourage the data producer to take action when a contract is violated. Chapter 11 goes into detail on how to identify the most important data assets.	**Broad visibility.** Data observability should reach into every aspect of your data stack, from ingestion and processing to serving. While one can refine data quality thresholds at later stages of implementation, the broad visibility of data observability enables baseline metrics and surfaces potential issues with respect to a data platform.

---

1 Melody Chien and Ankush Jain, "Data and Analytics Essentials: Data Observability," (Gartner, 2023) (*https://oreil.ly/tqIYv*), quoted in Andy Petrella, *Fundamentals of Data Observability* (O'Reilly, 2023), 28 (*https://oreil.ly/q8muz*) in an earlier version.

Data contracts	Data observability
Alerts before change.	**Alerts after change.**
Data contracts shift agreements between data producers and consumers from implicit to explicit. This enables the prevention of metadata changes that would result in breaking related data assets for known issues.	By definition, an event being observable means that it has already taken place, and thus can't be prevented. With that said, such workflows *after* an event are essential for surfacing unknown issues to inform future data contracts.

The key difference between data contracts and data observability is that contracts emphasize the prevention of known data quality issues, while observability emphasizes detection of unknown data quality issues. One is not a replacement of the other, but rather, both data contracts and data observability complement each other. Another way to think about the two is in terms of the flashlight and the laser pointer, as both illuminate an area to bring attention to it, yet serve different purposes. As illustrated in Figure 4-8, data observability is similar to the flashlight, illuminating the entire data system and workflows, where the alternative is being "left in the dark" about your data and waiting to bump into data quality issues. Data contracts can be viewed as the laser pointer. While its light is relegated to a small area, its value is in its ability to target and bring attention to a specific area within a system.

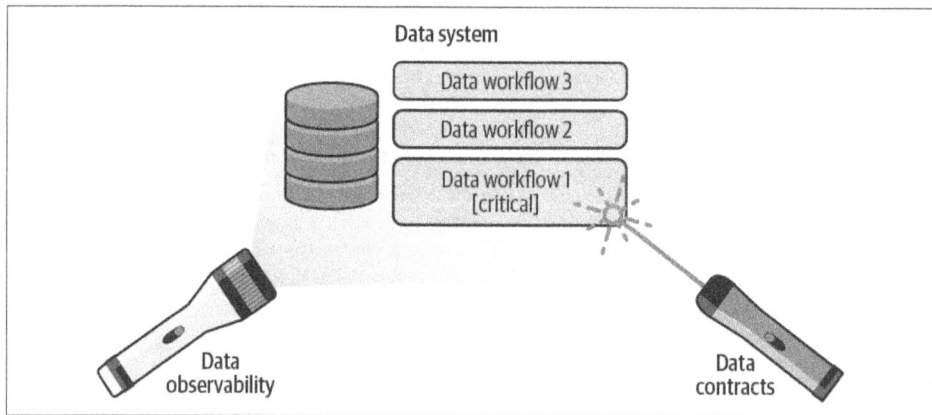

Figure 4-8. How data contracts and observability complement each other

Observability and contracts are individually useful for data teams, but using them together enables teams to work more efficiently. They become able to automate the process of understanding their entire data system with observability and then use this information to inform enforceable constraints with contracts.

Conclusion

This chapter provided the theoretical foundation of the data contract architecture, as well as discussed the key stakeholders and workflows when utilizing data contracts. Specifically, we covered:

- How collaboration is different in data
- The roles of data producers and consumers within the data lifecycle
- The current state of reactively resolving data quality issues.
- A high-level overview of the data contract workflow
- The various trade-offs between implementing data contracts throughout the data lifecycle
- The maturity curve of implementing data contracts and its outcomes

A main takeaway from this chapter should be the emphasis on placing data contracts as far upstream as possible. With the goal of preventing data issues, rather than reacting to them, it's prudent to place constraints where the data is originally sourced or generated, so that subsequent steps in the data lifecycle are not poisoned by issues. This key notion is central to shift-left data practices, which we will detail in Chapter 9, but also to how we discuss their components and implementation in the next few chapters.

## PART II

Implementation of the Data Contract Architecture

CHAPTER 5

The Data Contract Components: Data Assets and Contract Definition

In Chapters 1 to 5 we discuss data contracts from a theoretical perspective, and in Chapter 6 we will shift into actually applying data contracts with a real-world project. Specifically, in Chapters 6 and 7 we will provide the components of data contracts and our preferred open source tools needed to implement them. In Chapter 8 we will build on Chapters 6 and 7 with a guided project tying these open source components together to create the architecture for data contracts. We highly encourage you to reference our public GitHub repository (*https://github.com/data-contract-book/ chapter-7-implementing-data-contracts*) that complements these chapters and walks you through the technical implementation.

Let's start with our overview of the components of data contracts.

Overview of Components

What makes data contracts powerful is what also makes them challenging to get adopted beyond the data team. The power of data contracts is that they're designed to unite teams and disciplines across an entire company, while also integrating seamlessly into the individual tools and workflows at all stages of the data lifecycle. Thus, data contract architecture requires using a toolbox of infrastructure, in which components can be broken up into four main categories and their respective subcategories, as illustrated in Figure 5-1.

In this chapter we will only cover data assets and contract definition in depth, but we will provide a high-level overview of all components so it's clear how they all fit within the larger picture. Chapter 6 will cover the remaining components of detection and prevention.

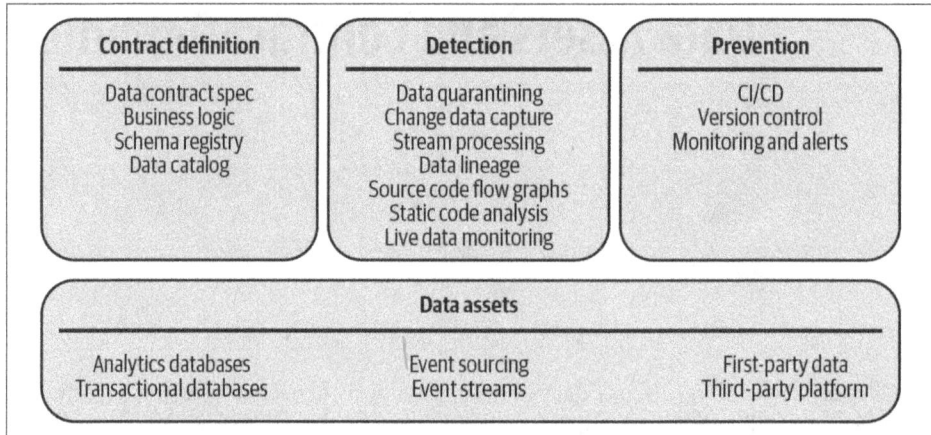

Contract definition	Detection	Prevention
Data contract spec Business logic Schema registry Data catalog	Data quarantining Change data capture Stream processing Data lineage Source code flow graphs Static code analysis Live data monitoring	CI/CD Version control Monitoring and alerts

Data assets		
Analytics databases Transactional databases	Event sourcing Event streams	First-party data Third-party platform

Figure 5-1. The building blocks of data contracts

Let's look at each building block in a little more detail:

Data assets

The foundation of all data infrastructure is databases, and while the range of databases is vast (*https://oreil.ly/w95tz*), we will focus on the following four categories for this book:

- Analytics databases
- Transactional databases
- Event sourcing and event streams
- First-party data, third-party platform

Contract definition

The surface to embed the expectations around schema and business logic (i.e., semantics) for a respective data asset, which is then compared to centralized sources of metadata. The three components are as follows:

- Data contract spec
- Business logic
- Schema registry and data catalogs

Detection

Detection needs to happen at the code level for schema and at runtime for data semantics to ensure changes are captured, ideally before data is written to the target database. The following seven categories represent the areas in which you can detect changes to data:

- Data quarantining
- Change data capture
- Stream processing
- Source code flow graphs
- Data lineage
- Static code analysis
- Live data monitoring

Prevention

While it's ideal for prevention to be automatic in handling contract violations, this is not possible given that the nature of many data quality issues are rooted in people and processes. Thus the automation is in alerting the right people at the right time within the developer workflow. The following three categories are typically where you can inform someone of potential breaking changes:

- CI/CD workflows
- Version control (data code review)
- Monitoring and alerts

While these are quite a few components, many of them are components already used within software and data infrastructure—thus, we're mostly repurposing existing infrastructure and/or adding additional workflows.

We'll start our in-depth review of each building block by digging deeper into data assets.

Data Assets

In Chapter 4, Figure 4-7 highlighted the considerations of implementing data contracts in the various touchpoints of the data lifecycle. We are bringing an iteration of that diagram with Figure 5-2, as we dive into the four categories of data assets: transactional databases (A), analytical databases (B), events data (C), and first-party data within third-party platforms (D).

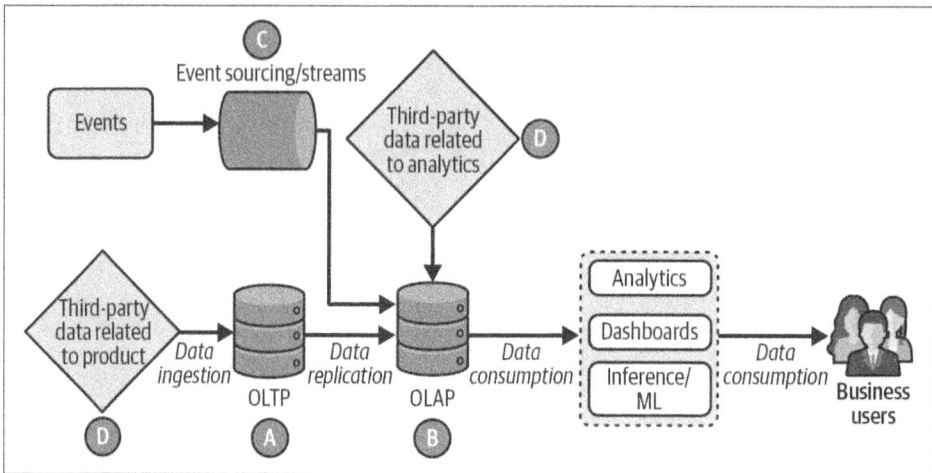

Figure 5-2. Data assets where contracts can be placed

Analytics Databases

Data developers are most likely found working within analytical databases—given their central role in analytics (as the name implies), machine learning, and AI—and storing the underlying data of dashboards presented to nontechnical business stakeholders. Analytical databases can include data warehouses, data lakes, data lake houses, and other variations where the emphasis is on being able to scan and aggregate large swaths of data. Furthermore, performance is centered around data quality and reliability rather than response time; for example, processing an extensive SQL query in minutes as compared to retrieving a specific data point in subseconds. Given this distinction, data contracts become quite useful in maintaining the reliability and quality of the data within an analytical database.

While earlier implementations of analytical databases centered primarily around data warehouses—which were subject-oriented, integrated, time-variant, and nonvolatile—the rise of big-data tools (e.g., Google File System and Apache Hadoop) changed these assumptions, and the Modern Data Stack further cemented this change. Specifically, MDS relies heavily on ELT, where minimal to no transformations are implemented to make upstream data useful for analytics. This has resulted in analytical databases becoming company-wide dumping grounds of data, via replication, where the hope is that one day the data may become valuable. In reality, it makes the small percentage of data that is truly valuable to the business much more complex to utilize and harder to find, like a needle in a haystack. In Chapter 8 we provide real-world case studies where multiple companies are pushing both batch and streaming data into the data lake post-ELT pipelines and discuss how this pattern causes challenges at scale (despite the substantial usefulness of data lakes).

Many data teams often put a patch on the issue by building numerous layers of transformations via dbt to quickly iterate and provide value to the business, but this doesn't solve the root problem. Specifically, modern analytical databases do not adhere to being nonvolatile, thus resulting in these layers of transformation being brittle. For example, an upstream table that's replicated into the analytical database has a schema change, resulting in all subsequent downstream transformation breaking.

This challenge is exacerbated even further by scaling both teams and infrastructure, where the number of assumptions and dependencies grows exponentially (as highlighted in Chapter 3). Mark experienced this firsthand in overseeing the analytical database at an HR tech startup. When he was initially hired to the data science team, it was relatively easy to manage the analytical database, as its use was relegated to just the few people on the data team, and the upstream engineering team was all under one manager. Two years later the analytical database was used by a data team that had doubled in size, it powered the majority of dashboards used by the business, and engineering was split among three different teams. What was once a simple set of tables had become a complex system that relied on three different upstream teams, supported numerous R&D initiatives and analytical workflows among the data science team, and was a source of contention among business users receiving the wrong data within their dashboards. While our manual workflows on the analytical database sufficed in the earlier stage, our ability to maintain these manual workflows suffered as we scaled.

Though these scaling issues were challenging, they are part of the growing pains of an evolving organization. As the number of dependencies increases for a data asset, so does the awareness of various edge cases and data quality issues among business stakeholders. It's not a matter of *if* a data issue will arise, but rather a matter of *when*, and increased scope leads to an increased probability of issues being highlighted. Though painful to deal with, these issues serve as a litmus test to determine if the underlying data aligns with the business stakeholders' expectations, especially when they are domain experts (e.g., a doctor reviewing clinical data). Specifically, such instances inform whether a data team's downstream transformations are wrong, if upstream data is being captured wrongly, or if the underlying assumptions of the data pipelines don't align with the reality the data represents. All of this makes data contracts useful in both documenting business logic and enforcing such constraints automatically as issues surface.

Transactional Databases

While data developers are found working within analytical databases, software developers are often found upstream in transactional databases, as this is most pertinent to the application and services layers of most businesses. As mentioned in Chapter 1, these transactional databases focus on CRUD operations, ACID compliance, and data in third-normalized form—all of which enable blazing-fast information retrieval (e.g., website actions taking subseconds). More importantly, transactional databases are where "snapshots of the truth" are captured by the business, such as product logs and user information (i.e., point B of Figure 5-2). This is why transactional databases serve as an ideal location for data contracts—they're the most upstream data source an organization controls, given that analytical databases are often replications. The challenge is that data quality is not a top priority for many software engineering teams, as their constraints revolve around the maintainability of the code rather than the underlying data. Thus a data contract initiative would be deprioritized unless driven by the engineering team itself.

Diving further into the concept of ACID is essential for understanding the importance of data contracts in maintaining data quality. ACID stands for atomicity, consistency, isolation, and durability, but the emphasis for data contracts will be on consistency for the following reason, highlighted in Martin Kleppmann's book *Designing Data-Intensive Applications* (O'Reilly):

> [This] idea of consistency depends on the application's notion of invariants [i.e., true conditions about your data], and it's the application's responsibility to define its transactions correctly so that they preserve consistency. This is not something that the database can guarantee: if you write bad data that violates your invariants, the database can't stop you. (Some specific kinds of invariants can be checked by the database, for example using foreign key constraints or uniqueness constraints. However, in general, the application defines what data is valid or invalid—the database only stores it.)
>
> Atomicity, isolation, and durability are properties of the database, whereas consistency (in the ACID sense) is a property of the application. The application may rely on the database's atomicity and isolation properties in order to achieve consistency, but it's not up to the database alone.

A great way to think of invariants in a database is to consider the question "Who is a customer?"

- Is it a company with an active contract with your organization?
- Is it a company that ever had a contract with your organization?
- Is it a company that doesn't have a contract but has made up-to-date monthly payments?

As you can see, the devil is in the details as to what exactly needs to stay consistent within your database, and data contracts are best equipped to uphold these constraints as the business (and ultimately the invariants) evolve.

An excellent real-world example of this comes from the hundreds of calls we have had with companies interested in data contracts. One consumer app company had the assumption that its business would be business-to-consumer (B2C), and thus this assumption was embedded everywhere from the software architecture to databases to documentation. Yet about 10 years later the company realized it needed to expand its offering to businesses, and thus it became business-to-business (B2B) in addition to B2C. In other words, its invariant of "each individual customer and user is a one-to-one relationship" ceased to be true as users could quickly switch between individual and company accounts (e.g., a freelancer joining a company for a three-month contract). The 10 years of revenue-driving assumptions and architecture quickly became data and tech debt with a single major business decision—resulting in an inability to properly bill customers and therefore a loss in revenue. Thus, the company explored data contracts as an avenue to put guardrails on its data system as it did a major refactor (see Chapter 3). By establishing contracts for the desired end state of data (e.g., expanding from consumer only to including business customers), the company could identify where in the transactional database these contracts were violated, and iterate until violations ceased to exist.

In addition to CRUD operations, transactional databases also serve as the ingestion point for third-party data relevant to the application layer (i.e., point A of Figure 5-2). For example, as noted before, Mark previously worked at an HR tech startup that ingested sensitive employee demographic data given directly by their respective enterprise customers. A key consideration through this workflow was: how can we handle differential data loading patterns from customers? While it's unlikely you can enforce a data contract on a third party, due to lack of leverage (e.g., an important enterprise customer is unwilling to change), data contracts are powerful between the raw data staging and the ingestion into the transactional database.

For Mark's HR use case, customers provided data as manual CSV files, Secure File Transfer Protocol, or a direct API—all of which were provided in varying intervals, such as daily, monthly, or quarterly. This ended up causing painful data quality issues, as the employee data determined org charts and manager statuses, which were key factors for product features. We had to deal with issues such as: why is a file missing? Did the customer shift from daily to monthly intervals? Did they change the format of the CSV file? These unexpected changes created data quality issues visible in the application and resulted in the engineering team spending copious amounts of time reactively debugging issues in the transactional database, manually fixing the third-party data, and doing backfills. In this situation, data contracts would enable:

- Documentation of differential workflows of the underlying third-party data assets
- Preventing data that violates a contract from entering the transactional database and creating customer-facing data quality issues in the application
- Logging contract violation patterns of provided third-party data, which can be used by the business team to highlight to customers the impact of providing poor-quality data

Not surprisingly, we have talked to numerous companies experiencing challenges with third-party data providers and see data contracts as an avenue to relieve their pain.

Finally, a less robust but simpler-to-implement pattern is pushing the outputs of data products in the analytical database back into the transactional database (i.e., point F of Figure 4-6). With the emerging category of generative AI, we expect this pattern to grow considerably as more companies expand their AI use cases. A great example of this is the "batch prediction" design pattern for machine learning models, as highlighted in Figure 5-3.

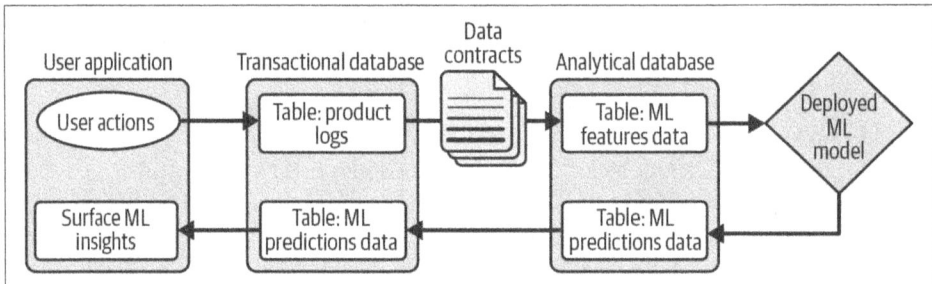

Figure 5-3. Machine learning batch predictions architecture with data contracts

There is already a tremendous amount of literature on machine learning (*https:// oreil.ly/1uXhp*) (which is out of scope for this book), but where data contracts fit within this use case is between the replication of a data asset between the analytical (OLAP) and transactional (OLTP) databases. In other words, a "data product" was developed using the analytical database assets, and now the transactional database has a major dependency on this data product for customer-facing surfaces. Some considerations include the following:

- Is the format of this data product output suitable for the transactional database?
- Would new data for the same users be overwritten or appended to?
- What happens if machine learning monitoring flags outputs with poor predictive power?
- Is the prediction data asset going to be versioned with the accompanying ML model versions?
- Are there any regulatory requirements for the predictions data (e.g., health or financial data)?

By placing constraints between the analytical database and the transactional database, organizations can ensure data maintains expectations before it reaches customer-facing surfaces.

Event Sourcing and Event Streams

Event-driven architecture (EDA) is a dense topic that deserves an entire book in itself, thus for the sake of brevity we will mainly focus on two facets: 1) event sourcing and 2) event streams and how they relate to data contracts. For a more in-depth discussion on streaming, we highly recommend reading Chapter 11 in Kleppmann's *Designing Data-Intensive Applications*.

It's best to understand streaming data in relation to batch data, which provides dumps of data from system A to system B in predetermined intervals (e.g., one day). This approach is the simplest and what many data teams default to. Yet there are cases where a set interval of time doesn't suit the use case, such as tracking changes when they happen in real time or when there is a high volume of data in a short period of time (e.g., telemetry data). In these use cases, the additional complexity of EDA is warranted. Examples of this additional complexity, and thus data quality issues, include:

Race conditions and concurrency
> Multiple conflicting database writes cause erroneous overwriting, which result in data targets becoming out of sync

Fault tolerance and durability
> Ability for a system to account for a node going offline and thus losing data (e.g., distributed computing)

Retention
> How long data within a stream should be retained to ensure accurate data but not cause memory issues

Latency
> An acceptable window of time the data can represent (e.g., seconds versus milliseconds)

Note that while these challenges can be present for batch processes, they're more pronounced within streaming.

These considerations bring us to the differences between event sourcing and event streams highlighted in Table 5-1. Both were used by Chad at a previous company, further described in his articles "An Engineer's Guide to Data Contracts," Part 1 (*https://oreil.ly/YG_gN*) and Part 2 (*https://oreil.ly/ykyvH*).

Table 5-1. Comparison of event sourcing and streaming

	Event sourcing	Event streaming
Use case	Immutable log that has every recorded event appended to the log	High volume of data captured in set intervals of times (i.e., "windows")
Data examples	Updates to self-reported user demographic information in an application Online shopping cart transactions Shipping status across a supply chain	Telemetry data for devices High-volume financial transactions (e.g., stock market) Click tracking on a high-traffic website

While there are numerous ways to implement EDA, we highly recommend the publish-subscribe pattern for data contract implementation—Apache Kafka is an example of an open source tool that enables this. Under this pattern, you have a service that sends events, a message broker that manages these events and essentially provides a buffer, and a set of event subscribers that read from the broker. Where event sourcing and streams differ is in how the event broker is utilized. As illustrated in Figure 5-4, event sourcing creates an immutable log of every event from the event publishing service, an example being updates to shipping status across a supply chain.

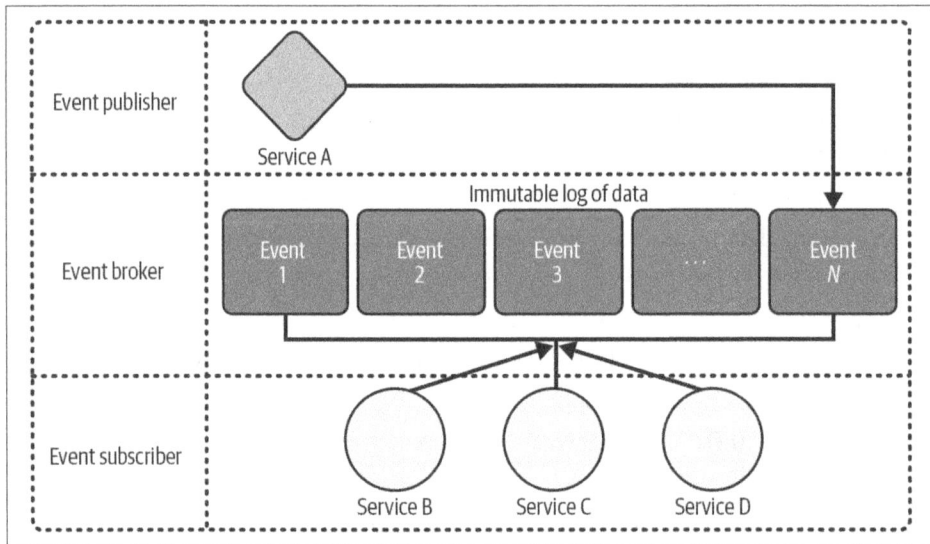

Figure 5-4. Event sourcing via publish-subscribe pattern

What makes this powerful from a data quality perspective is that the immutable log can re-create databases and event history in the instance of a downstream database going down. Furthermore, different downstream consumers can utilize the log for their respective use case, such as analytics reviewing all logs in a history or a user-facing app presenting only the most recent log in the UI. Pulling from the supply chain example again, the analytics team may want to know the average shipment wait time between each step in the supply chain, while an end user only wants to know where the shipment is currently located.

While event sourcing and streaming have many similarities, there are instances where creating an immutable log of every event is infeasible and would result in either an out-of-memory error or a very expensive cloud service bill. In instances where there is a high volume of data (e.g., telemetry data), windowing is leveraged to capture a log of data in set time intervals (e.g., every second), as illustrated in Figure 5-5. Though not all the data is captured, its general trends and patterns can be aggregated into a single value in a log, which then follows the similar pattern of a buffer via the event broker and a data consumer via event subscribers. For example, a site reliability engineering team might calculate site health metrics every second over the last 10 seconds of data to get a rolling, continuously updating picture of site performance.

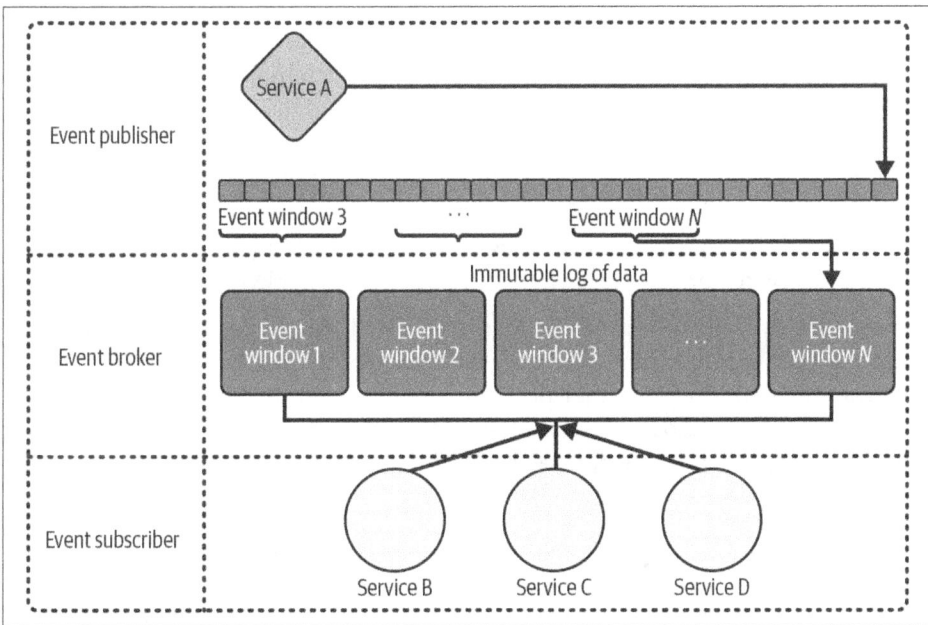

Figure 5-5. Event streaming via publish-subscribe pattern

Oftentimes, organizations will employ both event sourcing and streaming in the same data stack. Furthermore, EDA becomes more common as an organization scales and increases in data maturity. In Mark's previous role at a startup, he accomplished replication from a transactional database into an analytical database via daily batch loads. In earlier days, the batch operations were lightweight and reliable, but this changed once the company scaled the number of enterprise customers. The once-simple batch operations took hours to run, errors in the pipeline caused jobs to fail—resulting in stale data—and the batch would do full replacements of the table. The last point of replacements was most troubling, as breaking changes to schema and semantics were propagated into the analytical database and would require hours-long backfills. This resulted in days or weeks of the data science team being stalled in their work, and it was clear that it was time to start paying off the technical debt that was acquired via a trade-off for an initially simpler solution (and rightfully so at the time). The team heavily considered event sourcing via change data capture, as it would enable transactional integrity and shift them away from hours-long batch jobs toward incremental updates into the analytical database.

First-Party Data, Third-Party Platform

Typically you cannot enforce data contracts on third parties given the lack of leverage, but there is one edge case that doesn't apply: instances where the data is first-party and you can control the underlying data model, but the platform in which the data is stored and processed is third-party. Examples of this include customer relationship management software such as HubSpot and Salesforce, or enterprise resource planning (ERP) software such as SAP. These data sources are often business-critical, and many predate the implementation of analytical databases, thus being embedded with a tremendous amount of business logic without consideration of an underlying data model. While these systems don't have the same level of customizability as a traditional database, the underlying data objects can be modified and are replicated into an organization's analytical database (refer to point D in Figure 5-2), typically via batch jobs.

For example, in a former position, Mark replicated Salesforce data into BigQuery using the ELT tool Fivetran. He then generated reports that linked product usage, time-tracking data, and customer deal size and health (from Salesforce) to assist in reallocating staffing resources within the customer success team—ultimately aiming to optimize the number of employee hours dedicated per dollar of annual recurring revenue (ARR).

Given this nature of third-party platforms, CI/CD workflows are not typically possible and thus prevention shifts from preventing violations within source data, to preventing source data violations replicating into a target database. Figure 5-6 illustrates this, specifically steps 6, 7a, and 7b, where there is a prevention window between staging and execution of data replication into the target database.

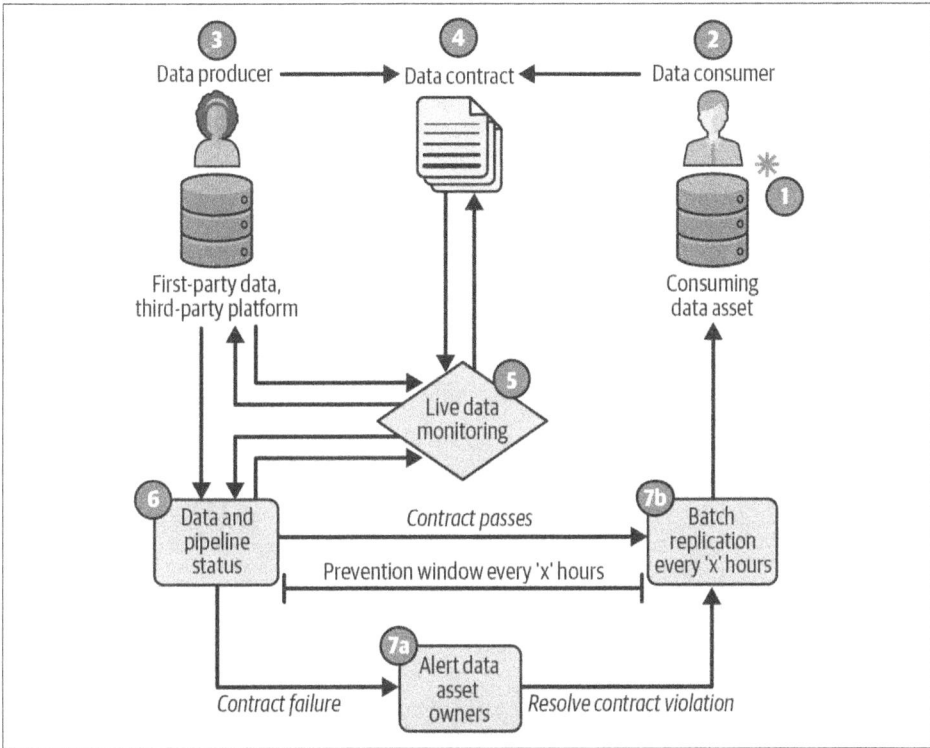

Figure 5-6. The data contract workflow: first-party data, third-party platform

Here's what this process looks like in detail:

1. Data constraints identified by the data consumer.

2. Data consumer requests a data contract for an asset.

3. Data producer confirms data contract is viable.

4. Data contract confirmed as code.

5. Continuous monitoring of data and relevant contracts.

6. Queue of batch replication jobs.

7. Depending on whether the contract passes or fails:

   a. Data asset owners are notified of data contract violation for a batch job and follow failure protocol.

   b. Data assets updated for downstream processes when the data contract passes tests for the batch job.

Figure 4-4 helps further visualize the difference between first-party data and platform versus first-party data and third-party platform use cases.

In Mark's example of optimizing employee hours and ARR, there was a one-week (i.e., 168 hours) window in which incorrect data in Salesforce could reach the reporting workflow and erroneously alter business decisions related to revenue. Without data contracts in place, these issues often fail silently until a business stakeholder notes that the numbers look off, given their domain expertise. Data contracts serve as a mechanism to surface the issue within the prevention window and implement a fix or block the replication before reaching the target database (as illustrated in Figure 5-6).

In this section we covered the four data asset categories you will likely encounter when considering data contracts, and where to place them. In the next section, we will expand to utilizing metadata to align expectations with the data assets via data contract specs.

Contract Definition

Now that we know what data assets we want to put under contract, we need to establish our expectations as code via a contract spec, codify business logic within the contract spec, and compare the expectations within the contract spec to the metadata of the data assets under contract via Schema Registries and/or data catalogs. This section details each of these and the various considerations you should account for.

Data Contract Spec

In our conversations with practitioners, a common but misplaced question revolves around the standardization of data contract specs. While the spec is an integral component of data contracts, it is a tool to help implement the architecture of data contracts—the spec is not a data contract itself. An analogy would be the question, "What database should we use to implement a data lakehouse?" Regardless of whether it's Snowflake, Databricks, BigQuery, etc., all that matters is what you have available and what works for your business use case.

As of this writing, open source data contract specifications are available, but they are not widely adopted. In our conversations with companies, many are developing their own specifications to address the unique nuances of their data systems. As this architectural pattern gains further adoption and matures, we anticipate that various standardized formats will emerge as popular choices. However, the purpose of this book is not to recommend a specific format, but rather to detail the underlying mechanisms, regardless of the specification used. A classic xkcd comic (927) (*https://*

xkcd.com/927) further illustrates why directing you toward a specific spec is a futile task.

To create your own data contract spec, we recommend utilizing JSON Schema (*https://json-schema.org*), "a declarative language for defining structure and constraints for JSON data," and pairing it with YAML. In addition, JSON Schema is also part of a larger ecosystem of tools that extend its power, such as validators for various languages and databases. This chapter will only provide a high-level overview, but we will provide further details and code in Chapter 8.

Key considerations of a data contract spec include the following:

- Ability to be technology agnostic to enable integration across the entire data lifecycle
- Ability to describe expectations of a data asset in a human-readable format—hence why YAML is a common format.
- Ability to cover both the schema of data and the semantics
- Ability for the contract spec itself be semantically versioned, as contracts will need to evolve over time
- Ability to account for the heterogeneity of the ways in which technologies define or constrain data (e.g., required typing in JavaScript versus optional typing in Python)

Here is a data contract spec from our implementation in Chapter 7 that uses a Postgres database to store information pertaining to museum objects. Note that while we are using JSON Schema, JSON and YAML can be easily converted one-to-one:

```
{
    "spec-version": "1.0.0",
    "name": "object-images-contract-spec",
    "namespace": "met-museum-data",
    "dataAssetResourceName": "postgresql://postgres:5432/postgres.object_images",
    "doc": "Data contract for the object_images table containing image URLs and
metadata for museum objects, including primary images, additional images, and
creation timestamps.",
    "owner": {
      "name": "Data Engineering Team",
      "email": "data-eng@museum.org"
    },
    "schema": {
      "$schema": "https://json-schema.org/draft/2020-12/schema",
      "title": "Object Images Table Schema",
      "table_catalog": "postgres",
      "table_schema": "public",
      "table_name": "object_images",
      "properties": {
        "object_id": {
```

```
            "description": "Identifying number for each artwork (unique, can be
used as key field)",
            "examples": [437133],
            "constraints": {
              "primaryKey": true,
              "data_type": "integer",
              "numeric_precision": 32.0,
              "is_nullable": false,
              "is_updatable": true
            }
          },
          "primary_image": {
            "description": "URL to the primary image of an object (JPEG)",
            "examples": ["https://images.metmuseum.org/.../DT1234.jpg"],
            "constraints": {
              "primaryKey": false,
              "data_type": "text",
              "is_nullable": true,
              "is_updatable": true
            }
          },
          "additional_images": {
            "description": "Array of URLs to additional JPEG images of the
object",
            "constraints": {
              "primaryKey": false,
              "data_type": "ARRAY",
              "is_nullable": true,
              "is_updatable": true
            },
            "array_element": {
              "data_type": "text"
            }
          },
          "created_at": {
            "description": "Timestamp when this record was created in the
database",
            "examples": ["2025-01-15T10:30:00.000Z"],
            "items": null,
            "constraints": {
              "primaryKey": false,
              "data_type": "timestamp without time zone",
              "datetime_precision": 6.0,
              "is_nullable": false,
              "is_updatable": true
            }
          }
        }
      }
    }
  }
```

In the subsequent subsections, we will break this contract spec apart into its key components of contract management, data schema, and data semantics.

Contract management

Key to infrastructure as code is the ability to manage the metadata being stored (i.e., meta-metadata) and keep track of its changes as it inevitably evolves. While technically this can be tracked via `git blame` and the version-controlled history, that only partially satisfies the necessary requirements of a data contract. In addition, we must be able to build automations on top of these changes, hence the following values:

`spec-version`
> The version of the data contract spec utilized within your system, where this value will change with each iteration to the spec structure as your use case changes or becomes more complex (e.g., adding further semantic constraints).

`name`
> The user-defined name of the respective data contract, where name and namespace form a combined unique identifier.

`namespace`
> A user-defined name representing a collection of data contracts, similar to a higher-level "folder" within a repository.

`dataAssetResourceName`
> The URL path of the data source under contract, where it aligns with the naming pattern of the data source (e.g., `s3://<your path>/<your file name>` or `postgres://db/<database-name>`).

`doc`
> The documentation that describes what the data contract represents, enforces, and any other pertinent information.

`owner`
> The assigned owner (either an individual or group) of the data contract, and the contact information used to notify when a contract is violated, when it needs a change, or if an individual is trying to determine a point of contact for further context:

```
{
    "spec-version": "1.0.0",
    ...
    "owner": {
        "name": "Data Engineering Team",
        "email": "data-eng@museum.org"
    }
```

```
      ...
    }
```

While we believe these are the essential components for contract management, there may be additional values that are pertinent to your specific business use case.

Data schema

Enforcement of data schemas will likely be the first use case implemented on a company's data contract journey and will protect the most obvious, yet most disastrous, upstream changes. When utilizing JSON Schema as the underlying language, you will need to map data typing to your standard (*https://oreil.ly/hFkov*) and/or utilize available extensions (*https://oreil.ly/3vH38*) for additional languages (e.g., Go, Rust, etc.). The standard JSON schema includes the following:

- string
- number
- integer
- object

- array
- boolean
- null

In addition to those standard types, it is also beneficial to enable optional and union typing to handle more complex typing use cases, such as where a null value is valid for a string value. For example:

```
schema:
  - name: aquarium_id
    doc: The id of the aquarium
    type: string32
  - name: exhibit_id
    doc: (Optional) The id of an exhibit within a specific aquarium.
    type: union
    types: ['null', 'string32']
  - name: exhibit_status
    doc: The status of the aquarium exhibit.
    type: enum
    symbols: ['OPEN', 'CLOSED', 'MAINTENANCE', 'FEEDING']
  - name: exhibit_location
    doc: (optional) The location of an aquarium exhibit.
    type: union
    types:
      - type: 'null'
      - type: struct
        alias: Location
        name: location
        doc: A geographic location
        fields:
          - name: latitude
            doc: The latitude of the location
            type: float64
```

```
          - name: longitude
            doc: The longitude of the location
            type: float64
  - name: last_exhibit_update_time
    doc: >
      The last known real-time update from the aquarium exhibit status
      (in milliseconds since the Unix epoch)
    type: date64
```

Data semantics

As a company moves forward with its data contract use cases, it may want to implement constraints beyond schema and on the underlying data itself, as well as use specific if-else conditions based on multiple data values. JSON Schema supports this via schema composition (*https://oreil.ly/-sfpe*) and subschemas (*https://oreil.ly/u2Zfc*):

```
schema:
  - name: aquarium_id
    constraints:
      - charLength: 32
      - isNull: FALSE
      - isNotEmpty: TRUE
  - name: exhibit_id
    constraints:
      - isNullThreshold: 0.8
  - name: exhibit_status
    constraints:
      - isNullThreshold: 0.3
      - length: 1
  - name: exhibit_location
    types:
      - name: location
        fields:
          - name: latitude
            constraints:
              - isNull: False
          - name: longitude
            constraints:
              - isNull: False
    constraints:
      - isNullThreshold: 0.45
  - name: last_exhibit_update_time
    constraints:
      - isNull: FALSE
      - max: today
```

This section serves as an introduction to the data contract spec, but we will provide a more in-depth description and use case in Chapter 8, where we will create a data contract spec from scratch and utilize it to prevent a breaking data change. In summary, data contract specs at a minimum need to support contract management and schema enforcement. For more complex implementations, you may consider the requirement of semantic enforcement that puts constraints on the data values themselves and conditional properties of one or more data values within the schema. While there are numerous ways to implement a contract spec, and a growing number of standards, we believe the JSON Schema framework provides a great avenue to understand the underlying mechanisms of a contract spec that you can continue using, or enable you to have a strong understanding of what to look for when choosing an emerging open source standard.

Business Logic

In the previous section we highlighted the role of managing data semantics via the contract spec, which serves as a means of codifying business logic. We define business logic as the the domain-specific knowledge of a particular business function, line of business, and/or sets of procedures that underline the operation of an organization. Similar to the existence of a data lifecycle, we argue that there is also a business logic lifecycle, as represented in Figure 5-7. Furthermore, like the data representing business logic, this logic is not static and is constantly iterated upon—though data quality issues arise when the data doesn't keep up in representing the business logic.

To summarize the business logic lifecycle:

1. Business domains establish the business logic that details the functions and procedures of the organization, such as standard operating procedures.

2. Upstream engineers operationalize this business logic and store the various steps and their timestamps within the transactional database.

3. Replication pipelines move the data from the transactional database (and other sources) into the analytical database, where the data is transformed to infer the business logic.

4. Downstream data teams provide recommendations to the business and inform others about how the business logic should be iterated upon by performing analytics on top of the data within the analytical database.

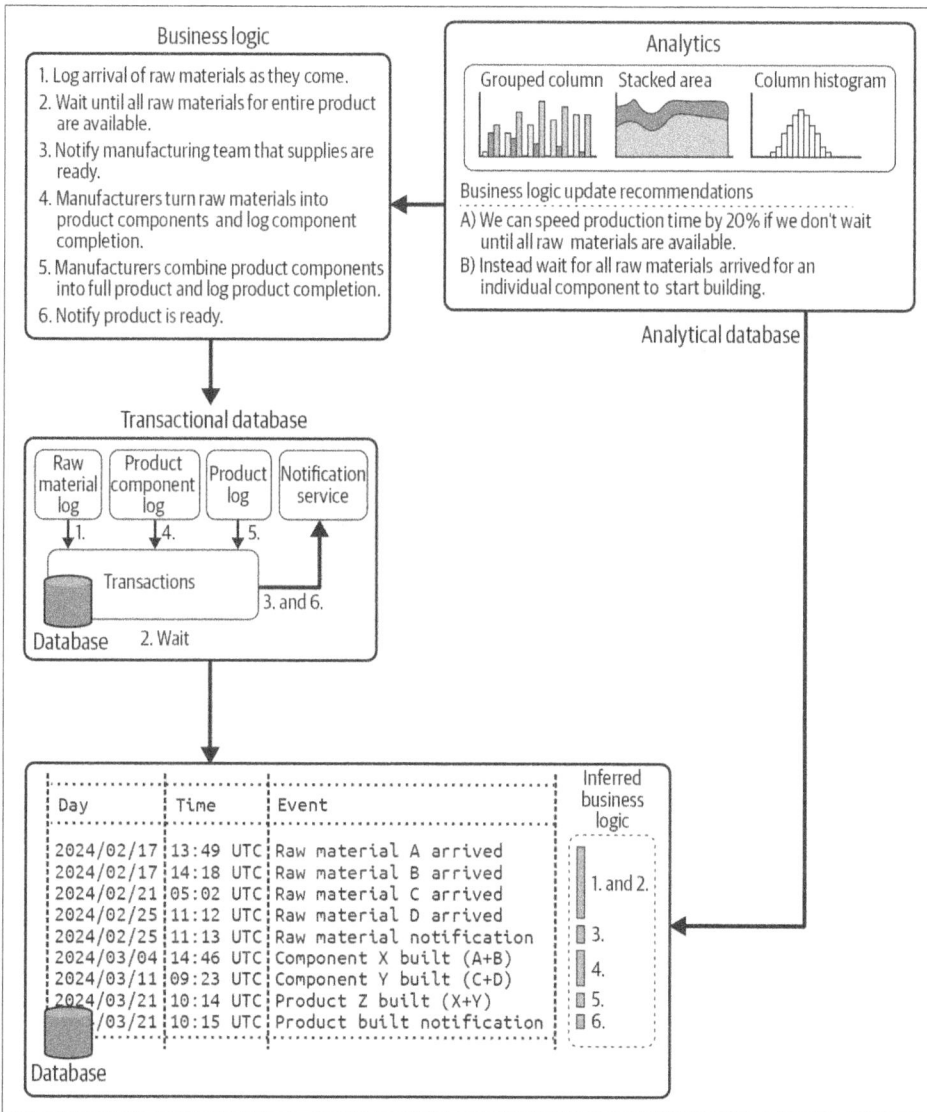

Figure 5-7. Business logic lifecycle

While this business logic is critical to the business, it's often maintained via institutional knowledge within teams and departments. If you're lucky, this knowledge is documented, maintained, and easily discoverable across the organization. Sadly, most people are not lucky. It's not uncommon for this knowledge to be shared via word of mouth, documented only in obscure Slack messages or emails, or worse, known only by a single person who left the organization years ago. This is what makes data contracts powerful, and why management fields within the contract spec are critical.

While data contracts are not a full replacement for documenting business processes, nor do they try to be, they do provide a means to maintain the critical business logic as it pertains to data processes.

Specifically, the "contract management" section of the data contract spec creates a composite unique identifier for a particular data asset and its respective business logic. Furthermore, since this logic is stored as a YAML file within a version-controlled repository, a history of changes to the data's business logic is maintained as discoverable code by any developer with access to the repository.

Schema Registry and Data Catalogs

The data contract spec captures the *expected* schema and business logic, but there needs to be a means of capturing the *actual* schema and business logic within an organization's data systems. While there are numerous ways to achieve this, ranging from hacky implementation to managed vendor tools, the two we will focus on are Schema Registry and data catalogs—where Schema Registry emphasizes stream processing, and data catalogs emphasize batch processing.

Schema Registry

Schema Registry provides a means for event publishers and subscribers to maintain consistency and compatibility of data assets, and thus are primarily focused on event sourcing and streaming data assets. Figure 5-8 provides a high-level overview of how we can utilize Schema Registry with data contracts within the CI/CD workflows. Confluent, the maintainer of the Kafka Schema Registry, defines the tool as the following (*https://oreil.ly/vEzUq*):

> Schema Registry provides a centralized repository for managing and validating schemas for topic message data, and for serialization and deserialization of the data over the network. Producers and consumers to Kafka topics can use schemas to ensure data consistency and compatibility as schemas evolve. Schema Registry is a key component for data governance, helping to ensure data quality, adherence to standards, visibility into data lineage, audit capabilities, collaboration across teams, efficient application development protocols, and system performance.

It is important to note that while we've placed our emphasis for this book on Kafka and Schema Registry, as they are both open source and widely adopted, the overarching concepts still apply to managed tools, such as AWS Kinesis and the corresponding AWS Glue Schema registry.

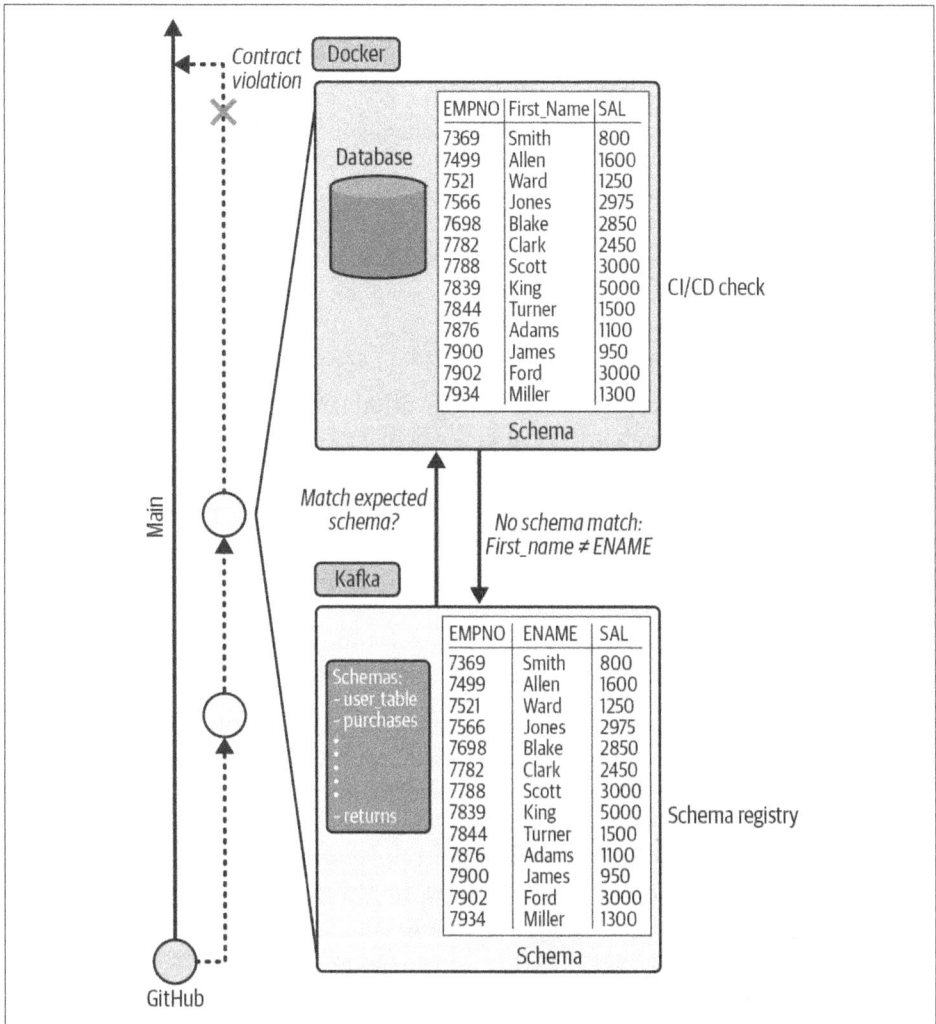

Figure 5-8. Data contracts: schema validation

Regardless of the tool, we'll use the same pattern to enforce schemas via data contracts:

1. A developer creates a pull request where a data asset under a contract is changed.

2. The pull request kicks off the CI/CD workflow, where a Docker image is spun up with a database.

3. The Docker database replicates a fraction of the changing data asset, where schema info can be extracted.

4. The extracted schema from the Docker database is compared to the source of truth of the respective data asset's schemas (e.g., Kafka Schema Registry).

5. The CI/CD test passes if the two schemas match, but will fail and block merging if there is a discrepancy between the two schemas.

This same workflow also applies to data catalogs, where the replicated database within Docker is compared to the metadata within the catalog. We will detail this further in the next section, as well as highlight when you would want to use Schema Registry over a data catalog for data contracts.

Data catalogs

Data catalogs serve as a centralized inventory of metadata within the organization, with emphasis on discoverability (what and where data exists), a data glossary (what this data means), data lineage between assets (how the data moves through a system), and defined governance (who has access to the data and how it should be used). As of this writing in 2024, data catalogs have become a hot topic, with the major data infrastructure vendors making their data catalogs open source, such as Databricks with its Unity Catalog (*https://oreil.ly/dyPfo*) and Snowflake with its Polaris Catalog (*https://oreil.ly/IbSiE*). With that said, any tool will suffice for data contracts as long as there is a means to extract the stored metadata within the CI/CD workflow.

Schema Registries and data catalogs both store schema metadata, but they differ in their implications for stream and batch processing. Specifically, data catalogs can consume metadata from Schema Registries, raising the question, "Which source should one reference for data contract enforcement?" Typically, data catalogs consume metadata via batch processing, which limits data contract enforcement to the timing of the batch intervals at the entire data asset level. In contrast, streaming data processes events in real time, allowing Schema Registries to enforce data contracts at the record level. Thus, if your architecture warrants it, we suggest utilizing both, as represented in Figure 5-9, where CI/CD workflows reference the Schema Registry and the data catalog.

Furthermore, data catalogs increase in importance for data contract enforcement once organizations move beyond just schema validation. As noted earlier, in addition to schema, data catalogs include other categories of metadata, such as lineage, definitions, governance policies, and locations of various data assets within different databases. Chapter 9 details advanced applications of data contracts, but examples include:

- Enforcement of PII protection on data asset changes, based on documented governance policies
- Impact analysis of upstream changes based on data lineage

- Data profiling thresholds to ensure data stays within expected ranges or follows specific regex patterns

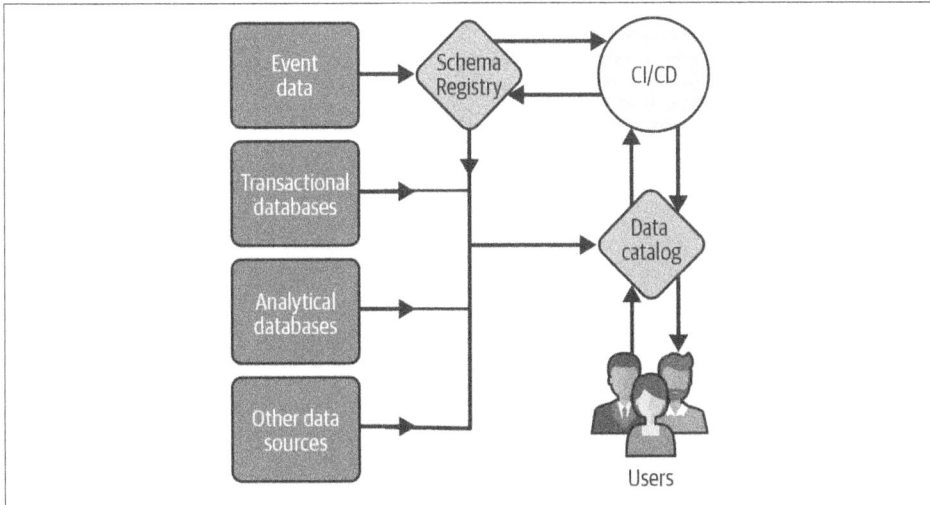

Figure 5-9. Flow of metadata consumption

These advanced use cases are ideal, but we still recommend a crawl, walk, and run approach to data contracts, where iterations of implementation build on each other and provide additional learnings for handling further complexity.

Conclusion

In this chapter, we covered the initial two components of the data contract architecture: data assets and contract definition. Among the data assets, we detailed the differences between analytical and transactional databases, event sourcing and streaming, and first-party data on third-party platforms. While the data itself has wide variability, these categories of data assets are the ones you will most likely encounter and want to place data contracts on. In addition to data assets, we also described the underlying foundations for data contract definitions via the data contract spec, business logic, and centralized metadata sources such as Schema Registry and data catalogs.

Furthermore, we highlighted the underlying structure of a data contract spec with the following key considerations:

- Ability to be technology agnostic to enable integration across the entire data lifecycle
- Ability to describe expectations of a data asset in a human-readable format

- Ability to cover both the schema of data and the semantics
- Ability for the contract spec itself to be semantically versioned
- Ability to account for the heterogeneity of the ways in which technologies define or constrain data

Chapter 5 focused heavily on the underlying data and metadata utilized by data contracts. In Chapter 6, we will continue describing the final two components of the data contract architecture—detection and prevention—which emphasize how to take action on the data and metadata covered in this chapter.

The Data Contract Components: Detection and Prevention

In Chapter 5, we provided an overview of the data contract components and discussed in detail the role of data assets and contract definitions within the data contract architecture pattern. In this chapter, we will provide an overview of all the architecture components and then spend subsequent sections focusing on the *detection* and *prevention* components of data contracts. By the end of this chapter, you will have a solid foundation of what you need in order to implement the data contract architecture—which we will do through a guided coding project in Chapter 7.

Recall from Chapter 5 that data contract architecture requires using a toolbox of infrastructure, with each component broken up into four main categories and their respective subcategories (you can refer back to Figure 5-1 for a visual representation):

Data assets
> The foundation of all data infrastructure is databases, and while the range of databases is vast, we will focus on the following four categories for this book:
>
> - Analytics databases
> - Transactional databases
> - Event sourcing and event streams
> - First-party data, third-party platform

Contract definition
> The surface to embed the expectations around schema and business logic (i.e., semantics) for a respective data asset, which is then compared to centralized sources of metadata. The three components are as follows:
>
> - Data contract spec

- Business logic
- Schema registry and data catalogs

Detection

Detection needs to happen at the code level for schema and at runtime for data semantics to ensure changes are captured, ideally before data is written to the target database. The following seven categories represent the areas in which you can detect changes to data:

- Data quarantining
- Change data capture
- Stream processing
- Source code flow graphs
- Data lineage
- Static code analysis
- Live data monitoring

Prevention

While it's ideal for prevention to be automatic in handling contract violations, this is not possible given that many data quality issues are rooted in people and processes. Thus the automation is in alerting the right people at the right time within the developer workflow. The following three categories are typically where you can inform of potential breaking changes:

- CI/CD workflows
- Version control (data code review)
- Monitoring and alerts

In Chapter 5, *contract definition* and *data assets* covered the required data and metadata needed for data contracts. The subsequent sections on detection and prevention will explain how to operationalize these components within your data lifecycle.

Detection

Under the lens of data contracts, we define detection as the ability to detect the metadata associated with data assets and the differences in expectations of a proposed change within the data lifecycle. The following categories are three of the methods we can use to detect these changes:

Code-level detection

Detecting what code is associated with a data asset under contract and how its changes would adhere to the expectations and constraints within the contract.

Data-in-motion detection

Analyzing live data, within a predetermined window of time between source and target databases, to ensure alignment within the contract expectation and constraints, especially with respect to semantic changes.

Historical detection

Surfacing data assets and/or code related to data assets that were changed *before* a data contract was in place but that violate the new enforced expectations.

Table 6-1 illustrates how the detection methods and data asset categories relate, as well as the various data assets that a data contract would protect.

Table 6-1. Detection methods and how they relate to data assets and their detection categories

		Detection method						
		Data quarantining	*Change data capture*	*Stream processing*	*Source code flow graphs*	*Data lineage*	*Static code analysis*	*Live data monitoring*
Data asset	*Transactional databases*	X	X		X	X	X	X
	Analytical databases	X	X		X	X	X	X
	Streaming data		X	X	X	X	X	X
	First-party data, third-party platform	X	X			X		X
Detection category	*Code-level detection*			X	X	X	X	
	Data-in-motion detection	X	X	X				X
	Historical detection	X			X	X	X	

But what exactly are the data quality issues we are trying to detect with these methods? This topic can be an entire book in itself, with many variations, depending on who you ask. One classic book we recommend is the *DAMA Data Management Body of Knowledge* (DAMA International) (*https://oreil.ly/GjfKH*), which categorizes data quality issues into the following nine dimensions:

Validity

The degree to which your data aligns with expected business logic (e.g., a timestamp showing occurrence during business hours)

Completeness
> Whether a value has all the required information to be considered complete (e.g., a birth date having day, month, and year)

Consistency
> Measurement of whether values are structured the same throughout the entire column (e.g., not having [1, 2, 3, 4, 5] and [a, b, c, d, e] both present in a column)

Integrity
> The plausibility of a data value (e.g., one wouldn't expect to see the city of San Francisco associated with the country of Germany)

Timeliness
> Whether data is received within an expected time frame with respect to the required business need (e.g., consistently receiving a data refresh within 24 hours given that there is a 1-day SLA)

Currency
> How recent the data is compared to the current time (e.g., a last refresh date beyond six months for a data asset with a one-month SLA would violate currency)

Reasonableness
> Whether a set of values can exist for a column (e.g., you would only expect 12 types of values max for a column representing the month).

Uniqueness
> Whether all data values within a column are distinct (e.g., all user_ids are unique)

Accuracy
> The degree of correctness of a value within a data asset, as determined by the business logic (e.g., an alcohol delivery service expects a user's age to be 21 minimum in the United States, as compared to European countries with lower age requirements)

Which data quality dimension you want to enforce is dependent upon your specific business requirements (again, "fit for use") and what threshold of errors is acceptable. Under the context of detection within data contracts, what's more important is understanding *how* these data quality dimensions manifest as errors. Many data professionals focus heavily on schema or semantics of the data itself, but while useful, that doesn't get to the root of where these issues manifest—the code itself.

To highlight the importance of code-level detection, Figure 6-1 shows a subset of the business logic lifecycle diagram from Chapter 5. At its core, data is an attempt at taking a snapshot of the real world, and business logic puts structure around what that data should look like. Code is the mechanism in which real-world events and the structure of business logic are transformed into data. Thus, this serves as the earliest point in which you can programmatically prevent data quality violations.

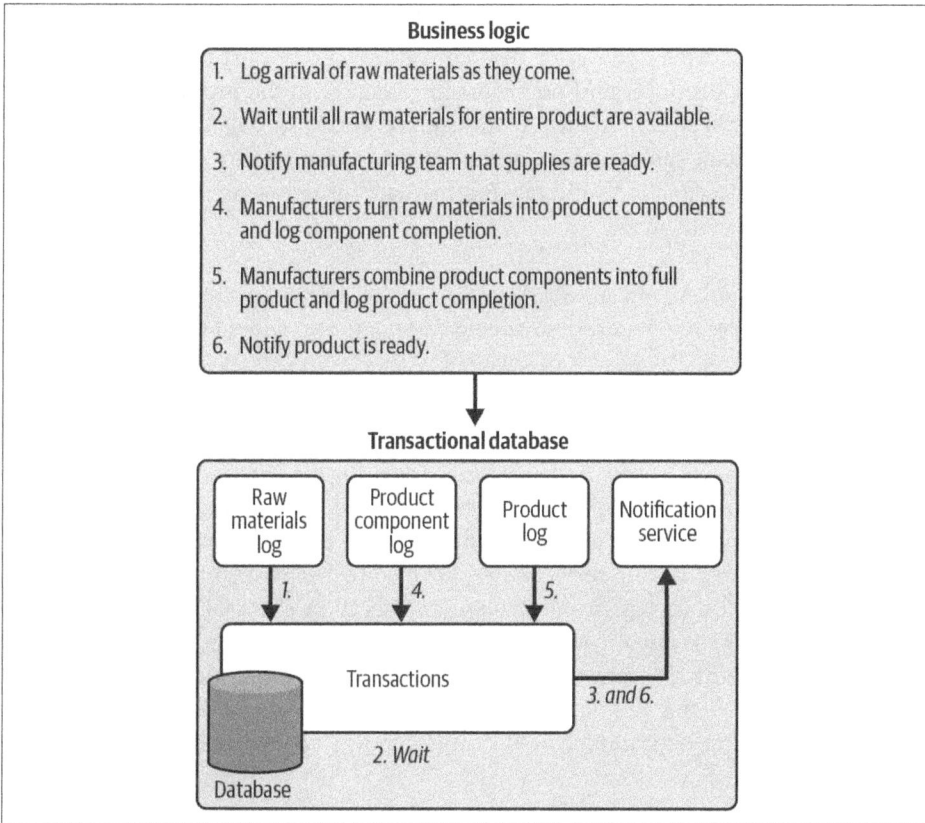

Business logic

1. Log arrival of raw materials as they come.

2. Wait until all raw materials for entire product are available.

3. Notify manufacturing team that supplies are ready.

4. Manufacturers turn raw materials into product components and log component completion.

5. Manufacturers combine product components into full product and log product completion.

6. Notify product is ready.

Transactional database

| Raw materials log | Product component log | Product log | Notification service |

1. 4. 5.

Transactions

3. and 6.

2. Wait

Database

Figure 6-1. Subset of the business logic lifecycle emphasizing code

While code-level detection is the most ideal form of prevention via data contracts, not all data quality issues can be detected via code nor do all organizations have the ability to inspect their code via automation. Data drift is a great example (see "How Data Drifts from Established Business Logic" on page 67), where the code has not changed but the business logic no longer aligns with the real world. In this instance, data-in-motion detection is necessary to prevent the data quality issue from propagating downstream, and thus the focus becomes how quickly you can detect that captured data has diverged from the real world you are trying to represent. Finally, data contracts will rarely be established before an organization has years of accumulated data, unless used for data migration efforts, so we must also account for historical detection, especially when putting an established data asset under contract for the first time. In this section we will dive into the various detection methods and their associated technology.

Data Quarantining

There are instances where you are a data consumer who doesn't have control of the data provided by a producer and no means to engage with the producer consistently (e.g., a data broker service). While a complete prevention of data asset change violations would be ideal, the next best option is data quarantining, or the process of monitoring for data violations and tagging the data for either separation or cautioning of downstream consumers.

Another name for quarantining is a "dead letter queue," especially under the context of streaming data. Our case studies in Chapter 8 provide two specific examples of their use with data contracts.

For example, in one of Mark's first jobs he worked on the management of ingestion files for health insurance eligibility. These files were critical and could mean the difference between someone getting needed clinical care or having to pay out of pocket for expensive health services despite having health insurance. Due to the sensitive nature, all data first went through an ingestion check at staging, and then was quarantined for manual review if it didn't meet specified requirements (e.g., a missing date of birth). These manual reviews were some of Mark's first introduction to diving into JSON data and navigating data quality issues—and a driver for exploring data contracts to determine a way to manage this change management process programmatically.

While manual processes sufficed for that job, it required an entire operations team to review and manage communication with external data producers over weeks. Furthermore, there were multiple times where the backlog became so large that the entire team had to drop everything and resolve the issues. Many of those issues were due to slight changes to the data's schema, which often caused entire file ingestions to fail for thousands of records in bulk. With data contracts, this manual process could be improved by:

- Creating more descriptive failures, given comparisons to the domain context from the contract spec
- Automating the communication to external parties and providing the necessary metadata to flag the issues
- Communicating the scope of impacted data under quarantine to internal downstream data consumers

Deciding whether or not to quarantine data once again depends on the business use case and the data quality dimensions valued for the use case. For example, in the health insurance use case, having no data was better than passing forward bad data. Specifically, while a patient not having access to care is a huge problem, there was a process for handling the use case and manually pushing the correct data through the system and instantly getting proof of coverage via a phone call. If instead we pushed the bad data through, the patient either would still not have care covered or would be billed wrong due to the data error—resulting in lower customer satisfaction scores. For the converse, having bad data pushed forward may be useful, such as in the case of telemetry data, where bad data can signal a faulty piece of hardware.

While data quarantining can be quite straightforward via batch ETL jobs like the health insurance use case, you can get even more fine-grained with your automations at the value level. The next subsections will dive further into this via *change data capture*, *stream processing*, and *live data monitoring*.

Change Data Capture, Stream Processing, and Live Data Monitoring

There are many business use cases where a traditional daily batch job via an ETL pipeline won't suffice, such as recommender systems, fraud detection, and telemetry analytics. Thus, organizations turn to streaming data methods to complement their batch processing. Three common techniques used for streaming are change data capture, stream processing, and live data monitoring (also called real-time data monitoring). They are defined as the following:

Change data capture
  A technique to monitor CRUD operations in an upstream database and propagate those database changes to downstream databases in real time, resulting in incremental changes

Stream processing
  A technique to both process and analyze ingested data in real time at the time of creation

Live data monitoring
  A technique to only observe and analyze real-time data for data quality

When combined with the write-audit-publish (WAP) pattern, these techniques allow the detection of data contract violations among data in motion, while also preventing violated data assets from propagating to downstream databases. The WAP pattern applies the software engineering best practices of staging and testing environments, before pushing to production, to data. Figure 6-2 illustrates how the WAP pattern works, and where:

1. New data is written to a staging database.

2. The data within the staging database is audited via various data quality checks and semantic tests within the data contract spec.

3. If the staged data passes the audit checks, it's promoted to a production database that downstream data consumers can access.

4. If the staged data fails the audit checks, it's sent to a "dead letter queue" to prevent breaking changes and provide the data team a chance to review the errors.

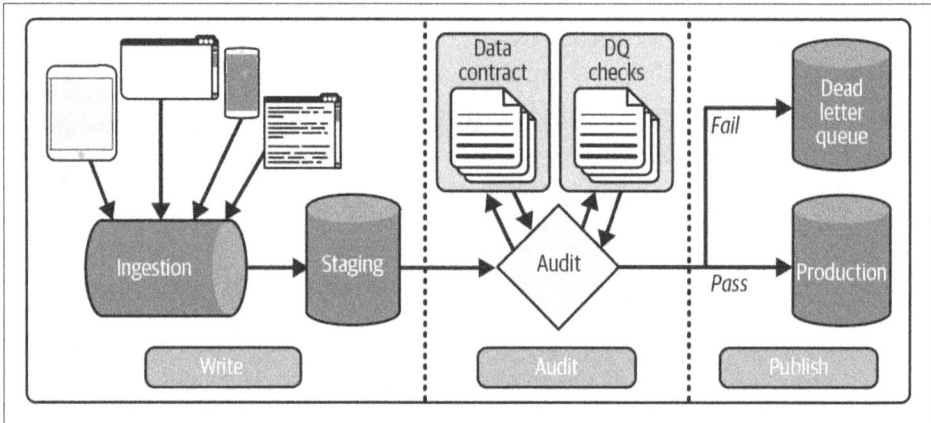

Figure 6-2. The write-audit-publish pattern and data contracts

In the next section, we will begin to describe how to move data contract checks further upstream and into the application codebase.

End-to-End Lineage: Source Code Flow Graphs and Data Lineage

In Chapter 9 we will discuss the role of software engineers in implementing the data contract architecture in more detail. One of the key language differences we saw between software and data developers in describing the movement of data was *source code flow graphs* and *data lineage*. We would reference data lineage whenever we discussed the impact of contract violations on downstream data workflows to software engineers. In return, they would often provide us with a blank stare until we showed a visual example, and then they responded: "Oh, you mean a code flow graph." Thus, we quickly pivoted to using their language. While this is useful for explaining the movement of data to your upstream colleagues, it's important to recognize there are differences in both terms, illustrated in Figure 6-3 and defined as the following:

Source code flow graph
   A directional graph representing how objects and/or files are referenced between each other within a codebase with respect to function calls

Data lineage
   A directional graph representing how data is sourced, transformed, and/or
   moved across tables within databases—especially pertinent in understanding
   what data to use and/or where to look for debugging issues

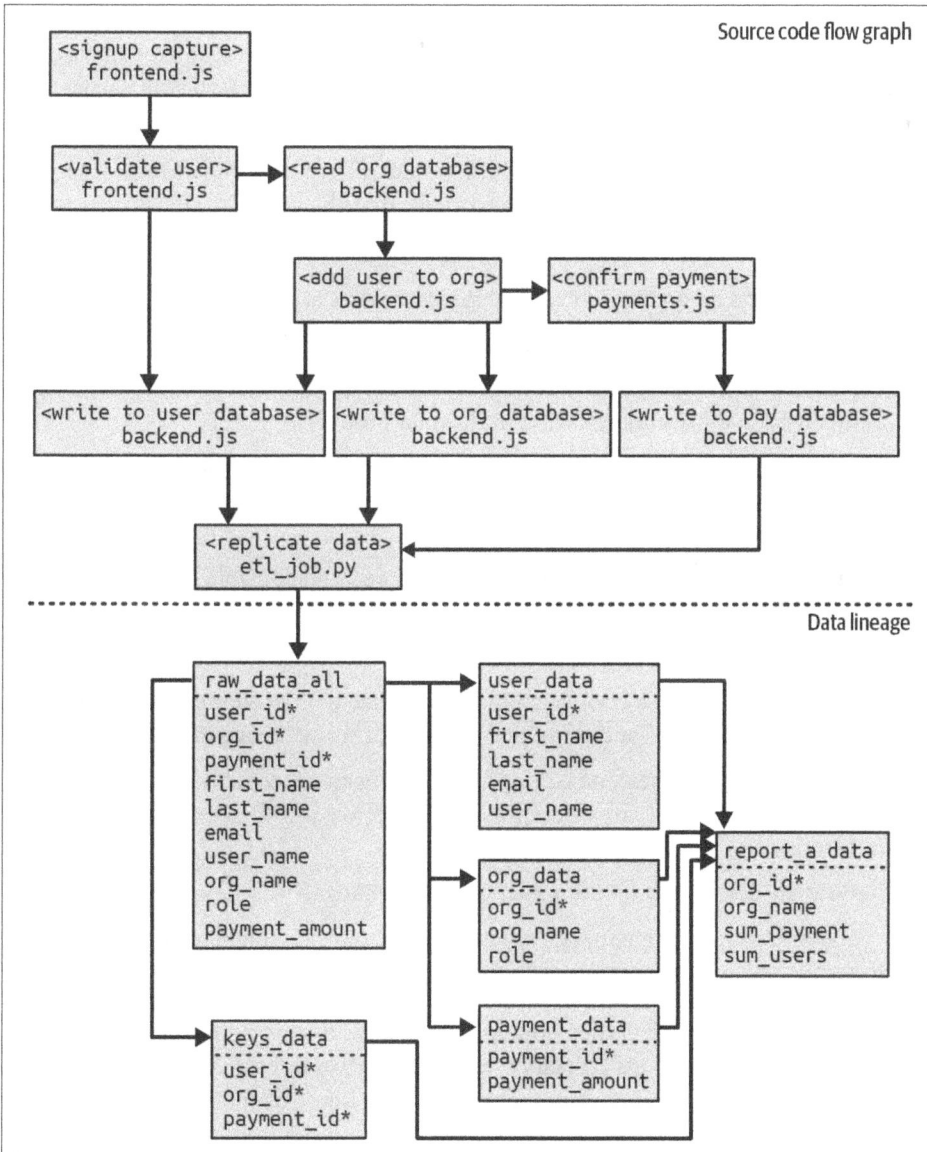

Figure 6-3. Source code flow graph and data lineage

Moving forward, we will describe the combination of the source code flow graph and data lineage as *end-to-end lineage*.

What became clear to us in our data careers was that data lineage in its current state wasn't enough to solve the root cause of data quality and governance challenges. If you have read up to this point, then it's clear our stance is that to do so we must shift left as far as possible and ideally into the operations of the transactional database. Yet most data lineage tools only provide information within the analytical database after it's been replicated from the transactional database.

In a previous data engineering role, Mark would often manually trace downstream data to upstream code that generated and replicated the data. Specifically, he would follow this path for resolving data quality issues that arose due to upstream changes:

1. Replicate the data quality issue in the downstream data product.
2. Determine which data assets were causing the errors.
3. Utilize the data lineage to understand all the points the data assets touched between replication and surfacing in the data product.
4. Review the transformation code (e.g., SQL and/or PySpark) to determine if the issue is due to incorrect transformation logic or if an upstream change is breaking assumptions.
5. Identify the raw replicated data assets and the code responsible for replication.
6. Trace the code function calls from the replication code back to the function responsible for generating the code for the data assets of interest.
7. Along the various files and function calls, utilize `git blame` to determine if any of the highlighted files and functions changed and who changed them.
8. Pull up the PR to review the `git diff`, read any comments on the PR describing the changes, and find any references to tickets (e.g., in Jira) or product requirement docs.
9. Review the documentation to understand the changes.
10. Work with upstream engineers, specifically the ones highlighted with `git blame`, to resolve the upstream issue.

Note how steps 1 through 5 focus on *data lineage*, and steps 6 through 10 focus on *source code flow graphs*. This workflow would take days at best, and weeks at worst, to go through, and it is what ultimately convinced Mark of the importance of data contracts.

With respect to the data contract architecture, the better you are able to capture and connect the metadata of end-to-end lineage, the more robust your enforcement logic can be. We argue that this is by far the most important metadata you can capture beyond the changes that trigger enforcement. It provides a clear line of sight for upstream software engineers to see the impact of their code on downstream reports.

For example, referencing Figure 6-3, the shortest path between nodes `<signup capture> frontend.js` and `report_a_data` within the end-to-end lineage is six edges—or six degrees of separation between the upstream producer of `frontend.js` and the downstream consumer of `report_a_data`. It's unreasonable to expect either party to be aware of these dependencies for this simple mock example, and it's impossible once you scale this to a real-world instance of an enterprise with thousands of function calls and tables!

Figure 6-4 highlights how the data contract architecture helps unify these silos.

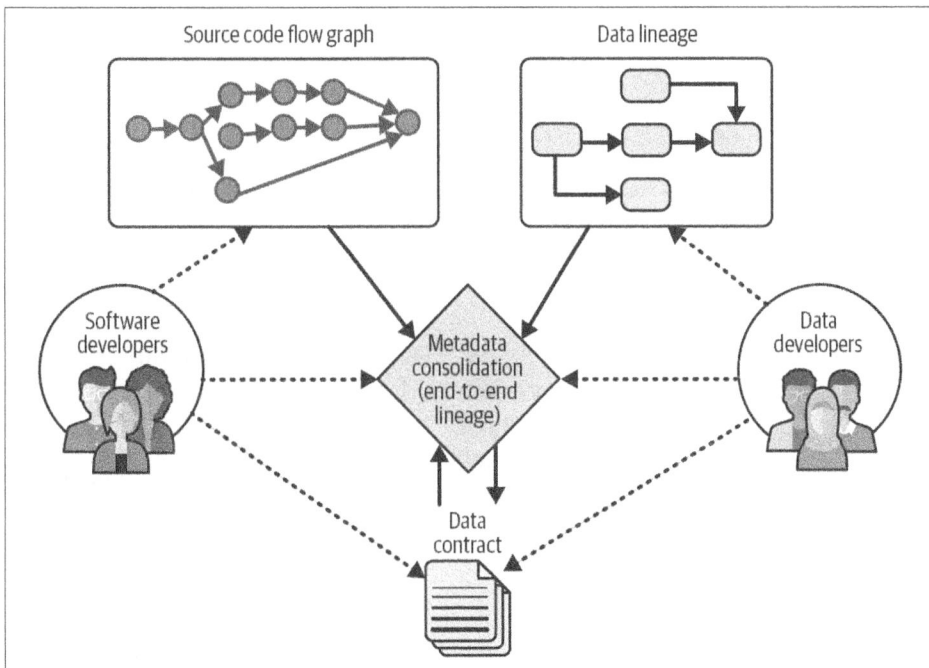

Figure 6-4. Data contracts and end-to-end lineage

Individual developers are no longer required to manually trace through dependencies and lineage, and instead are only presented the most pertinent metadata to the problem they are solving as surfaced by the data contract enforcement.

> We recommend *Fundamentals of Metadata Management* by Ole Olesen-Bagneux (O'Reilly), which provides an in-depth look at how the need for bridging metadata silos is growing via what he describes as *meta grid architecture*.

This all sounds great in theory, but how does one actually achieve end-to-end lineage? Thankfully, the data lineage side is a solved problem with many open source tools available (such as OpenLineage (*https://openlineage.io*)). What becomes difficult is pulling the metadata for source code flow graphs within codebases that are rapidly evolving and utilize various coding languages. In the next section, we will discuss the method that will allow you to build a source code flow graph—static code analysis.

Static Code Analysis

Static code analysis (SCA) is a niche subset of software engineering that determines how code should behave. This has been very useful for compilers since the 1960s, and you have probably experienced SCA when using a debugger or linter in an IDE. To be clear, the topic requires an entire book to explain, and this small section will only focus on its intersection with data contacts.

We recommend *Static Program Analysis* by Anders Møller and Michael I. Schwartzbach (*https://oreil.ly/6-BZd*), which describes SCA as:

> [T]he art of reasoning about the behavior of computer programs without actually running them. This is useful not only in optimizing compilers for producing efficient code but also for automatic error detection and other tools that can help programmers. [A] static program analyzer…aims to automatically answer questions about the possible behaviors of programs.

Thinking back to the previous section on source code flow graphs, this is why we believe SCA to be one of the most powerful tools in generating the metadata for the data lifecycle. The following three problems pushed us toward SCA when we were first implementing data contracts across companies:

- Problems with data quality happened before the analytical database, and thus we needed to shift left to truly be preventative.

- Most data teams don't have visibility into the code that generates, transforms, and moves data throughout the data lifecycle before analytical databases—thus we need involvement from software engineers.

- If we want software engineers to be involved, we need to make it unbelievably simple to use and provide value immediately.

SCA checked all the boxes for this problem as it 1) extracted metadata well before database touchpoints, 2) provided value to software engineers by quickly mapping their code across systems, and 3) was automatic and thus unbelievably simple to use for software engineers.

With that said, actually building SCA tools is extremely difficult and requires specialized knowledge in software engineering. As of this writing, we have created a substantial amount of proprietary custom code for the purpose of data contracts, and this method is an advanced application of data contracts. A great starting point for SCA tooling comes from Meta (Facebook when released), which made its Pysa and Infer open source in 2020 and 2015, respectively. Pysa is the Python SCA tool used by Meta's Instagram team (*https://oreil.ly/5HwHw*) to identify security vulnerabilities on its servers, while Infer is the SCA tool used by Meta (*https://oreil.ly/VlSD5*) to identify bugs before mobile code is shipped for Java and C languages.

SCA works for data contracts by embedding itself within the CI/CD workflow, specifically code review, where data contracts apply SCA to the main and the branch of the proposed change. Then the determined code behaviors are compared with respect to their impact on data assets by the data contract. If the data contract identifies a change that impacts a data asset, then the data contract enforcement workflow takes place. Figure 6-5 illustrates this via a simple example of a frontend logging event being changed from first_name and last_name to only full_name, resulting in a data contract violation.

We will provide more detail within the case study of Glassdoor's data contract implementation in Chapter 8, where we mention that it utilized SCA as one of the earliest steps in its data quality checks via data contracts. Figure 6-6 is adapted from the Glassdoor Engineering Blog article "Data Quality at Petabyte Scale: Building Trust in the Data Lifecycle" by Zakariah Siyaji (*https://oreil.ly/7ur5L*), detailing the implementation.

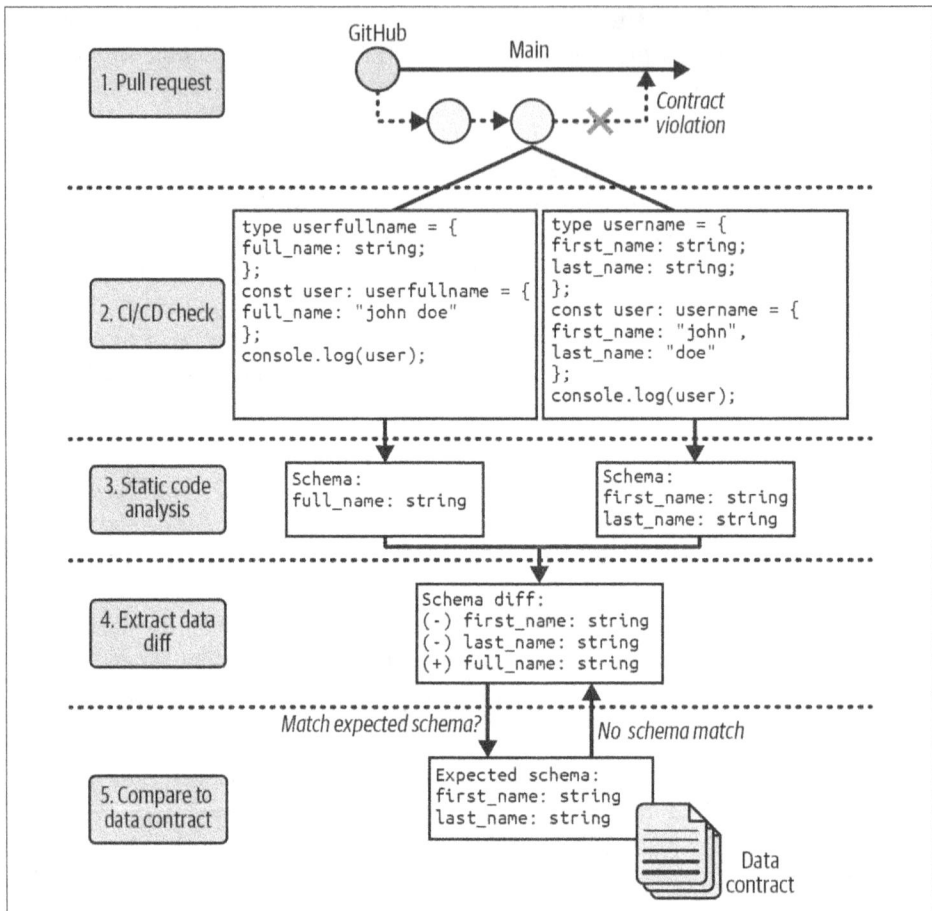

Figure 6-5. How static code analysis fits within the data contract workflow

While we believe SCA provides the most useful metadata for *early* detection of changes to data assets, we also recognize the difficulty of such a method. You can still get tremendous value from data contracts without SCA, especially around schema evolution and live data monitoring, but SCA is imperative to enforce data contracts at the code level and can dramatically reduce data contract violations in production.

In the next section we will describe how to automatically enact data quality prevention methods once a data contract detects a violation.

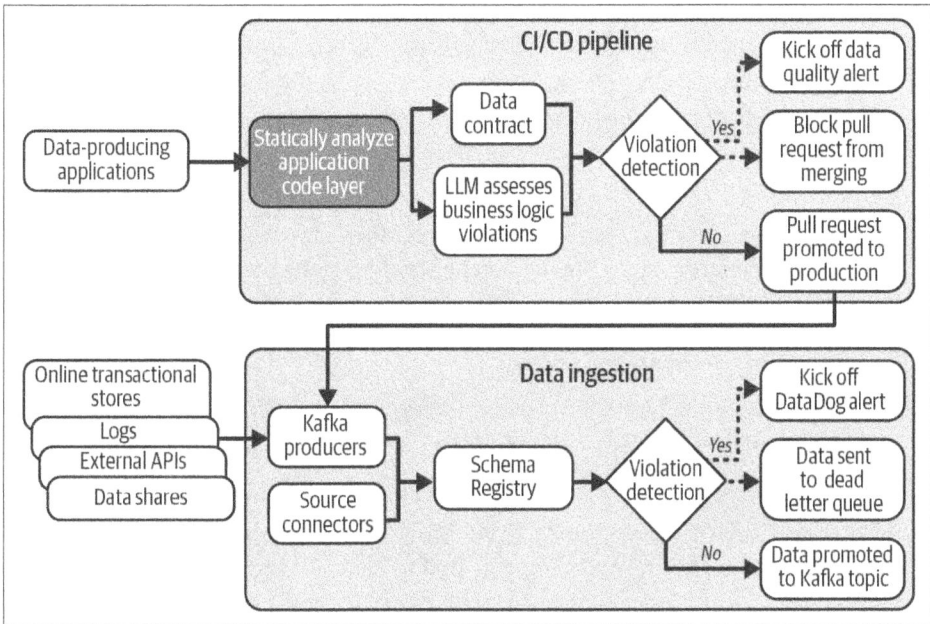

Figure 6-6. Glassdoor's static code analysis use case (adapted from "Data Quality at Petabyte Scale: Building Trust in the Data Lifecycle" by Zakariah Siyaji)

Prevention

In the context of data contracts, we define prevention as the ability to programmatically prevent incorrect data within an upstream data source being written to a downstream target database. The three primary means of prevention via data contracts are version control, CI/CD, and monitoring and alerts. The subsequent sections provide more detail about each prevention function with respect to the data contract architecture.

Version Control

If you have worked on code at any company in the past 10 years, you have most likely used version control to manage your codebase across multiple independent developers—specifically Git. What sets Git apart from other software is its sheer level of adoption and ubiquity among developers today. Git became the most dominant version control software between 2005, when Linus Torvalds shared his first official Git merge via the Linux email list (*https://oreil.ly/7PDrv*), and 2015. Ten years later, in 2025, most developers can't imagine not using Git unless working on a legacy system using a less popular version control software.

Git fundamentally transformed change management among developers and made it trivial to make small iterative changes distributed across multiple people, compared to developing without Git. The amount of active coordination among developers to manage codebases became negligible. Furthermore, changes required only the necessary context of the increasingly smaller pull requests and their diffs, making reviews and iteration possible.

We believe the data contract architecture can do for data what Git did for software. With respect to data contracts, the main benefits of version control are the following:

- Having a mechanism to update the data contract spec file, and having a history of its changing constraints and context

- Providing the foundation for change management within the software development lifecycle we build the data contract architecture upon—specifically with respect to CI/CD workflows

Given the ubiquity of version control, we won't belabor the point, but if you want to learn more we highly recommend this 2007 video of Linus Torvalds sharing his thoughts on Git (*https://oreil.ly/4Hb-A*) two years after creating it.

CI/CD

This section will focus primarily on the intersection of CI/CD and data contracts rather than describing the component in detail itself. With that said, Henry van Merode provides the following excellent summary of the core literature on CI/CD that we can build upon, taken from his book *Continuous Integration (CI) and Continuous Delivery (CD): A Practical Guide to Designing and Developing Pipelines* (O'Reilly):

> Continuous integration is based on the fact that application code is stored in a source control management system (SCM). Every change in this code triggers an automated build process that produces a build artifact, which is stored in a central, accessible repository. The build process is reproducible, so every time the build is executed from the same code, the same result is expected. The build processes run on a specific machine, the integration or build server. The integration server is sized in such a way that the build execution is fast.
>
> Continuous delivery is based on the fact that there is always a stable mainline of the code, and deployment to production can take place anytime from that mainline. The mainline is kept production-ready, facilitated by the automation of deployments and tests. An artifact is built only once and is retrieved from a central repository. Deployments to test and production environments are performed in the same way, and the same artifact is used for all target environments. Each build is automatically tested on a test machine that resembles the actual production environment. If it runs on a test machine, it should also run on the production machine. Various tests are performed to guarantee that the application meets both the functional and the nonfunctional requirements. The DevOps team is given full insight into the progress

of the continuous delivery process using fast feedback from the integration server (via short feedback loops).

The last sentence calling out "the DevOps team" is the most relevant aspect of CI/CD with respect to the implementation of data contracts. It bears repeating that the data contract architecture serves to bridge silos across the data lifecycle, and thus it's important to work with disparate stakeholders with various constraints to warrant them taking action to maintain acceptable data quality. The majority of this book focuses on software engineers who work on application code that changes data assets, but at this component of data contract architecture we begin working with DevOps engineers. We have found that the most common next step among software engineering teams finally bought into data contracts is for them to then pull in the DevOps team. Thankfully, we have found that DevOps engineers rarely push back on the implementation of data contracts, but they often serve as the engineering org's first impression of data contracts.

> While it's possible for application software engineers to also focus on DevOps functions, our assumption is that the investment into data contracts is mainly warranted for organizations with larger workforces (refer to Dunbar's Number in Chapter 3) and thus the need for the division of labor warranting the hiring of specialized roles such as DevOps.

What makes CI/CD so powerful for the data contract architecture is that now the needs of data teams are embedded directly within the software development lifecycle and within a process familiar to software developers. It bears emphasizing that the constraints of most software engineers do not include data, and thus the person implementing data contracts needs to make taking the desired action for data quality as easy as possible. For further detail, Figure 6-7 illustrates the classic CI/CD figure-eight cycle and where data contracts fit within the cycle.

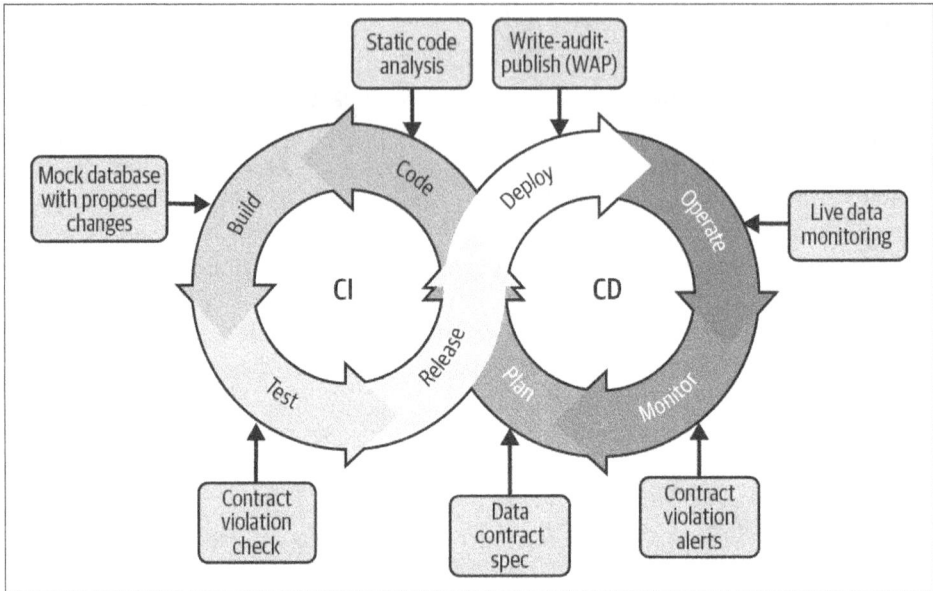

Figure 6-7. How data contracts fit within CI/CD

Once embedded within the software development lifecycle, CI/CD supports the following aspects of the data contract workflow:

- A mechanism to trigger the workflow for data contract violation detection on each new branch of proposed code
- The capacity to block the merging of code into the main branch if a data contract violation is detected
- The ability to provide real-time alerting to the relevant parties established within the contract spec

Given these capabilities, we argue that CI/CD is the most critical component of the data contract architecture as it operationalizes the enforcement of the expectations codified within the data contract specs. Without CI/CD, one simply has a list of desired constraints and a fragile handshake agreement that all parties will adhere to the document.

Violation Monitoring and Alerts

Similar to other challenges we've presented in this book, violation monitoring and alerts is a people and process problem on technical scaffolding. The most advanced and detailed alerts become worthless if people within your organization ultimately ignore them.

As a starting point, use journalism's five Ws and one H framework (*https://oreil.ly/ 3F2VT*) as a means to develop meaningful violation monitoring and alerts:

- *Who* are the most relevant stakeholders that need to be notified?
- *What* is the most relevant information for the presented violation?
- *When* should the violation alert take place?
- *Where* should your target stakeholder receive violation alerts?
- *Why* should the target stakeholder care with respect to their needs?
- *How* should the target stakeholder resolve the violation?

Table 6-2 describes how you can apply the framework to the various stakeholders with respect to data contract violation alerts.

Table 6-2. The five Ws and one H of data contract violation alerts by stakeholder

Alert component	Software developers	Data developers	Business stakeholder	Leadership	External customers
Who	The developer making the code change.	The developer responsible for the impacted data asset as denoted by the data contract.	Stakeholders who are blocked from completing a critical business workflow. Business domain experts who agreed to be included within a data contract spec.	The designated leader for SEV-0 resolution (no active communication otherwise).	Active product user at the time of impact. Customer point of contact.
What	What specific lines of code are in violation. Which key stakeholders are impacted downstream. The meaningful impact to the business. The contract spec(s) associated with the violation.	The specific data assets at risk. The contract spec(s) associated with the violation. The pull request of the proposed change causing a violation.	The specific business workflow impacted. The point of contact for further questions on the data team. Expected timeline to resolve the issue. What actions need to be taken to account for the impacted workflow.	Aggregated information that ties to their key metrics of interest.	What service and or product is impacted. The status of the resolution.

Alert component	Software developers	Data developers	Business stakeholder	Leadership	External customers
When	When a code change is committed to a pull request branch via the CI/CD workflow.	When a data asset they manage and/or depend on is impacted. When associated with the violated data contract.	When a data asset they depend on is actively impacted. When domain knowledge of the specific stakeholder is needed, as defined in the data contract.	Set interval dependent on business need. SEV-0 incidents that threaten the business.	When a meaningful number of active users are impacted. When there is meaningful risk event (e.g., breaching service agreement).
Where	PR comment	PR comment Business messaging (e.g., Slack, email, etc.) Dashboard and reports	Business messaging (e.g., Slack, email, etc.)	Dashboard and reports	Within product Stakeholder management communication (e.g., customer success)
Why	The code change will cause meaningful impact to the business (backed up with data).	A data asset they are responsible for is at risk.	A specific business workflow dependent on the impacted data asset is no longer viable.	Meaningful changes to a key metric they own. Imminent risk to the viability of the business function they lead.	Meaningful impact to the usability of the product and or service.
How	Update the code based on feedback from the violation and or tagged stakeholders *before* merging into main.	Provide support to the software developer within the pull request. Provide communication to impacted data consumers (if not already alerted automatically).	No action if only a consumer of the data asset. If necessary, provide domain knowledge of the business to the developers.	Strategic decisions based on aggregates of violations and alerts data.	No action should be taken by the customer.

While this communication framework may seem obvious, its execution is often an afterthought for many data products. In Chapter 10 we'll discuss data contract adoption and specifically the analogy of building airplanes versus airline experiences, where we highlight how the success of flying is now less about the technology and is instead focused on the experience of using the airline. Thus, you must be deeply aware of how your target stakeholders will react to violation alerts for them to be accepted.

A real-word example that illustrates this best was the failed launch of Epic's Sepsis Model. Epic, the largest hospital electronic health record company in the world by market share (*https://oreil.ly/EAS9v*), launched an ML-based classification product to alert clinical staff of patients at risk for sepsis. What resulted was huge safety concerns and an entire research paper from *JAMA* (one of the most prominent medical journals) calling out its issues with alert fatigue. The paper "External Validation of a Widely Implemented Proprietary Sepsis Prediction Model in Hospitalized Patients" by Andrew Wong et al. (*https://oreil.ly/rNQEa*) highlighted the following:

> An [Epic Sepsis Model (ESM) alert]...occurred in 18% of hospitalizations...even when not considering repeated alerts. If the ESM were to generate an alert only once per patient when the score threshold [used alert minimization strategies]...clinicians would still need to evaluate 8 patients to identify a single patient with eventual sepsis (Table 2). If clinicians were willing to reevaluate patients each time the ESM score [alerted]...to find patients developing sepsis in the next 4 hours, they would need to evaluate 109 patients to find a single patient with sepsis.

While most data products are not life-or-death, this example highlights how providing alerts that are not meaningful to the target stakeholders quickly erodes trust—completely defeating the purpose of implementing data contracts.

With *what* and *why* established for violation monitoring and alerts, the next paragraphs will describe *how*. Within the data contract workflow, violation monitoring and alerts consist of the following:

Version control interface
  The surface where developers leverage Git to do code change management (e.g., GitHub)

CI/CD
  The triggering mechanism to run the data contract workflow when a code change is proposed on the version control interface

Data contract spec
  The source of truth for expectations of a data asset, and with respect to mentoring and alerts, provides the user IDs of individuals who need to be notified via PR comments and or business communication surfaces

Logging service
  Scripts that log the results of the data contract workflow for debugging and analytics

Alerting service and webhooks
  Scripts that determine who needs to be alerted and what surface(s) to provide the alerts, as noted by the data contract spec, which are executed via webhooks

Business communication surface
  The surfaces in which nontechnical stakeholders can receive alerts for data contract violations (e.g., Slack, email, etc.)

Figure 6-8 illustrates how these components work together to provide timely alerts of data contract violations to stakeholders in their respective communication surfaces.

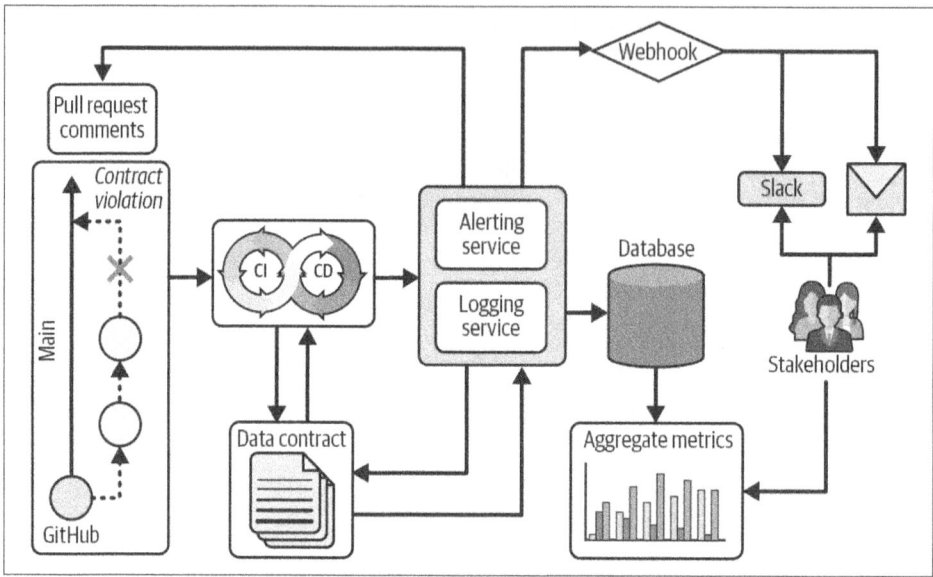

Figure 6-8. The data contract violation and monitoring workflow

A developer triggers the CI/CD workflow by pushing a code change via Git and the version control interface. The CI/CD workflow triggers the execution of the data contract workflow by assessing if the proposed change is associated with an existing data contract spec and whether it violates the contract—all of the logs for the CI/CD workflow are typically visible within the version control interface. If a violation occurs, the alerting service looks to the data contract spec to determine who needs to be notified and sends the alert payload to both a comment on the pull request within the version control interface and the relevant webhooks for the business communication surface. In addition, the logging service captures the data contract workflow logs and stores them within a database for analytics and reporting.

Conclusion

In this chapter, we covered the final two components of the data contract architecture: detection and prevention. Among the detection methods, we detailed the various surfaces and methods for code-level detection, data-in-motion detection, and historical detection. We emphasized the need to ingest disparate forms of metadata, where the more types of metadata you capture across your business's systems, the more robust your data contracts can be. In addition to detection methods, we also described the mechanisms for prevention via the data contract workflow: version control, CI/CD workflows, and violation monitoring and alerts.

Furthermore, we highlighted the need to be intentional with alerting to prevent loss of trust in the data contract workflow due to alert fatigue. We suggested using the five Ws and one H framework from journalism by framing alerts as the following:

- *Who* are the most relevant stakeholders that need to be notified?
- *What* is the most relevant information for the presented violation?
- *When* should the violation alert take place?
- *Where* should your target stakeholder receive violation alerts?
- *Why* should the target stakeholder care with respect to their needs?
- *How* should the target stakeholder resolve the violation?

Another way to view detection and prevention is through the lens of developer experience. Many times, the detection and prevention components are developers' first interaction with data contracts (if they were not the ones to implement them). It's also the first time you will set the impression of the value that data contracts can provide to developers. Pay special attention to this consideration in how developers expect to be notified of a violation and what additional work they are willing to do in accounting for your data needs (ideally it's minimal, given the contract provides the necessary context).

Chapters 5 and 6 detailed the components of the data contract architecture and the various considerations you should make. In Chapter 7 we will tie everything together by providing a hands-on coding tutorial of creating a data contract spec, detecting changes to data assets on a mock data stack with real-world data, triggering the data contract workflow via CI/CD, and surfacing violation alerts.

Implementing Data Contracts

Chapters 5 and 6 covered the four components of the data contract architecture in depth. In this chapter, we'll move from theory to actually implementing data contracts via open source tools. Our corresponding GitHub repo (*https://github.com/ data-contract-book/chapter-7-implementing-data-contracts*) provides a full sandbox environment you can run locally or in the browser via GitHub Codespaces with:

- A full walkthrough of a data contract architecture implementation and its corresponding scripts
- Implementation of a data contract spec
- A scenario project simulating a data contract violation workflow

While we highly encourage using the code repository, this chapter is sufficient as a stand-alone, featuring architecture diagrams, the corresponding tools, and highlights of relevant code snippets. The goals of this chapter are for you to:

- Understand how to implement the four data contract components: data assets, data contract spec, detection, and prevention
- Create a data contract spec via JSON Schema as a means to understand how to evaluate available specs on the market or whether to build one of your own for specific use cases
- Learn how to leverage the metadata of databases to create your own "data catalog" that you will compare data contract specs to
- Embed data contracts within unit tests for local testing and embedding within the CI/CD workflow
- Fully walk through the data contract violation workflow on a pull request

Finally, we suggest the following three ways to work through the material in this chapter, going from simplest to most involved:

Sandbox exploration
Read this chapter and then go explore the sandbox environment on your own.

Follow along
Follow along with this chapter with an active sandbox environment on the side.

Create your own implementation
Leverage Chapters 5 and 6 to create your own implementation (how we created this chapter) and then compare it to the sandbox environment.

There is no right or wrong approach, and we often use a mix of these approaches when learning new technology ourselves. In the next section, we will introduce the mock scenario that will frame the entire project and corresponding scripts.

Mock Data Contract Scenario Intro

In this scenario, you are a data platform engineer supporting the backend software engineering team, which is tasked with creating the OLTP database that will support a new product line for the entertainment software business. Specifically, the product line is an AI assistant to use at museums that leverages computer vision to identify objects, and then provides context-specific information—your own personal museum guide.

Of course, the AI application is all aspirational, and the early work requires setting up the database to start processing images and relevant metadata of objects within museums. In addition to building the foundation of the application, this image data is essential for the downstream data scientists who are developing the models for the application.

Given the importance of this database to the soon-to-be-built application, and the strong downstream dependency of the downstream data science team, you were able to get buy-in to implement data contracts, as other parts of the enterprise have experienced data quality issues in similar scenarios. (We'll talk more about buy-in and adoption in Chapters 9 to 12.)

Thus, in this mock scenario the data platform team previously created documentation on the dataset, the museum application, and the data pipelines you oversee that will be covered by the data contract implementation.

Dataset

Though the ultimate goal is to have this application integrated with all major museums, the minimum viable product of this application will focus on the Metropolitan

Museum of Art in New York City. Specifically, the Metropolitan Museum of Art Open Access dataset (*https://oreil.ly/G50o6*), which includes "more than 406,000 hi-res images of public-domain works from the Met collection, all of which can be downloaded, shared, and remixed without restriction."

To simplify your early development work, a sample of around 3,000 records has been pulled from the Metropolitan Museum of Art Collection API (*https://metmuseum.git hub.io*) (Museum API) and stored as a JSON array to seed your Postgres database (note that you can run the script get_data_subset_from_met_api.py, but with API rate limits it takes hours). As of right now, the database has the schema pictured in Figure 7-1, where every table has the primary key object_id.

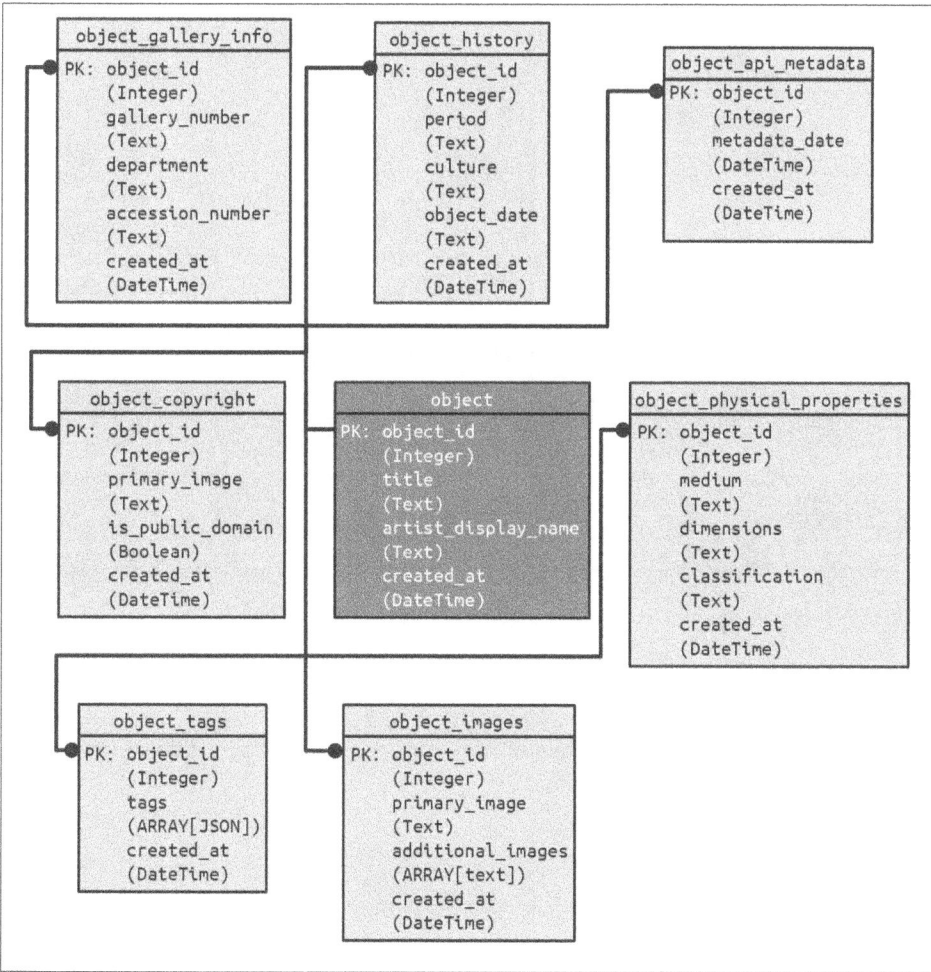

Figure 7-1. Met museum database schema

Note that in this mock scenario there is still a lot of work left to get to the final data model for the OLTP database, and this is why you want data contracts to help track changes and expectations as they evolve with the application.

Museum Application

The high-level architecture of the museum application, as pictured in Figure 7-2, consists of a Postgres database that sources data from the Museum API. In addition, the Postgres database handles CRUD operations from the museum object product interface—which is the main focus of development work right now.

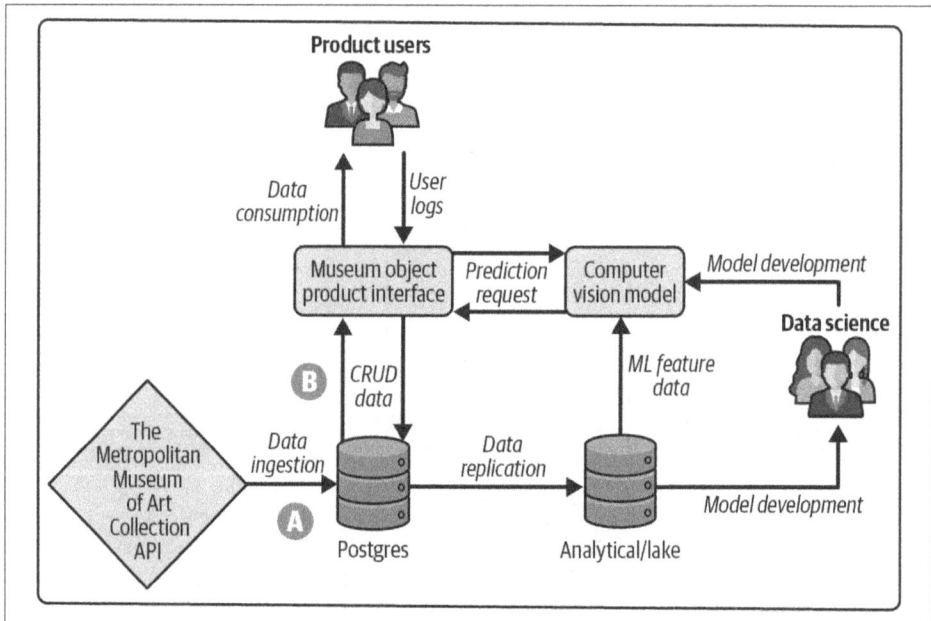

Figure 7-2. High-level museum application architecture diagram

As highlighted in Figure 7-2, our only focus for this mock scenario is the data ingestion and CRUD operations, labeled as A and B, respectively. We can assume the replication pipeline and ML-related activities are working as expected (as long as there are no data contract violations).

Project Repo Overview

The following directory tree provides an overview of the data contract architecture implementation at the file level, as well as brief descriptions. At a high level, the project is composed of the following:

- Configuration files (e.g., *docker-compose*) for the sandbox environment and CI/CD workflows
- A simple notebook as a lightweight means to query the Postgres database and test scripts
- The data contract architecture itself, organized by its respective components:
  — Data assets
  — Contract definition
  — Detection
  — Prevention

We suggest taking a moment to make yourself familiar with this directory tree before moving forward with the chapter:

```
/workspace
├── .devcontainer.json                      # VS Code dev container config
├── .gitignore                              # Git ignore rules
├── README.md                               # Project documentation
├── docker-compose.test.yml                 # Docker compose for testing
├── docker-compose.yml                      # Docker compose for development
├── requirements.txt                        # Python dependencies
├── run_sql_queries_here.ipynb              # Jupyter notebook for SQL queries
├── .github/                                # GitHub configuration
│   └── workflows/                          # GitHub Actions workflows
│       └── docker-image.yml                # Docker image build workflow
└── data_contract_components/               # Data contract components
    ├── contract_definition/                # Data contract specifications
    │   ├── __init__.py                     # Python package init
    │   └── object_images_contract_spec.json # Contract spec for object_images
    ├── data_assets/                        # Data management and assets
    │   ├── __init__.py                     # Python package init
    │   ├── _query_postgres_helper.py       # PostgreSQL query helper
    │   ├── alembic.ini                     # Alembic database migration config
    │   ├── seed_db.py                      # Database seeding script
    │   └── db_migrations/                  # Database migration files
    │       ├── __init__.py                 # Python package init
    │       ├── env.py                      # Alembic environment config
    │       ├── script.py.mako              # Alembic migration template
    │       ├── raw_data/                   # Raw data files
    │       │   ├── __init__.py             # Python package init
    │       │   ├── get_data..._api.py      # Met Museum API data fetcher
    │       │   └── objects.json            # Met Museum objects data sample
    │       └── versions/                   # Database migration versions
    │           └── 00e9b3375...tables.py   # Migration to create tables
    ├── detection/                          # Data contract violation detection
    │   ├── __init__.py                     # Python package init
    │   ├── _get_data_catalog.py            # Data catalog retrieval
    │   ├── _get_data_contract_specs.py     # Contract specifications retrieval
```

```
│   ├── contract_coverage_detector.py      # Contract coverage analysis
│   └── contract_violation_detector.py     # Contract violation detection
└── prevention/                            # Prevent data contract violations
    ├── __init__.py                        # Python package init
    └── test_data_contract_violations.py   # Contract violation tests
```

Now that we've established the scenario and provided the background information, let's move on to walk through the data contract implementation.

Implementing Data Contracts

As stated earlier in the mock scenario, this data contract implementation focuses on upstream data between ingestion from a third-party API (represented as the *data_assets/db_migrations/raw_data/objects.json* file) and the transactional database (i.e., Postgres) that will enable CRUD operations with the museum object product interface. For our first data contract, we are going to protect our most important data asset: object_images. This data asset is critical, as it's planned to surface pictures to the user once the machine learning model identifies a museum object from the user-provided photo. In addition, object_images.primary_image and object_images.additional_images provide the text links used by the downstream data science team to access the image files for model training (which is outside the scope of this tutorial).

It's important to note that while we tried to make as realistic an implementation as possible, the reality is that most companies are not going to be fully open source or use just a single database. Thus, this implementation is intended to teach you the architecture *pattern* of data contracts that you can extrapolate to other tools within your respective use case. Furthermore, there are instances where we build tools that we could have integrated with a more robust external tool (e.g., data contract specs, data catalogs, etc.). This is intentional to help better illustrate the pattern of data contracts and manage simplicity for readers, but we will be sure to highlight where, so you can better evaluate what would be the best implementation and/or integration for your use case.

Data Contracts Architecture Overview

Referring back to Chapter 4, Figure 7-3 illustrates the data contract workflow that we have implemented within our repository. This workflow is broken up into four distinct components:

- Data assets
- Contract definition

- Detection

- Prevention

With this implementation, we are able to define our expectations for the object_images data asset via our contract spec, detect changes to the metadata within our Postgres database (with special attention to object_images), compare our data contract spec to this metadata via a unit test, have this unit test run via CI/CD checks, and automatically alert of violations via a pull request comment.

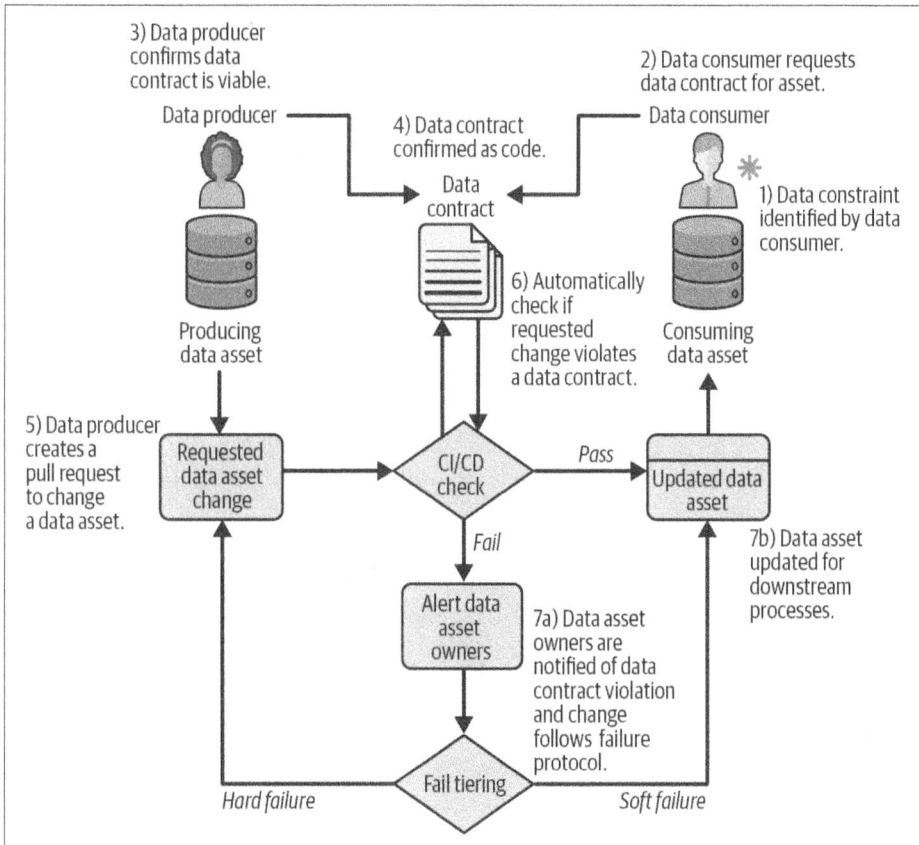

Figure 7-3. The data contract workflow

In the subsequent sections, we will provide more detail on each respective component and discuss considerations you should take for your own implementation.

Component A: Data Assets

The foundation of all data contracts is the data assets themselves. It's important to note that while you can explore seeded data within the database yourself, via *run_sql_queries_here.ipynb*, the data contract implementation only requires metadata to function. This is critical, as it greatly lowers the barrier needed for security implications to not read the actual data, given that data contracts span across multiple departments (i.e., in this mock scenario, backend engineering, data platform engineering, and data science). The following code snippet is a subset of the full directory tree as it pertains to data assets:

```
/workspace
├── docker-compose.test.yml              # Docker compose for testing
├── run_sql_queries_here.ipynb           # Jupyter notebook for SQL queries
└── data_contract_components/            # Data contract components
    └── data_assets/                     # Data management and assets
        ├── _query_postgres_helper.py    # PostgreSQL query helper
        ├── alembic.ini                  # Alembic database migration config
        └── db_migrations/               # Database migration files
            ├── env.py                   # Alembic environment config
            ├── script.py.mako           # Alembic migration template
            └── versions/                # Database migration versions
                └── 00e9b3375...tables.py  # Migration to create tables
```

At a high level, our *docker-compose.test.yml* file is Docker's instructions for setting up the devcontainer, Postgres database, and data assets. As illustrated in Figure 7-4, containers with Postgres and Python are spun up at the same time, and once the database returns a "healthy" check from Postgres, the Python container (i.e., `devcontainer`) executes the database migration to create all of our tables for our application's transactional database within the Postgres container (i.e., `postgres`). Next to the diagram in Figure 7-4 is a code snippet from the database migration file *data_assets/db_migrations/versions/00e9b3375a5f_create_met_museum_seed_tables.py* for creating the `object_images` table and assigning schema and primary keys.

It's important to highlight that you will likely come across other database migration tools or even SQL scripts with `CREATE TABLE` rather than the database migration tool we chose (i.e., Alembic) for this sandbox (*https://oreil.ly/gEoSs*). A key point here is that you are able to represent a data asset as code and have a means to extract metadata from this data asset. In addition, we are using Docker as it will make integration into the CI/CD pipeline at a later stage easier—which is also another reason we opt for just using metadata.

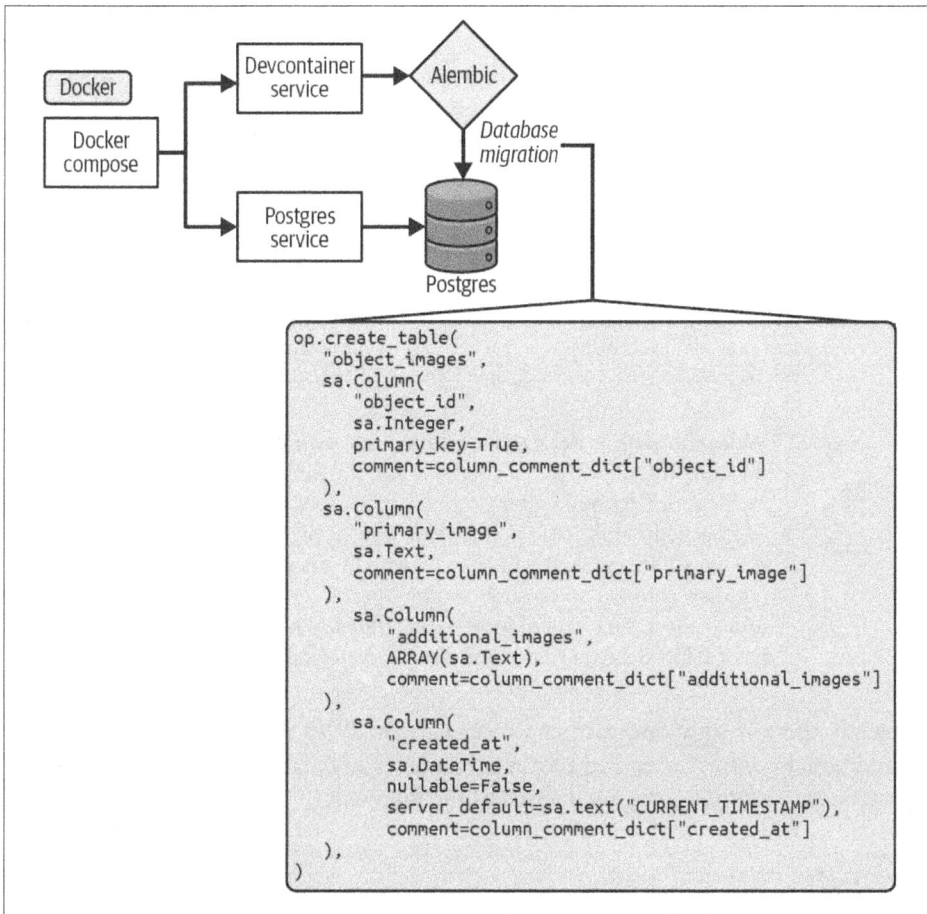

Figure 7-4. Data contract component: data assets

Note that the sandbox environment has two similar files, *docker-compose.test.yml* and *docker-compose.yml*. The former is used within our CI/CD pipelines and includes calls to run the test scripts, while the latter is used by the sandbox environment itself and runs scripts to seed the Postgres database with *data_assets/raw_data/objects.json*. In the next section we will discuss how we can use the metadata defined by the database migration file to inform what to put within the data contract spec.

Component B: Contract Definition

Once we have our most important data assets identified, we need to establish our expectations via a data contract specification file. A typical starting point is to use the current state of the data asset as the baseline for the contract spec (as in this current implementation), but you can also use it to establish a desired state to inform your database migrations, which we highlight in a later section. The following directory tree subset highlights the components related to contract definition:

```
/workspace
└── data_contract_components/           # Data contract components
    └── contract_definition/            # Data contract specifications
        └── object_images_contract_spec.json  # Contract spec for object_images
```

> We again want to iterate that creating our own data contract specification for this mock scenario is for learning purposes. It may make sense to build your own if your needs are fairly simple (e.g., schema-only enforcement) or you have a company-specific use case. Otherwise, it will be substantially easier to leverage existing data contract specs such as the Open Data Contract Standard under the Linux Foundation (*https://oreil.ly/Ks0TO*), which also has a JSON Schema adaptation (*https://oreil.ly/CWxBO*).

Currently there is only one data contract spec for object_images, but we will add an additional contract spec for another data asset in a later stage. The contents of *object_images_contract_spec.json* consist of the following:

```
{
    "spec-version": "1.0.0",
    "name": "object-images-contract-spec",
    "namespace": "met-museum-data",
    "dataAssetResourceName": "postgresql://postgres:5432/postgres.object_images",
    "doc": "Data contract for the object_images table containing image URLs and
metadata for museum objects, including primary images, additional images, and
creation timestamps.",
    "owner": {
      "name": "Data Engineering Team",
      "email": "data-eng@museum.org"
    },
    "schema": {
      "$schema": "https://json-schema.org/draft/2020-12/schema",
      "title": "Object Images Table Schema",
      "table_catalog": "postgres",
      "table_schema": "public",
      "table_name": "object_images",
      "properties": {
        "object_id": {
          "description": "Identifying number for each artwork (unique, can be
used as key field)",
```

```json
          "examples": [437133],
          "constraints": {
            "primaryKey": true,
            "data_type": "integer",
            "numeric_precision": 32.0,
            "is_nullable": false,
            "is_updatable": true
          }
        },
        "primary_image": {
          "description": "URL to the primary image of an object (JPEG)",
          "examples": ["https://images.metmuseum.org/.../DT1234.jpg"],
          "constraints": {
            "primaryKey": false,
            "data_type": "text",
            "is_nullable": true,
            "is_updatable": true
          }
        },
        "additional_images": {
          "description": "Array of URLs to additional JPEG images of the
object",
          "constraints": {
            "primaryKey": false,
            "data_type": "ARRAY",
            "is_nullable": true,
            "is_updatable": true
          },
          "array_element": {
            "data_type": "text"
          }
        },
        "created_at": {
          "description": "Timestamp when this record was created in the
database",
          "examples": ["2025-01-15T10:30:00.000Z"],
          "items": null,
          "constraints": {
            "primaryKey": false,
            "data_type": "timestamp without time zone",
            "datetime_precision": 6.0,
            "is_nullable": false,
            "is_updatable": true
          }
        }
      }
    }
  }
}
```

As covered in Chapter 5, there needs to be metadata associated with managing the contract spec across its lifecycle and enabling a means to use it programmatically without conflicts. We suggest the following (also highlighted in Chapter 5):

spec-version

> The version of the data contract spec utilized within your system, where this value will change with each iteration to the spec structure as your use case changes or becomes more complex (e.g., adding further semantic constraints)

name

> The user-defined name of the respective data contract, where name and namespace form a combined unique identifier

namespace

> A user-defined name representing a collection of data contracts, similar to a higher-level "folder" within a repository

dataAssetResourceName

> The URL path of the data source under contract, where it aligns with the naming pattern of the data source (e.g., `postgres://db/database-name`)

doc

> The documentation that describes what the data contract represents, enforces, and any other pertinent information

owner

> The assigned owner (either an individual or a group) of the data contract, and the contact information used to notify when a contract is violated, needs a change, or if an individual is trying to determine a point of contact for further context

We also have the `schema` field, which has the metadata `table_catalog`, `table_schema`, and `object_images`. We want to call out that this metadata is for making it easier to work with Postgres for this mock scenario. A more robust implementation and/or tool would account for different data assets such as application code or multiple database types, or for connecting directly to a data catalog. In addition, emphasis should be on adhering to the pattern illustrated here rather than treating the specific naming and structure as dogma.

Finally, we want to call out the need to account for nested variables such as `object_images.additional_images`, which is an array of strings, and its metadata nested under that value. While it is a relatively straightforward task to extract the metadata of a single-layer nested value from Postgres, adding further layers and different types of data asset sources increases the complexity substantially—especially in the detection component of data contract violations. In the next section, we will detail how this sandbox environment detects changes to the Postgres database, and create a simple "data catalog" for the purpose of data contract validation.

Component C: Detection

Detection of data contracts requires three key steps: 1) detect what exists in the current state of the data asset, 2) detect what data contract specifications exist, and 3) compare these two sources and detect violations if they exist. The following subset of the directory tree highlights the detection component:

```
/workspace
└── data_contract_components/          # Data contract components
    └── detection/                      # Data contract violation detection
        ├── _get_data_catalog.py        # Data catalog retrieval
        ├── _get_data_contract_specs.py # Contract specifications retrieval
        ├── contract_coverage_detector.py  # Contract coverage analysis
        └── contract_violation_detector.py # Contract violation detection
```

As illustrated in Figure 7-5, within this sandbox the scripts *contract_coverage_detector.py* and *contract_violation_detector.py* extract metadata from Postgres and the contract specs from the *data_contract_components/contract_definition/..* directory. The two sources of metadata are compared, where the contract spec is treated as the source of truth and any violations are returned as a list.

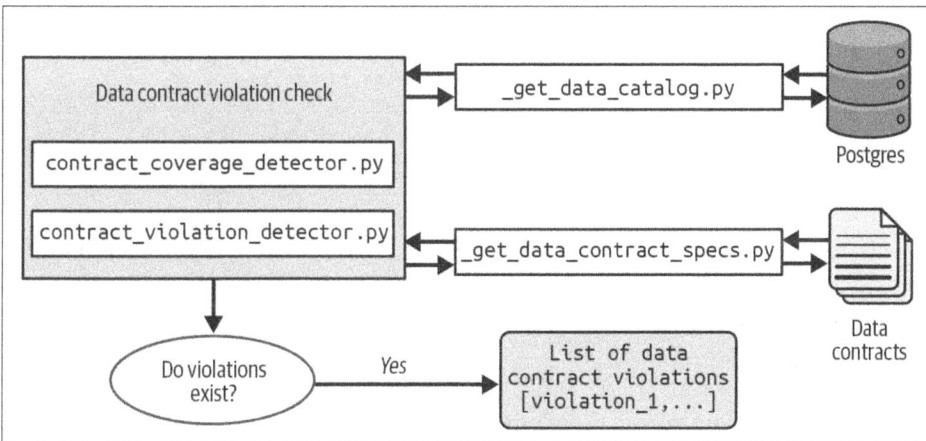

Figure 7-5. Data contract component: detection

We can dive further into the two previous scripts to understand how these comparisons are made. In both of the following script snippets, we turn the metadata from our "data catalog" and our data contract specs into two respective DataFrames that both have the columns table_catalog, table_schema, and table_name. In the case of *contract_coverage_detector.py* we do a left join, where data assets that are present in the contract spec directory but not the "data catalog" are flagged as a violation:

```
# contract_coverage_detector.py
...
def detect_coverage_in_data_catalog(self) -> List[str]:
```

```
coverage = self.get_contract_spec_coverage()
coverage_df = pd.DataFrame(coverage)
catalog_df = get_data_catalog()

merged = coverage_df.merge(
    catalog_df,
    on=['table_catalog', 'table_schema', 'table_name'],
    how='left',
    indicator=True
)

missing_assets_df = merged[merged['_merge'] == 'left_only']
missing_table_names = missing_assets_df['table_name'].tolist()

return missing_table_names
```

Within *contract_violation_detector.py*, we use a similar process of creating two Data
Frames from the "data catalog" and contract specs, but this time we are also joining
on column_name for further granularity:

```
# contract_violation_detector.py
...
def detect_constraint_violations(self) -> List[Dict[str, str]]:
    contract_specs_df = pd.DataFrame(
        self.transform_contract_specs_to_catalog_format()
    )
    catalog_df = get_data_catalog()

    merged = contract_specs_df.merge(
        catalog_df,
        on=['table_catalog', 'table_schema', 'table_name', 'column_name'],
        how='left',
        suffixes=('_contract', '_catalog'),
        indicator=True
    )
...
```

As stated earlier, comparing violations beyond a single type of data asset increases
complexity considerably. While we won't go into depth on this comparison logic
here, note that *contract_violation_detector.py* has an entire function, transform_con
tract_specs_to_catalog_format(), dedicated to parsing the data contract spec to
match the format of the "data catalog" metadata. Again, this is one of the moments
where we are erring on simplicity and explicitness for teaching purposes.

Furthermore, this is also why we highly encourage the use of a dedicated data
catalog tool (there are many open source options available), so that the various data
asset sources are abstracted into a single metadata format to compare against. You
might have noticed throughout this chapter that we have been using the term "data
catalog" in quotation marks so that it's clear we are *representing* a data catalog, but in
reality our implementation is quite simple. Specifically, *_get_data_catalog.py* is a SQL

script with a Python wrapper that reads the information_schema table from Postgres (where its metadata is stored). While Postgres offers even more fine-grained metadata tables, the information_schema table is common across many SQL-based databases. In short, this is essentially how the core functionality of data catalogs works under the hood, and we encourage you to check out the script to see for yourself. The key difference is that data catalogs manage the metadata collection, collect metadata from multiple sources, and automatically update metadata consistently (this would be quite the endeavor to self-code).

In the next section, we will detail how we embed these detections within the CI/CD workflow via unit tests, and then trigger pull request comments if violations are detected.

Component D: Prevention

Finally, the last component is detection, as highlighted in the following directory tree subset. For this implementation, we are using GitHub Actions for our continuous integration test, as denoted by the *.github/workflows/docker-image.yml* file. Under the hood, GitHub actions is spinning up a Docker container and running two jobs: build and test. The build job is to ensure the sandbox dev environment is working properly for our repo—therefore, we will focus on the test job, which gets its container configurations from *docker-compose.test.yml* (this sets up the Postgres database with schema but does not seed the data).

```
/workspace
├── docker-compose.test.yml                # Docker compose for testing
├── .github/                               # GitHub configuration
│   └── workflows/                         # GitHub Actions workflows
│       └── docker-image.yml               # Docker image build workflow
└── data_contract_components/              # Data contract components
    ├── detection/                         # Data contract violation detection
    │   ├── contract_coverage_detector.py  # Contract coverage analysis
    │   └── contract_violation_detector.py # Contract violation detection
    └── prevention/                        # Prevent data contract violations
        └── test_data_contract_violations.py # Contract violation tests
```

At a high level, *docker-compose.test.yml* sets up the necessary infra and installs requirements, runs the database migration file, and then performs a unit test check via the following command, which then exports its log to a folder in the container that can be surfaced in a pull request comment:

```
python -m unittest \
   data_contract_components/prevention/\
   test_data_contract_violations.py -v \
   > /workspace/test_output.log 2>&1
```

Figure 7-6 illustrates how *test_data_contract_violations.py* works within the CI/CD workflow on a GitHub pull request that wants to merge onto main. Where the unit test fails is if the returned violations list from either *contract_coverage_detector.py* or *contract_violation_detector.py* has a length greater than zero.

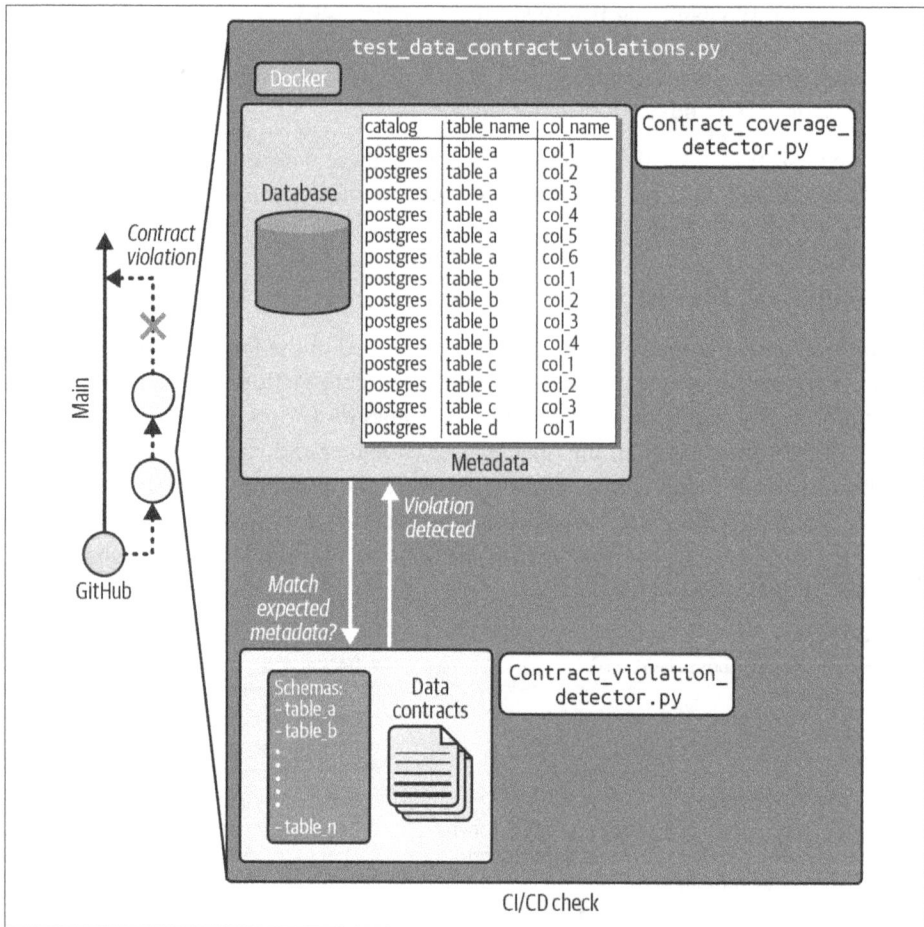

Figure 7-6. Data contract component: prevention

Finally, if the test returns a violation, the log is saved and passed to GitHub via a script command in *.github/workflows/docker-image.yml*. Figure 7-7 provides an example of a data contract violation message via a GitHub pull request comment. This is a forced error by changing the values within the data contract spec to values that don't make sense (e.g., text -> integer).

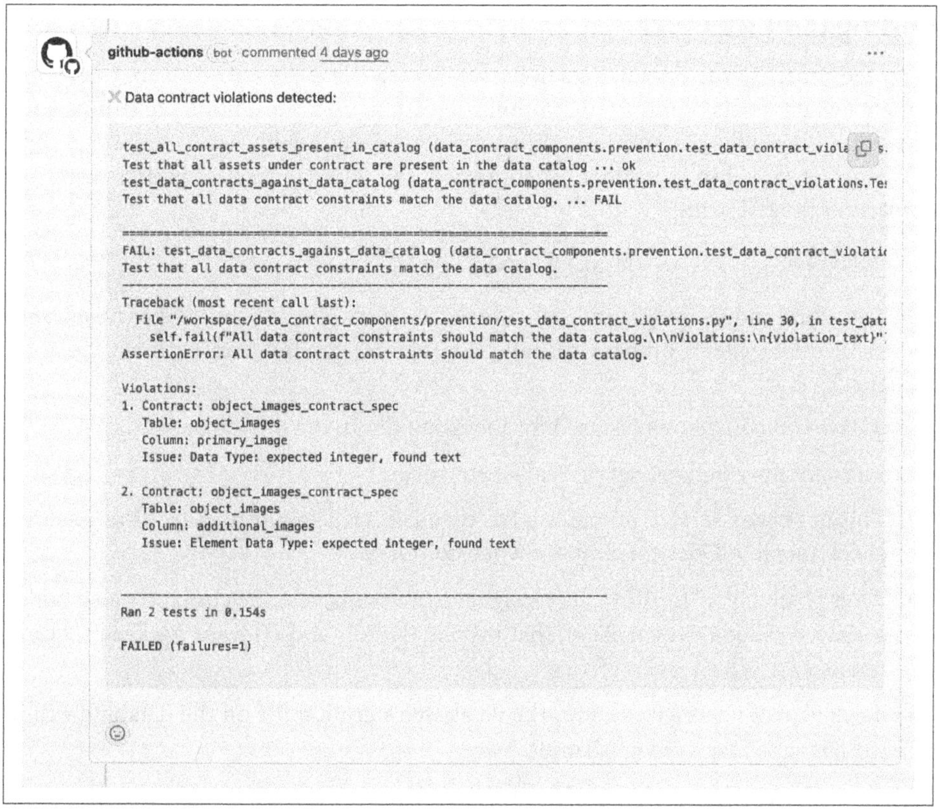

Figure 7-7. Example: data contract violation message via GitHub pull request comment (see it on GitHub (https://github.com/data-contract-book/chapter-7-implementing-data-contracts?tab=readme-ov-file#component-d---prevention))

We have now completed the full data contract workflow, and hopefully you feel comfortable navigating the sandbox yourself to create additional data contracts or building off this repository to test out data contracts on different data asset sources. In the next section, we will summarize the entire workflow and provide a source code flow graph that highlights which files to look further into when going through the data contract violation workflow.

Putting It All Together

Over the course of the previous sections, we have detailed the four data contract components (data assets, contract definition, detection, and prevention) and how each important file within the project directory corresponds with each component and the contract violation workflow. In summary, the data contract violation workflow consists of the following:

1. GitHub Actions kicks off the CI/CD workflow.

2. The continuous integration job (test in *.github/workflows/docker-image.yml*) kicks off Docker Compose to build a container for the data contract violation check.

3. *docker-compose.test.yml* is used for the container in the infrastructure layer.

4. The container builds a service called postgres.

5. This postgres service prepares a PostgresSQL17 database and sends a "healthy" check signal to Docker Compose when complete.

6. After receiving a "healthy" check signal from postgres, the container also builds a service called devcontainer that installs Python and relevant package requirements.

7. devcontainer service executes the database migration file on the database within the postgres service via Alembic.

8. Once devcontainer completes installing dependencies and confirms the database has been set up successfully, it runs the unit test via *test_data_contract_violations.py*.

9. *test_data_contract_violations.py* executes *contract_coverage_detector.py* and *contract_violation_detector.py* via Python's built-in unit test.

10. These two detector functions pull relevant metadata from the database within the postgres service and data contract spec directories via *_get_data_catalog.py* and *_get_data_contract_specs.py*.

11. The data contract spec *object_images_contract_spec.json* is referenced by *_get_data_contract_specs.py*, which enables the comparison between the database metadata and the data contract spec expectations.

12. If a data contract violation is detected, Python saves the logs from *test_data_contract_violations.py* as *test_output.log* on the devcontainer service.

13. The continuous integration job, test, finishes by checking if a test failure occurred, and if so, returns *test_output.log* as a comment within the respective GitHub pull request.

Figure 7-8 summarizes this entire workflow as a graph that you can use as a guide to navigate a data contract workflow step and know which file to reference.

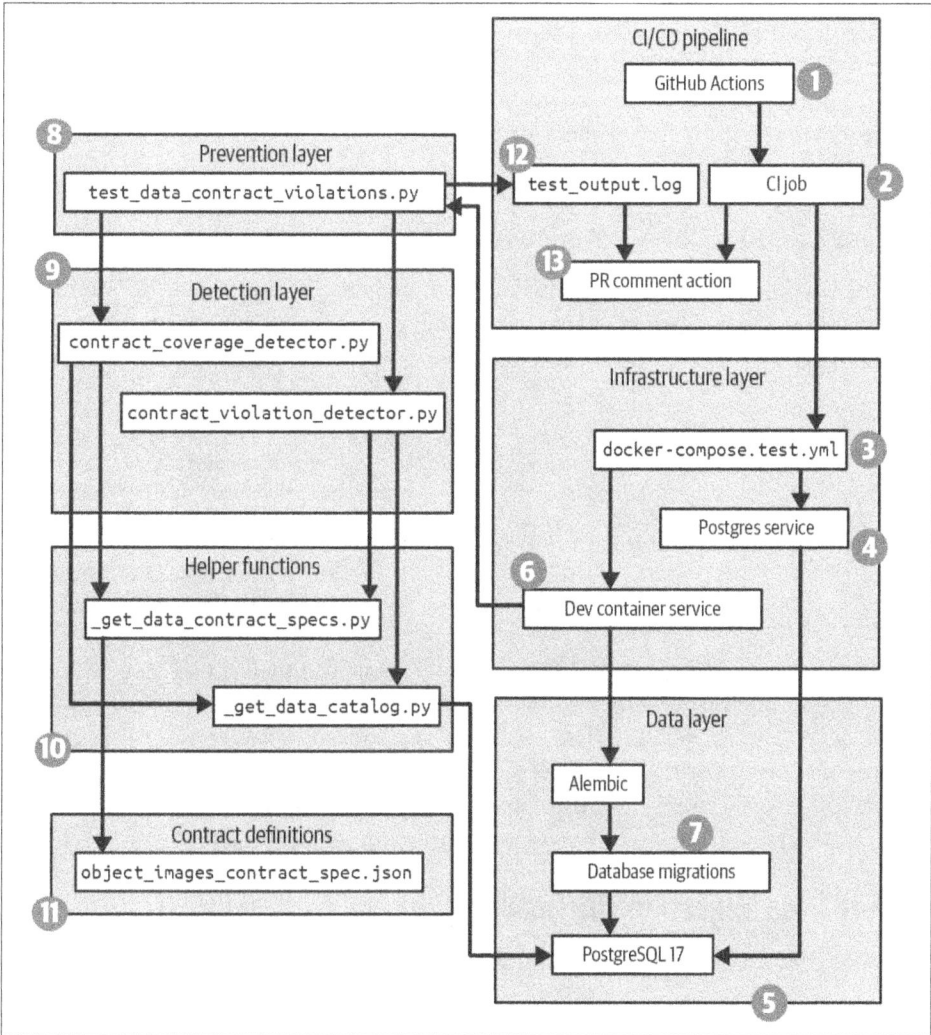

Figure 7-8. Data contract violation workflow graph

In the final section of this chapter, we will build on our understanding of the data contract components and their respective files to conduct a mock scenario of creating a contract-violating change, going through the violation process, and then using data contracts to inform what changes should exist.

Data Contract Violation Scenario

Again, in our mock scenario the backend software engineering team is tasked with creating the OLTP database that will support a new product line of the entertainment software business. In the previous section we took on the persona of the data platform engineer who implemented the data contract components. Moving forward, we are now taking on the persona of the backend software engineer who is going through the contract violation workflow.

Received Request to Normalize the object_images Table

You received a request to normalize the `object_images` table by unnesting `object_images.additional_images`, renaming `primary_image` to `image`, and creating a boolean called `is_primary_image`:

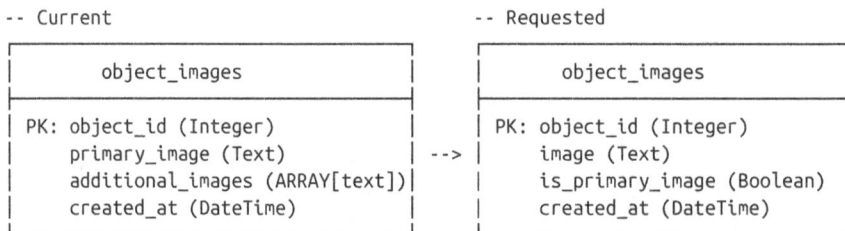

```
-- Current                                   -- Requested
┌─────────────────────────────────┐          ┌─────────────────────────────────┐
│         object_images           │          │         object_images           │
├─────────────────────────────────┤          ├─────────────────────────────────┤
│ PK: object_id (Integer)         │          │ PK: object_id (Integer)         │
│     primary_image (Text)        │   -->    │     image (Text)                │
│     additional_images (ARRAY[text])│       │     is_primary_image (Boolean)  │
│     created_at (DateTime)       │          │     created_at (DateTime)       │
└─────────────────────────────────┘          └─────────────────────────────────┘
```

The request makes sense as this aligns with the goals of this database and will make working with the images data more straightforward. In addition, since it's early days of the development, you are only aware of the backed software engineering team needing this database that's not even connected to the application yet. Thus, you also believe it makes sense to drop the table completely, so you implement the most up-to-date version of `object_images` within the transactional database.

Update Data Migration File for New Schema

First, you create a new branch with the following command in your terminal:

```
git checkout -b 'update-objects-images-schema'
```

Next, in a development branch within *data_assets/db_migrations/versions/00e9b3375a5f_create_met_museum_seed_tables.py*, you update the database migration file to reflect the correct schema of the `object_images` table by replacing this code with the following update:

```
# old schema to replace
    op.create_table(
        "object_images",
        sa.Column(
            "object_id",
            sa.Integer,
```

```python
            primary_key=True,
            comment=column_comment_dict["object_id"]
        ),
        sa.Column(
            "primary_image",
            sa.Text,
            comment=column_comment_dict["primary_image"]
        ),
        sa.Column(
            "additional_images",
            ARRAY(sa.Text),
            comment=column_comment_dict["additional_images"]
        ),
        sa.Column(
            "created_at",
            sa.DateTime,
            nullable=False,
            server_default=sa.text("CURRENT_TIMESTAMP"),
            comment=column_comment_dict["created_at"]
        ),
    )

# new schema for `object_images`
    op.create_table(
        "object_images",
        sa.Column(
            "object_id",
            sa.Integer,
            primary_key=True,
            comment=column_comment_dict["object_id"]
        ),
        sa.Column(
            "image",
            sa.Text,
            comment=column_comment_dict["primary_image"]
        ),
        sa.Column(
            "is_primary_image",
            sa.Boolean,
            comment="Identifies if it's the primary image for the object."
        ),
        sa.Column(
            "created_at",
            sa.DateTime,
            nullable=False,
            server_default=sa.text("CURRENT_TIMESTAMP"),
            comment=column_comment_dict["created_at"]
        ),
    )
```

You then run the following commands in your terminal to remove all the tables and seeded data from Postgres in your development area, and then implement new database migration with `object_images` updates:

```
cd ~/../workspace/data_contract_components/data_assets
alembic downgrade base
alembic upgrade head
```

You should expect the following logs from Alembic:

```
(update-objects-images-schema) $ alembic downgrade base
INFO [alembic.runtime.migration] Context impl PostgresqlImpl.
INFO [alembic.runtime.migration] Will assume transactional DDL.
INFO [alembic.runtime.migration] Running downgrade 00e9b3375a5f -> , create met
     museum seed tables

(update-objects-images-schema) $ alembic upgrade head
INFO [alembic.runtime.migration] Context impl PostgresqlImpl.
INFO [alembic.runtime.migration] Will assume transactional DDL.
INFO [alembic.runtime.migration] Running upgrade  -> 00e9b3375a5f, create met
     museum seed tables
```

Check Unit Tests and Trigger Contract Violation

Before pushing your change to your remote branch, you first go back to your root directory folder, `workspace`, and run your unit tests locally via the following commands:

```
cd ~/../workspace
python -m unittest data_contract_components/prevention/test_data_contract
_violations.py -v
```

To your surprise, you receive the following failed test for the exact two fields you updated. It looks like the data platform engineering team has finally implemented data contracts in this repository:

```
(update-objects-images-schema) $ python -m unittest data_contract_components/
prevention/test_data_contract_violations.py -v
test_all_contract_assets_present_in_catalog
(data_contract_components.prevention.test_data_contract_violations.
TestContractViolations.test_all_contract_assets_present_in_catalog)
Test that all assets under contract are present in the data catalog ... ok
test_data_contracts_against_data_catalog (data_contract_components.
prevention.test_data_contract_violations.TestContractViolations.
test_data_contracts_against_data_catalog)
Test that all data contract constraints match the data catalog. ... FAIL


======================================================================
FAIL: test_data_contracts_against_data_catalog (data_contract_components.
prevention.test_data_contract_violations.TestContractViolations.
test_data_contracts_against_data_catalog)
Test that all data contract constraints match the data catalog.
```

```
----------------------------------------------------------------
Traceback (most recent call last):
  File "/workspace/data_contract_components/prevention/test_data_contract_
violations.py", line 30, in test_data_contracts_against_data_catalog
    self.fail(f"All data contract constraints should match the data
catalog.\n\nViolations:\n{violation_text}")

Violations:
1. Contract: object_images_contract_spec
   Table: object_images
   Column: primary_image
   Issue: Column 'primary_image' is defined in contract but missing from
          data catalog

2. Contract: object_images_contract_spec
   Table: object_images
   Column: additional_images
   Issue: Column 'additional_images' is defined in contract but missing from
          data catalog


----------------------------------------------------------------
Ran 2 tests in 0.240s

FAILED (failures=1)
```

Push to Remote Branch and View Error Logs

So that this violation is logged on the pull request, you push your local branch to your remote branch via the following commands:

```
git add .
git commit -m 'adding updates that caused contract violation'
git push --set-upstream origin update-objects-images-schema
```

As expected, the CI/CD checks via GitHub Actions fail, as seen in Figure 7-9.

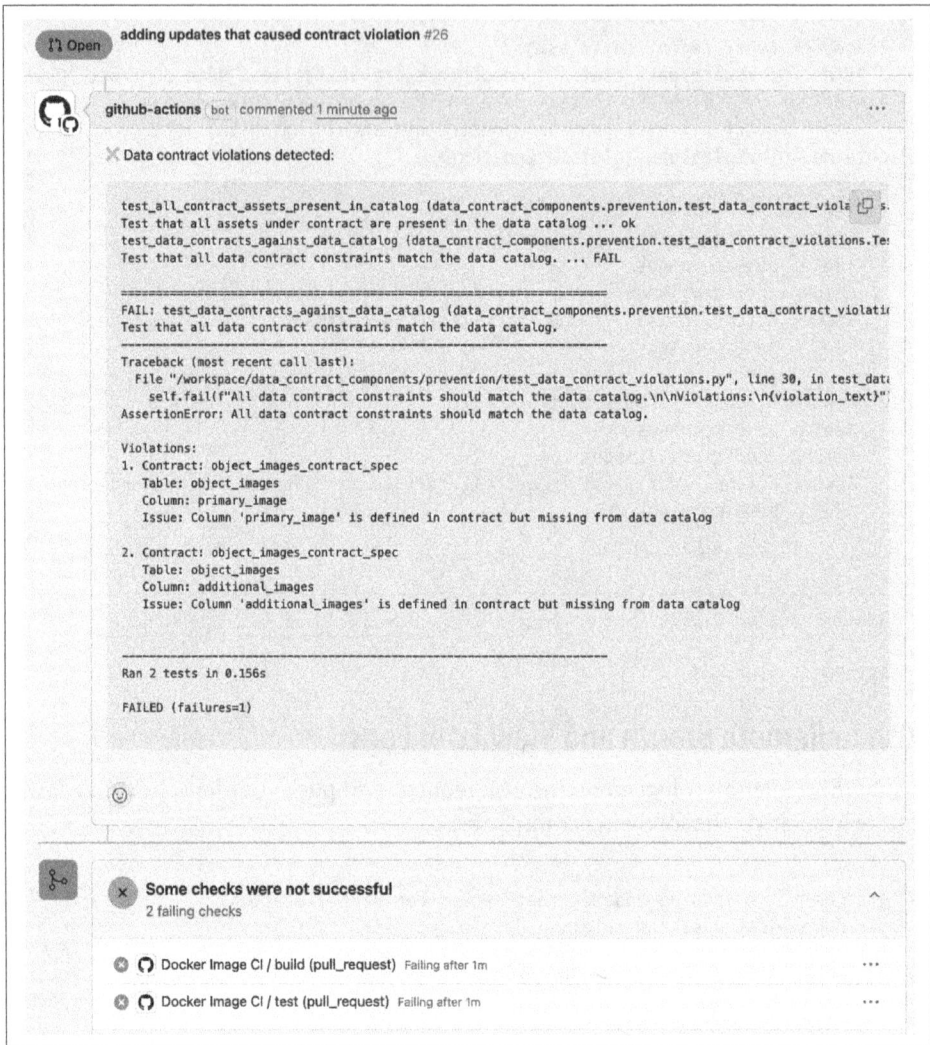

Figure 7-9. Data contract violation message with failed CI/CD tests (see it on GitHub (https://github.com/data-contract-book/chapter-7-implementing-data-contracts?tab=readme-ov-file#iv---push-to-remote-branch-and-view-error-logs))

This will also be useful when trying to explain the issue to your colleagues.

Revert Database Migration Changes

You undo this commit pushed to your remote branch by using the following commands:

```
git revert HEAD
git push
```

> The way you approach managing Git branches and changes will depend on your specific organization and/or team. This approach was chosen for simplicity for this walkthrough.

You also confirm that the CI/CD tests pass again, as seen in Figure 7-10.

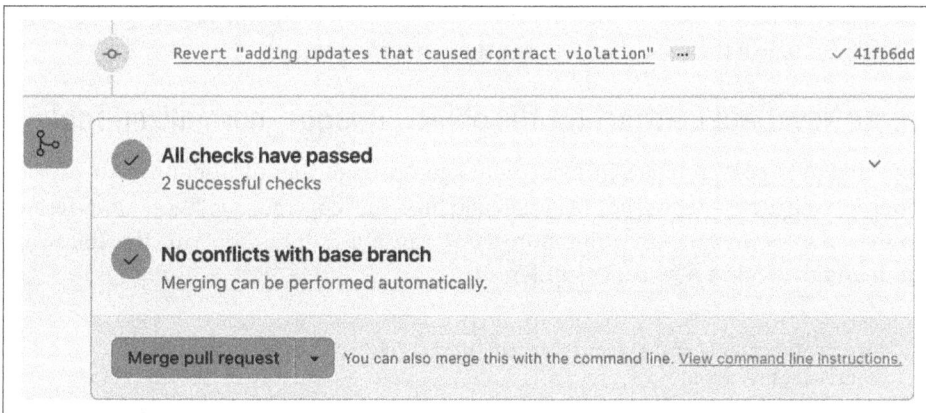

Figure 7-10. CI/CD tests passing again

Your next steps are to find the data contract spec that is causing your violations and to determine which team you need to talk with to learn more about their needs.

Discuss with Downstream Team to Learn Use Case

You locate the contract spec at *data_contract_components/contract_definition/object_images_contract_spec.json* and identify from the spec that the owner is the following:

```
"owner": {
    "name": "Data Engineering Team",
    "email": "data-eng@museum.org"
},
```

You reach out to the data engineering team and learn the following new information:

- The data science team started its model training last week and heavily depends on object_images.

- With that said, having images split between object_images.primary_image and object_images.additional_images, the latter being an array, requires additional data pre-processing and business logic the data science team has to maintain.

- The data science team is excited to learn about the normalized table and agrees on the change, but it needs time to update its data pre-processing pipelines to account for the new schema of object_images.

Thus you and your stakeholders decide to 1) not drop object_images, 2) create a new table called object_images_normalized, and 3) maintain object_images for one month to give the data science team time to transition.

Create New Data Contract for the object_images_normalized Table

Now that data contracts are in place, you can leverage them to define your expectations for object_images_normalized and use the contract violation unit test to confirm that your database migration won't cause a failure. You run the following command to create a new contract file:

```
touch
data_contract_components/contract_definition/object_images_normalized
_contract_spec.json
```

Before reading further, attempt to create your own data contract spec for object_images_normalized by adapting the existing spec *object_images_contract_spec.json*. Alternatively, you can just copy and paste the following into *object_images_normalized_contract_spec.json*:

```
{
    "spec-version": "1.0.0",
    "name": "object-images-normalized-contract-spec",
    "namespace": "met-museum-data",
    "dataAssetResourceName": "postgresql://postgres:5432/postgres.object_
images_normalized",
    "doc": "Data contract for the object_images_noralized table containing
image URLs and metadata for museum objects and creation timestamps.",
    "owner": {
      "name": "Data Engineering Team",
      "email": "data-eng@museum.org"
    },
    "schema": {
      "$schema": "https://json-schema.org/draft/2020-12/schema",
      "title": "Object Images Normalized Table Schema",
```

```json
      "table_catalog": "postgres",
      "table_schema": "public",
      "table_name": "object_images_normalized",
      "properties": {
        "object_id": {
          "description": "Identifying number for each artwork (unique, can be
used as key field)",
          "examples": [437133],
          "constraints": {
            "primaryKey": true,
            "data_type": "integer",
            "numeric_precision": 32.0,
            "is_nullable": false,
            "is_updatable": true
          }
        },
        "image": {
          "description": "URL to the image of an object (JPEG)",
          "examples": ["https://images.metmuseum.org/.../DT1234.jpg"],
          "constraints": {
            "primaryKey": false,
            "data_type": "text",
            "is_nullable": true,
            "is_updatable": true
          }
        },
        "is_primary_image": {
          "description": "Boolean flagging if the image is a primary image
for the museum.",
          "constraints": {
            "primaryKey": false,
            "data_type": "boolean",
            "is_nullable": true,
            "is_updatable": true
          }
        },
        "created_at": {
          "description": "Timestamp when this record was created in the
database",
          "examples": ["2025-01-15T10:30:00.000Z"],
          "items": null,
          "constraints": {
            "primaryKey": false,
            "data_type": "timestamp without time zone",
            "datetime_precision": 6.0,
            "is_nullable": false,
            "is_updatable": true
          }
        }
      }
    }
  }
}
```

Our next step is to see what errors occur now that we have a new contract spec, but the database migration file doesn't reflect the new table yet.

Run Unit Tests and See Error for Missing Asset in Catalog

Again, you run the following commands to reset your Postgres database based on the most up-to-date database migration file:

```
cd ~/../workspace/data_contract_components/data_assets
alembic downgrade base
alembic upgrade head
```

Afterward, you also run the unit test command again:

```
cd ~/../workspace
python -m unittest data_contract_components/prevention/test_data_contract
_violations.py -v
```

As expected, you get the following error message, highlighting that your new data contract exists but is not present in the data catalog:

```
AssertionError: False is not true : All assets under contract should
be present in data catalog.
Missing: ['object_images_normalized']


======================================================================

AssertionError: All data contract constraints should match the data
catalog.

Violations:
1. Contract: object_images_normalized_contract_spec
   Table: object_images_normalized
   Column: object_id
   Issue: Column 'object_id' is defined in contract but missing from
          data catalog

2. Contract: object_images_normalized_contract_spec
   Table: object_images_normalized
   Column: image
   Issue: Column 'image' is defined in contract but missing from data
          catalog

3. Contract: object_images_normalized_contract_spec
   Table: object_images_normalized
   Column: is_primary_image
   Issue: Column 'is_primary_image' is defined in contract but missing
          from data catalog

4. Contract: object_images_normalized_contract_spec
   Table: object_images_normalized
   Column: created_at
   Issue: Column 'created_at' is defined in contract but missing from
```

```
        data catalog


----------------------------------------------------------------
Ran 2 tests in 0.213s

FAILED (failures=2)
```

Again, you push the local changes to your remote branch so that the errors are logged on the pull request:

```
git add .
git commit -m 'added new contract, but need to update the db migration
file still'
git push
```

Thus, your next step is to update the database migration file to add the data asset `object_images_normalized` until you no longer receive data contract violations from the unit tests.

Fix Database Migration Until All Checks Pass

Run the following commands to reset your Postgres database via `alembic downgrade base`:

```
cd ~/../workspace/data_contract_components/data_assets
alembic downgrade base
```

Before reading further, attempt to update *data_contract_components/data_assets/db_migrations/versions/00e9b3375a5f_create_met_museum_seed_tables.py* to include the creation of the `object_images_normalized` table. When you are done, you should have the following code snippet added under `def upgrade() -> None::`

```python
op.create_table(
    "object_images_normalized",
    sa.Column(
        "object_id",
        sa.Integer,
        primary_key=True,
        comment=column_comment_dict["object_id"]
    ),
    sa.Column(
        "image",
        sa.Text,
        comment="URL to the image of an object (JPEG)"
    ),
    sa.Column(
        "is_primary_image",
        sa.Boolean,
        comment="Identifies if it's the primary image for the object."
    ),
    sa.Column(
```

```
        "created_at",
        sa.DateTime,
        nullable=False,
        server_default=sa.text("CURRENT_TIMESTAMP"),
        comment=column_comment_dict["created_at"]
    ),
)
```

You should also have the following snippet under def downgrade() -> None: to ensure you properly clean the database with the new table:

```
def downgrade() -> None:
    """Downgrade schema."""
    op.drop_table("object")
    op.drop_table("object_history")
    op.drop_table("object_physical_properties")
    op.drop_table("object_gallery_info")
    op.drop_table("object_tags")
    op.drop_table("object_images")
    op.drop_table("object_images_normalized") #add this line
    op.drop_table("object_copyright")
    op.drop_table("object_api_metadata")
```

Run the following commands to set up your Postgres database with the new object_images_normalized table:

```
cd ~/../workspace/data_contract_components/data_assets
alembic upgrade head
```

Finally, you run the unit test command to confirm there are no more violations:

```
cd ~/../workspace
python -m unittest data_contract_components/prevention/test_data_contract
_violations.py -v
```

You can confirm that the unit test returned no failures for the data contract violation check:

```
test_all_contract_assets_present_in_catalog
(data_contract_components.prevention.test_data_contract_violations.TestContract
Violations.test_all_contract_assets_present_in_catalog)
Test that all assets under contract are present in the data catalog ... ok

test_data_contracts_against_data_catalog (data_contract_components.prevention.
test_data_contract_violations.TestContractViolations.
test_data_contracts_against_data_catalog)
Test that all data contract constraints match the data catalog. ... ok


----------------------------------------------------------------------
Ran 2 tests in 0.176s

OK
```

Your final step is to push your change to your remote branch to confirm the CI/CD checks will pass.

Push to Remote Branch and See It Pass

You run the following Git commands to push your local branch to remote and view the GitHub Actions logs:

```
git add .
git commit -m 'adding updated spec and db migration file for object_images
_normalized'
git push
```

As confirmed in Figure 7-11, all of our tests are passing now for both the new contract spec and the new data asset `object_images_normalized`.

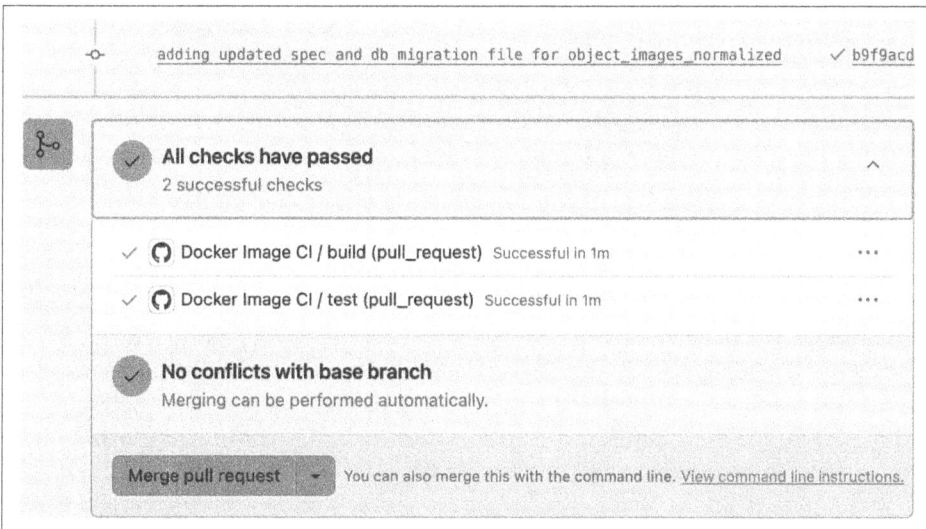

Figure 7-11. CI/CD tests passing again after database change

With the tests passing, it's now time to ask a colleague for code review and ultimately merge this code to the `main` branch.

Conclusion

Congrats on implementing your first data contract and completing the tutorial! In this chapter, we provided a full walkthrough of a data contract architecture implementation and its corresponding scripts. In addition, we detailed how to implement your own data contract specs for the purpose of learning, and provided you the trade-offs of managing your own data contract spec. Finally, we closed out the chapter with a mock scenario imitating what a data producer will experience throughout the data contract violation workflow.

Walking away from this chapter, you should be able to achieve the following:

- Understand how to implement the four data contract components: data assets, data contract spec, detection, and prevention.
- Create a data contract spec via JSON Schema as a means to understand how to evaluate available specs on the market or whether to build your own for specific use cases.
- Learn how to leverage the metadata of databases to create your own "data catalog" that you will compare data contract specs to.
- Embed data contracts within unit tests for local testing and embedding within the CI/CD workflow.
- Fully walk through the data contract violation workflow on a pull request.

Again, we want to highlight that this implementation and sandbox environment are intended for learning purposes. Scaling beyond a few data contracts increases the complexity of managing their lifecycles, and thus you should strongly consider the trade-offs of building your own, leveraging an open source tool, or buying a dedicated product (e.g., a data catalog service) for each component of the data contract architecture.

Furthermore, we were adamant about having a code repository for this book, as one of the earliest complaints we heard about data contracts was "They're too theoretical." Especially among other technical teams, such as upstream software engineers, having code available for exploration can help you quickly build buy-in and illustrate how this work differentiates from unit tests, quality assurance testing, and data observability. In addition, you can leverage this repo as a launch pad to quickly get a proof of concept running to help build buy-in within your organization (which we will discuss in Chapters 9 to 12).

In the next chapter, we continue moving away from theory and present three real-world case studies of data contracts in production from companies we interviewed for the book.

## CHAPTER 8

Real-World Case Studies of Data Contracts in Production

As this chapter stands between the second and third sections of this book, we've designed it to help us transition from the practical and technical aspects of data contract implementation to the human and organization-centric aspects needed to initiate, fuel, and maintain lasting adoption. To do this, we'll share three stories about data contract adoption, each involving a different instance where data professionals confronted the reality that the data management status quo in their organization was no longer viable.

Presented as parts of a greater whole, these stories make it easier to see the parallel trends running through each—trends reshaping the data world in real time. You may have sensed these trends within your own organization, perhaps inspiring you to pick up this book in the first place. As we'll confirm, you aren't imagining them. These stories act as evidence that data leaders like yourself are rethinking how they approach data quality itself, how they structure their teams, and what's required within an organization to shift from reactive autonomy to proactive accountability.

The examples evidence a shift taking place, where a growing number of leaders, practitioners, and teams find themselves making tough calls, challenging long-standing assumptions, and taking a smart, strategic, informed chance on something new. This is change, and change can be intimidating if not outright scary.

Change can also be very difficult to recognize when you're sitting right in the middle of it. We posit that these stories, in addition to the similar ones data professionals share in Slack channels, blog articles, and on social media, aren't just stories. They're signals. Not loud signals, necessarily, but most certainly persistent ones. And when we place them side by side, as we've done in this chapter, they become easier to read.

Like sedimentary layers in rock, these adoption stories form a pattern and act like strata. Accumulated experiences from different teams, industries, and inflection points, when viewed in sequence, reveal the deeper ripples of a movement already underway. They offer more than anecdotes—they offer evidence. The shift in data work isn't imagined, isolated, or confined to a niche. It's happening right now, across the industry. And if you're experiencing it too, you're not alone.

We begin with coauthor Chad Sanderson's own data contract adoption story at Convoy, informed by his first-person account of what happens when the old way of doing things breaks down under the pressures of a brand-new startup. Next, we'll shift to Glassdoor, where the need to rethink data ownership and operational accountability emerged not from one voice, but instead from leaders collectively heeding a broader internal need. Finally, we travel around the world to Adevinta Spain, where similar pressures occurred under very different circumstances, confirming that this movement isn't limited to one network, one geography, or one domain.

Convoy Data Contract Story

Through its proprietary software platform, Convoy enabled instant booking, transparent pricing, and automated matching of loads to available trucks—Uber for freight. The goal was to reduce the industry's previously accepted amount of waste and inefficiency while providing faster payments and better data insights to all involved. At its core, Convoy used data and machine learning to build a competitive marketplace where suppliers placed their bids and truck drivers accepted jobs.

When Chad joined Convoy, the company had 250 employees and had just completed its Series C funding round. However, no one could have predicted the intensity of growth Convoy would soon experience, exploding to roughly 1,000 employees over the subsequent two years. The data platform team Chad was hired to lead expanded from just 4 to more than 40 people during this time.

This parallel expansion of the data team was no accident, however, as Convoy built itself as a data-first organization, laying a robust foundation comparable to today's Modern Data Stacks. It began with data teams utilizing Amazon Redshift before eventually adopting Snowflake. For data orchestration, Convoy relied on AWS in concert with other tools, including Airflow, Spark, dbt, Fivetran, and Census. Additionally, the culture as a whole was very data-driven, with highly engaged executives regularly using dashboards tied to OKRs and KPIs.

Yet, as Convoy continued to grow, cracks became more apparent and numerous around its data products. As data quality became shaky, executive dashboards slowly began fueling more questions than answers. And as these questions worked down the chain, passing from the C-suite to managers and from managers to analysts, the

Convoy employees at the end of the chain were increasingly unable to explain what was going wrong.

In addition to Chad recounting the situation, we also interviewed his colleague Adrian Kreuziger, a principal software engineer within Convoy at the time who helped lead its data contracts implementation. As Adrian stated:

> Once we started expanding out the data science team, making it easier for people to write dbt models, and then also doing this kind of microservice migration, just the complexity of the data got a lot worse…. What I tell people is that Convoy's problem was not scale. There are only so many shipments that happen every day in the US. Convoy's problem was data model complexity. You are modeling the entire trucking industry from abstract concepts like shipments all the way down to facilities, drivers, and geolocation. The freight industry is insanely complicated. And so as we expanded out the business and product offerings, we had to model more and more of the trucking industry. And now you have 150 developers each changing this data model to ship new features on this incredibly complex data model while data scientists are trying to build something on top of it. It was just moving constantly.

As data teams brought more systems online, they found it increasingly difficult to trace ongoing issues to their source. One moment in particular made this painfully clear, serving as a wake-up call for the company as a whole.

While Convoy's service offering and need to continuously innovate grew more pressing, even relatively small changes upstream soon had the potential to cause unexpected downstream failures. "Garbage in, garbage out" was how Chad would later describe the problematic loop Convoy found itself in at the time—where one silent schema change had the potential to completely break a production system. It was a reality the company had to confront, and one where no one had any reliable ways to detect these business-critical risks in advance.

Despite expanding its offerings over time, the freight marketplace remained the company's core engine. However, data issues cascaded to such a point that ultimately, perhaps inevitably, a key dashboard suddenly began indicating to stakeholders that auction engagement was dropping. Company leaders concluded that this was likely a marketing problem. Desperate to correct it, they instructed the organization's marketing managers to invest heavily in a campaign designed to boost participation and nullify the drop in engagement. Weeks and hundreds of thousands of dollars later, the real problem was uncovered—the drop had been due to a bug in the data table feeding the dashboard. The system hadn't failed—the data had, thus rattling the company. Not only had things gotten to the point where issues could arise from seemingly anywhere, now leadership couldn't be sure in its ability to correctly diagnose what was happening in order to correct the issues.

From a technical perspective, Adrian described how the turning point was the introduction of Kafka:

> I think that the actual big driving point was the introduction of Kafka and trying to get our developers and our engineering team to start emitting more semantic events instead of CDC events. Previously, all we had was basically change data capture events of how things got changed in the database. CDC events are great at telling you the state of the world at a certain point in time. But they're not great at telling you why the world changed for that state to change.
>
> And what ended up happening was that we would have people trying to reverse engineer real-world events that happened based on a string of CDC events. So you might have a shipment and you get a CDC event where the status has changed from "in progress" to "canceled." And then you can kind of conceptually say, "OK, the shipment must have been canceled." You can reverse engineer that from the history. That also gets very, very complicated and very error prone.

The truth was now painfully clear. Everyone was working hard, but no one had the full map. Fixes didn't last. Visibility tools helped surface symptoms, but not causes. So Chad, Adrian, and the data platform team tried to rally, doing what any good data professional does when they're out of answers—they started checking assumptions. As part of these efforts, Chad began talking to other data professionals and trying to piece together what was working, what wasn't, and how other teams were thinking about similar problems—anything that might help them understand what was really going on.

Bringing this learning back in-house, Convoy's data teams first started trying to improve visibility by investing in better lineage tools to trace how data moved through the system. This helped to some extent, but didn't solve the root problem Convoy was facing. So, they pivoted, focusing instead on documentation. Internal tooling was built to make data sources and definitions more accessible. However, again, overall impact was limited, with new tools adding clarity in some places but issues continuing to slip through.

Eventually, through this tireless trial-and-error process, and some first-principles thinking, the team eventually realized the deeper issue wasn't technical per se. It stemmed from a lack of accountability—no one owned the full lifecycle of datasets at Convoy. Therefore, there was no mechanism in place to enforce quality expectations between teams—no shared understanding of what data was supposed to look like, and no clear lines of accountability for who was responsible when something broke. As Chad remembers, "This realization just hit us all right upside the head. We didn't just need better tools. We needed an agreement, something in place upstream that could define what 'correct' even meant."

This realization led Chad and the Convoy team to begin piloting data contracts as enforceable agreements between a select group of data producers and consumers, shifting quality checks upstream so they would happen as early in the data lifecycle as possible. To do so, they began working with software engineers to implement data contracts directly into the CI/CD pipeline. Figure 8-1, from Chad and Adrian's article, "An Engineer's Guide to Data Contracts: Pt. 1" (*https://oreil.ly/w1zJh*), illustrates their implementation at Convoy.

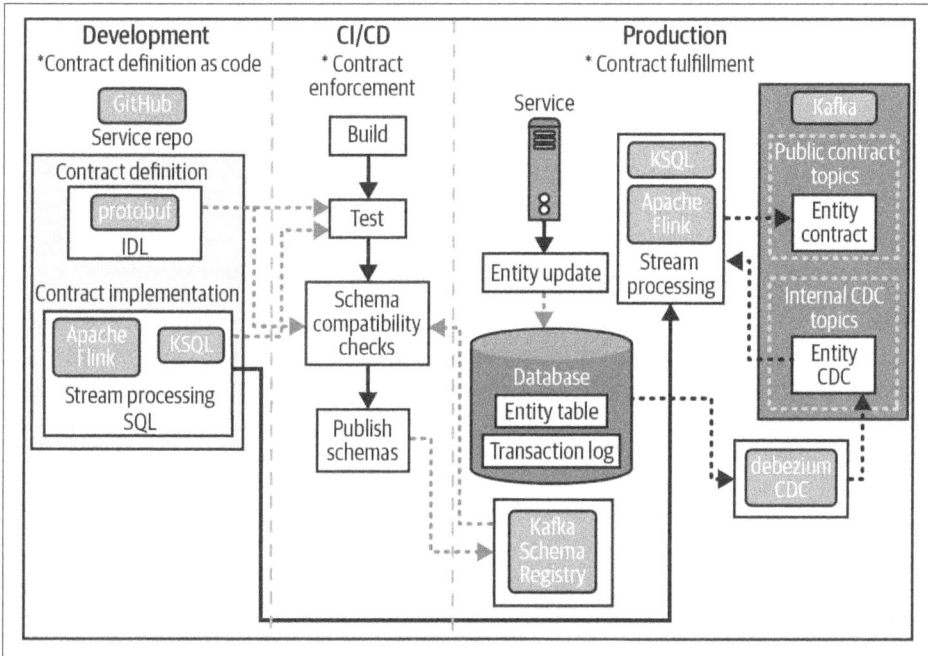

Figure 8-1. Convoy's data contract implementation

Contracts were versioned and separate from operational databases, creating a more stable and predictable interface between upstream and downstream teams. As a result, data contracts began providing an abstraction layer. Consumers defined what they needed, and engineers implemented against a clear interface.

As data contract adoption gained traction in Convoy, it became clear to teams across the organization that this had been an alignment problem, not simply a tooling problem. As Adrian describes:

> It basically made data much more like a first-class citizen in developers' minds. So except for select teams with a big ML focus where the engineers and the data scientists worked really well together, other engineers had no idea that their data was even being sent to the warehouse. They were just focused on building their service and production database. The fact that it got kind of mirrored into the warehouse and used downstream…[was a] black box.

> By going through this exercise with a team of saying, "Hey, let's rethink your data model, let's figure out what you want to expose to the rest of the world," suddenly, as engineers are making changes for a new feature, they're immediately thinking about

things such as, "Oh, we should probably add some new events here" or "We need to go and update that event and probably go talk to the data science team." So that made it much more up front and apparent. And because we built dev tooling around this, it made it much more like their standard workflow. They got compile time feedback when they were making changes that we knew weren't allowed.

So contracts at Convoy changed all this on a fundamental level, creating shared expectations enforced by code, not contingent on conversation. They enabled data producers and consumers to agree on schema, meaning, and responsibility. And by shifting data left in the greater organization, it became normal for these expectations to be part of the development process moving forward. This created confidence downstream, as teams began to trust that their work wouldn't break without warning. Yes, contract adoption got data management back in gear at Convoy. But its success also drove the importance of data quality deep into the culture itself.

The bigger change, though, was psychological: teams stopped waiting for the next issue to crop up or the system to break down. Analysts stopped second-guessing the data. Engineers had fewer reactive tickets and more confidence in the impact of their code. Conversations shifted from patching to planning. The entire system felt more stable, because it was.

The outcomes weren't just about preventing errors. They were about giving Convoy's teams the ability to keep their attention on the expectations of their data and code.

In addition to the Convoy story, Adrian also shared additional advice he has reflected on since moving on from Convoy:

> From my experience, you need to make the data contracts part of the normal developer flow. They need to feel like just another developer tool to really gain adoption. And then the other big thing I want to reiterate is that contracts shouldn't be viewed as if we're going to take everything that we have and put it all under contract all at once. First, you should attack it vertical by vertical, or only put contracts where they really make sense. And then you can use contracts as a way to rethink your existing data and help drive the data model that you want, versus the data model you're stuck with.

Glassdoor Data Contract Story

Glassdoor is one of the first companies to implement data contracts that are not only in production but also use advanced metadata capture, such as static code analysis, to drive prevention. This case study dives into the public information made available regarding their implementation via "Data Quality at Petabyte Scale: Building Trust in the Data Lifecycle (*https://oreil.ly/lMdQn*)," a post on the Glassdoor Engineering blog by Zakariah Siyaji, data platform engineering manager at the time of writing. In addition, we were lucky enough to have Zaki join our Shift Left Data Conference as a speaker, where he provided further information on the implementation via his talk, titled "Shifting From Reactive to Proactive at Glassdoor" (*https://oreil.ly/uggPf*).

Glassdoor is an online platform for job listings and writing reviews of employers, either as an employee or as someone who went through an interview. One of its revenue-driving business lines is to sell ads for jobs on their platform. With respect to data, this means that impressions for its specific brand ads are critical, and thus have a higher standard of data quality. This flow was best described in Zaki's conference talk as the following:

> And so for us, brand impressions are really important…[as] its…flow of [data]…goes through many hands [at Glassdoor]. So it goes from data producing applications, through another application, then through [an] API gateway and a variety of systems within AWS, and then it goes through ETL. And so when there's so many hand-offs, the question that we have is, "Well, what's the flow of data and what are all the points at which…there could be data failure?"

The quote highlights the problem that Glassdoor aimed to address via data contracts. According to Zaki's talk, Glassdoor had three unique components that positioned it to take on shift left data practices and therefore adopt data contracts:

- Adopting write-audit-publish (WAP), where each batch of data undergoes review in a staging area before being moved to production
- Embedding static code analysis (SCA) within the CI/CD workflow, where teams can determine how changes to frontend code impact backend systems and thus data assets
- Using large language models to take the metadata captured via data contracts and SCA, and provide additional business context to surface any meaningful business logic impact as well

This further resonates with a point our coauthor Chad makes throughout the book, in that culture change, such as shift left, needs to be enabled through technology. Specifically, automation that makes the required behavior change of upstream teams minimal to further incentivize the continued use of new tools such as data contracts.

In Zaki's conference talk, he addressed the cultural change:

> [One] really interesting thing that we found at Glassdoor was that folks naturally gravitated towards the shift left paradigm. And so oftentimes when I preach about shift left at Glassdoor, the question that I often get from data folks is, how are you going to be able to drive adoption of the shift left paradigm within product engineering and QA orgs?
>
> And so what we found was that product engineering teams are intrinsically motivated to build reliable systems. And QA teams, by their very nature, are focused on defect prevention. And so ultimately these teams taking responsibility for data production means that teams are better informed and data outages can be prevented instead of actively addressed.

This all goes into seamless collaboration. 'Cause when you have your data producers talking to your data consumers, you're able to effectively ensure that the data steward isn't stuck in the middle trying to figure out what it is that folks actually want.

In short, both upstream and downstream teams were already aligned on the value of data within the company and specifically what data products were important for protection. Yet, despite this alignment, teams still struggled without the technology in place to enable collaboration at scale (remember our discussion in Chapter 3 on Dunbar's Number and Conway's Law). Zaki highlights this pain in his article, where he states:

> Historically, Glassdoor's data engineering teams have been reactive, learning about issues only after they disrupt downstream systems. This challenge is compounded by the fact that the data engineering team often serves as the first line of defense against all data failures, even when the root cause lies in upstream data quality issues. Consequently, this scenario results in wasted time, duplicated efforts, increased costs, and a loss of trust in the data as teams rush to fix problems that could have been addressed earlier in the pipeline.

Glassdoor had the "perfect storm" for ensuring the successful adoption of data contracts. Specifically, first, the company had a shared understanding of how data assets, specifically brand views, were important to the business. Second, pain was felt both by reactive data platform teams and upstream producer teams that were flagged by data stewards regarding issues due to data changes. Finally, and most importantly, leadership (according to Zaki's conference talk) was able to see that "fewer drops in [brand] impressions...means that there's less revenue loss," and thus they had top-level buy-in.

The pain was present, the pain led to a meaningful impact on revenue, and the pain was attributed to the many handoffs within the brand image data lifecycle. A problem perfectly aligned to shift left data practices and data contracts.

This created the opening Glassdoor's data platform team needed, one that allowed them to make clear that the company's data issues were not the result of minor bugs or tooling gaps. The true problem, as they explained to stakeholders, was due to the absence of a clear, enforceable agreement between the organization's data producers and its consumers—a "handshake" between both stakeholders.

To illustrate how their implementation worked, the following architecture diagram (Figure 8-2) is adapted from Glassdoor's engineering blog article, "Data Quality at Petabyte Scale: Building Trust in the Data Lifecycle" (*https://oreil.ly/ZnITs*), and highlights the four data contract components detailed in previous chapters:

- Data assets
- Contract definition

- Detection
- Prevention

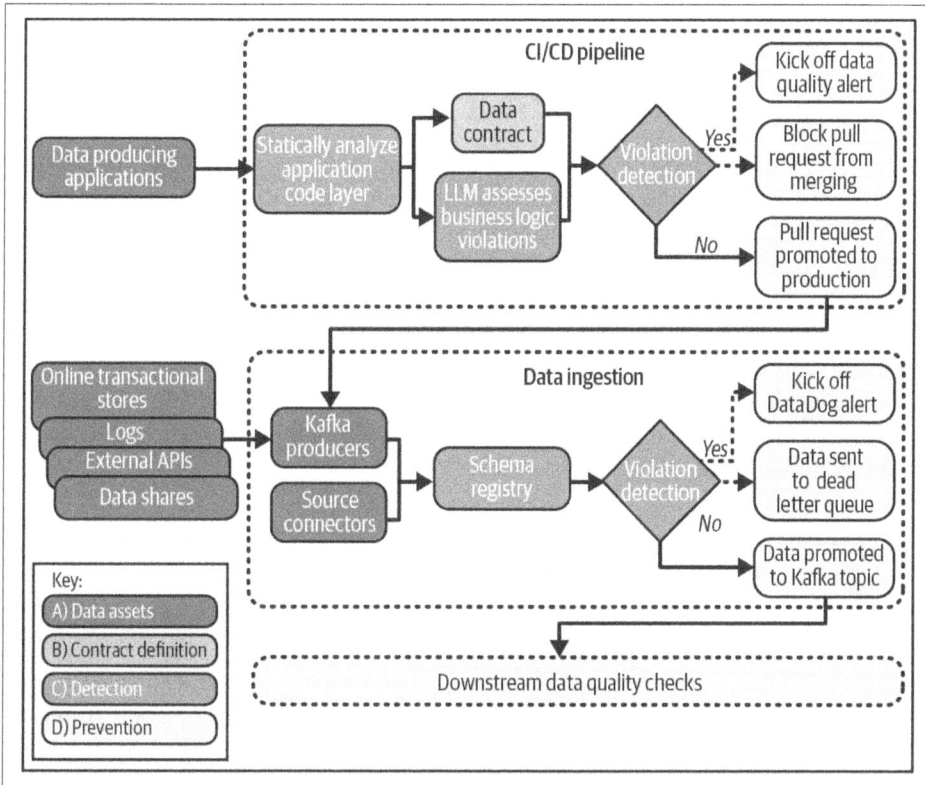

Figure 8-2. Glassdoor's data contract implementation

Glassdoor's post describes the success the company found with this approach:

> Proactive data quality isn't about imposing rules at the last minute; it's about instilling confidence in both the producers and consumers of data—an approach [they've] integrated throughout the data lifecycle.

> [Furthermore, by] addressing the psychological dimension of trust through shared responsibility, transparent validation, and confidence-building checks, [they're] scaling to petabytes without compromising [their] data's essential sense of faith.

So, here again we see evidence of data contract adoption leading to much more than mere technical upgrades. These changes quickly began to evidence a deeper cultural transformation within Glassdoor. Where Chad's time at Convoy demonstrated data contract viability, Zaki and Glassdoor have demonstrated repeatability. Two different companies, at two different times, could both scale their operations with confidence, leveraging data contracts to shift left, delivering data management and data quality out of chaos.

In the next case study, we will highlight an implementation that occurred outside our awareness but that we came across while researching this book.

Adevinta Spain Data Contract Story

Our third and final data contract adoption story adds an interesting layer to the growing awareness among data professionals around upstream data ownership and accountability. At roughly the same time as the Glassdoor implementation, a story involving Adevinta Spain took place completely independently almost five thousand miles away. While doing research for this book we came across the article "Creating Source-Aligned Data Products in Adevinta Spain" (*https://oreil.ly/3mEwM*), written by Sergio Couto, and we knew we had to get in contact with this team and feature their implementation. The following is based on our interview with Sergio and his data engineering colleague Christian Herrera, as well as the article and public conference talks on their implementation.

> While Sergio and Christian are the ones being interviewed, they made it extremely clear throughout how the work they describe was a huge team effort at Adevinta Spain.

Headquartered in Barcelona, Adevinta Spain operates a variety of popular online marketplaces for European audiences, including those specific to jobs, cars, and real estate. As part of its business model, the organization collects behavioral event data—clicks, publishes, deletes, etc.—through the activity on each marketplace. Due to the collective popularity of these sites, teams found themselves dealing with significant amounts of data, with internal systems ingesting roughly four terabytes of marketplace data per day.

Originally, Adevinta Spain utilized Segment (still in use today) to ingest real-time events data via Kafka and, in turn, into a central data lake. While this ingestion workflow may seem like standard practice, we have to remember that the company is working at scale across multiple independent business units, which makes tracking and resolving upstream issues quite difficult. Sergio and Christian described the challenge:

> Sergio: "We're consuming a lot of events and the typical daily [state of engineering is that]...something is broken.... [We] have a lot of problems [finding] the producers of any of the topics that we are consuming. So...[putting contracts] first...[enables] a place to store the topic name, owner of the topic, and the events they are sending to it."

Christian: "We started with a full open source architecture...[where] we were consuming all the events, domain events, and behavior events into the data platform. So we had a lot of problems here in order to do it automatically and do the schema evolution in all the tables. So it was very, very hard...[and thus,] we decided to change to a push architecture."

It's worth noting the emphasis on the former architecture being "fully open source" and becoming a bottleneck to manage. Adevinta Spain eventually switched to a paid tool that offered a fully managed platform, thus enabling it to reduce the efforts of trying to manage numerous integrations between systems. This aligns with our discussion in Chapter 7 on how validating contract spec expectations to numerous forms of data assets is quite complex compared to validating against a data catalog that aggregates the metadata.

While these talking points are quite technical, the core challenge around the company's data quality was cultural. Specifically, the events data, and how it's processed, are central to the success of Adevinta Spain while also already providing tremendous business value. Yet to continue growing and evolve, the data platform team recognized the business needed to change its understanding of how data should be leveraged, highlighted by Christian's comment on Adevinta deciding "to change to a push architecture." Where a pull architecture relies on consumers accepting whatever data they receive, the push architecture puts ownership in the hands of the producer, who must decide who receives the data and the subsequent use cases they plan to support.

To better understand this cultural change, we asked Sergio and Christian to explain their four guiding principles from Sergio's article:

You produce it, you own it
Shifting to a push architecture, where data producers treat data assets as a product they maintain, rather than the exhaust of logs from their software and business operations

Data-driven teams without data analysts
Not relying on manual efforts of analysts to validate data quality for internal data products

Data governance by design
Recognizing that manual governance is less effective than embedding governance into the code itself, and subsequently your software design

Data people working as software engineers
Taking the extra effort to treat data the same way you maintain code, via rigorous testing, version control, and other software engineering best practices

This all falls in line with what Chad often highlights as the importance of technology to drive cultural change. Heavily manual changes rarely find success given that changing a behavior is already quite difficult. That's why you need to focus on leveraging technology to automate as much as possible, to reduce the friction for behavior change and thus cultural change (e.g., instituting data contracts). Sergio and Christian shared nearly identical sentiments, stating that "focusing on automation is key because otherwise people won't engage with your project" and "the user experience…is the most important" for adoption. We will discuss navigating cultural change in much more depth in the next few chapters.

Eventually, the cumulative weight of these issues did not rest only on the shoulders of the data platform team. It began to press down on the entire organization. Putting out fires bordered on normal, and manual enforcement couldn't scale. Internal trust in the system eroded. Morale and culture were stretched thin. The team needed a way to build alignment and accountability into the platform itself—not through more hours allocated to manual triage, but within the code.

> Sergio: "I remember…every day [being filled] with alerts, errors, [and] missing data…. [We one day] realized there…[was a] month of missing data when an analyst realized there was no communication, no alerts, [and] no awareness about the state of the data ingestion. I don't know if that was a tipping point, but it was hard to work…[where] you went to the office in the morning [and] you see…[only] message errors, that's it."

> Christian: "I remember two big problems here with the old architecture. First…in order [for] people without software engineering knowledge [to] query [specific] tables…[we had a] pipeline read these tables in JSON with SQL and [then] write in another layer in parquet…. So it was very…hard because the rules are different in the JSON layer and in the parquet tables. And some…users complained that the data is in JSON tables but are not in the parquet because the schema is not correct…. Another is that our consumer in the pool architecture raises a lot of topics…from Kafka, where the process…lasts…[a long] time…. [When] dealing with errors, we don't want…to stop the process if one table fails."

These challenges that centered around business-critical data gave Adevinta Spain's data platform team the leverage to start implementing data contracts across the data lifecycle. They viewed data contracts as a means to shift toward becoming data product oriented, where data isn't just dumped in storage but actively serves a purpose and is maintained across a lifecycle among a set of users. This requires ownership of the data assets, agreement between producers and consumers, automation of work related to change management, standardizing data processing patterns across the business, and ensuring this is all secure since the company operates under GDPR.

Adevinta Spain's data contract implementation consists of two key stages: definition time and runtime ingestion. Similar to diagrams we have shown in previous chapters, Figure 8-3 (adapted from Sergio's conference talks) illustrates the following process:

1. Data producers define their data via JSON Schema and upload it to the schema repository on GitHub.

2. They then leverage generative AI to transform the schema into a contract specification proposal that is sent via Slack to the producer and consumer for review.

3. Data producers and data consumers agree on the data contract constraints, which then kicks off an automatic contract validation step.

4. If the data contract passes validation, then an Airflow DAG (i.e., directed acyclic graph or data pipeline orchestration) is automatically created to execute the data ingestion based on the contract spec, create or update the data asset, and upload the data contract to Amazon S3.

5. The data consumer merges and activates the DAG created in the previous step to operationalize everything.

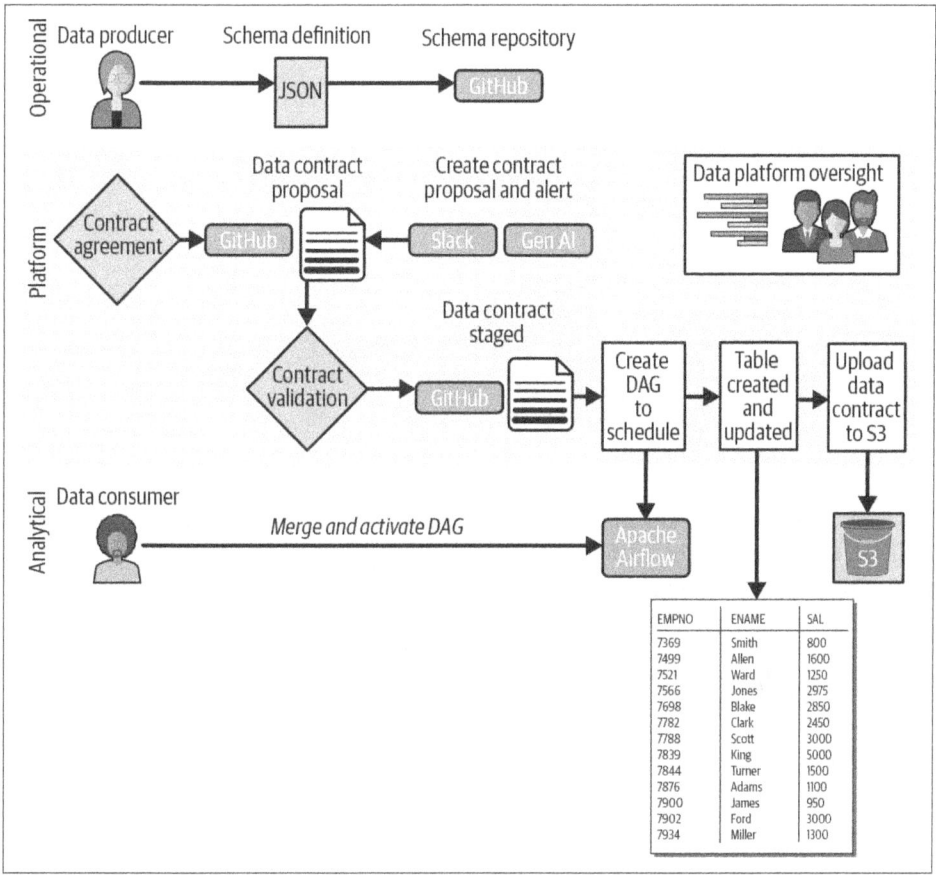

Figure 8-3. Adevinta Spain data contract implementation: definition time

In addition, Sergio's article provided the actual data contract spec template that their generative AI tool uses to create the proposal, which is also similar to what we implemented in Chapter 7. Note that, given his team are early adopters of this architecture pattern, they had to build their own contract spec, as prebuilt tools and formats were not widely adopted yet:

```
{
    "contract_name": "MyNewEvent",
    "contract_version": "1",
    "description": "Event published from microservice",
    "start_date": "2024-10-01T00:00:00+00:00",
    "schema": {
        "source": "url",
        "version": "1",
        "location": {
          "url": "https://schema.…/events/…/MyNewEvent-Event.json/1.json"
        },
        "format": "jsonSchema"
     },
    "landing_source":{
        "kafka_topic": "pub.mytopic"
     },
    "pii_fields": [<FILL or leave empty if there are no private fields> ],
    "source": "ms-mysource",
    "slas": {
      "owner": "team-myteam",
      "contact_support": "<FILL>",
      "data_periodicity": "<daily/hourly>",
      "Execution_hour": <FILL or remove if hourly>,
      "time_to_recover": "<FILL>",
      "retention": "<FILL>",
      "provider_ids": ["mymarketplace"]
    }
}
```

Once the contract is validated and the orchestration ready, it will trigger a daily/ hourly (as defined in the data contract) process that will ingest data assets via the following steps, as illustrated in Figure 8-4:

1. Each event triggers an Airflow DAG that pulls the relevant data contract and Kafka pipeline into Databricks, where they run Spark operations.

2. Data contract specs are pulled from S3 and filtered down to active contracts for the relevant events data.

3. The defined schema is applied to the data asset, and violations result in the data being quarantined.

4. PII data that is not used for analytics is deleted, and the remaining PII data is separated for GDPR compliance.

5. PII data and non-PII data is stored in the analytical database.

Furthermore, Adevinta Spain leverages Delta Lake's time-travel features as it's particularly useful in allowing ingestion writes to be atomic and rollback-safe.

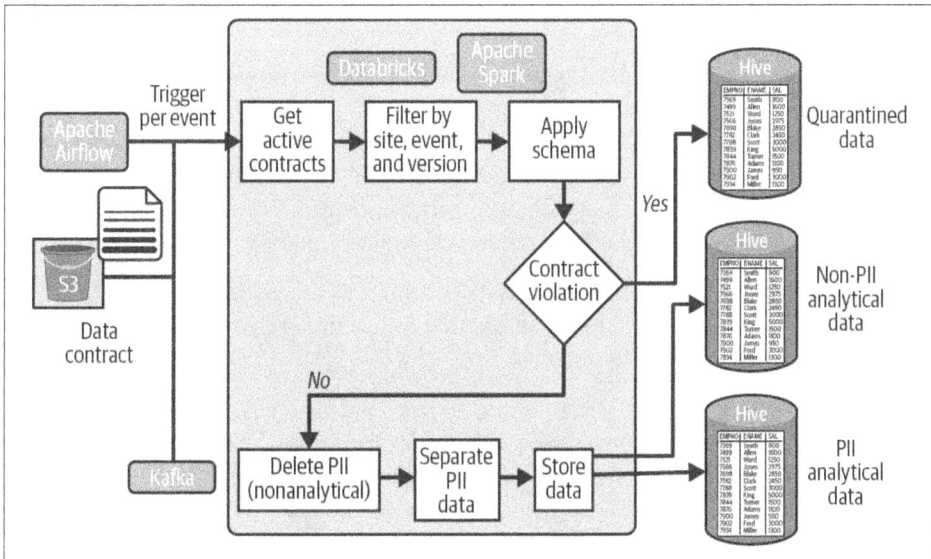

Figure 8-4. Adevinta Spain data contract implementation: runtime ingestion

As the team worked to layer these improvements together, visibility into contract health, ingestion status, and data usage also received the attention they deserved, supported by dedicated Grafana observability dashboards and Slack alerts.

One thing we greatly appreciated from talking to the Adevinta Spain team was their transparency around the initial challenges of getting this process adopted, which matched similar challenges we have encountered when getting data contracts adopted across an entire business. Specifically, the challenge of determining who would be the best team to roll out the initiative within Adevinta when the organization has numerous business units that leverage the events data. Here's how Sergio described it:

> We were serving several websites selling stuff, and each team was almost independent—we have a real estate team, a motor team, and [other] miscellaneous teams…. Each of the teams came with different responses…[where] some teams [were already using best]…practices and software engineering principles, and some others are less engaged in that.

Furthermore, the data platform team had to educate the wider business on how their work is coupled with the data platform, and also persuade them that implementing across the thousands of tables wouldn't be labor-intensive. Here's Christian:

> I think from the beginning, all the teams understood the value of the data contracts. But the concept was a new way of working. And for example, another problem was [that no]…data consumer…is capable [of consuming] all the events dealing with

schema evolution…. Another concern…was, "OK, I like data contracts, but I have thousands of tables that already don't have a data contract." So we started to…do an automated migration for all these tables and create a data contract in an automatic way so the work of doing this…was small.

Diving further into Christian's comment, their minimum viable product faced numerous complaints related to the manual effort of adopting data contracts, which is why their next iteration, shown in Figure 8-3, has so many automation steps. In particular, the steps include reusing the schema definition already being used by data producers, reducing the manual effort of creating a contract spec by using generative AI, and automating the alerting around data contract creation via Slack.

The wider company ultimately viewed data contracts as a success, as it finally enabled GDPR compliance to become more automated rather than relying heavily on manual work. As Christian and Sergio noted:

> Christian: "The GDPR compliance of the process…[is] very important because it's a challenge for the company and it's difficult to deal with it in data."

> Sergio: "Yeah, that's right. That's a huge issue here in Europe, and before [GDPR requirements] we had no idea of where the private data was, in which tables, and how many…. It was a lot of manual work to apply GDPR…. We now have a way and a place to specify the private and personal fields. [For example,] 'What is a private field and what is a personal field?… Is the name private? Is the address OK? The address may be yes, but [what about] the province?' There are a lot of issues, doubts, and discussions with that. [Thus,] being able to check the schema validity in the very beginning of the process instead of at the end when you are consuming data was something huge for us because we…avoid errors instead of fixing them."

For the data platform team itself, the change to their work was a dramatic improvement. For example, the average time an engineer spent on data quality issues dropped from two days a week to only half a day. In just months, 40% of PII is now correctly identified and governed automatically (instead of needing full manual efforts), with 65% of producers reporting they now understand the analytical value of their data (their baseline was 0% before). Teams are now evaluating cost versus value before ingesting new datasets—tempering the artificial scaling of data volumes and related storage costs. And dashboards at Adevinta Spain now consistently show ingestion volume, error rates, and cost breakdowns, which further reinforces transparency and cross-team accountability.

Adevinta Spain had been suffering from a lack of alignment, trust, and accountability, just as Convoy and Glassdoor had, as opposed to some failing related to infrastructure. And, just as in our other adoption stories, a straightforward and pragmatic embrace of data contracts helped create a single source of truth around schema, data value, and responsibility. Considering their predicament prior to data contract adoption, Adevinta Spain's data platform team finally felt they'd passed a critical milestone as overall governance evolved from reactive policing to proactive system design—a system that, in relatively short order, regained the trust of the organization as it proved itself transparent, self-validating, and predictable.

Conclusion

In this chapter, we examined three distinct instances where data professionals at Convoy, Glassdoor, and Adevinta Spain adopted data contracts to address data-related breakdowns in their organizations. While the industries and business models of these three organizations were strikingly different, the inciting drivers of these issues were strikingly similar. Namely, the drivers included schema instability, increased needs for downstream firefighting, manual governance enforcement, and eroding trust in data.

Across the course of these three stories, several patterns emerged:

- Data teams lost unacceptable amounts of time and focus reacting to issues instead of proactively creating value.
- The impact of reactive triaging was severely limited, relying on guesswork, trial and error, and limited internal documentation.
- Upstream misalignment between data producers and consumers was the root of much, if not all, of the downstream chaos data teams were dealing with prior to data contract adoption.
- Organizations were not truly open to change and new ways of thinking until the right people (i.e., leadership, most often) could tangibly feel the fear, stress, and pain of business-critical functions beginning to falter.

Data professionals at each organization independently discovered that, ultimately, tools or technology alone could remedy their situation. Allowing the organization to go along its current path was unacceptable. In each story, the data team realized what their organization needed was a system-level handshake—a means to both codify expectations as early as possible in the data lifecycle and hold those expectations to account through automation, versioning, and visibility. Therefore, these layered accounts benefit our efforts in two ways.

First, the parallels they share among issues, efforts, turning points, and subsequent successes evidence a greater truth, that the closer to the point of data creation that expectations are aligned, the more resilient systems and teams become downstream.

Second, the stories provide information you can use to guide your own potential adoption efforts. As you think about the needs, drivers, and organizational changes required to shift data left, it's worth resisting the natural instinct to overengineer a solution. Additionally, you must extend your efforts beyond the technical comfort zone many data professionals operate within by default.

Start thinking of data's relation to the business as a whole. Begin thinking of data products in your organization by how and how much they support key business functions and drive business success, which we provide guidance on in Chapter 11.

Finally, begin thinking about the people, culture, and operational challenges that must be involved in enacting lasting change in an organization. Because once you realize you have a major role to play in the shift left data movement, the next step becomes learning how to create and maintain the momentum needed to drive data contract adoption forward.

With the end of this chapter, we move on to Part III of the book, where we detail in Chapters 9 to 12 how to build buy-in among leadership, get your first wins with data contracts, measure your impact, and ultimately get data contracts adopted across the entire organization.

## PART III

Getting Leadership Buy-in
for the Data Contract Architecture

## CHAPTER 9

Shift Left: The Cultural Change Needed for Data Contracts

In Part I, we described the data challenges that organizations face today and made clear why they need data contracts to address those problems. Part II addressed the technical details of data contracts, provided a hands-on coding project that implemented data contracts with open source tools, and described three real-world implementations in industry. One undercurrent throughout Parts I and II is the emphasis on how the data contract architecture pattern is tightly coupled to a cultural change in how data is managed throughout the organization.

Part III (Chapters 9 to 12) is where we detail how to bring forth the cultural change to enable the data contract architecture, develop a strategy to get buy-in and your first data contract win, and, finally, measure the success of your implementation. We have labeled this cultural change *shift left data*, drawing parallels to the DevSecOps (i.e., DevOps applied to security) space, which faced challenges around security management and enforcement, much like our industry's data challenges.

In this chapter, we want to zoom in and focus on what needs to take place leading up to and during the cultural shift left data moment within an organization. We'll cover what we are doing to set up data contract implementation for success and gain adoption across the wider organization beyond data teams. Many of the lessons we'll share stem from encountering and overcoming numerous setbacks across implementations among various organizations that we hope you can avoid.

We'll then touch on how we realized the need to explicitly address the perception gap between software developers (e.g., data producers) and data developers (e.g., data consumers) before any in-code data contract implementation takes place, all on software engineers' (SWEs') terms. Finally, this chapter will include relevant lessons from Chad's first data contract implementation at a previous digital freight brokerage startup, Convoy, where the foundation of our understanding of the data contract architecture and shift left data movement formed.

What Needs to Be True: What We Missed About Shift Left Data

Despite the clues—from Chad's time working at Convoy and Mark's professional shift from data science to data engineering—our initial hypothesis for how shift left data adoption should take place in organizations turned out to have one minor flaw. We underestimated the depth and complexity the adoption process itself would have in practice.

In speaking with early adopters—those initial data teams we supported through their own shift left data efforts—we quickly realized the adoption process was far more involved when it comes to working with software engineers to get a proof of concept off the ground. We faced a much higher adoption curve, and as a result, it quickly became clear that software engineers needed to take much more responsibility and ownership of the adoption process itself. When they didn't, the adoption process failed to take hold, or stalled out altogether. This means software engineers need to have a stake in ownership and understand what's in it for them to take on more complexity and constraints.

Regardless of how data teams tried adjusting their own strategic approach to foster adoption, we had overlooked how critical it would be to persuade software engineers to become data contract champions. The question then became how exactly to lead this change.

Thankfully, it was at this point that we opted to revisit our prior assumptions around data contract adoption with some much-needed first-principles thinking, or the process of breaking a situation or problem down into its most basic elements. In our experience, first principles are given lip service far more often than they are pressed into service—the former being much easier than the latter.

An analogy that Chad often uses around first-principles thinking is the question, "Can you reach the bottom of this body of water?" Without digging further (e.g., "Bottom of a pool?," "Bottom of an ocean?," etc.), one is likely not set up for success. Say it is the bottom of the ocean—then the question becomes, "What needs to exist to ensure success?" Without going into detail, it's clear to see how each layer reveals more and more assumptions around requirements for success. It's often why we constantly ask ourselves, "Can we go deeper?"

In our context, we needed our application of first principles to help us drill down to a core truth, and to get to it as quickly as possible. Therefore, we forced ourselves through this reasoning in its purest form—focusing on the following key question:

"What must be true to solve the problem of the lack of software engineer adoption of shift left data?"

After much iteration, we landed on the following: to solve shift left data adoption, software engineers would need to see it as something so beneficial to their role as to be worth fighting for. But for that to happen, however, we first needed to fully understand and appreciate why, by default, they didn't already see it that way. That led to our realization that not only did a significant perception gap exist between software and data teams, but we were also attempting to execute on the wrong side of it by focusing on the data team first. Table 9-1 highlights the key differences between these two groups with respect to working with data.

Table 9-1. Comparing the work of software and data teams

Attribute	Software engineering teams	Data teams
Individual contributor titles	• Frontend engineer • Backend engineer • Full stack engineer • QA engineer	• Data engineer • Analytics engineer • Data analyst • Data scientist
Scope	Developing scalable and maintainable code that provides discrete actions (e.g., create a user) that are repeatable	Providing the organization, and/or stakeholders, relevant insights and/or recommendations based on past information
Key internal stakeholders	• Product managers • Other engineering teams from different services • Security and DevOps	• Business stakeholders consuming data • Engineers who put data products into production • Domain experts to inform data assumptions
Interactions with data	Upstream transactional databases for CRUD operations, logs pertaining to captured events within code, APIs, and potentially ingestion of third-party data. Putting data products in production within the services they own.	Downstream analytical databases utilizing large table scans, aggregates, and statistics R&D around data products, such as developing ML models, product analytics, etc.
How value is created	Adding to and/or optimizing the functionality of a product and/or service that directly drives revenue for the business. In addition, creating internal tools for improving developer experience and developer velocity—many popular open source tools from Big Tech have come from such internal tools.	Providing insights that create a strategic advantage in the market, identify potential risk, or optimize the customer experience (e.g., recommender systems). Data teams *can* drive direct value and substantially higher revenue than software teams, through deployed data products (e.g., recommender systems), but this requires substantial initial investment as compared to software.
Working style	Clearly scoped deliverables (ideally) for discrete units of change within a product and/or service's application code. While less experimental than the data teams, the complexity arises in the need to coordinate a high volume of changes across multiple engineers, teams, and/or microservices—hence why ubiquity of version control is an expected standard.	Experimental R&D with the understanding that projects may lead to a dead end and be hampered by available data and/or data quality. This unpredictability is offset by the outsize impact of successful projects in creating a strategic advantage. Furthermore, this is why it's rare to see data teams adopt methodologies such as Agile.

You may be wondering, "Why do software engineers need to learn data best practices when we already have data engineers?" Scaling data engineering capabilities is not a linear process—managers can't afford to hire a new engineer for every data team, compliance role, or business function added as their organization grows. Even if operational budgets could enable this, hypothetically, it would lead to bloat and inefficiencies.

In fact, Fred Brooks, in his book *The Mythical Man-Month* (Addison-Wesley), highlights how development, by its very nature, relies upon an ongoing whirl of complex interrelationships—making communication overhead a feature, not a bug. Budgetary constraints aside, this is why throwing more people at a software engineering problem has the opposite of its intended effect—the time SWEs need to manage communication begins increasing faster than individual task time can be reduced through more hands being on deck. Brooks concludes that "adding more [SWEs] to a project often lengthens rather than shortens the schedule, because the increased complexity of coordination outweighs any gains in productivity."

In summary, software engineering is a discipline that cannot cleanly scale up along with a growing organization. The overwhelming focus in this world is tightly wound around the daily demands of the software development lifecycle. These daily demands necessitate that the SWE bounce back and forth repeatedly between product-related collaboration and production-specific tasks. Because of this, they are overtasked and often working in the dark—from a data utilization perspective—as anything that isn't helping a software engineer code, test, ship, or debug an existing product threatens to complicate or delay those waiting to be worked on next.

And it's here, having just a glimpse of the world through the software engineer's eyes, that we ask ourselves: is it still surprising that some new data-related request or initiative posited as an "opportunity" would, in fact, feel like yet another responsibility being added to their overflowing plates? One that is delivered by teams or departments that barely, if ever, interface with their daily challenges, hurdles, and expectations? Is it hard to understand why a reflexive response of "I didn't sign up for this" is fully warranted, if not completely natural?

No, of course not.

In the next section, we will explore what these perception gaps look like in practice based on Chad's experience leading the data platform team at Convoy.

Understanding the Stakes: Three Real-World Examples of Perception Gap Complications

Now that it's clear that a perception gap will naturally exist between data and software developers, our operative goal shifts. We need to resolve said gap before we begin any attempt to shift data left in an organization. Because when highly specialized teams fail to bridge the divide between their different ways of thinking, the consequences can be enormous—crippling the ability for high-purpose initiatives like shift left data to ever get off the ground.

To thoroughly illustrate the stakes at hand, we'll examine relevant high-stakes projects. We'll take a look at situations Chad experienced implementing data contracts at Convoy. We'll also walk through the catastrophic dangers of unattended gaps and provide practical, shift left relevant insights regarding data contract implementation.

Perception Gaps Fuel Faulty Assumptions

Convoy's goal was to leverage machine learning and automation to optimize freight logistics and reduce empty miles—ultimately to increase earnings for carriers while lowering costs for shippers. Convoy's founders designed it to function as the first two-sided marketplace of the freight logistics world, its contemporaries being Uber and Airbnb.

The first issue related to perception gaps at Convoy began simply enough, with internal teams taking what they thought was a straightforward approach to estimating the time it should take to get from Point A to Point B. With Convoy installed on their phones, functionality like a dashboard that could help carriers plan their routes made perfect sense. Internally, when the analytics team at Convoy needed to calculate the estimated time of arrival, recommended routes, or load-to-drive assignments for its carriers (i.e., truck drivers), it also made sense to combine available distance data with average speeds.

What didn't occur to these internal teams, however, was that the reality of their carriers was much more complicated in practice. Due to a variety of uncontrollable factors—traffic congestion, parking availability, and even distance between rest stops—carriers constantly adjusted and readjusted their routes in real time. Data dashboards that made absolute sense in their original spreadsheets fell apart when put into practice. Convoy's goal with the dashboard was to help carriers handle more shipments more efficiently. But the exact opposite happened, causing late pickups to soar.

Moreover, the startup suffered reputational damage. Carriers who tried to use this early iteration of the dashboard felt like Convoy didn't get them. Data teams, thanks to those seemingly logical assumptions made at a distance, quickly realized they'd been operating out of ignorance—and had, quite literally, engineered a feature of the Convoy app that actively alienated half of its user base.

Internal analytics teams at Convoy thought they could plan carrier routes using a formula that made sense to them. But what made sense to internal teams overlooked commonly experienced, real-time constraints that carriers experienced every day. This demonstrates that when perception gaps exist between key parties, even the most "straightforward" assumptions can be critically flawed.

Perception Gaps Obscure Real-World Complexity

One reason the shipping and freight industry was ripe for disruption was that so many milestones in a given supply chain were either recorded manually or not at all. A prime example arrived at the operative Point B, when a carrier reached their destination for delivery. Ideally, a carrier will always arrive at their destination at an estimated time or earlier. However, the earlier a driver arrived, the higher the chance they'd have to wait at their destination to unload their shipment. This, in turn, punished drivers for being efficient. Time spent waiting around stuck in a queue was time they weren't making money.

The industry then sought to correct this with "detention pay," where shipping companies would compensate carriers who lost time while waiting to unload their shipments in this way. This was a well-intentioned solution, but it was a bit too easy to fudge, and it was difficult for shippers to account for remotely. In another attempt, Convoy's data engineers proposed how the app could potentially make detention pay work as intended. To do so, Convoy partnered with loading facilities in the app's network to install geofencing hardware. Once these digital boundaries were online, the Convoy app on a given driver's phone would ping when they arrived at their destination, confirming the truck had, in fact, physically arrived at a given time. This would keep detention time honest. This new arrival timestamp could also be an invaluable internal data point, feeding into everything from the on-time performance dashboard to Convoy's cost and labor models.

Again, though, the ongoing perception gap between Convoy and its carriers clouded underlying issues with the logic of the geofencing solution. And, just like the route optimization dashboard, these issues became readily apparent when Convoy deployed this new solution—as internal teams soon learned that "arriving" at one's destination contained many shades of gray. For example, in reality many carriers who arrived to find they'd be waiting for an open dock opted to park nearby while waiting for their turn. Since the geofencing was limited to the loading facility and not the surrounding area, these carriers hadn't reached their destination, according to the app, even though a driver might be stationed right outside it.

Alternatively, it wasn't uncommon for a carrier's phone signal to drop upon reaching the facility, showing a driver as en route when, in fact, they'd already unloaded and driven off to pick up their next load of cargo. Some drivers, understandably, didn't like knowing there was an app on their phone tracking where they were at every moment of the day. Many drivers began to change how they used the app, making sure it only pinged when they personally felt like they'd "arrived" to dock. Others turned off location sharing altogether.

As a result, the much-coveted arrival metric grew increasingly skewed—with actual arrivals sometimes being an hour off or more. This began causing chaos for many of Convoy's downstream data consumers until, after much time and effort, root cause analysis traced the source of the discrepancies back to the geofencing feature.

Like all of Convoy's initiatives at the time, offering a geofencing solution to keep detention pay honest was well-intentioned. However, while a driver and cargo being at their destination was a clear and simple concept internally, the realities of arriving were much more fluid for carriers. The perception gap experienced in Convoy prevented engineers from clearly thinking through the whole situation. As a result, nuanced user perspectives—like a want for privacy and concerns that Big Brother would be watching—never made their way into key internal conversations.

However, Convoy's challenges with the perception gaps weren't limited to internal teams and external users—though any impacts to the app would, of course, impact shippers or carriers (or both). Sometimes the gap would lead to situations where two teams would end up working at cross-purposes. This is exactly what happened with our final example, which involved Convoy's job auction and the advent of the auto-bid feature.

Perception Gaps Can Pit Teams Against Each Other

Convoy's auction feature was arguably the heart of the app experience, acting as a mini-marketplace for shippers and carriers. Carrier companies and individual drivers could use the app to see a list of shipments (i.e., loads) in need of transport. Each of these loads had bidding windows during which a carrier would pay the price they'd be willing to haul the load for.

During the bidding window, Convoy's system would simultaneously compare bid variables while accounting for related factors—the route, timing constraints, driving reliability, etc. The app then awarded a bidder the job, having ensured the winner had time to travel to the shipper and secure the load. All things being equal, this was effective—at least for the shippers.

Carriers, on the other hand, had to work a little harder to get the Convoy auction working for them. The auctions were manual, meaning carriers had to watch the app closely during open bidding windows—adjusting their bids in real time to remain competitive. Few drivers had time to continuously check and rebid when they were on the road handling existing business.

This is exactly why Convoy introduced the auto-bid feature. This was, in a sense, a productive example of a team iterating on needs and perspectives that were not their own. The problem, however, was the team failed to consider the perspective of how the auction itself would function if things shifted into automatic.

The challenge fell to a team of internal software engineers, and the thinking was this: auto-bid would allow drivers to set an initial price to haul a load. Once this amount (let's say $500) was locked in, Convoy would automatically bid on behalf of the driver, undercutting competing bids in real time until it reached a floor the driver also specified (let's say $200). On a case-by-case basis, this made sense—as the driver went about their business, they knew that Convoy's auto-bid would stay within set parameters.

This worked well for drivers. However, since it worked well, it became popular, meaning the amount of bidding within the auction soon exploded. Unfortunately, no one had considered the effects of this, least of all on the functionality of the auction itself. Remember, the status quo in most software engineering environments involves SWEs having little awareness, if any, of what happens downstream with respect to data.

Practically overnight, exponentially more bids began flooding each auction window, as driver auto-bid accounts fought against each other to secure shipments on their owner's behalf. To the engineers who created auto-bid, user adoption and the subsequent explosion of bids that started taking place in a relatively short time seemed like enormous success.

This caught the data team responsible for the auction house itself off guard—the abrupt and massive change in bidding volume resembled either bad data or a pipeline anomaly. The pricing machine learning models they'd meticulously trained on the comparatively glacial pace of manual, human-paced bids quickly grew confused and started mispricing the ceiling and floor prices for each shipment. This, in turn, resulted in each auction window running longer than it should have. With the data team thinking this was an anomaly at first, it took months and millions of dollars to trace the issue back to the implementation of the auto-bid functionality.

Technically, the auto-bid feature worked precisely as its designers had envisioned, lifting the burden of staying on top of the bidding process off drivers' shoulders. But they had no visibility into the auction house bidding algorithm's functionality, as the team with that knowledge sat firmly nestled on the opposite side of this particular perception gap. Because of this separation, it never occurred to the auto-bid team what a sudden, exponential increase in bids per user would do to the auction process itself.

Now, to be fair, Convoy, in classic fashion as a startup, had buckled up and was moving fast and breaking things. Its successes, especially those of the data teams, definitively outnumbered the setbacks noted. And, just as it often is with any high-stakes opportunity, smarts and experience also weren't directly at fault. We described this pattern in Chapter 6, specifically the business logic lifecycle repeated in Figure 9-1. Specifically, we called out how "data quality issues arise when the data doesn't keep up in representing the business logic."

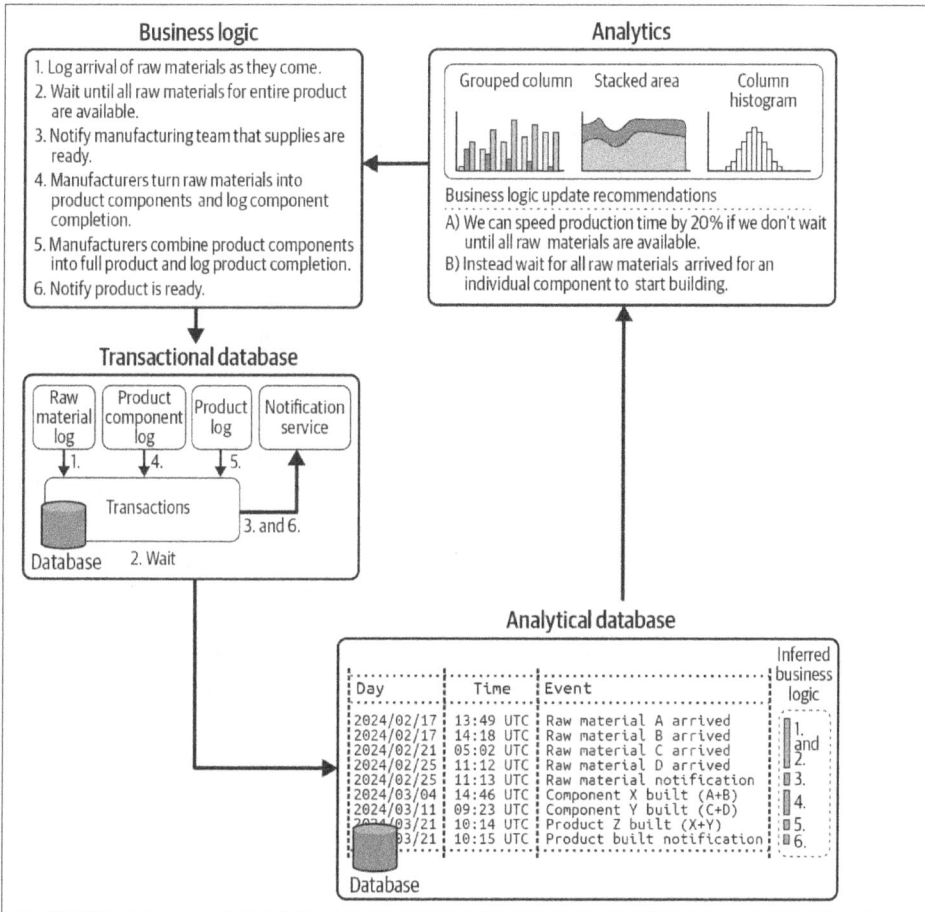

Figure 9-1. Business logic lifecycle

Unfortunately, what Convoy experienced in the breakdown of the business logic lifecycle is the norm for most organizations working with data, and why we turned to data contracts. Collectively, these three examples from Chad's formative, fascinating, and, at times, white-knuckling-the-dashboard experience at Convoy serve as a firm and final real-world lesson as to why perception gaps need to be identified and resolved in any data-driven organization—especially when the stakes are high.

Failure to do so leaves shift left data adoption in an unacceptably unclear position. But being aware of the gaps is not enough, thus the next section describes how to start closing them.

Enabling Adoption: A Strategic Approach for Closing the Software-Data Gap

In our eyes, and in accordance with our first-principles thinking, the following must be true to solve this second shift left data problem:

- Data teams need to take the first step: work to find a bridge between themselves and software engineers and then initiate the process of building trust.
- All parties involved in closing the perception gap with SWEs must insist on evidence-based decision making.
- Once all parties agree on and understand how to move forward, regular and productive feedback meetings with key stakeholders interested in adopting data contracts must be established to sustain momentum in collaboration.
- Data teams establish key milestones in advance (with leadership buy-in) so that shift left efforts evolve alongside the needs of the organization.
- In addition to moving the needle on data contract-related performance metrics, SWE buy-in and quality-of-life improvements must occur during those critical phases of shift left data adoption.

Note that all this assumes you have executive sponsorship for driving change within the organization (which we detail how to get in Chapter 11). It's particularly important to have a top-down directive to set incentives for software engineers to care about data contracts; closing the software-data gap helps you identify what those incentives should be.

We'll now flesh out each step for you with practical advice and learnings we've acquired to date.

Finding a Bridge and Fostering Trust

The best software engineers, Addy Osmani informs us in his book *Software Engineering: The Soft Parts* (self-published), think of the user first:

> Let customer needs guide every decision and prioritization. Putting users front and center means starting with empathy. It involves deeply understanding the problems users face and the impact our work can have on their lives.

This is fitting, as our goal, in a simple sense, is to successfully and sustainably posit software engineers as the "users" of shift left data in modern organizations. For our purposes, your first users should be key stakeholders in the software engineering process. Although it may seem counterintuitive, don't rely on org charts to identify the first key individuals.

As Lili Duan, Emily Sheeren, and Leigh M. Weiss discuss, writing for McKinsey & Company (*https://oreil.ly/efdWk*) "hidden influencers" within software engineering teams and departments may function as better internal catalysts and co-advocates for shift left data. Aim to "bring them into such efforts in the earliest stages and…get their input and guidance on planning and direction—as well as help with execution. Changes made with the support of these influential employees are vastly more likely to succeed in the long run than changes delivered from on high."

To make first contact with software engineering teams and individuals to begin this discussion, the 1-10-100 rule of data quality is an excellent way to establish common values between the worlds of data and software engineering.

Developed by Yu Sang Chang and George Labovitz (*https://oreil.ly/faZfQ*) in 1992, data professionals know of the rule as a means to quantify the escalating cost of poor data quality. But it has been readily adopted by software engineers, as the same cost-escalation principles apply: SWEs can spend $1 fixing a bug during the coding or design phases (for instance, during unit testing). Or $10 fixing the bug during quality assurance testing, perhaps during debugging or regression tests. Or, comparatively, $100 to fix the bug post-release, through hotfixes or reputation damage management. A software engineer who appreciates this thinking appreciates shift left data. They simply don't realize it yet.

To be extremely clear at the outset—shift left data will not be an everything, every-where, all-at-once situation. This approach would diminish the chances of success for all involved. As we'll cover in Chapter 11, the data contract adoption and implementation must be intentionally conservative and strategic—focused on the organization's Tier-1 data products at the outset, aiming to transform each into what we refer to as production-grade pipelines.

In addition to maximizing the chances of lasting shift left data success, the advantages of this highly restrained approach are legion. Most notably, it will become easier and quicker to align on and lock down mutual goals and shared expectations together. Software engineers involved in these early stages will experience the net-positive impacts of shift left data sooner, the initial improvements to Tier-1 products (and related ROI) will become apparent faster, and you and your software engineering counterparts will begin building a shared vocabulary together.

For example, in Mark's previous role as a product data scientist, he was tasked with creating the funnel analytics infrastructure for the product onboarding process. Thankfully, this team ensured that SWEs consulted with the data project lead during the product scoping phase. Initially, SWEs only wanted to pass the URL slugs (e.g., company.com/app/onboarding/step-1) without an ID for the iteration of the onboarding funnel; the SWEs emphasized simplicity given this was v1 of the new onboarding. This would be problematic on the data side, as it requires complex and hard to maintain business logic accounting for any subsequent (and inevitable) changes to the funnel, A/B testing, or even special funnel edge cases for enterprise customers—ultimately making the product funnel analytics slow and unreliable. With that said, adding a funnel ID would require a refactor that would extend the project well past the deadline, which was something the SWEs were unwilling to do.

Mark thus focused on making a case for preventing slowed down iteration cycles for a key product they oversee, rather than emphasizing the impact of the quality of the data itself. He compromised on its implementation: it would not be part of the v1 but would be coupled to the first change to the funnel. If he knew of them back then, Mark would have wanted data contracts on this key data product.

Charting the Course with Objective Information

When shift left data wayfinding and decision making begin, all parties must agree that this will be evidence-based. Data leaders must then ensure SWEs will honestly perceive all actions moving forward as irreproachably fair and unbiased. It's not enough to know it to be true.

We've taken on the task of *showing* it to be true. Moreover, we know that teams that engage in transparent decision-making processes—such as evidence-based approaches—are more likely to build trusting relationships over time.

As teams agree upon objective, data-driven definitions of success, these definitions naturally become part of the shared vocabulary that will continue to grow between data and software engineers. They will prove invaluable once shift left data is under-way—a common language for evaluating whether or not given initiatives are on track will, thankfully, already be in play.

When working with data teams, one of the first sets of data we want to capture are:

- The number of data incidents per week, grouped by their severity
- The average number of staff involved in root cause analysis and resolving the issues, stratified by role (e.g., data analysts, SWE, etc.)
- For each role involved, the average salary (we often use public salary metrics not from the company to maintain privacy, and give leadership the option to input accurate salary numbers)
- The average number of hours spent resolving an issue, grouped by role
- If possible, the incurred cost (e.g., data backfills) or lost revenue of a data asset and/or product being unavailable due to a data incident (note that many data teams we talked to struggle with this and thus turned to data contracts)

With this data, you can build a financial model of the impact of data incidents with respect to work hours multiplied by staff salary, compute and storage costs, and revenue impact. In addition, you can quantify the opportunity cost based on the work hours spent on data incidents grouped by role, which is especially pertinent to leaders who feel the strain of required work but can't get the budget for additional headcount.

Evolving Shift Left Data Alongside Your Organization

As shift left data adoption begins, data leaders need to take a technology-forward approach to keeping data teams in sync with SWEs who are, and will continue to be, directly responsible for data contract implementation.

Additionally, while the adoption process does begin through the direct collaboration of these two departments, it cannot end there. Data leaders must also keep the shift left movement aligned with the ongoing trajectory of the organization itself. Just as Chad's time at Convoy clearly illustrates, ongoing iteration and change must be embraced as a constant. Fortunately, it often takes only a few strategic initiatives to keep shift left aligned with the business as its objectives ebb and flow over time.

With that said, sustaining these efforts manually will ultimately lead to momentum slowing down—which is why many data governance programs that rely solely on people and processes struggle to scale. In addition to executive sponsorship, there needs to be an emphasis on automatically detecting changes among data assets to continually highlight the need for data contracts (often the first step data teams take when building a case for software engineering involvement).

Furthermore, leaders involved in the shift left initiative need to build off the foundation between data and software engineering teams—adding in a governance mechanism that includes key product managers, line-of-sight product owners, and relevant domain leads. This will ensure these tertiary parties can weigh in on how to support and scale the adoption process. Again, emphasis should be placed on how technology can drive the cultural change of shift left, as compared to relying solely on recurring check-in meetings. For example, the collected metadata, the data assets' subsequent changes, and the impacted parties of such changes can be automatically highlighted with data contracts, and thus these signals should guide discussions with these tertiary stakeholders when most relevant. We have already seen a similar pattern among SWEs with branch protections for merging code, where automatic tests enforce the expectations of what quality code entails, and culturally it's extremely frowned upon to manually override this protection.

Thus, remember our fundamental question of "What must be true to solve the problem of the lack of software engineer adoption of shift left data?" The previous paragraphs address this by highlighting how leveraging technology reduces the friction of adopting these new practices by meaningfully reducing the minimum overhead to operationalize and maintain them. In the next section we will cover how to measure this adoption among software engineers.

Measuring SWE Quality-of-Life Improvements During Shift Left Data Adoption

Assuming you have continued executive sponsorship, the success or failure of shift left data in your organization will ultimately boil down to one thing—how quickly and tangibly the software engineers you've convinced to take necessary ownership of the adoption process begin to benefit from it. That is, when the net-positive effects of data contract implementation in the software development lifecycle begin to make their lives better. Ideally you'll quickly hear about this firsthand. But it's certainly worth the effort needed to actually measure the effects of these benefits as they begin to manifest. And this means measuring the moment of shift left ignition by looking at three key areas: SWE satisfaction and engagement, reduced rework and friction, and downtime and incident reduction.

An easy way to begin doing so is to deploy brief pulse surveys (two to three questions) monthly or quarterly during the adoption period to efficiently keep a day-to-day sense of how your key SWEs feel about the shift left data adoption process. In these surveys, track ongoing "satisfaction" as a KPI with a blend of data points relating to topics like perceived collaboration quality and levels of impact on existing projects/expectations. Finally, compare the pulse survey results to the more qualitative data gained from scheduled milestone reviews, progress check-ins, and feedback sections that take place during the adoption process.

Next, once initial data contract implementation on the organization's Tier-1 products is complete, related incidents due to unclear or breaking data requirements should drop. Concurrently, the frequency of SWE work related to these products should also drop. Therefore, ticket volume related to SWEs revisiting or redeploying code during the adoption makes for a simple yet informative way to measure improvements. For tickets related to products that do occur, shortened time-to-fix during shift left adoption becomes an indicator of better alignment and improved collaboration within the software development lifecycle—which should correlate in feedback meetings to SWEs feeling less burdened and more able to focus on their projects in pipeline.

Fewer data-related issues (i.e., less stress) involving an organization's key products can boost morale and collaborative bandwidth, quickly improving operations between software and data teams. As a result, the amount of time required for teams to recover from issues should begin to lessen as day-to-day working conditions improve for software engineers and teams.

Production incidents linked to Tier-1 product data issues should also fall off precipitously during shift left data adoption, as data contracts control and account for root issues previously caused by flawed data ingestion, schema mismatch, and other data quality–related root causes. Having fewer data-driven production issues on even a few strategically selected data products means fewer late-night or weekend fire drills for software engineers, quickly becoming a tangible and much-appreciated quality-of-life improvement for SWEs.

In this way, data leaders can ensure pivotal SWEs are the first to experience the benefits of shift left data success. Furthermore, software engineers need to see themselves as part of the success of data products and be incentivized to do so. For example, data teams are traditionally credited for the successful performance of a machine learning model. If an ML model leveraged data assets under contract, then one can connect its success to the availability of the data assets generated by upstream software teams.

This all said, there may still be software engineers scratching their heads at all this, wondering, "Yeah, but how can you be sure this will all go like you say?"

"That's the best part," Chad often says when fielding this question. "In DevSecOps, it already has."

What the Rising Need for DevSecOps Demonstrated

We began this chapter asking what really needs to be true to solve the shift left data problem. Answering this question involves data leaders leveraging understanding and empathy to close the gaps in perception between their teams and the software engineers in their organizations.

We now address software engineers directly (hello there) to approach the second question of our first principles thinking. That is, if data leaders embrace what we've discussed and suggested throughout this chapter, will it actually solve the shift left data problem through the lens of software engineers it must, by necessity, affect?

We believe so, especially as evidenced by the shift left movement that coalesced into what we now know as DevSecOps around 2014. In our opinion, the details regarding the need for and successful shift of security from a reactive, downstream process up into the software development lifecycle are instructive, mirroring the data quality issues we face in organizations today.

To understand the parallels between the two shift left patterns, we need to look back a bit before 2014—circa 2012, where the workplace pressures experienced in the software engineering world were similar to what they are today. The experience of a software engineer at this time was much the same as it is now—tight sprint deadlines, on-call rotations, and ever-growing backlogs were the norm. And, just like now, software engineers a decade ago also had to be good at maintaining a respectful, "not my problem" mentality to protect their ability to get their own job done.

What someone in another department proposed as a new and shiny opportunity (e.g., real-time everything, more big data platforms, using machine learning for this, etc.) was viewed with healthy and self-preservational suspicion by the average SWE.

In these before shift left times, security lived far right in the deployment chain. This meant that security concerns and testing took place a comparatively long time after the code was written.

However, three key shifts in the industry—involving technical shifts, process gaps, and evolving tooling demands—caused major issues for those charged with data security and compliance. Let's review those shifts:

Accelerating development cycles
> The ascension of DevOps and Agile methodologies was compressing development timelines dramatically. As a direct result, relying on traditional late-stage security checks was quickly becoming impractical. As CI/CD pipelines began deploying code to production multiple times per day, vulnerabilities discovered post-development by security teams were quickly going from $10 to $100 in more organizations. Delays and subsequent costs to fix increased rapidly. Security leaders in the midst of this faced a reckoning, realizing they could no longer afford to act as gatekeepers at the end of software development lifecycle. This prompted their thinking to shift upstream.

Expanding cloud and container attack surfaces
> Security teams in the early 2010s grappled with how the proliferation of modern, cloud-native architectures—like microservices and containers—introduced new vulnerabilities that perimeter-based security models couldn't address. For example, early containerization (Docker, LXC) and cloud platforms (AWS EC2, OpenStack) introduced new attack vectors by 2012. These risks directly expanded the attack surface in organizations that adopted them, forcing security integration earlier in development. Additionally, popular CI/CD pipelines in heavy use at the time often lacked native security tools for cloud or container workflows. Exploitable gaps surfaced—unpatched base images and secrets in plain text, for example.
>
> The widening adoption of cloud-native architectures brought with it a tidal shift in how regulation was written and enforced. As a result, static IP/host-based security approaches were further rendered obsolete—forcing security teams to look further left. These teams needed to build and maintain automated compliance toolchains to codify policies in their organizations.

Increasing regulatory and compliance pressures
> At this same time, stricter data protection laws (e.g., GDPR, HIPAA, PCI DSS) and high-profile breaches dragged data compliance and governance into the spotlight—making it clear that they needed to become business-critical requirements. More importantly, this garnered the attention of CEOs and nontech executives as they began to understand the potentially catastrophic consequences of a security breach or data leak. This spotlight was uncomfortable for many overseeing data security as, increasingly, manual audits couldn't scale with

DevOps velocity. Compliance-as-code practices were quickly becoming the only alternative.

These three factors coalesced into a definitive paradigm: security could no longer follow some after-the-fact process. Shifting security left and into the software development lifecycle, along with the formalization of DevSecOps, was, as we know, the solution. But even with this inevitability, there was still resistance.

Security teams couldn't mandate this solution—it took time, collaboration, and integration. Where security teams saw the future (the same future we now operate in), software engineers and developers had every right to resist what they said was the addition of more security tasks in their daily workflows.

Here, again, was a perception gap that had to close before shift left security could occur. This required security teams to employ empathy and understanding. Considering both the stakes and the shifting security landscape, DevOps adoption was far more important than perfection at the outset.

Thinking through things from the perspective of software engineers and developers made it clear that proposing smaller, more phase-specific security measures implemented during the early stages of the software development lifecycle—like static analysis, dependency management, or unit tests—would be much more productive (not to mention developer-friendly) than insisting on manual penetration testing or full-scale integration testing. Additionally, shift left leaders acknowledged that introducing a new and separate security system that software devs would have to learn or monitor in isolation would be a nonstarter. Instead, they focused on solutions that utilized tools already in use—like Git and CI/CD pipelines.

Embracing this home-field advantage proved instrumental in formalizing DevSecOps. Shifting left was now firmly in the purview of those most affected, making adoption a natural and ongoing process.

Seeing (and Embracing) Shift Left Data for What It Truly Is

Now, in coming back to the future, we have evidence that our proposed approach to shift left data will solve a shared problem for data and software engineering teams. But how best to leverage details from the DevSecOps story to the benefit and advantage of software engineers and departments? Let's start by looking at how we shift our thinking to get the most out of data shifting left:

Adoption as ownership
Software engineers, collectively, aren't looking for more responsibilities. But they certainly should be seeking recognition. As a result of being boxed into roles by the increasing demands of data products, the impact and influence your work has throughout an organization can be largely invisible. Shifting data left is also

an opportunity to shift more credit to where credit is due, as the output of software engineers' produced data is transformed into valuable data products downstream. Own the code, sure. But, in doing so, welcome this chance to own and benefit from how the essential work you're doing is helping your organization thrive. Furthermore, this recognition needs to come from leaders who set the directive for SWEs to own more data responsibilities upstream.

Data quality as a feature, not someone else's bug
Shift left data makes much more sense if we simply think of data as a product itself, not an afterthought. As software engineers, the products you design generate data essential to analytics, customer insights, and machine learning initiatives. If the data these products produce is unpredictable or malformed, this reflects poorly on the product. And on you. While this may seem daunting, given the scale of data within some organizations, teams can start small by only focusing on not breaking the data assets pertaining to Tier-1 data products.

Prioritizing keeping things whole over cleaning up messes
As your data friends should keep in mind, software engineers have been trapped in the old pattern of after-the-fact $100 problem-solving for far too long. Instead, they can embrace a new way of working, one where discovering broken datasets weeks after deployment—requiring emergency patches, reverts, or investigation—becomes a thing of the past.

SWEs can easily catch inconsistencies or unintended logic changes in code reviews, integration tests, or runtime checks. Just like DevSecOps proved, and continues to prove, shift left is the optimal way to operate. Why wouldn't we want the same?

It's undeniable—data is heavily coupled with code. And the sooner that software engineers get on board, the sooner shift left data will begin to benefit them directly. It won't be easy. But it can be a win-win. So, when data leaders call a meeting to discuss getting adoption started in your own organization, do your best to drop your guard a bit, engage in some first-principles thinking, and bring the data team into your world.

Conclusion

This chapter began with our detailing how we had to rethink our approach to shift left data—realizing we needed to ensure that software engineers would be willing to take on much more responsibility during the adoption process itself. We then covered how we corrected for this error, what we learned by doing so, and finally addressed software engineers directly. A parallel process that led to DevSecOps is evidence that our recalibrated approach to shift left data does, in fact, point the right way forward.

Details we covered in this chapter include:

- First-principles thinking helped us diagnose why data professionals were struggling to implement shift left data in their organizations.
- Data leaders must work to understand shift left data through the lens of software engineers and the software development lifecycle.
- Perception gaps compromise progress in data-driven environments, and three instructive examples of this happened during Chad's tenure at Convoy.
- Data leaders should strategize to close the perception gap between data and software engineering teams before the shift left data adoption process begins.
- The DevSecOps origin story should encourage software engineers that shift left data doesn't just stand to benefit them directly—the benefits are instrumental to the success of the adoption process itself.

One key aspect to highlight here is that while we emphasized the importance of the software engineering perspective at an industry-level overview, we strongly encourage you to understand the unique processes and constraints of SWEs within your organization. If you are a software engineer yourself, recognize that these processes and constraints may not be obvious to your downstream counterparts (see "OLTP Versus OLAP and Its Implications for Data Quality" on page 34). Regardless, for the shift left data initiative to succeed, both the data and the software teams must have a desire to work with each other, with leadership buy-in and key SWE champions supporting the efforts.

Now that we've covered what's needed to set shift left data adoption up for success, we move on to the next chapter to address change management comprehensively: how managing the combination of people, process, and technology within an organization is mission-critical for realizing long-term shift-data success.

## CHAPTER 10

Change Management: The Crux of People, Process, and Technology

In Part II of this book, we covered how to implement data contracts from a technological perspective. While that's extremely useful, the reality of getting a new process adopted within an organization relies heavily on people. This is especially true for data contracts since they serve to bridge silos across the organization, with each silo having different motivations and constraints (e.g., software and data teams).

Part III of this book details how to get leadership buy-in for the data contract architecture, and specifically creating a data quality strategy, getting your first wins with data contracts, and measuring your impact. We have spent years learning how to build adoption of data contracts within organizations, ranging from Chad implementing the architecture within his previous job at a startup, to us working on implementations at *Fortune* 100 companies. We hope this section of the book helps you navigate the journey of adoption, and ideally avoid the hard lessons we learned along the way.

One lesson that stood out the most to us was that while it was relatively easy to get buy-in for data contracts from data engineers, leadership was still hesitant to invest. It's obvious to us now that leaders don't invest in technology—they invest in solving strategic problems, and technology is one of many levers to do so. Time and time again, the strategic problem that got the attention of leadership and ultimately investment in data contracts was *change management*.

This chapter details this key lesson, and will serve as the framing for subsequent sections of this book. To be clear, the idea of change management is not new, but it's extremely powerful as a concept that easily translates pains felt between software engineers, data developers, and nontechnical business stakeholders. Building on the foundation of change management, we will finish the chapter with how you can create your data quality strategy.

The Importance of Change Management

What type of product is GitHub? Most people might say it's a DevOps platform. After all, everything GitHub facilitates is a component of DevOps: code review, unit tests, integration tests, code diffs, repos, merging and branching, subscribers, and change-logs. But we see it differently. GitHub might be a DevOps tool, but it's a federated change management platform. Its raison d'être is to create automated processes that reduce the risk of changing code across a complex, heterogeneous codebase.

Branching and merging? You're parallelizing change. Pull requests, code review, and code diff? Human-in-the-loop change review. Subscribers, changelogs, notifications? Systems for being notified of change.

Why is change management important? Because unmanaged change is the primary cause of quality and governance problems. Whether it's data quality issues, gover-nance issues, compliance, or other regulatory problems, every one of these can be tied back to change: change to the codebase, change to business logic, change in data users, change in expectations, change in producers, and change in consumers.

This is a problem for software systems because technology doesn't prevent change. In fact, it shouldn't. Change is an inevitable part of our industry. As highlighted in the business logic lifecycle in Chapter 6, the product and company will evolve, as will our tools, infrastructure, frameworks, and ideas. This very book represents a change that may motivate you to create systems for managing change.

Given that change is such a ubiquitous part of the data industry, it's surprising that change management isn't discussed more openly. After all, according to change management consultant Al Lee-Bourke (*https://oreil.ly/8kr-h*), "the most common percentage given to adoption and change management [within large projects] is 10% [of its budget]." Many companies have undertaken data migration projects from on-prem systems to the cloud, costing billions, yet data change management remains an elusive component of those projects.

Data contracts, data products, data governance, and other techniques we've discussed all fall under change management. As mentioned earlier, the intent of data contracts is not to prevent change but to help teams understand it, communicate when changes are happening and their impacts, and prepare for changes that would otherwise cause downstream systems to fail. That is change management, through and through.

Companies that need change management the most are typically larger organizations. The larger a company becomes, the more data it generates. The more federated a business becomes, the more complexity and replication occur. As data becomes more valuable, more spaghetti code emerges over time, increasing the impact a single change can have on downstream consumers. We covered this in more detail within Chapter 3, where we discussed the implications of Dunbar's Number and Conway's Law.

That isn't to say small companies don't need change management. After all, GitHub is the global standard for code change management. Even in small companies, code change management is necessary from day one because the code is crucial to the company's existence, so processes like pull requests and code review are seen as necessary to ship any functionality. The risk of simply connecting to a repo and merging code directly into the main branch is too great.

In companies where the core product is a physical good, like a sofa or a television, change management is an important part of the product lifecycle. Want to change how the brake system works in a car? Prepare for months or even years of reviews, testing, regulatory confirmation, communication to customers, and so on. In other words, the more critical the system is to the company, the more change management becomes a no-brainer.

While it might surprise some readers in 2025, many engineering teams still don't use a DevOps platform or have version-controlled code. Can you guess why? If you guessed because those companies prioritize physical products or service-based relationships that don't rely on code, you'd be right.

So what does that mean in the data space? Fortunately, thanks to data products (i.e., the packaging of data, models, and/or insights as a product), we're seeing a rise in the utility and value of data. With generative AI on the rise, we expect AI will become a revenue engine equivalent to applications and websites. Furthermore, since data is absolutely essential to all models, the criticality of data increases significantly, and precepts of change management will likely become more prevalent.

Meanwhile, framing your data management initiatives in terms of business-critical data products provides the strongest rationale for investing in this space. We'll cover that more in Chapter 11 where we discuss creating your first wins with data contracts. For now, let's switch gears to discuss another subject close to our hearts: the data supply chain.

Data as Supply Chains

In 1975 Nintendo's Gunpei Yokoi coined the term "lateral thinking with withered technology" (*https://oreil.ly/8BZL0*). He developed the concept after a string of hits from the video game company at a time when most games were straightforward and fell into a few distinct categories: puzzle games, fighters, racing games, and so on. But Yokoi found fun gaming experiences in unexpected places—fields with repetitive tasks that weren't seen as enjoyable at all! Yokoi discovered that applying an old idea in a new context could breathe new life into it. He found inspiration in everyday surroundings instead of following common patterns in the video game industry.

We think the data field could use a bit of lateral thinking as well. It's common for us data developers to look to our cousins in software engineering and try to learn from their best practices. However, even software engineers are novices in change management! Other industries, like health care, manufacturing, and logistics, have been dealing with quality issues for hundreds of years, with far greater stakes. Changing how you treat a patient for a dangerous disease risks doing harm if you're not extremely careful. Changing a shipping lane might delay delivery, or the ship could hit rocky waters and potentially capsize. When lives are at stake, change processes are taken seriously.

One of the most sophisticated areas where change management comes into play is the supply chain. A supply chain is an interconnected network of producers and consumers working together to ensure a physical product reaches a customer with a certain degree of quality and timeliness (sound familiar?). Producers start by extracting raw materials from the earth—think farming, mining, and woodcutting. Once collected, the material is transported to a manufacturer. Since people can't use raw logs or iron ore, a processing facility turns the materials into something useful. Usually, there are steps between transforming the raw material into a good that is consumable by an end user. One plant may treat a chemical, another might handle bottling and packaging, and a third might test the quality of the mixture. After manufacturing, the product is shipped to a distributor. The distributor typically owns a warehouse or central store where it holds various transformed materials, making them available to retailers on demand.

Retailers are consumer-facing. They are the interface between buyers and products. When you walk into a business like Walmart, consider the problems it must solve: maintaining a large inventory with high availability, ensuring the products it sells are of good quality and not contaminated, understanding who is purchasing which products, and which supplier provided a certain product at what price. It must track all its costs, including for storing goods and moving them between physical locations. The company also needs to ensure its wares are clearly labeled and discoverable so any shopper can find what they need quickly and check out.

Finally, consumers are the stakeholders getting utility from the product. They are the ones going to the store, handling the browsing, shopping, and item selection. If what they picked doesn't meet their needs, they might return it or complain.

Figure 10-1 illustrates these parallels between supply chains and data workflows. Every component of a supply chain is present in the data space. The miners or farmers are equivalent to data producers; the trucks transporting goods between processing centers and retailers are the data pipeline; the manufacturers are the data engineers, accepting raw data and turning it into something usable by a downstream customer; the distributor is our data warehouse. Heck, it's even called a *warehouse,* if the parallel wasn't obvious enough. The retailers are the tools and systems providing utilities to leverage data in valuable ways, like Tableau, Microsoft Power BI, Amazon SageMaker, and so on. And of course, our end customers are the data scientists, analysts, and product managers we serve every day.

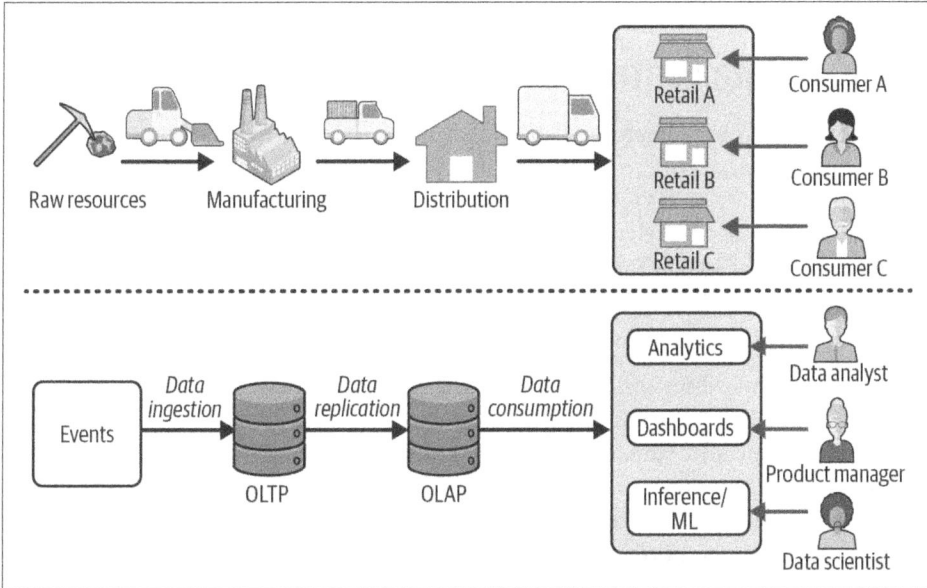

Figure 10-1. Parallels between supply chains and data workflows

Why is it useful to think about our work in the context of data supply chains? It starts to dawn on us that supply chain management is as much (if not more) a people problem as a tech problem! In fact, supply chain managers leveraged contracts between producers and consumers long before they existed in software engineering. A farmer will sign a contract with a cereal company, for example, to provide a certain amount of grain on a particular schedule, to a degree of quality defined by the consumer (remember our Chapter 2 definition of data quality being "fit for use by consumers"). After all, it's the restaurants that understand what is fit to serve their guests, not the farmers who sit far from the line cooks!

What is essential is understanding how changes ripple across the supply chain, who is impacted, what that means for affected teams, and what action each party must take next. Freely communicating this information, tracking how changes have been applied, and creating open communication is a must in a fast-moving supply chain where disruptions are common and teams need the ability to collaborate in real time as climate disasters or geopolitical events change their ability to produce or consume.

Good data change management puts people at the core—not tech. Facilitating conversation and the free flow of information is more important than tests. Helping people understand how they are impacted is more important than catalogs, and giving all impacted parties the right distribution of power for what decisions to make next is essential. In the following section, we will discuss what this actually looks like across the stages of implementing data contracts.

Levels of Data Contract Implementations

The first step with implementing data contracts is to require they be placed on source data in order for that data to be pushed into a platform. This is a great starting point for a few reasons. First, it's within the control of the data platform team. You built the platform, so you decide what goes into it. Simple enough! If a data producer wants their data to be available for querying—perhaps because a product manager needs it for analytics—they have to go through the process of creating a contract, taking ownership, and managing change communication to the broader team.

A great pattern we've seen implemented successfully at several large-scale enterprises is for the data platform team to maintain a group of data product managers. When someone fills out and submits a new data contract through a portal (or catalog), the data product manager collaborates with the producer to define the data, clarify its meaning, establish the producer's perspective on ownership, and even create the YAML version of the contract stored in Git. There are more sophisticated implementations where teams require producers to upload a snapshot of their data, and the platform team automatically collects useful statistics and descriptions about the data. This can be used as a baseline for building the initial specifications of the contract and data quality rules.

There are some major challenges to this approach, which we will cover in a moment. But first, there's a metaphor we are going to use that we hope will make the different levels of implementation easier to understand. These categories are not unique to data contracts but represent how teams typically think about the internal implementation of technologies in various fields, potentially explaining why many of these initiatives tend to fail.

Airplane and Airline Projects

In 1903, Orville and Wilbur Wright flew the first functioning airplane, taking off from Kitty Hawk, North Carolina, and landing 120 feet later. This invention was a seminal moment in aviation history. The brothers discovered that arranging wings with a specific airfoil shape, control surfaces like elevators and rudders, and a lightweight yet strong frame allowed the vehicle to achieve lift, maintain balance, and be steered in flight. The design causes air passing over and under the wings to create differential pressure, generating lift. These factors together enabled flight.

A decade later saw the dawn of the first airline, the St. Petersburg–Tampa Airboat Line. Created by Percival Fansler, the airline faced different problems. How do you make people feel safe enough to fly between cities? After all, airplane safety during the early 1900s wasn't at today's level. Airplanes lacked advanced navigation systems and were made of wood and fabric, and accidents were common. Fansler needed to address this. The company invested in safety measures like rigorous pilot training, regular aircraft maintenance, and establishing standard operating procedures.

But that was just the beginning. Airlines had to consider the *incentives* that drove people to purchase tickets: great customer experience, affordability, and awareness relative to competing options. Comfort is extremely important in travel, for example, as a person is often willing to sacrifice time for an enjoyable experience. Seating that wasn't stiff or painful, in-flight meals, and attentive flight attendants made the experiences superior to train rides or sea travel. The industry later adopted technologies like pressurized cabins and more-reliable aircraft to reduce turbulence and noise.

Second came ticket prices. Airlines addressed affordability through offering classes like economy to make flying accessible, and using government subsidies to lower ticket prices. They made it a goal to achieve an economy of scale, offering flights to many cities, states, and countries in order to drive down prices to be competitive with other forms of transportation. To do this they needed to create schedules, follow strict flight paths, and improve ticketing systems and boarding speed to get people on and off faster.

To *convince* people to fly more frequently, airlines launched marketing campaigns that emphasized safety records, showcased the speed and convenience of air travel over trains or ships, used celebrity endorsements, and portrayed flying as a glamorous, modern experience. For example, the 1950 ad by Eastern Air Lines with the tagline "'Tried and Proven'...There's no substitute for Eastern's Experience" included the following highlights:

- "Fly Eastern's New-Type Constellations, the world's most dependable airliners."
- "Eastern's experience gives you double dependability, dependable airliners, dependable personnel."
- "'Tried and proven' over billions of passenger miles."

You can view the ad in reference (*https://oreil.ly/wLqjz*) via the Ad*Access collection of Duke University's John W. Hartman Center for Sales, Advertising & Marketing History.

In short, the Wright brothers focused on proving *technical viability*, while Percival Fansler focused on *business viability*, or adoption. Technical viability is a subset of business viability. Just because you've proved something can be done does not mean you've solved the myriad requirements necessary for customers to regularly use your invention instead of alternatives. To that end, what we've termed an *airplane project* focuses on implementing a particular technology without considering other factors, while *airline projects* go beyond providing a technological capability and focus on what incentivizes customers to use that technology.

Some projects are primarily technical endeavors. For example, most ETL/ELT tools are airplane projects. As long as you can move data in near real time between systems, the data engineering or platform team that built the technology can roll it out wherever it makes sense. Other examples might be cost optimization tools. If you can optimize the cost of your Snowflake instances, then you've solved the most critical problem. You don't need to think much about the interaction layer because you're unlikely to have users outside the team who created the project.

However, approaching an airline project as an airplane project can be disastrous. One reason most data catalog implementations fail is because they are airplane projects. It is less about whether or not some system *can* catalog all the data in your analytical database, and more about what will incentivize business stakeholders and data teams to use and derive value from the catalog. There's a long tail of problems and challenges your customers might experience that have nothing to do with technical feasibility. For example, maybe your tool can facilitate adding descriptive metadata for each table, but do customers go through the effort of doing that? Why or why not?

Data contracts fall into the airline project bucket. On the surface, implementing a contract is simple, perhaps even trivial. An Excel spreadsheet can contain your contract, or a Confluence page could. But the purpose of a contract is for producers to take ownership and for consumers to gain value from it. Software engineers must be willing to create and manage these contracts iteratively. Thus, data teams need to ask themselves:

- Why would software engineers work with data contracts?
- Why might working with data contracts be challenging?
- Where might software engineers resist that ownership?
- Do software engineers have the time to own more surface area?
- Do software engineers even know what the data contract should be?
- How do software engineers decide what goes into a data contract?
- Are the created contracts useful to consumers?
- Does implementing data contracts solve downstream problems?

- Are contracts applied to the datasets consumers actually need?
- Are violations actually addressed in a timely fashion?

The answers to these hypothetical questions are dependent on your specific use case and organization, but regardless, all data teams need to consider the implications of the data contract beyond the data team itself.

Forward- and Backward-Looking Problems

With the airline context in mind, let's return to our earlier implementation of data contracts. For an initial implementation, it's not bad as an airline project because it accounts for the *why*. The reason a producer fills out a contract is because they want to move their data into the data platform team. Great. But that raises the following questions:

- What if the data producer doesn't want to expose their data to the broader business?
- What if they don't have a product manager pushing them to use the data for analytics?
- What happens if the producer decides to change their data from the initial contract?
- What happens when contracts are out-of-date?
- What about all the old data that doesn't have a contract?
- How do data producers communicate when changes have to happen?
- How do data consumers know which data has a contract and which doesn't?

We call these the *forward-looking problem* and the *backward-looking problem*. Forward-looking problems are about how we deal with changes to data or new data being added that isn't included in the platform. Backward-looking problems deal with how consumers access the data they want that isn't under contract, or even learn what source data is available and how they should use it.

Another big problem is a lack of scalability. Generally, there aren't many data product managers or data engineers on a team. These central data platform organizations are already bottlenecks, overwhelmed by data quality issues and outages they have to handle. If this already swamped team now becomes the central change control agents for every data change made in the entire company, it results in a situation not much different from centralized DevOps teams being responsible for approving every PR. What we need to do is *shift left* (there's that phrase again) and distribute some of the responsibility of data management to everyone.

Challenges of Technology-First Implementations

The second implementation we've seen is more technological. Teams might build an automated testing framework or use tools like Protobuf and Apache Avro to manage schemas, then document those schema-based contracts in some central catalog that the data producer maintains. This is definitely shifting left, but these implementations typically run into a different set of challenges, such as:

- Why would the data producer adopt a system like this? What's the incentive?
- How does the producer understand what the contract should be?
- What happens when the producer needs to make a breaking change?
- What happens when nonschema changes occur? Semantic or context changes?
- How do you scale a system like this to every engineer in the company?

Companies going down this route usually say the same thing: "We built the technology, but we're struggling with onboarding." In engineering-driven organizations with lots of build decisions being made, you encounter this sentence often. This is because the problem is being treated as an airplane project when it's actually an airline project. It's equivalent to asking: "Hey, we built a rickety plane that can cram a couple of people inside with no safety precautions and doesn't take people where they want to go...why isn't anyone flying with us?"

To answer that question better, it helps to explore a concept called *friction*, or blockers that prevent your target audience from engaging in a desired action and or workflow. Chad first learned about friction from Peep Laja, who ran the CXL institute for conversion optimization back in the early to late 2010s. Click-rate optimization is a discipline of analytics and website development that focuses on examining user experiences, creating hypotheses on how to improve those experiences, testing various options, and measuring the results with the end goal of increasing conversion, or the percentage of users who complete a task from the total population of users who *could* complete that task.

Let's use an example from this author's personal experience: donating to charity. I (Chad) don't always donate to charity as often as I should because I find the process of finding and vetting charities, and then deciding how much to give and how often, overwhelming. However, when I shop at a grocery store, the credit card scanner frequently asks if I'd like to round up my purchase to support one of two or three charities that have been preselected for me. When this happens, I almost always donate. Why? Friction.

If I were to donate to charity on my own, I'd need to first find a charity to donate to. This can be overwhelming given there are thousands of charities, with some being significantly more reputable than others, all working on projects that may be more or less important to me. I'd need to research these charities and find one with a compelling cause. Then I'd need to choose the donation amount. Should I donate a dollar (seems too low), or enough that it could be a tax write-off? If it's a higher amount, then do I need to have a conversation with my partner first? Then I need to go through the actual process of making the donation. Hopefully it's easy, and there is a PayPal integration, but if not I'd need to add my credit card number and other details, at a minimum filling in the billing address plus potentially additional details.

Compare that to the donation experience when shopping. I've swiped my credit card to pay, so I don't need to enter any additional information. The charities and the amount are preselected for me. The amount is negligible such that it doesn't require any additional outside confirmation. The cost of donation (outside the 45 cents or so) is pressing a button on the screen that says "I'd like to donate." The difference in friction between the two options is night and day.

The concept of friction is incredibly important in airline-oriented projects. Whenever you are asking a customer or a stakeholder to do something they are not naturally inclined to do, any friction in the user experience will significantly decrease the likelihood of it. If you are attempting to encourage data producers to be owners of their data and be more thoughtful of downstream consumer teams, there are many examples of potential friction points you will run into, such as asking engineers to:

- Manage systems they are not familiar with
- Be thoughtful about the data they are producing
- Understand who is using their data and to derive contracts from that
- Adopt a process that slows them down from shipping code
- Adopt a solution that prevents them from making needed changes
- Adopt a process that relies on humans making consistently correct decisions
- Care about consumers when they don't know who those data consumers are

Ultimately, adoption of data contracts boils down to incentives and friction. If you can align the incentives of the various stakeholders in the data supply chain while *making the right thing to do the easy thing to do*, you will be far more effective than if you simply propose using certain technologies and hope that "If we build it, they will come." (Pro tip: this never happens.)

The Trap of Standards

We want to spend a bit of time addressing standards. Inevitably, for all new software engineering or data engineering paradigms, some system emerges that claims to be a standard or aims to become one. We can respect the effort of the teams pushing these standards onto others—whether it's Protobuf, Avro, Iceberg, or one of the many opportunistic data contract standards that have emerged over the last few years as this concept has gained popularity. However, in our experience, the winners of standards wars emerge naturally over time as developers understand the use cases and actively solve problems using that standard.

For example, OpenAPI has become a standard because it provides a unified way to describe RESTful (representational state transfer) APIs, making it easier for developers to build, test, and integrate services. Data build tool (dbt) is another open source technology rapidly becoming the standard for analytics engineering. Standardization doesn't arise because the industry makes an explicit decision to follow one tool, but because the tool adds so much value that everyone adopts it to solve their problems. We have worked with many companies following a data contract standard, and to be frank, that kind of standard adds very little additional value compared to simply defining your own YAML specification with your own use cases baked in. The far larger problem is not which spec the industry decides to use, but how you solve the problems of adoption, ownership, visibility, and change management we've been discussing throughout this chapter.

In other words, focus on the difficult existential problems that will determine whether your data contract implementation succeeds. Once the issues we've discussed are solved, the industry will rally around a specification that makes sense for the common use cases we've uncovered collectively.

Requirements of a Successful Data Contract Implementation

Now that we know the challenges, let's lay out some of the requirements of a successful system. In the following section, we'll get into the weeds about how to implement such a system starting from scratch, but let's start by focusing on the high-level needs based on what our data producers need for adoption and what data consumers need to improve their data usability.

Visibility

Data producers need to know where their data is going and who is using it. In other words—a source code flow graph! Engineers are familiar with the concept of a source code flow graph and use it in many areas of their day-to-day work, like API management and security. If you understand the services, systems, applications, teams, and products that leverage the data being produced, you can begin to make choices proactively with the context of how your system is impacting others in the organization.

The second phase of data visibility is impact analysis. As mentioned in other chapters, data producers rarely understand how their data is being used. Without this context it is difficult to make informed decisions. If I am making a change to schemas or business logic, who should know about it? When should I tell people? Who should I tell? What information must I communicate? What actions should I take to minimize any damage being done?

Change communication

When data sources change, producers need to understand who to speak to, what to communicate, and when to communicate. Engineers are good at communicating their changes, but if the change management process is to push updates to a central Slack channel or email, that is simply not going to get the job done. The primary reason is that there are many transformations between the producer and the team that ultimately uses the data. If software is making changes in Java, which pushes data into a MySQL database, which pushes data to a Kafka topic, which pushes data to an S3 bucket, where an ELT pipeline is set up to dump data into Snowflake, where this data is transformed in a data model again and again and ultimately ends up in training data for a critical pricing model—neither side of the data supply chain will have the context that is useful to them.

One option to solve this problem is to funnel all change communication to the central data platform that operates as the "gate" to the data warehouse, but ultimately this runs into the challenges of scale we mentioned before. If data is changing all the time, and it is the responsibility of an overencumbered platform organization to manage communication on behalf of the producers, they become the bottleneck. We recommend this approach for smaller companies and startups where the rate of change or the number of downstream use cases is low.

Policies

A quote from a distinguished engineer at a large bank: "We have lots of policies. The problem is enforcement." A policy is a requirement for how data is managed, analyzed, modified, or created. Policies lay out regulatory and compliance requirements, access-control specifications, querying allowances, and more. In order to have a successful data contract implementation, you must have a way to define the rules and policies that can be cataloged and referenced in data contracts. The company must create these policies centrally, must have executive sponsors, and must be explicitly tied to a mechanism of enforcement in the data management system of choice. Policies should operate at a higher level of abstraction, with the ability to transpile to and from the underlying technologies where enforcement occurs. This allows governance teams to build policies based around business rules without needing to become full-fledged software or data engineers themselves.

Context evolution

In most cases, the evolution of schemas is relatively straightforward. Depending on the events being populated by application developers, they may evolve data types, update specific values for CRUD operations, and/or create or remove new schemas.

However, there are other changes to business logic that fall outside this context. For example, what happens when the underlying meaning of a field changes, or features are built that modify how a property should be leveraged elsewhere in the codebase? As an example, imagine the field promo_code changed so that it is only valid if promo_expiry_date is in the future. This is a logic change that could significantly affect the number of valid promo codes moving forward. Simple checks against schemas would not be enough to detect this change, as no types are being modified or removed. Software systems must exist to not only catch schema and row-level data shifts, but also to have the means to detect semantic drift in important business objects.

Contract management

Adoption will stall if there is no management system created for handling the evolution of the contracts themselves—even if all the other implemented requirements of data contracts are put in place. Contracts must be owned, highly visible, and versioned. There must be a way to associate data contracts with the underlying assets they support—systems to track how those assets have evolved over time and whether the changes were in compliance with policies. In addition, contract management must record ownership changes, document incidents, and communicate outages. The contract is your source of truth for what a data product represents, but that truth is only valuable if the full context of change is made visible and clear to all parties. Equivalently, there must be mechanisms to detect when data contracts are missing or need to evolve. There must be systems to make requests for data that currently does not exist, or requests to alter existing data. As we have stated previously, the power of data contracts is in their ability to promote collaboration around what the data means and how it is governed. However, this requires processes that allow a variety of different technical and nontechnical actors to make their voices heard and participate in the process of data management.

In the next section, we will discuss in more depth how to bring technical and nontechnical actors together by providing a framework for introducing data contracts to your organization.

Developing a Strategy for Introducing Data Contracts

In the previous sections of this chapter, we detailed the considerations of a successful data contract implementation, but how do you actually get buy-in from leadership to start? The following sections will illustrate a set of frameworks you can use to start building buy-in through the lens of introducing data contracts within your company. These are the frameworks (*https://oreil.ly/GBjUe*) that the management consulting firms McKinsey & Company and Boston Consulting Group use, following what's called the *hypothesis-led approach*. As described by former consultants from both, the approach has the following steps:

1. Define the problem: what key question do we need to answer?
2. Structure the problem: what could be the key elements of the problem?
3. Prioritize issues: which issues are most important to the problem?
4. Develop an issue analysis [and] work plan: where and how should we spend our time?
5. Conduct analyses: what are we trying to prove [or] disprove?
6. Synthesize findings: what implications do our findings have?
7. Develop recommendations: what should we do?

We will use this framework to conduct a thought exercise to illustrate how you could develop your data contract strategy. Note that this is only one of the many frameworks we can use, and subsequent sections mainly explain how to adapt it to the needs of your data contract implementation.

Define the Problem

A phrase we use with each other when formulating problem statements is the idea of "going deeper" when trying to understand what's worth solving. This process is deceptively hard, as one can quickly settle on an appealing problem statement that ultimately doesn't address the root of the issue. This process is exactly what led us to change management as the key driver of data contracts among organizations that have adopted the architecture.

The following list of statements is an example of how going deeper led us to change management as the core issue, where each subsequent statement goes deeper into the issue:

1. Data quality is difficult for data teams despite data being their specialization, and this problem has persisted for decades.
2. Data governance exists and is effective in providing a framework to manage data quality issues, but is limited in its enforcement.
3. Data governance is challenging to enforce as many breaking changes to data come from upstream workflows—such as application code and business logic, both of which are not owned by data teams.
4. Teaching data best practices to upstream teams would be ineffective, as there is high inertia to change current workflows, especially when downstream issues don't directly impact those who made the change.

5. There needs to be a mechanism to automatically enforce expectations of data to all parties who plan to make data-impacting changes (i.e., data contracts).

6. Inertia in changing workflows and taking on additional dependencies will likely not be well met by upstream teams without proper context of what's in it for them.

7. Having data contracts managed programmatically and enforced via the CI/CD workflow is key for fitting within the developer workflow and addressing the issue of inertia.

8. If we position data contracts to enforce workflows only on the most important data assets (e.g., revenue-driving or risk-mitigating ones), we can explain *why* it's important and *what's* in it for them.

9. The root of the change that we are requesting of our upstream stakeholders is the process of change management.

10. We need to determine how to create the most effective change management workflow with respect to changes that impact the data that's important to the organization.

Now you may be asking yourself, "At what point do I stop going deeper in trying to find the root of a problem?" You can always go deeper, but we found that it's mainly warranted when you have not found traction with the level you are currently engaging with. For example, our chain of sequentially deeper thoughts was the culmination of four-plus years of trial and error in implementing data contracts at various organizations.

We once stopped at statement 5, "There needs to be a mechanism to automatically…," as we initially thought it was sufficient in resolving data quality issues. While this was true among data teams, expanding implementation beyond them left us stuck once again, prompting us to revisit and validate our assumptions more deeply. A few years after publishing this book, we may very well have found that we *still* need to go deeper as we uncover more information through additional implementations.

Structure the Problem

From the process of going deeper, we have identified the problem statement of "How do we create the most effective change management workflow with respect to changes that impact the data that's important to the organization?" With this question in mind, we must identify the key levers we can pull to solve this question. The folks at McKinsey suggest utilizing an "issue tree" where you break a problem down into its subcomponents. Figure 10-2 provides a simplified example of this exercise.

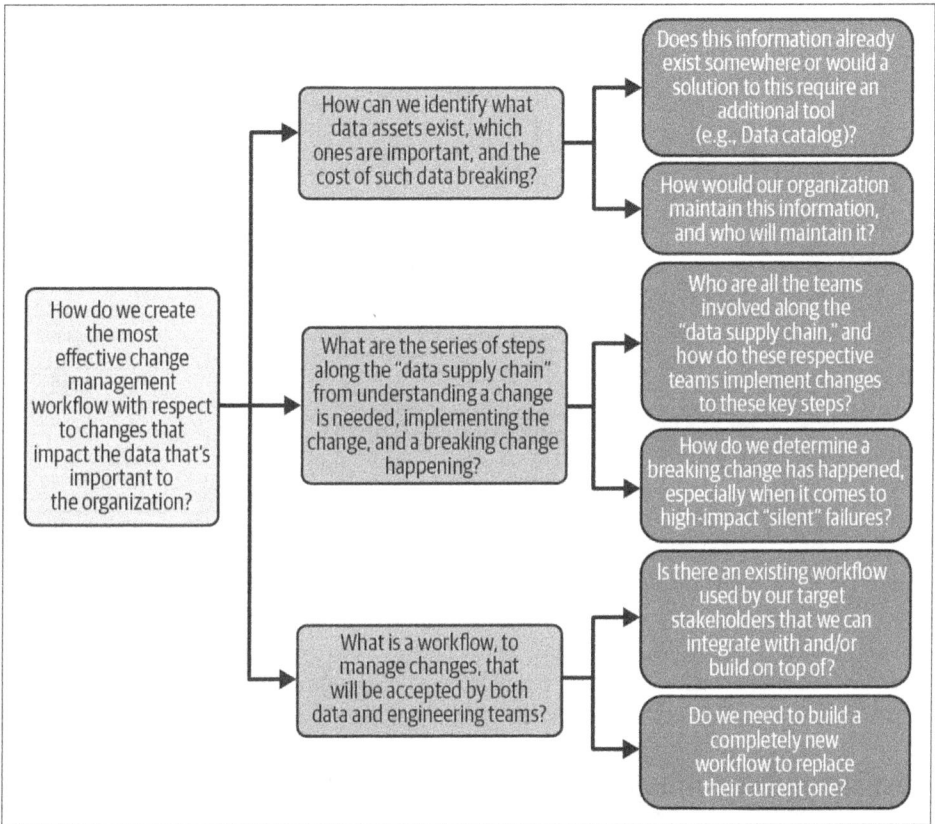

Figure 10-2. Issue tree example applied to the change management use case

One important note for creating this structure is the presence of a hierarchy in how the issues are organized. Having a hierarchy further informs us of the prerequisites of solving a particular issue and thus is a starting point to explore a question further.

Prioritize the Issues

In the previous step in the thought exercise, we determined the key elements of a problem that needs to be understood to take action on. While our simple example resulted in only six elements, a real-world implementation would likely result in substantially more elements, and with even more limited resources constraining which questions to pursue. Thus, it's best to take these elements and prioritize them via a matrix, such as in Figure 10-3, with relevant criteria as the axis (e.g., impact and ease of implementation).

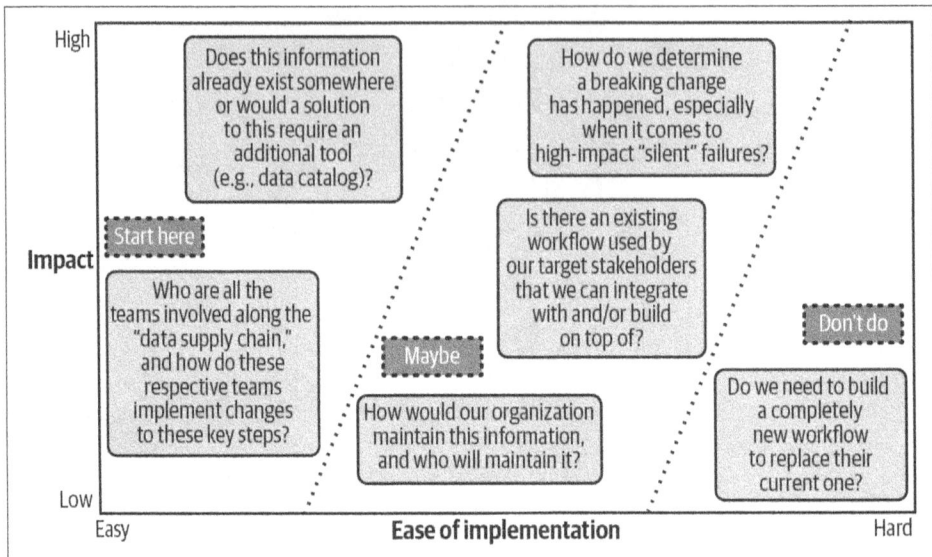

Figure 10-3. Prioritization matrix applied to the change management use case

Based on the position of the elements of the matrix, we can determine where to start and delegate tasks across a team in the subsequent step. Furthermore, such prioritization also quickly identifies which elements we would not pursue.

Develop an Issue Analysis Work Plan and Conduct the Analyses

This is the stage where the strategy development moves from thinking to execution, and where we will establish a work plan to validate the various questions and assumptions within the strategy. Following are examples with the "start here" elements we identified within the prioritization matrix:

"Does this information already exist somewhere, or would a solution to this require an additional tool (e.g., data catalog)?"

- Search for existing documentation related to the data assets we utilize.
- Determine if the organization already uses an existing tool to manage this information, and whether this tool is used across the entire organization or within specific teams.
- Among the data assets we utilize, identify the various databases within the organization where the data is created, ingested, replicated, and transformed.
- If an existing tool isn't present, scope out the requirements of such a tool and determine if it's a build or buy decision.

- If determined to be a buy decision, begin researching various vendors and starting early procurement conversations.

"Who are all the teams involved along the data supply chain, and how do these respective teams implement changes to these key steps?"

- Among the data assets we utilize, identify the various databases within the organization where the data is created, ingested, replicated, and transformed.
- Among the identified databases, identify which teams within the organization interact with the databases, manage the databases, and are held accountable for the respective data within the databases.
- Among the identified teams, identify who we already have an existing relationship with, who we need to build a relationship with, and who are the key decision makers among these teams.
- Identify any existing internal documentation regarding how these respective teams implement changes for workflows related to the databases.

All of these tasks will generate further information that will need to be synthesized in the next step.

Synthesize Your Findings

Another framework heavily utilized by McKinsey consultants is the Pyramid Principle (*https://oreil.ly/jrbNa*), where information is synthesized in a way that emphasizes persuasion. The principle is structured in three layers:

1. The decision you want the audience to make.
2. Supporting arguments for the decision.
3. Supporting data for the arguments.

In Figure 10-4, we illustrate the Pyramid Principle, utilizing our previous steps in this thought exercise.

Note that you will need to adapt the arguments and evidence you present based on the audience you want to persuade. With that said, the previous guidance is a means to structure your synthesis, but the next step will focus on how to present it.

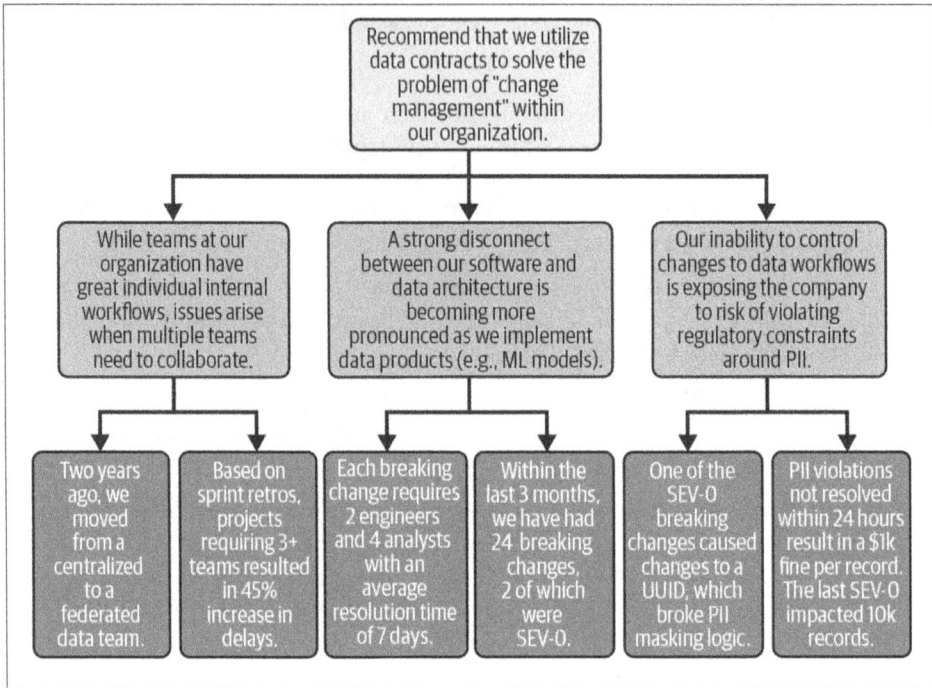

Figure 10-4. The Pyramid Principal applied to the change management use case

Develop Recommendations

The final framework used by McKinsey consultants is SCQA (also known as the SCR framework), which stands for "situation, complication, question, and answer." Applied to our use case, it would look like the following:

Situation

Numerous breaking changes have occurred in the past three months that at best require around eight thousand person-hours to resolve, and at worst exposed the company to a $10 million regulatory fine.

Complication

A strong disconnect between software and data teams has arisen with our shift to federated team structures, where it has been identified that change management between teams is the root cause. We've seen this in sprint retros, where it was noted that projects requiring three or more teams resulted in a 45% increase in delays.

Question

Is there a way to resolve this issue without reverting our decision on federated teams that we have invested heavily in?

Answer

> Yes, we can better handle change management across multiple teams at scale via data contracts, which would prevent breaking changes such as the recent SEV-0 that exposed the company to a potential $10 million fine if it wasn't resolved in less than 24 hours.

Throughout this thought exercise we applied the hypothesis-led approach to develop a strategy to introduce data contracts into an organization, and develop messaging to persuade stakeholders that this strategy is worth pursuing. If you want another example of this process, Mark wrote the article "How to Make Leaders Pay Attention to Your Next Data Initiative" (*https://oreil.ly/grkF_*), where he applied the same process to a failed AI initiative use case.

Conclusion

In this chapter we discussed the importance of change management when considering the implementation of data contracts, as well as how we came to this conclusion via our implementation of data contracts at various companies. In addition, we applied the frameworks used by the management consulting firms McKinsey & Company and Boston Consulting Group to illustrate how to develop a strategy to introduce data contracts within your organization. In summary, this chapter covered:

- The importance of change management and how it's the root of the problem that data contracts solve
- Viewing data workflows as supply chains within your organization
- The levels of data contract implementations and their various trade-offs
- Developing a strategy for introducing the implementation of data contracts

While we provided concrete examples, it is paramount that you apply these concepts through the lens of your organization's specific nuances. We believe data stacks are akin to thumbprints: there are categories of thumbprint patterns, but each thumbprint is different. The specific nuances of your organization, and how your organization manages change, are the key levers you can pull to get adoption of data contracts. In the next chapter, we will discuss exactly how to get your first wins with data contracts.

Creating Your First Wins with Data Contracts

We want to make it clear that this chapter is intended for the specific audience of leaders implementing data contracts within enterprises. While you may find value in this chapter even if you are not an enterprise leader, note that this chapter dives deep into the management side of implementing data contracts with this assumption. Our reasons for the special attention to this facet of data contract implementation are the following.

The past few years devoted to writing this book and implementing data contracts across different organizations have made it abundantly clear that *the technology of data contracts is relatively straightforward, but the adoption of this technology is quite complex.* If you recall in Chapter 3, we highlighted Conway's Law (i.e., how team structure and communication shape systems) and Dunbar's Number (i.e., the breakdown of communication among more than 150 employees) as driving forces that make data contracts necessary for change management in data-enabled software systems.

While organizations of any size can implement data contracts, we have found that enterprise-scale organizations are the ones most likely to earnestly pursue them. Enterprises have a large number of software and data developers distributed across multiple teams and locations (sometimes even countries). Furthermore, beyond the scale of the systems, the diversity in tooling and maintenance of legacy systems within enterprises is vast. All of this is coupled with the fact that enterprises also have higher governance needs (e.g., audits, regulations, etc.) and exposure to risk. Thus, enterprise-scale organizations have clear ROI that warrants the effort of implementing, maintaining, and driving adoption of data contracts across multiple teams and business units that are typically siloed.

In the previous chapter, we focused on why change management ties together the key elements of shifting data left in organizations—people, processes, and technology. We also discussed how effective communication forms the crucial foundation for change management itself.

Now, in this chapter, we'll build on that foundation by outlining a straightforward, pragmatic approach you can use to strategically select the right data product, around which you'll center an initial data contract proof of concept (POC). Furthermore, we will detail how leaders gain the information and buy-in needed to sell that proof of concept and, ultimately, build on its subsequent success to drive data contract adoption throughout the organization.

Determining Your First Data Contract Use Case

First, and most importantly, you must select a candidate to serve as the cornerstone of your data contract pilot, a proof of concept that will provide critical success you can build on in the near future.

But before we select a candidate, we require a clear and actionable definition of what a data product actually *is* within your organization. You'll need a definition that will enable you to filter and parse through hundreds, if not thousands, of data assets. As it turns out, settling on a definition can be a surprisingly difficult thing to do.

Defining Data Products

Ask 10 data professionals what constitutes a data product in their own organizations, and you'll receive 10 different answers that—while sharing common intent—have distinct entities.

In the right setting, with the right group of data professionals, participating in the cognitive effort required to reconcile different opinions and experiences regarding a comprehensive data product definition can make for an enjoyable exercise. We believe this should not be your goal, as only data professionals enjoy digging into the pedantic nuances.

For our purposes here, we simply need a working definition that filters all possible data products in your organization to an initial and manageable consideration set. The nascent stages of an organization's data contract maturity curve thrive on iterative progress, not perfection.

So, as a minimum viable definition to serve our purposes of determining your first data assets to protect, we propose the following definition of data product:

> A packaged workflow and/or process that consists of a data asset, a means to operationalize this data, and a method of serving the data to a consumer. Furthermore, it

must be reusable, domain-owned, and tied to a verifiable high-value outcome within the organization.

Applying this definition ensures that any data product involved in the next phase of the filtering process will be quantifiably relevant to the business—and that its business logic lifecycle will involve data producers and data consumers who are highly invested in the data product itself.

This last point is especially crucial for the designs of your data contract pilot, chiefly because levels of investment correlate to levels of feedback. The more feedback you receive as the pilot process unfolds, and the more often you receive it, the better positioned you'll be to make the small yet vital adjustments that determine its success or failure.

Our friends in software engineering circles have long recognized the power of continuous, real-world feedback in this sense. So much so, in fact, that they refer to it in a very specific way: "tracer bullets." Here's how David Thomas and Andrew Hunt's book *The Pragmatic Programmer* (O'Reilly) describes tracer bullets:

> Tracer bullets show what you're hitting. This may not always be the target. You then adjust your aim until they're on target. That's the point. You use the technique in situations where you're not 100% certain of where you're going. You shouldn't be surprised if your first couple of attempts miss: the user says, "That's not what I meant," or data you need isn't available when you need it, or performance problems seem likely. So change what you've got to bring it nearer the target.

Therefore, our working definition of data products will get you through the first phase of focusing on the assets in your organization that you can safely consider pilot worthy. To focus further, we'll borrow another concept from the software engineering world that will help you separate high-value outcomes from those that are mission-critical in your organization.

Identifying Your Steel Threads

Through the application of our data product definition, any asset included on your list of potential pilot candidates will tie to high-value outcomes in your organization (i.e., "Tier 1" data products). To cull the list further, you should now identify which of these data products qualitatively function as organizational steel threads.

The term "steel threads" originated in bridge building—specifically, suspension bridges. Construction relied upon cables of varying materials strung between anchorages on either side of a given expanse, as illustrated in Figure 11-1. Once secured, these cables act as a vital substructure, enabling the construction of the bridge itself—across and over them. As such, these steel threads are critical to the structural integrity of bridges.

Figure 11-1. Manhattan Bridge, March 23rd, 1909, Irving Underhill

Software engineers have adopted the concept of steel threads, applying it to systems architecture (we highly recommend Jade Rubick's article on the topic (*https://oreil.ly/UTGzp*)). It's used in organizations to identify and demonstrate end-to-end execution paths that support core functionality and align with business objectives. By "walking the thread," engineers trace critical workflows, document key system components, uncover potential risks, and validate any potential architectural decisions before scaling a given system.

For our purposes, data products qualify as a steel thread if their failure would cause immediate and measurable disruption to business operations, decision making, or customer experience.

To illustrate the stakes we're referencing here, imagine working as a logistics manager in a large automotive manufacturing company. In your role, you are responsible for overseeing the supply chain—ensuring parts and finished vehicles get delivered efficiently.

You start your week early each Monday with the help of a dashboard that integrates data from multiple sources, including real-time production data, inventory levels, and data from the manufacturer's supply chain. Using this dashboard, you produce a report that highlights any manufacturing bottleneck due to any number of potential problems—equipment overloads, inventory shortages, or transportation delays, for example. In turn, you deliver this report to your suppliers—each of whom relies on it to optimize their own production schedules and reallocate resources as needed to ensure the timely delivery of critical components.

Due to the scale and complexity of the supply chain, any delays or inaccuracies in the report you provide could result in shipment delays, production slowdowns, or even full stoppages on the manufacturing floor. In this sense, the singular and seemingly straightforward report this data product enables isn't just critical, it's essential to business operations.

Now imagine the data fueling the dashboard becomes unreliable due to schema changes, data ingestion discrepancies, or an upstream system failure. Unnoticed, you may have no way of detecting that the weekly report you're generating is inaccurate. You send the report out without realizing the data product you rely on is compromised. And the damage compounds quickly. Your suppliers begin to make misinformed adjustments, and the production process breaks down with impacts rippling across the entire organization. How long before the problem can be identified and corrected? Minutes? Hours? Entire working days?

Considering that the costs of manufacturing stoppages in the automotive industry averaged $22,000 in profit per minute (*https://oreil.ly/Y_Chp*) over 20 years ago (we can assume it's substantially more today), it's an understatement to say even the smallest of issues that impact steel thread data products can cascade into substantial financial losses and reputation damage.

But this is the point of our example, as this is precisely the level of business impact that should inform which data products in your own organization you choose to identify as steel threads and which you do not. As the second phase of our iterative filtering process, your list of data contract pilot candidates should now seem much more manageable.

There is, of course, a chance that you've already arrived at your primary candidate. If so, feel free to skip to the next section. But when facing a handful of compelling steel threads, leveraging a simple weighted decision matrix can make the ensuing selection process clear.

Making Your Final Decision

The weighted decision matrix is a simple yet highly versatile tool within multicriteria decision making (*https://oreil.ly/QLvvu*). As our third and final phase of filtering data product candidates, it provides an effective way to evaluate and compare the criteria of those steel threads that remain in contention for your pilot, and doing so with as little bias as possible. Your goal is to go from a small group of good pilot candidates to that which is best—and do so in a way that considers your organization's unique needs.

First, define your steel thread comparison criteria with a dual focus on business impact and pilot feasibility. Related factors commonly include:

Business criticality
    Higher operational impact correlates to more potential buy-in and the urgency your data contract pilot can generate.

Producer and consumer engagement

Highly engaged data producers and consumers will be more inclined to see the potential benefits of data contract adoption. As such, they're more likely motivated to act as valuable sources of key details needed for planning your proof of concept and maximizing tracer bullet feedback while it's underway.

Low data volatility

Highly dynamic steel threads may require frequent updates, either increasing risks during the pilot process itself or necessitating more versioning compared to other candidates. Note that this is a balance of risk, as the volatility of a data asset is the reason it would benefit from data contracts.

Existing data quality issues

It's entirely possible for high-value, steel thread data products to be plagued by data quality issues. The degree to which data contract implementation could fix these issues determines if this category is a benefit or a hazard.

Complexity of dependencies

As a rule, data products with fewer interdependencies lower their risk of use in a data contract pilot. With that said, there could be reduced complexity if the multiple dependencies fall under a single team.

Ease of implementation

This gauges approximately how much tooling and engineering effort setting the pilot itself up will require. This is where we have often received the most pushback from upstream software engineers.

Organizational visibility

Ultimately, the more teams rely on data from a particular data product, the clearer the benefits of a data contract adoption pilot stand to be.

Once you capture all key criteria, you then determine a weight for each criterion on a scale from 1 to10, with 1 being a weak criterion and 10 being a strong criterion for the steel thread selection. The more important a given criterion is to your pilot's chances of success in your organization, the higher that weight should be. Next, score each of the steel threads remaining in your consideration set from 1 to 5 based on how well it meets your listed criteria, with 1 being a poor fit and 5 being an excellent fit.

As a thought exercise, we will illustrate the weighted decision matrix in practice by once again bringing forth the automotive company logistics example. Table 11-1 represents the potential decision matrix of raw numbers created by the leader exploring potential steel threads.

Table 11-1. Decision matrix raw values

Data product	Business criticality (weight: 10)	Producer and consumer engagement (weight: 7)	Low data volatility (weight: 2)	Existing data quality issues (weight: 6)	Complexity of dependencies (weight: 4)	Ease of implementation (weight: 4)	Organizational visibility (weight: 7)	Total
Logistics Cost Ledger	4	4	3	4	5	5	3	28
Dealer Sales Forecast	4	5	4	3	5	5	1	27
Carrier Performance Metrics	4	4	4	2	3	5	3	25
Shipment-Lifecycle Events	5	2	2	3	2	5	2	21
Dealership Customer Reviews	1	4	3	4	5	1	3	21
Automotive Parts Inventory Management Database	5	2	2	3	4	1	4	21
Safety-Incident Reports	3	2	5	1	4	1	4	20
Warehouse Inventory Snapshot	5	2	2	2	3	1	4	19
Machine Maintenance Logs	3	1	4	2	4	3	2	19
Vehicle Telemetry Stream	1	1	1	2	3	5	3	16

After recording the score justification for each potential steel thread, one can then tabulate total values per steel thread (i.e., score × weight value) for each criterion and add them all together.

The steel thread with the highest aggregate amount is the data product with the highest relative chance for success, and the choice that will produce the maximal amount of proof from your proof of concept. In the case of Table 11-2, it seems like the logistics cost ledger data product is the most promising steel thread.

Table 11-2. Decision matrix weighted values (top steel thread highlighted)

Data product	Business criticality (weight: 10)	Producer and consumer engagement (weight: 7)	Low data volatility (weight: 2)	Existing data quality issues (weight: 6)	Complexity of dependencies (weight: 4)	Ease of implementation (weight: 4)	Organizational visibility (weight: 7)	Total
Logistics Cost Ledger	40	28	6	24	20	20	21	159
Dealer Sales Forecast	40	35	8	18	20	20	7	148
Carrier Performance Metrics	40	28	8	12	12	20	21	141
Automotive Parts Inventory Management Database	50	14	4	18	16	4	28	134
Shipment-Lifecycle Events	50	14	4	18	8	20	14	128
Warehouse Inventory Snapshot	50	14	4	12	12	4	28	124
Dealership Customer Reviews	10	28	6	24	20	4	21	113
Safety-Incident Reports	30	14	10	6	16	4	28	108
Machine Maintenance Logs	30	7	8	12	16	12	14	99
Vehicle Telemetry Stream	10	7	2	12	12	20	21	84

This process can take a bit of experimentation to get right. But it's time well spent, as you can add to and expand your weighted decision matrix during the initial phases of your pilot process—revising, adding to, and broadening your overall knowledge. You'll grow more certain as you meet with data producers and data consumers and fully map out the data product's lifecycle, while ensuring you're making the right pick for your data contract pilot.

The next section will walk you through exactly how to approach that.

Determining Your Business Case and Requirements

Once you've got the right steel thread in your sights, you must shift gears to build a bulletproof business case around it. As established in the previous chapter, leaders invest in solutions, not technology. You'll need to demonstrate the technical viability of your first data contract implementation. But the chance to demonstrate the raw potential that data contracts will have in this initial use case rests on your ability to align all necessary leaders and decision-makers in your organization with your cause.

You need to do more than just outline the problems, outcomes, and implementation steps of the pilot. You also need to compel leadership in your organization to not just sign off but also become personally vested in ensuring your success. This can all seem like a lot. It is a lot. Going from the candidate you've chosen for your pilot and getting to the pilot itself is its own journey.

To support your efforts, we have distilled into four steps the process of creating a strong foundation for your initial steel thread implementation:

1. Gather information and plan to engage.
2. Map out where key stakeholders fit in the data lifecycle.
3. Determine key stakeholder influence, interest, and risks.
4. Gain leadership alignment and buy-in.

Notice how three of the four steps revolve around *people*. The next sections will go into detail on how to enact each step based on our experiences and those of people we spoke to from across the industry.

Gather Information and Plan to Engage

Your first step should entail gathering information specific to your chosen data product's system and its related processes. Key here is learning critical assumptions and requirements that you need to validate, as well as identifying crucial stakeholders.

Sketch out a sense of who produces the data that fuels the data product, individuals who consume it, and how this all connects to business needs. And we're very intentional in our use of the term "sketch" here, as the goal is to get your bearings. Those bearings will keep you from trying to wayfind and solicit buy-in in a contextual vacuum. Furthermore, this prep work shields you against misunderstandings and pushback by prioritizing the needs and existing commitments of everyone else first.

In many organizations, you can gather a substantial amount of information by analyzing a given data product's technical artifacts and operational patterns, especially since you've already invested the time needed to make sure the product in question is business-critical for your organization. With that said, we also spoke to many data teams that didn't know where to start or worried that such data wasn't captured. If you find yourself in the latter situation, we suggest the following as starting points:

- Who has read/write access to databases of interest
- Audit logs of a database (e.g., "Who has read from XYZ database in the past 90 days?")
- Recent contributors to specific code repositories (e.g., `git blame`)
- Determining metrics related to the data product and leaders held responsible for such metrics
- Data ingestion patterns and orchestration logs (e.g., daily versus weekly batch jobs)
- On-call incident reports that mention code and/or data assets related to the data product
- Product requirement docs related to code and data used for the data product

Additionally, attempt to work out what appear to be the key constraints related to the product domain. Read past tickets. Review Slack and other related communication channels. And be realistic, as these initial efforts may represent only a quarter of the total organizational reality surrounding your pilot. In previous roles, Mark would often create a Slack channel where he forwarded key messages he found (he also encouraged others to add to it). He would then pull in screenshots of these company-public conversations within his proposals to make the issue feel more real.

Ultimately, this process of sketching our initial slice of knowledge will enable you to plan how to engage with your data producers and consumers and identify who exactly to start with. Ideally, leverage the information you've gathered to establish a basic engagement plan. This plan should include the following components:

- The mission, goal, and scope of your pilot proof of concept
- Separate listings of all data producers, data consumers, and related personnel you've identified during your information-gathering process, whom you may need to reach out to, and in what order
- Relevant domain-specific knowledge you've gained to date

- Succinct, elevator-pitch versions of your mission and goal, which you can use when first reaching out to data producers and consumers

- A clear way to articulate your need to set up brief, initial conversations, tailored as needed to be immediately clever and relevant to either data producers or data consumers

- A consistent way to conduct these meetings and conversations (Mark would often pull from his background in qualitative research by using semistructured interviews (*https://oreil.ly/TBduI*))

- Clarity on how you will document the data producer and consumer pain points, in addition to how a successful pilot could benefit all relevant parties

- A rough working timeline, which you can easily update and use to recap next steps, interviews, and plans

In the next step we will describe how to organize and leverage this collected information and engagement plan.

Map Out Where Key Stakeholders Fit in the Data Lifecycle

The process of mapping the business logic to your steel thread data product will help you bridge technical-focused rigor and business-focused priorities. This process forces you to shift your perspective up and away from the function calls and data transformations you may initially gravitate toward when meeting with your first data producers and consumers. That data is, of course, important. But it's the business meaning behind that data you now must draw into focus. You can't allow your pilot to be only the pile of "technical fixes" that get lobbed at leadership all too often.

Thus, we suggest mapping out the series of steps required to deliver your data product to a data consumer, also known as value stream mapping. As you visualize your data product's value stream, you will naturally capture what key actions take place at each stage and begin to understand which are business-critical. In addition, your key domain owners should also be clear by this point.

Going back to the automotive company logistics example, Figure 11-2 illustrates what a potential high-level value stream map would look like for the logistics cost ledger data product chosen as a steel thread.

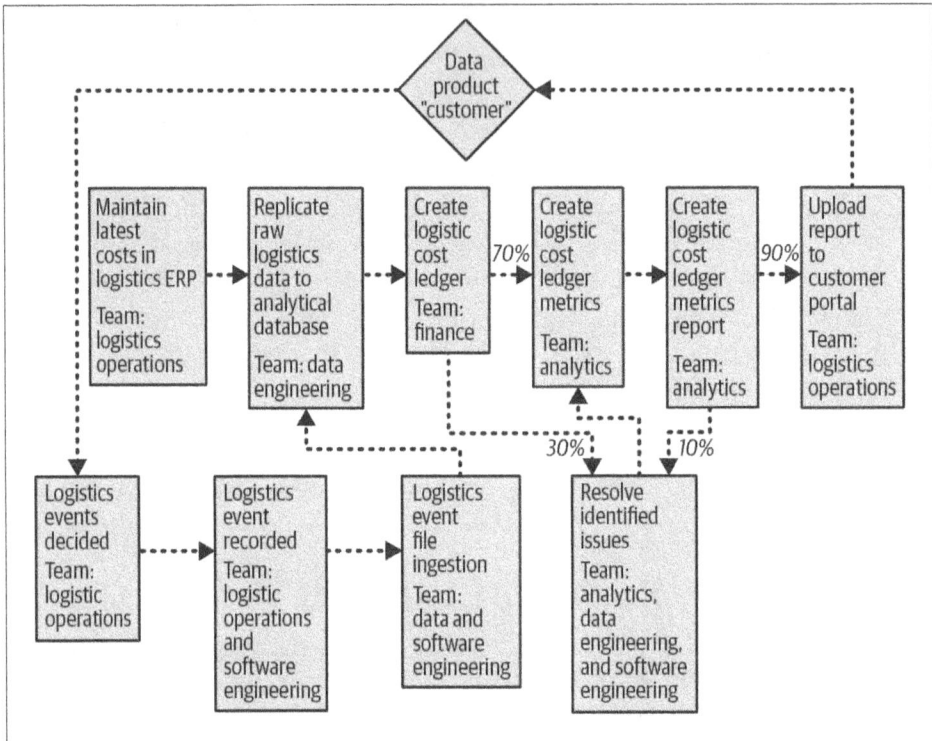

Figure 11-2. Value chain mapping example: logistics cost ledger

In the next section, we will utilize this high-level value stream map to identify your key stakeholders' influence, interest, and risks as it pertains to your data contract implementation.

Determine Key Stakeholder Influence, Interest, and Risks

You must understand how to manage your key stakeholders and any issues that could potentially impact the course of the pilot in progress. We recommend you use a simple 2 × 2 matrix in two different ways. The first will determine which stakeholders are potential blockers or enablers. The second will highlight which issues (i.e., risks) you should be prepared to manage or mitigate.

Begin with the conversations you conducted with your data producers and consumers, and plot all stakeholders across the four quadrants of an influence versus interest matrix, as shown in Figure 11-3.

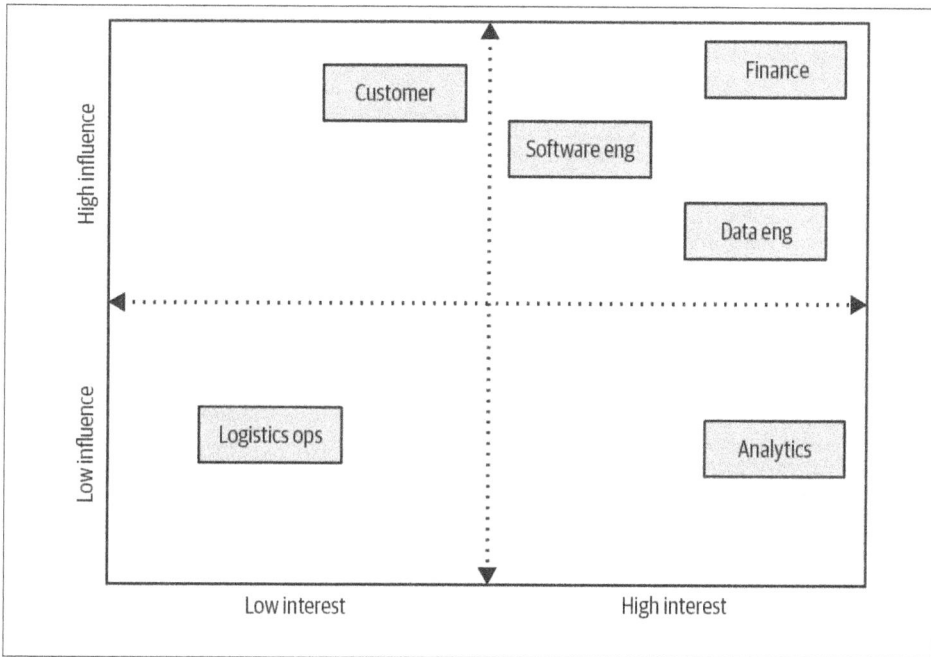

Figure 11-3. 2 × 2 matrix: influence versus interest

You can interpret the various quadrants as the following in this matrix:

High influence, high interest

The stakeholders in the upper right quadrant are your pilot champions, your enablers. Provide these individuals with regular updates and ongoing decision making, as they have significant influence and are most interested in your pilot's success. Chances are good these individuals will, at this point, already be aligned with your vision and goals for your data contract pilot. But it's worth the time and effort required to maintain that alignment as they help you move forward.

High influence, low interest

These stakeholders should receive periodic updates as you move forward in the pilot process. Your goal is to maintain their high-level support without overwhelming them. Additionally, make sure low-interest stakeholders in this quadrant will not inadvertently work against you. Classic blockers in this sense are often framed as open antagonists. Influential low-interest stakeholders can potentially impact key resources, decisions, or opinions if left unchecked.

Low influence, high interest

> Such stakeholders are those who are very invested in your pilot and its success in the organization. While their impact may be limited, work to keep each as informed and involved as you can to ensure their voices are heard. This can prove especially important post-pilot when you begin to scale data contract adoption throughout the greater organization.

Low influence, low interest

> These stakeholders require the least amount of your attention moving forward. But you should still monitor them up to and through the pilot process. As stakeholders related to a steel thread in your organization, they can still shape informal sentiment. Providing these stakeholders with a baseline courtesy (e.g., a short monthly status update about the data contract pilot process) fosters trust and goodwill.

Next, dive further into the stakeholders in the high influence, high interest quadrant by utilizing a probability versus impact matrix, as shown in Figure 11-4. Use the same 2 × 2 approach and plot all potential issues accordingly, whether they are stakeholder-related, technical, or purely operational. Note that the example matrix is much sparser than what you may create.

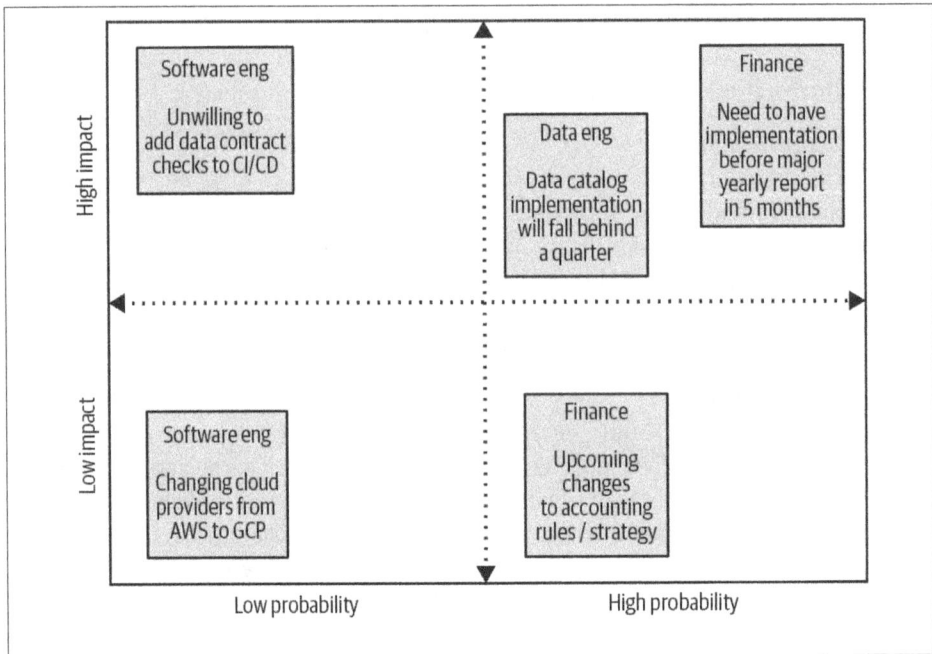

Figure 11-4. 2 × 2 matrix example: impact versus probability

Again, here is how you can interpret the following quadrants:

High probability, high impact

Risks require immediate attention. Any issue mapped to this quadrant that cannot be handled before presenting your pilot proposal deserves its own concrete mitigation plan—as it may actively prevent or erode alignment and buy-in at the leadership level.

High probability, low impact

Risks may be likely or even expected. Therefore, consider establishing small safeguards for issues you map to this quadrant, as they (individually or collectively) should not actively put your pilot presentation or execution at risk.

Low probability, high impact

Risks deserve contingency planning, since any issue in this quadrant would be catastrophic (were it to occur). Create a clear "if-then" plan for each issue and, when possible, establish a means of monitoring for any relevant early warning signals.

Low probability, low impact

Risks are still potential factors that can impede or affect your efforts. For this reason, note each one on a "watch list" you can reference and revise as needed.

Keep in mind that stakeholder influence and interest can shift, and thus you may need to revisit this exercise as new pertinent information emerges.

Note that this advice is suggestions to handle stakeholder challenges that may arise. You must balance efforts around strategy and analysis with pragmatic ways of achieving results.

Ultimately, the goal is to create a compelling narrative for your best-suited key stakeholders and determine their must-have deliverables or assurances for them to confidently back your data contract implementation proposal. In the next section we will detail how to utilize this narrative to gain leadership buy-in for your proposal. and provide a presentation template.

Gain Executive Leadership Sponsorship

Leaders rarely have time to spare and are balancing numerous demands outside your use case. Thus it's critical that you distill your business case into a narrative that can easily do the following:

- Lead with the problem (or key problems) and business case alignment.
- Position pilot outcomes as solutions.
- Communicate what to expect and when.

- Reassure decision makers that your approach mitigates risks.
- Make the ROI clear, as it will be compared with the ROI of competing proposals.

We suggest using a slide deck, as it's an asset that's easy to share with your stakeholders, but always defer to your organization's norms (e.g., Amazon prefers documents (*https://oreil.ly/sKwOh*)). The following sidebar is a slide deck outline we have found success with in getting a data contract proposal accepted. Note that this deck is a great format for directors, vice presidents, and leaders at similar levels, but it will need to be adapted to a brief summary or one-pager for C-suite executives.

The following slide deck template is based on successful decks we have used to gain approval from C-suite leadership for data contract implementation.

Shift Left Data's Lean Deck Outline for Pilot Approval

Title slide
- Lead with a short, relevant, attention-grabbing title.
- Include your name, the date, and any key pilot sponsors.

Executive summary
   A high-level overview that details the problem, proposed solution, and business benefits that are tailored for an executive audience who may not review the full deck.

Problem and use case alignment
- State the core business or operational problems your pilot is designed to address.
- Provide your main evidence about the problem (current-state affected metrics):
  — Clearly outline the impact your steel thread has on the needs of the business.
  — Establish the current state of the data product's relationship to the business, provide context, and create urgency while leveraging issues, friction, and pain points.
- Provide supplementary evidence of the problem (current-state secondary effects).
- Lay out the issue lineage: provide prior evidence of the problem (legacy issues/past incidents).

Use cases (repeat per use case, max of three)
- Name the use case.
- Offer a quick, real-world scenario illustrating how the pilot (solution) will benefit the business (alignment) by solving the/a problem.
- Mention the expected metrics that will be affected.

Outcomes (max of three)
- List expected business outcomes: summarize the business-level benefits (ranked by immediacy/time-to-value).
- List expected technical outcomes: summarize the technical-level benefits (ranked by immediacy/time-to-value).

Implementation phases
- Give a high-level overview of the process.
- Map the individual phases to the timeline and teams involved.
- Offer a detailed overview of key factors: current state, ongoing issues, proposed solution, and proposed impact.

Furthermore, include any deeper dives that may or may not be useful on the day in an appendix section at the end of the presentation. They will be easy to reference if needed but won't, by default, impede the urgency and clarity of your approach.

Finally, plan the presentation itself. Determine whether you'll present your pilot live in a leadership meeting (ideal) or circulate the deck asynchronously with a short summary. Don't let success catch you off guard. Outline post-approval next steps as thoroughly as is reasonable. Having these details thought through and ready will underscore to leaders that they're placing their trust in the right person and process.

Post-approval, someone may ask you if the success of your proof of concept can scale. "Yes" is the correct answer here, as you can build on the wins of your steel thread pilot by modifying and repeating this journey until you've successfully implemented data contracts on every business-critical data product in your organization.

At this point, you may or may not get a moment to celebrate before leadership begins asking, "Where do we go from here?"

It's a great question. The answer, in our opinion, involves formalizing your approach to taking steps forward and shifting from doing pilots to changing the organization's culture around shift left data practices. In the next section we will outline how you can approach such organizational change.

Eight Steps Toward Organization-Wide Shift Left Adoption

You now understand how to undertake the journey from identifying steel threads to gaining the alignment and buy-in needed for data contract implementation. The wins produced in each instance don't just directly benefit the business; they are necessary both for your ability to move data contract adoption forward and for scaling shift left data practices throughout the organization as a whole.

Steel threads are a beginning, a way to make progress possible. Despite their substantive value in the organization, they can't create the broader infrastructure required to drive lasting change on their own. This infrastructure needs to connect teams, sustain energy, and compel individuals to change how they work, think, and relate to each other. Said organizational infrastructure, then, will be the focus of this section.

To guide you through these efforts, we turn to a well-established framework for organizational change: John Kotter's eight-step process. Originally developed to help leaders address large-scale business transformations, we find his approach especially relevant due to its emphasis on the value of vision and leadership. The eight steps, as highlighted in Kotter's book *Leading Change* (Harvard Business Review Press), are the following:

1. Establishing a sense of urgency
2. Creating the guiding coalition
3. Developing a vision and strategy
4. Communicating the change vision
5. Empowering employees for broad-based action
6. Generating short-term wins
7. Consolidating gains and producing more change
8. Anchoring new approaches in the culture

However, know that what follows in this section is not meant to be a checklist. Nor is it a comprehensive breakdown and analysis of Kotter's approach, research, and methodologies. Instead, view it as a way forward—a proven methodology to adapt and adopt when it's time to transition from proving shift left data practices work to ensuring their longevity.

Establishing a Sense of Urgency

Once you've established steel threads, the time will inevitably come to pivot to scaling data contracts throughout the organization. Your first step in doing so must involve cultivating and managing shift left–related urgency as you move forward.

Urgency is nothing short of foundational to organization-wide management initiatives, and it fuels the engine that drives change forward. Per Kotter's research, you will need to convince at least 75% of management in your organization that the status quo is untenable to affect change at scale. And as this buy-in is one of the key data contract adoption metrics we'll cover in the next chapter, you'll need to maintain it over time.

Another way Kotter frames urgency is a "removal of complacency" so that the organization recognizes the true urgency a situation warrants. For example, in Mark's previous role, the main daily batch data replication pipeline from the application to the analytical database kept going down and halting much of his team's data work. Month after month his team would face extraordinarily stale or incomplete data, work with downstream stakeholders to determine alternatives, and then provide results with the data at hand.

The data team accepted complacency around the lack of dependability of the data replication pipeline, and therefore the wider business didn't recognize the issue—until Mark's manager had enough. With the approval of leadership, the data team stopped utilizing workarounds and simply didn't provide work to downstream teams unless the data was adequately fresh and complete. After a month of the data pipeline being inoperable, the business could no longer ignore the issue and quickly allocated a software engineer to update the problematic data pipeline.

As a quick aside, a common trap we see is attaching urgency to another complex project. Countless times we've come across organizations that were in the planning phases of a huge migration, and thus had high excitement for data contracts given that they finally had budget and executive sponsorship to improve their infrastructure. Every time, the data contract implementation was ultimately deprioritized as the migration inevitably went over budget and had timelines extended extensively. We believe implementations such as data contracts and other large changes make much more sense as gradual buildouts rather than huge migrations.

Finally, proximity in large organizations complicates the natural impact of urgency. At any given moment, as you scale, some individuals will be closer than others to the key stakeholders, pain points, and breakthroughs that all play a role in the adoption process itself. In large organizations, urgency cannot be everywhere or felt by everyone all at once.

Therefore, your goal in adopting Kotter's first step involves learning to rely less on the valuable but limited boosts produced to date from your initial proof of concept and pilot phase wins. Instead, to begin to scale, you will need to begin cultivating urgency through eliminating complacency around the business's status quo.

Creating the Guiding Coalition

With urgency providing momentum, you will then need to build cross-functional coalitions to establish traction. In doing so, you'll build your ongoing data contract adoption efforts in the right direction over time.

This means you must strategically select the members of your coalition. Resist what may be a natural urge to focus on technical experts alone, and also include senior executives for their budgetary and policy authority, in addition to influential mid-level leaders who understand frontline realities. It's a bonus if these executives or mid-level leaders have a data analytics background and can immediately understand the problems you point out, even if they no longer run queries day-to-day.

Taking a strategic approach to coalition building in the way that Kotter outlines ensures you won't build a more gilded version of what is, in actuality, another temporary project team. Instead, you'll orchestrate a dynamic group of individuals with a shared purpose, which will help you bridge the gap from pilot success to organization-wide adoption via their expertise, credibility, and/or authority.

Developing a Vision and Strategy

We've already covered how to develop a strategy in Chapter 10, so the emphasis here will be on how we extend those ideas under the context of growing company-wide adoption. Specifically, your cross-functional coalition should require its members to align on a shared vision that remains relevant to the wider organization over time. This will serve as a foundation for planning and ensure ongoing data contract initiatives remain aligned with your desired end state, as well as facilitate better ongoing communication and decision making. Your vision is ideally easy to understand and share, and it should refer back to why a shift left approach matters and relates to day-to-day business decisions.

More importantly, wider adoption requires teams and individuals throughout the organization to actively see themselves playing a part in this vision. A great real-world example of a successful shared vision and strategy is JPMorgan Chase's data mesh implementation. We highly recommend the company's blog post, "Evolution of Data Mesh Architecture Can Drive Significant Value in Modern Enterprise" (*https://oreil.ly/InIBn*), which details how the firm aligned its data architecture to its data product strategy.

Furthermore, this quote from Kotter's book summarizes exactly why a strong vision is essential: "[It serves] to facilitate major changes by motivating action that is not necessarily in people's short-term self-interests." For example, in the case of software engineers, they are often under immense pressure to constantly deliver new features and ship code. The developed vision must resonate with both leaders, who must change the incentives to enable data quality to shift left, and engineers, who must accept that adding more constraints today will increase developer velocity tomorrow.

Communicating the Change Vision

While previous steps build to this point, communication of your vision in adopting shift left data practices within your organization will make or break your initiative. This task is deceptively challenging. Don't underestimate the amount of refinement that messaging will require, nor the amount of effort needed to disperse and internalize the message throughout the organization.

This is especially true for technical leaders who may fall back on the comfort of their specialized knowledge. Communication efforts regarding your vision must be both robust and adaptable enough to influence strategic decisions among leaders and the operations of individual contributors who are outside your domain.

For example, let's go back to the automotive company logistics example to demonstrate the difference:

Bad communication
> "We must fix our logistics reporting, as poor data quality within the logistics cost ledger data asset is resulting in high error rates within our logistic metrics. This has led to wasteful spending for our supply chain, which further exacerbates the risk posed by the rising cost of steel."

Good communication
> "It's paramount that we reduce waste within our supply chains to counteract the rising cost of steel."

The former message relies on lengthy jargon and places the emphasis solely on the analytics team despite our value stream mapping exercise illustrating there are six different stakeholders. Furthermore, the accountability is also mainly placed on the analytics team and does not show a connection to leadership. The latter message is concise, implies a sense of urgency via "paramount" and "rising cost of steel," and establishes a company-wide initiative that needs to be adhered to by individual roles while attaching it to a strategic outcome owned by leadership.

Now, this example was a simple thought exercise, and ideally you spend more time on refining your own messaging than what we spent here. But even with that effort, you should not stop there. Your strategic messaging needs to be repeated often and in multiple contexts for it to hold. Done correctly, this messaging will play a key role in your ability to mitigate resistance to your efforts, prevent ongoing efforts from becoming fragmented or misaligned, and foster a commitment to the shift left cultural change at all levels of the organization.

Empowering Employees for Broad-Based Action

With your strategy established and vision well communicated, there will be teams who are ready to take action. Great—having a wide pool of on-the-ground practitioners excited about your vision is critical for success. Yet, like any move toward change, there will be inertia given the current state of the business. Your guiding coalition must identify potential blockers and bottlenecks in adopting data contracts within respective teams. Following are some of the blockers we have identified in the adoption of data contracts:

Unsupported technology
> One of the earliest bottlenecks of the wide adoption of data contracts is the *detection* component, given its variability. This is exacerbated even more in large enterprises, where IT sprawl is commonly compounded by decades of technical debt and legacy systems. Do you support the homegrown ERP system? How many coding languages can you realistically cover with static code analysis? Maybe it's a NoSQL database with complex nested JSON blobs? Having a clear roadmap is key for overcoming this.

Skeptical software engineers
> As stated in earlier chapters, software engineers are one of the most important stakeholders to buy into the change toward shift left and data contracts. Thankfully, data contracts already align with their best practices of version control, testing, and API agreements between services (which they also call contracts— this is where the term originated). Thus, their skepticism isn't about the solution, but rather about whether the solution is worth prioritizing given their competing demands. Countless software engineers have told us that proper data design of their services makes subsequent development easier, but they are not incentivized to pursue it. This consideration for data must come from engineering leadership to incentivize shift left data practices.

Poor onboarding experience
> Even with your initial success with your first steel thread, it is likely that it required substantial effort to get your data contract implementation working end-to-end. This is expected as you formalize what this implementation looks like within your own company. Unfortunately, you won't have this luxury as you conduct subsequent implementations across new teams. Don't discount the role of developer experience, and work to ensure the time to a first-deployed data contract becomes shorter until an acceptable time is reached.

Territorial leadership
> Despite how technologists aspire to be logical and merit based, the reality is that business is heavily emotional. We have encountered times where key stakeholders become strong detractors despite us believing they would benefit from

data contracts. Digging further, we've found they often worry that data contracts may make their team's important work obsolete. At best, you can work with the stakeholder to understand how their work fits within the shift left vision, and give public credit to the hard work they were already doing. At worst, you may need higher leadership to take action.

Finally, Kotter recommends taking a systemized approach to blocker identification, whether that be surveys, workshops, or interviews. Each touchpoint creates opportunities to analyze processes, cultural norms, and systems that may conflict (or already conflict) with shift left efforts. As such, blocker identification will serve double duty in this sense, helping you work with leadership to ensure sufficient budgets and resources are prioritized and allocated as needed. Employees on the front lines of data contract adoption get what they need—the tools, training, and information—to actively contribute to the process.

Generating Short-Term Wins

While the success of organizational change is measured in years, it's prudent to remember that success isn't a binary only seen at the end, but rather a portfolio of success with short-term wins interspersed. As Kotter establishes, successive repeatable wins stand to benefit every other key aspect of your efforts to scale—when properly leveraged—in a few ways:

- They add practical details, specifics, and nuance to the corpus of information needed to refine your vision and keep it blisteringly relevant.
- They build increasing credibility for new and further changes that your prior proof of concept and steel thread pilot experiences alone don't directly support.
- Collectively, they make it easier for stakeholders to support you and to keep leadership bought in at all levels required to see adoption through.

Kotter provides a straightforward methodology for generating volumes of wins sufficient to scale. Plan for successes by defining key milestones and breaking longer-term goals into smaller, more achievable targets. Furthermore, strategize for allocating resources, monitoring progress, and celebrating data contract wins in ways that actually matter. While "planning for success" may seem obvious, having an organization-wide agreed-upon definition of wins and long-term success is rather difficult.

By going through the process of establishing relevant criteria, focusing on strategic alignment, and judiciously engaging stakeholders, you'll be able to prioritize the types of success that are most likely to produce lasting change. This again further highlights why it's critical to have the guiding coalition consist of diverse organizational viewpoints and leaders with influence.

Consolidating Gains and Producing More Change

The last stages of organizational change are always the most difficult. This is because the distribution of effort becomes a primary challenge. Progress depends on the commitment and contributions of individuals increasingly removed from your original pilot teams. In some cases, they'll be even more removed from those core data and engineering functions that have served as the beating heart of your efforts to date.

In line with Kotter's approach, this stage of adoption will signal a shift in strategy from providing top-down direction to supporting bottom-up discovery. Thus, you may need to help more data engineering–adjacent individuals adopt a "build-measure-learn" mindset in their own roles in the organization. This includes their asking more data-related questions, testing in their own context, and coming to their own realization that data contracts are less of a one-off custom solution and more of an internal product within the company—one that they can use to address their own pain points, needs, and goals.

Depending on the size of the organization, supporting this phase might involve encouraging your internal champions to challenge some of their assumptions by posing key questions like:

- Can teams self-serve as needed?
- Are we providing discoverable and understandable data contract examples?
- Are our communication resources for the shift left vision helping people learn from early adopters and influencers?
- Are we strategically creating clear ways for those with less direct involvement to observe what we're doing and participate?

Thankfully, this bottom-up discovery pattern has already happened within DevOps, which can serve as a guiding example. DevOps emerged around 2008, and similar to data teams, IT operations and developers were working in siloes. In addition, similar to data contracts, there was a need for monitoring changes to code and enforcing expectations within the CI/CD workflow. Thus the same pattern of shifting these enforcement mechanisms to the left and embedding them closer within the development workflow was needed. While a top-down directive from executive sponsorship is needed to kick-start such an initiative, the bottom-up adoption among developers stemmed from the fact that DevOps provided them value as it made deployments quicker, more incremental, and caught major issues before code was deployed.

Ultimately, you'll need to ensure your champions and stakeholders remember that the closer you can keep the shift left vision to the work, the more relevant it remains.

Anchoring New Approaches in the Culture

With the bottom-up approach in full effect, again, we need to make it easy for the wider organization to adopt and anchor data contracts as a formalized practice within the company's operating model (*https://oreil.ly/mw4s-*). There are many frameworks, but the one most relevant for our purposes is the target operating model (*https://oreil.ly/G-68q*), as the concept of "people, process, and technology," which we have already discussed, stems from this framework. Furthermore, our exercises in stakeholder and value chain mapping serve as inputs into this framework. With that said, detailing this framework and developing an operating model is outside the scope of this book, but we believe it's worth noting here the mechanism of embedding the changes of shift left and data contracts within business operations.

In addition, successful anchoring establishes shift left data practices as a cultural signal. In practice, as clearly documented prime value drivers, data contracts will be cited in launch reviews, discussed during employee performance reviews, and noted as "just how we do things here."

In short, leaders must recognize desired behavior as the culture, because this behavior has demonstrated great results. This is the root of anchoring data contracts into the way you work.

Data contract adoption may never have a definitive end point. But the end game happens when shift left data practices inform culture in addition to organizational outcomes. For these reasons, Kotter's eighth and final step does not involve effectuating closure. Instead, it will guide how you achieve shift left continuity, and how data contracts will survive changes to technology, team structures, leadership, or the business itself.

As Kotter himself emphasizes, this anchoring won't hold unless leadership continues to recognize shift left–related behaviors as key drivers of success. And this necessitates adopting a near-obsessive relationship with attribution of the more qualitative occurrences that act as positive symptoms of the data contract adoption process.

You must ensure leadership isn't just aware that your overall efforts make a difference. Rather, the connection between shift left efforts and organizational excellence is undeniable. By leveraging Kotter's entire framework, you will develop more than just a data contract adoption roadmap. You will also establish a dynamic pattern that enacts lasting change and is tuned to the unique needs, challenges, and goals of your organization.

All this is moot, however, without recognition. Individuals at your organization will want to feel and measure the effects of adopting data contracts. Therefore, in the next and final section of this chapter, we'll touch on those initial qualitative indicators that will appear as data contract adoption begins to work.

Attribution in Action: The Importance of Making Success Tangible

Lasting cultural change doesn't come from just understanding data contracts and shift left data practices—it comes from feeling their value. No amount of early success guarantees that change will stick. And early wins won't necessarily dictate how quickly the organization will embrace shift left data practices as a whole. This makes it challenging, if not impossible, to establish precise timeframes.

Your primary role as a change leader is to keep the adoption momentum alive by doing everything you can to prevent change from dragging on longer than necessary or stalling out completely. You'll do this by endlessly repeating, reinforcing, and recognizing the key milestones and behaviors that signal progress, especially when they begin to occur on their own.

As the shift left data culture blooms throughout your organization, ongoing data contract implementations should become as common as their mention in casual work conversation, how your peers think about solving problems, and how teams collaborate across boundaries. Cultural shifts make themselves known when success is observable, not just possible, and therefore are easily attributable to the right behaviors occurring at the right time.

At this point in your journey, organizational adoption may still be somewhat uneven. Some teams may directly drive or maintain data contract adoption. Others may still be working out how to approach it. This is natural. Because, again, visibility should always take precedence over uniformity.

Shifts like these often begin to take place before they're noticed. They emerge first as patterns, then as more uniform behaviors, and eventually as organizational norms. Therefore, consistent self-reflection, informally or as part of engaging with your cross-functional coalition, can prove invaluable for gaining a sense of how deeply entrenched the adoption process is at any given moment.

To do so, ask yourself:

- Are you noticing a shift in the organizational atmosphere as you progress through your own eight steps?
- Are people growing more open to trying, adopting, and evolving shift left data practices in their own domains?
- Are incidents becoming fewer? Postmortems calmer?

- Are data producers discussing potential downstream concerns more often, unprompted?
- Are data consumers starting to ask about contract coverage while their product managers reference contracts during feature planning?

None of these are formal milestones. And they certainly aren't metrics in the classical sense. But they do all matter. They serve as informal signals that contract adjacency is occurring and that the logic of shift left data practices is holistically echoing beyond the traditional barriers of data contract implementations.

For example, going back to our case studies from Chapter 8, success looked like the following:

Convoy

Data became a "first-class citizen" in developers' minds, with the culture change among developers resulting in them thinking about the underlying data model and how their changes impacted others. This was critical, since the main challenges Convoy was facing stemmed from the massive endeavor of modeling the entire freight trucking industry.

Glassdoor

Implementation of data contracts restored trust in the data that calculated revenue, and enabled Glassdoor to increase the complexity and volume of data to the petabyte scale. Specifically, technology such as static code analysis, write-audit-publish data patterns, and data contracts drove automation that made adoption of shift left data practices feasible both downstream and upstream within product engineering workflows.

Adevinta Spain

Beyond reducing data quality issues, the introduction of data contracts resulted in the automation of a substantial portion of GDPR compliance. Specifically, before data contracts, significant time was spent reactively addressing GDPR issues manually to maintain compliance—to the point where this was nearly all the data platform team was working on. The team went from reactively fixing tickets to focusing on making the data platform more robust.

These early, qualitative indicators can also be easy to miss if you aren't looking for them. Which is why promoting active attribution becomes so important during the final phases of the data contract adoption curve. Your own role becomes about deepening guardianship, while also protecting and expanding on the conditions that keep these occurrences thriving. As adoption deepens, you'll also anticipate the need to quantify how this is all working, how well, and what should happen next.

Conclusion

In this chapter, we covered the three main phases leaders will progress through in their data contract and shift left adoption journey. First, select the best data product for an initial data contract proof of concept. Second, go from product selection to a proof-of-concept presentation and fast-follow pilots (i.e., steel threads). Finally, pivot to scale shift left data practices throughout an entire organization.

We explored the following ideas:

- The importance of defining data products as the first phase of an iterative filtering process
- How information gathering and engagement plans are instrumental in the first phases of proof-of-concept planning
- Invaluable, effective ways to map stakeholder influence and potential risks
- A minimum-viable-product approach to creating a proof of concept and pilot presentations that speak the language of leadership and business needs
- Why Kotter's eight-step change management framework's core focus on maintaining leadership buy-in and producing lasting change makes it a perfect fit for scaling data contract adoption
- Why each of Kotter's eight steps matter, and how data leaders can anticipate needing to apply them
- How change needs to be experiential (not simply understandable), and how qualitative examples indicate when data contract scaling efforts deliver on their promise

Kotter's work, specifically, should be viewed as a potential solution to scale by the reader, and not a prescription. Any change management framework needs to be studied, interrogated, understood, and adapted to the specific needs of the reader and their organization.

In the coming years we expect adherents of shift left data practices to coalesce around a shared framework for scaling data contracts through their respective organizations, and thus we can spend much more time working together on testing, learning, and sharing how best to use it—as opposed to endlessly debating which framework could be the best to use.

In the next chapter, we will shift to exploring the metrics at play beneath change phases and frameworks. Furthermore, the chapter focuses on what needs measuring during the adoption process, how best to measure it, and why leveraging metrics to tell compelling stories will play such a large role in achieving your goals.

## CHAPTER 12

Measuring the Impact of Data Contracts

Measurement isn't just a reporting function; it's a mechanism for supporting the organizational change we outlined in Chapter 11, the culture changes we discussed in Chapter 10, and the perception changes we highlighted in Chapter 9. In addition, leaders understand that metrics aren't created in a vacuum, and thus require thoughtful planning and communication. Specifically, leaders recognize that people within the business need to accept their metrics' validity and agree on their meaning.

Throughout this chapter, we'll explore how you can complement the qualitative results surfaced in previous data contract implementations with quantitative measurements. In addition, we will detail how you can effectively communicate these numbers and ensure the wider business understands the positive impact of shift left data practices and data contracts.

What's Worth Measuring?

With respect to data contracts, we group measurements into the following three categories:

Technical
Metrics that are indicative of the coverage, reliability, and functionality of any data contract implementation itself (e.g., test time length, number of assets covered, etc.)

Team
Operational metrics tied to efficiency, behavior, or workload of teams related to data products and/or implemented data contracts

Business

Bottom-line metrics that directly demonstrate the business value of one's data contract implementation

As a starting point, Figure 12-1 outlines potential measurements you can use in quantifying the impact of data contracts among the three categories.

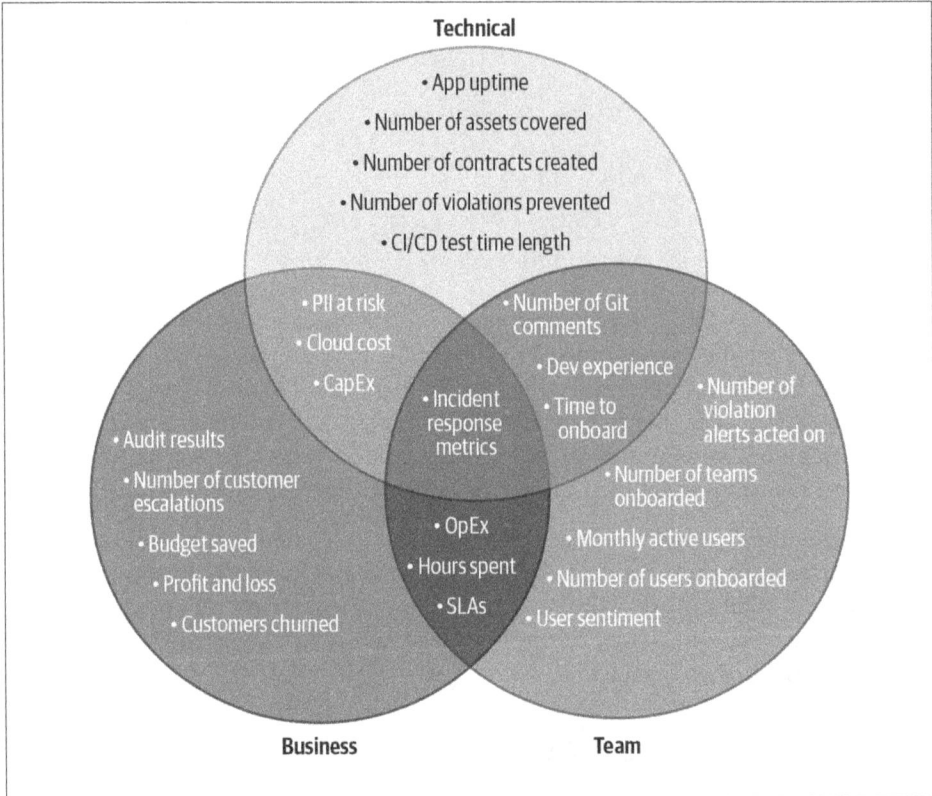

Figure 12-1. Potential data contract impact measurements

But we would also caution readers here to avoid the foreknowledge trap. It becomes far too easy to assume that because you understand the value of what should be measured and why, this value will be both shared by and equally apparent to everyone else throughout the organization.

Where to Start If You Have Minimal Existing Measurements

An invaluable first step in understanding why metrics tend to get mentioned much more than measured involves POSIWID—an acronym that stands for *the purpose of a system is what it does.* Coined by Stafford Beer (*https://oreil.ly/q9ETX*), the term acts as a heuristic lens. It encourages a focus on a system's behavior and results rather than on the intentions of its creators, helping to counter biases and facilitate more-objective evaluations.

For our purposes, POSIWID correctly sets expectations that while measurement is praised in the business world, its practical application often falls short. This is because organizations are designed to generate profits, not measurements. This misalignment manifests as everyday hesitations, biases, and resistance when people are asked to measure what truly matters.

Echoing the contents of Chapter 10, and rigorously demonstrated in *How to Measure Anything: Finding the Value of Intangibles in Business* (Wiley) by Douglas W. Hubbard, most, if not all, of this dissonance can be decomposed into hesitations. In his book, Hubbard details how misinformation and cognitive biases related to measurement create significant barriers. For example, organizations that have grown comfortable with individuals relying on inconsistent and imprecise methods such as intuition alone or available but incorrect data.

Collectively, these organizational hesitations over time can make change difficult, leading to feedback and comments such as:

- "We already know this is a problem."
- "I think that's too fuzzy to quantify."
- "It won't matter, as nothing's going to change if we measure this."
- "Without a baseline, we can't measure improvement."
- "OK. Well. No one's ever tried to measure that before."
- "We don't trust your metric—you should rely on ours instead."

In our own experience working with companies implementing data contracts, we've found instances where data teams often held similar sentiments, such as "We know we have a problem with data quality but we have never measured it, nor do we know where to start." This highlighted an even bigger problem when conversations dragged on at this juncture. Simply put, it was unclear how the data team provides value to the wider organization beyond being seen as a necessary cost of running the business. This is all the more reason why figuring out how to measure their impact becomes critical. Data contracts center the conversation on which of the business's critical data assets are worth protecting first.

So where can a team start if they find themselves in this position? Pulling from Hubbard's concept of *clarification chains*, our first step is recognizing that if people care about an output or process in an organization, then that entity is, by definition, detectable. As Hubbard states in his book, "If we have reason to care about some unknown quantity, it is because we think it corresponds to desirable or undesirable results in some way."

His clarification chain then progresses as follows:

1. If an entity is detectable, it must be observable.

2. If an entity is observable, one can observe more of it.

3. If an entity is more observable, then it must be measurable.

This logic provides a simple yet logical justification for needing to measure the impact of a critical data asset. Applying Hubbard's own distillation of his heuristic under a data contract perspective, we can say:

- A data product being deemed business-critical is, in itself, showing value is detectable.

- Since this value is detectable, we can further observe the data product and express these observations as quantities or ranges.

- As expressible quantities or ranges, these are data contract metrics we can measure (e.g., "incident tickets related to the data product reduced from a rate of 14 to 2 tickets per month").

In conjunction, Beer's POSIWID and Hubbard's clarification chains provide any team with a starting point on what to measure, advice on measuring what's observed rather than what's intended, and a business justification as to why it's worth measuring.

But remember, we stated earlier that metrics aren't created in a vacuum. It needs to be clear how they tie to the overall business objectives that are already deemed valuable to the wider business. To support you in making this connection, the next section details what we call *minimal viable metric trees*.

Minimal Viable Metric Trees

Metric trees have been popular in some analytics circles (with Abhi Sivasailam driving the concept, described in his 2023 Data Council conference talk "Designing & Building Metric Trees" (*https://oreil.ly/JWwDN*)), and have parallels with DuPont analysis, which was created by the eponymous DuPont company in the 1920s, and Bernie Smith's 2010s concept of KPI trees (*https://oreil.ly/ODThY*). We call this out to explicitly highlight that the minimum viable metric tree (MVMT) is not a new concept we created, and more importantly, we want to emphasize the word "minimum" here. DuPont analysis and KPI trees can be quite extensive, and similar to Chapter 11, we want to focus on practicality and opt for informed action over deep analysis.

Thus, we argue that MVMT provides a lightweight, structured view of how your data contract efforts connect to measurable business outcomes. It starts with a clear North Star metric that reflects the goal of your data contract implementation and builds downward to map contributing inputs and their dependencies.

Furthermore, MVMTs help teams focus on what matters in the moment without getting lost in what *could* be measured at some point in the future. They also create shared visibility by clarifying the logic of impact for both technical and nontechnical stakeholders. Additionally, they ensure the feedback you generate stays meaningful as conditions around you continue to evolve. Figure 12-2 provides a high-level overview of what this looks like, and we will provide a data contract example in subsequent sections.

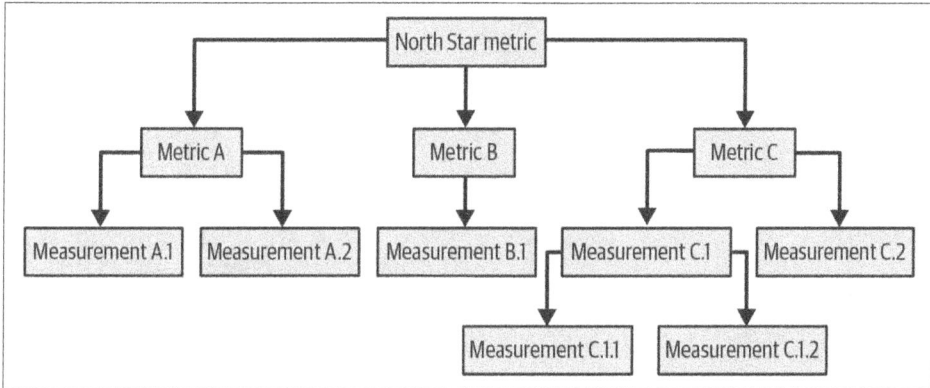

Figure 12-2. High-level MVMT example

As an example, let's bring back the automotive company logistics use case from Chapter 11, where leadership stated, "It's paramount we reduce waste within our supply chains to counteract the rising cost of steel." Figure 12-3 illustrates what a potential MVMT would look like.

Here, we can see that our North Star metric is total supply chain cost, which we decompose into inventory costs, logistics costs, and manufacturing costs. This first layer is relatively straightforward, but the next set of layers is where the complexity starts to arise and where we emphasize *minimum*. You will need to work with your stakeholders to determine the key drivers of the metrics they care about. In the case of the example automotive company, this would be the team held responsible for supply chain costs—the logistics operations team. Repeat this process until you get to a node that is directly impacted by the data product you are trying to protect via data contracts, in this instance the logistics cost ledger metrics report.

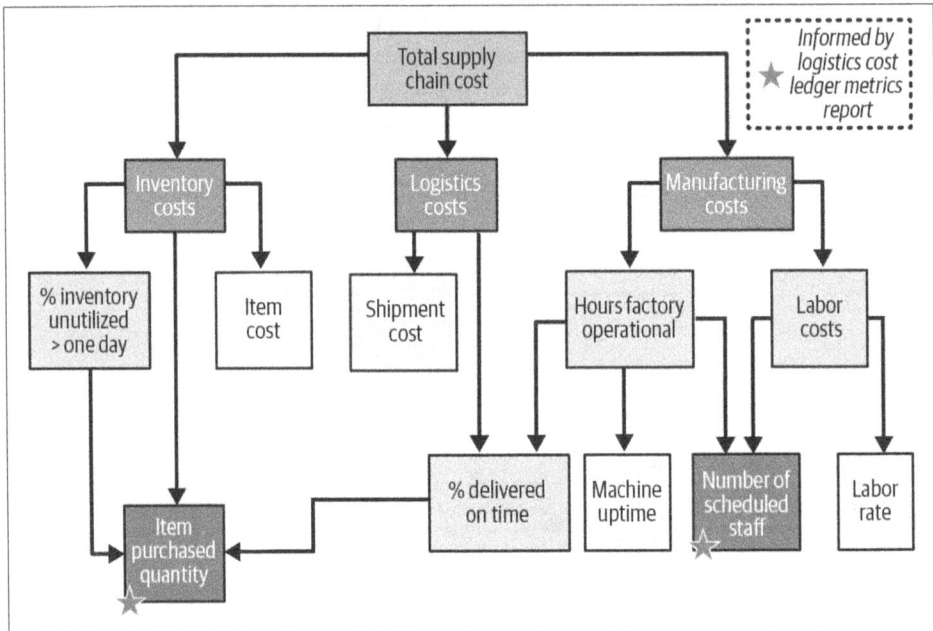

Figure 12-3. MVMT example: logistics cost ledger

Note that there is a huge assumption that this process will eventually lead to your data product of interest as a node. We are confident this assumption will hold given the effort put in to strategically decide what data product is worth protecting. If you are struggling to come to such a point, it may be a signal that the data product is not as business-critical as originally thought. With that said, there may be instances where measurements and metrics can't be derived from internal data, and thus organizations will instead leverage available data such as former baselines, reporting from similar practices or industries, or even public information from competitive firms.

In this example, we can clearly tie how the protection of the logistics cost ledger metrics report, via data contracts, ties to the overall company goal of "reduce waste within our supply chains." Specifically, the logistics operations team uses the report to inform the item purchased quantity and the number of scheduled staff, which in turn impact factory operations and inventory utilization. It could be argued that reducing errors on this report would empower the logistics operations team in improving resource allocation within the supply chain and ultimately reduce waste.

With this thought exercise as scaffolding, the following sections will bring all of this together by walking through how measurement evolves across each of the three main measurement phases of the data contract adoption journey: 1) measuring for viability, 2) measuring for repeatability, and 3) measuring for scalability.

Measuring Across the Three Phases of Adoption

In Chapter 11, we broke down the adoption journey into three phases precisely because of the different evolving facets in each. Each phase—the initial proof of concept, extending those wins to additional pilots, and, eventually, scaling data contract adoption across the organization—also corresponds to a distinct measurement objective: data contract viability, repeatability, and scalability. So, with this framing in mind, we suggest the following framework that can be applied at each phase of adoption:

1. Adopt a measurement point of view.

> A simple yet meaningful snapshot of the business that supports you in identifying business-relevant outcomes that a given data product supports or is responsible for. As part of your measurement strategy, you'll select these outcomes to act as North Star metrics.

> *Align on a North Star metric.*
>> Each MVMT begins with a North Star metric that all inputs ladder up to. Furthermore, this business-relevant outcome must be both highly visible to the company and related to the data product you want to put under contract.

> *Decompose all key related inputs.*
>> Break down each of the guiding business outcomes into its key contributing metrics and levers. As part of the MVMT diagramming process, this helps you clearly diagnose how an outcome actually happens and, by extension, validate its related metrics and stakeholders.

2. Outline a metric tree.

> At this point, your goal is to codify information gained in the previous steps into a metric tree. These simple, hierarchical, context-specific maps can prove invaluable, as they will help you and your data contract champions keep all implementation efforts firmly bolted to the business outcomes you're ultimately working to impact.

> *Map data contract intersections.*
>> With inputs defined, now trace how each metric logically builds on others (no more than is needed for the purposes of a specific implementation opportunity). This keeps your MVMT grounded in observable outcomes that you can directly point to.

> *Collaborate iteratively.*
>> Again, metrics don't happen in a vacuum. Periodically get feedback from your key stakeholders to understand what's worth prioritizing for the respective data contract implementation.

3. *Validate your assumptions.*

   While North Star metrics in an organization may be quite obvious, the web of key metrics that feed into each may not be. Ensure those in play will be meaningful, observable, and relevant to your phase-specific adoption needs.

   Validate selected metrics.

   Once you map the MVMT structure, assess whether each metric and relationship still reflects the issue you're trying to solve. Avoid the temptation to set and forget your measurements. Focus instead on adjusting your metrics over time to better reflect what success looks like as adoption progresses.

   Prepare to monitor and report.

   Prioritize consistent and concise communication with stakeholders identified within your metric tree.

By leveraging this practical framework, you'll be able to adapt your measurement strategy as your implementation efforts mature. But what does that look like across the phases? Table 12-1 provides a guide that you can reference along your own data contract adoption journey.

Table 12-1. Measurement considerations across the data contract adoption journey

MVMT framework step	Measurement considerations		
	Phase 1: Viability	Phase 2: Repeatability	Phase 3: Scalability
1. Align on a North Star metric	At the POC phase, this must be laser-focused on the key metric related to your steel thread's primary business outcome or impact.	North Star metrics in this phase should increasingly center on cross-team outcomes to highlight their generalizability across the organization.	How does the adoption of a shift left data practice support overall business goals? Your North Star metrics are thus now centered around overall organizational change and how such a change better repositions the business.
2. Decompose inputs	Identify and decompose no more than three critical downstream outcomes, along with their key contributing metrics or levers. Ask yourself, "Which inputs in my set of considerations would be most painful to get wrong?"	Remember, you're now dealing with organizational signals and shared pain points. Therefore, work to decompose each North Star into recurring measurements that surface across teams.	Decomposition needs to account for cross-domain contributors. At the same time, you'll need to be mindful of ambiguities creeping into your metric definitions, namely inputs that behave differently depending on team contexts (e.g., "Who is considered a customer?").
3. Map data contract intersections	In Phase 1, focus only on the minimum necessary metrics. These are one to two key sources that feed your selected North Star metric, directly affecting the outcome of the POC.	Focus on dependencies across systems and ownership boundaries—identifying, for instance, where a single metric is fed by different pipelines, or where enforcement will require coordination.	This phase requires focusing on known failure points, enforcement boundaries, and system interdependencies. While this begins to show in Phase 2, in Phase 3 it's the expectation as you view contract coverage at an org level.

| MVMT framework step | Measurement considerations | | |
	Phase 1: Viability	Phase 2: Repeatability	Phase 3: Scalability
4. Validate metrics	Ensure the metrics you want to surface will prove the viability of the implementation and will also ladder up to the north star metric.	Emphasis here focuses on shared understandings and beliefs in metrics across teams. One metric may be critical for one team and an afterthought for another.	Scaling into and through the latter phases of the data contract maturity curve as a whole requires validation that is automated, integrated, and continuous. It's the only way to ensure the overhead doesn't become the blocker of sustaining efforts.
5. Collaborate iteratively	Work closely with your champion or one to two stakeholders, prioritizing informal yet direct and honest feedback.	In Phase 2, shifting data left becomes a collaborative effort. Full stop. As such, you should begin to maintain shared definitions and document decisions, in addition to creating feedback loops across teams. Formalization here can evolve as the organization moves along the data contract maturity curve.	As collaboration evolves into governance structures, be on the alert for signs of overhead creep. Collaborative efforts themselves should always and actively support resilience, not slow it down. Therefore, endeavor to design for autonomy with accountability.
6. Monitor and report	Based on your measurement POV, deliver a clear, focused, observable outcome that makes the impact of data contract implementation easy to understand.	Phase 2 reporting needs to begin enabling comparison and pattern recognition. Work to build dashboards or trackers that begin to demonstrate where data contracts are being applied, which teams are benefiting from your ongoing efforts, and where violations occur.	In this phase, it becomes crucial to ensure your metrics maintain their ability to help tell compelling, outcome-related stories that can be used by leadership.

In the next sections, we will break down each phase, provide additional considerations for within a phase, and suggest potential metrics you can use.

Phase 1 Goal: Measuring for Viability

In Phase 1, your goal is simply to show that a data contract can function as intended when applied to a business-critical, well-scoped use case. This phase of the data contract adoption journey arguably requires the most discipline, as your goal is to do nothing more than demonstrate the viability of a data contract on a strategically selected steel thread (as discussed in Chapter 11). Before things get more complicated, you want to validate that the data contract implementation can function as intended in a contained area of the business. This shows that it delivers reliable performance and measurable value under limited and clear conditions.

Here are some potential questions that can guide you:

- "What is the business risk we're trying to mitigate or prevent?"
- "Is this metric close to something that's already being tracked or felt?"
- "Who ultimately needs to be convinced of the efficacy of this POC, and what will they trust as evidence?"

> If answers here prove elusive, we suggest reviewing Chapter 11's criteria for selecting your POC steel thread. Additionally, you may also need to revisit and revise the stakeholder influence/interest matrix developed as part of the POC proposal process itself. This is all part of the process as you learn more about what really matters to your stakeholders.

In addition, here are some potential metrics that may be useful beyond the business-specific measurements tied to your steel thread:

- Number of data assets detected
- Number of data contracts drafted, accepted, implemented, changed, or archived (i.e., a funnel)
- Time to first contract (the date of the start time is often negotiated)
- Number of developers onboarded to data contracts
- Number of CI/CD runs that started, errored out, passed checks, or surfaced violations
- Number of alerts that were accurate or false positives
- Likert score for developer satisfaction (e.g., "On a scale of 1–5...")

The emphasis on these measurements is on the *viability* of data contracts, in contrast to the metric tree exercise that focuses on the *impact* of data contracts.

Post-POC implementation, the pain related to your steel thread should be noticeably lesser. In this operational wake, stay tuned to signals of increased trust from previously hesitant stakeholders, particularly those upstream or adjacent to the steel thread. Are they asking fewer clarifying questions? Do they seem more confident in the system's output? These subtle shifts matter.

Also pay attention to early signs of adoption momentum, specifically, interest or alignment that begins to emerge organically from parts of the organization you haven't actively engaged. This might take the form of casual inquiries, references to your POC in adjacent team meetings, or a willingness among noninfluential participants to advocate for similar adoption efforts elsewhere. These moments of unsolicited support are often the earliest signs that Phase 2 will be easier to initiate than anticipated.

It's worth calling out that reporting goes beyond documenting what happened and changed. Reporting also serves as a feedback mechanism to inform teams of potentially new metrics (or ones not worth measuring). This is critical as you move toward repeatability of your efforts.

Phase 2 Goal: Measuring for Repeatability

In Phase 2, your focus must shift to repeatability as you apply your initial approach to additional high-value data products and domains, testing whether your approach is viable under broader, more varied conditions. Post-POC, you should now sit in a prime position thanks to all the hard work, planning, and peer wrangling you've done. You will have proven the viability of data contract implementation in your organization, and you'll have done so with one of your most valued data products.

Your operative goal is now different. You've shown that data contracts can work in a highly controlled context. Now it's time to expand that success. This means pushing beyond the POC and recalibrating your approach to implementation, ideally with as many remaining steel threads as possible. You're no longer trying to prove that data contracts can work—you're now proving they can work again and again, with different data products, domain owners, and continued real-world pressures.

By extension, this means preparing yourself to tackle more organizational complexity, more stakeholders, and stakes that, while already high due to your steel-thread-first approach, will only continue to increase as your organization matures along the data contract curve. As you push ahead with pilots, you may find yourself quickly needing to extend your efforts out beyond your early adopters and influencers. In doing so, you will begin to encounter more hesitancy or even pushback among the data producers and consumers you're pitching your ongoing adoption efforts to.

Because of this shift to a broader, less naturally inclined audience, your measurement efforts must now center on metrics that highlight consistency, cross-team alignment, and operational trust—not just those tied to direct business outcomes. Some examples are:

- Time to resolution of an incident across multiple teams
- Number of teams denoted as owners within contract specs
- Number of customer-related escalations versus internal escalation
- Reduction in repeated escalations over time
- Time spent managing contract violations

- Decrease in reactive on-call events per X-week window
- Estimated engineering hours saved through violation enforcement quarter-over-quarter

In addition, after a successful POC, it's tempting to rush forward. But in Phase 2, you must pause and realign around what success looks like under broader conditions. Therefore, make time to, once again, self-interrogate based on what you've now established through your evolved goals, snapshot, and measurement POV:

- "What would it mean if [metric] improved in one place in the organization but not in another?"
- "Does every team define [metric] this way? Or will it require translation?"
- "Would this metric make sense to someone outside of data?"
- "Can we measure this often enough to inform decision making? Or is it too delayed or manual?"

Additionally, it can be tempting to standardize your measurement efforts too early and too rigidly. There will be ample time to refine in Phase 3, where the long game of organization-wide adoption begins. In Phase 2, by comparison, you're still in implementation learning mode. Forcing consistency before you're able to validate fit can foster unnecessary resistance and data contract implementations that lack the flexibility needed to build on them.

Lastly, as successful implementations multiply, it's easy to deprioritize the time and energy required to maintain stakeholder engagement. As covered in Chapters 10 and 11, leveraging measurement is mission-critical but requires clear communication for expanding the confidence and trust others have in your efforts. By design, MVMTs should be as lean and effective as humanly possible. But if your measurement efforts begin to omit the human context behind the data—the real needs, risks, and relationships driving each use case—you risk losing the underlying point of your efforts entirely.

By contrast, successfully expanding your efforts through the second phase of the data contract adoption journey provides more success signals of which you should take note. Implementation should begin to edge toward being proactive, with more teams over time seeking you out to request data contracts. Far fewer should still be trying to justify it by asking, "What's in it for me?"

As you move closer to Phase 3, shared metrics should begin to hold their meaning, and dashboards should show trends across teams. Once you've defined a key metric, you should see more teams reporting against it, with less confusion or translation overhead required over time.

Phase 3 Goal: Measuring for Scalability

Finally, in Phase 3, broader adoption efforts become possible, and your attention turns to scalability and embedding measurement and enforcement practices across systems and into culture.

For the final phase of the data contract adoption journey, you will begin to shift to scale. It's now time to evolve your data contract adoption efforts from crafting single implementations to establishing cultural practices. In progressing from proof of concept to repeatable success across steel threads and additional data product pilots, your measurement efforts must now embed enforcement, governance, and observability into the broader systems and practices of your organization.

In practice, this will mean navigating complexities as they naturally compound. Yes, teams may begin to embrace and implement data contracts independently. But as adoption spreads, so do the risks of implementation drift, enforcement inconsistencies, and signal fatigue. Therefore, the role of measurement in this phase is not just to support adoption; it must also help reinforce trust, surface invisible breakdowns, and fortify long-term resilience.

As data contract adoption practices begin to embed themselves in the organization, and the value of data contracts and shift left data practices become capable of self-reinforcing, your measurement efforts can serve a broader, but no less vital, purpose. Therefore, metrics at this phase should increasingly speak to the needs of leadership by showing the value of data platform teams as a whole. This looks like providing visibility into ROI, shaping roadmap decisions, and supporting data governance policy development.

As such, this may involve a focus on metrics like:

- Percentage of all steel threads under full data contract enforcement
- Quarterly cost savings from prevention
- Percentage of the company's data assets under contract (i.e., contract coverage)
- Mean time to resolution for issues related to data products
- Onboarding time for new teams
- Volume of recurring violations over time
- Percentage of alerts resolved without escalation

It is also important to call out that Phase 3 requires accepting that motivating pressures from Phases 1 and 2 will grow more distributed, if not entirely deferrable to competing priorities. Now, you must push back against assumptive thinking, blind trust, and, as noted in Chapter 11's adoption of Kotter's eight-step framework, the anti-momentum effects of complacency.

In addition to your vigilance in complacency, you must focus on your ability to detect if data contract maturation is, in fact, taking place and maintaining momentum:

- "What's going on under the surface of our efforts that we've stopped seeing clearly?"
- "Are the metrics we're reporting still driving action? Or are we just fulfilling expectations?"
- "If [steel-thread-related team] stopped complying with their data contact tomorrow, how long would it take us to notice?"

First and perhaps foremost, be aware of the challenges that come with data contract adoption at scale. Automation is essential, but it can also create blind spots if you measure the wrong things or ignore failure signals. This risk overlaps with that of a subtle cultural slide into the assumption of trust, as teams and stakeholders scale adoption across the organization. Similarly, dashboards and agreed-upon metrics can degrade into organizational noise if they're not revalidated regularly against real business risks and outcomes.

With these points in mind, success signals in the final phase of the data contract adoption journey can prove exceptionally rewarding because, in addition to furthering the overall health and wellness of business operations, they become increasingly visible throughout the organization's culture itself. Self-correcting behaviors should appear and go on to become increasingly common. Teams should proactively update contracts, flagging violations, and refining metric definitions from the bottom up instead of requiring top-down initiation. In addition, thinking back to Phase 2 challenges, new teams should continue to onboard faster while contract-violation false positives decrease.

Ultimately, metrics and measurement evolve too, from being a backward-looking obligation to being a forward-facing strategic advantage and paving the way for ongoing implementation and adoption momentum. Regardless of which phase you find yourself operating in, remember the core insight from Hubbard: measuring anything, especially those things that seem intangible, is ultimately about reducing uncertainty to make better decisions.

But in order to drive an organization through the data contract maturity curve, we need to communicate those insights clearly and persuasively to others. Journeys, by definition, require forward momentum. Measurement successes from each data contract adoption phase need to contribute to establishing and maintaining constant and consistent forward progress. In the next section we will provide you with a framework for supporting your communication efforts and keeping the forward momentum.

Storytelling for Measurement Impact

One reason that measurement isn't more self-sustaining within organizations is that insights and information cannot sell themselves. In fact, as Hubbard also discusses in his work, while data-driven information certainly reduces uncertainty in organizations, it's unable to overcome human biases, misunderstandings, or resistance to change all on its own. Those at the helm of data contract adoption efforts are inclined to appreciate the potential of data contracts and are the first to witness data contracts begin to succeed, but re-proving one's efforts over time can be frustrating. You may wonder:

- "Why don't people just get what we're doing here?"
- "Can't everyone see why this is working so well?"
- "Why do I need to keep proving the value again and again?"

These frustrations are understandable. As detailed in Chapter 9, gaps of perception between teams and individuals working in different parts of the organization can be surprisingly wide. The one proven way to span these gaps is empathy.

Ultimately, you need to reduce the resistance of others by approaching issues in ways that make sense to them. Use themes, issues, and perspectives that resonate with the realities of their professional experiences. In addition to being prepared to measure and use metrics as proof, we also need to be ready and able to use them to persuade. To do so, we now shift from the science of measurement to a complementary discipline—the art of storytelling.

Just as metric trees offer a structured formula for measuring what matters to the business, we propose a similarly intentional structure for storytelling. Here, we introduce storytelling as a strategic, repeatable mechanism for getting your message across to the wider business. Done well, it becomes a way to surface alignment, build confidence, and cut through competing priorities and political friction in ways metrics alone often can't. And, as we'll show shortly, this story structure doesn't just support the narrative; it mirrors the practical realities of the data contract adoption journey itself, aligning naturally with the three core phases we've already established.

Thus, we draw on the pioneering insights of Joseph Campbell in creating a captivating story. Through his lifetime of work studying mythology, religions, and cultural archetypes, Campbell discovered that certain characters, plot points, and narrative themes appear repeatedly throughout history in the stories people seem most drawn to.

In *The Hero with a Thousand Faces* (*https://oreil.ly/j1eKm*) (Princeton University Press), Campbell synthesized the most common story patterns into the "monomyth," also referred to as the "hero's journey." His goal in doing so was entirely practical: to provide a mythological roadmap of near-universal appeal, rooted in shared human psychology and timeless cultural rites. In short, he devised the ultimate storytelling formula, one that's proven invaluable to thousands of writers and filmmakers and, yes, business professionals, who all need effective and repeatable ways of persuading others that are bracingly simple yet exceedingly adaptable.

This highly persuasive storytelling structure has been directly credited with shaping some of the most influential and enduring narratives of our recent era. It is no coincidence that, in 2012, Disney felt it worth spending $4.04 billion to purchase *Star Wars*, one of the most successful film franchises in history. George Lucas, its creator, credits the successes of the franchise to Campbell's story structure (*https:// jcf.org/learn/star-wars*).

These storytelling tactics help audiences understand why a story matters and why it's worth paying attention to. We'll use the monomyth to do the same here in ensuring our measurement efforts are not just concise and clear, but optimally compelling.

Before pushing Campbell through the data contract lens, let's first crack apart each act of the monomyth—departure, transformation, and return.

Departure

First, establish a sense of normalcy. This helps the audience appreciate the change that's about to unfold. We meet the main characters and learn about their basic needs and goals. But then, something unexpected happens that confronts the protagonists. A change, event, or disruption forces them to leave the world they know in order to try to save it.

Transformation

Next, a journey unfolds. The protagonists face trials, encounter resistance, and are forced to face either internal or external change. The moment our heroes face the moment of transformation is the apex of the monomyth story, where positive character traits like trust, resilience, or faith are tested.

Return

A successful transformation in the monomyth story results in death and rebirth, with the protagonist often making a great sacrifice in order to accomplish something heroic. In doing so, they thwart that which drove them to depart the normal world in the first place. They then return home, and the world around them is changed to the benefit of everyone within it.

Let's now build on those three acts and break down how you can apply different phases of the data contract adoption journey to this structure. We'll ensure measurement-relevant storytelling as needed.

Departure

The goal of the first phase of the monomyth story, the *departure*, is to make it clear to your audience that something new needs to happen. This requires establishing background. The background needs to include identifying our main characters—a steel thread or data product and its related key stakeholders, data producers, and consumers—and the world they operate in. Providing this information to your audience first is vital because it creates the context for everything else that happens in the story. The background makes the story make sense and, by extension, matter to the audience.

The key to establishing the first part of a monomyth pattern is to introduce a complication that functions as a catalyst. It is a failure for our characters to address that risks the stability of the world we've established and our characters' goals and needs. This is where our immediate or retroactive issues come into play, where we make it clear to our audience that failure to act is not acceptable. We must together take action, departing from the safety and security of how things have been in order to, quite literally, prevent bad things from occurring.

Transformation

This brings us to the second part of the storytelling structure, when a *transformation* must occur. In the monomyth, this classically involves our heroes gaining a magic potion, tool, or the help of a mentor or support character. The heroes go on to sacrifice themselves only to be reborn anew—transformed with the power, knowledge, or skills to make the pivotal difference needed in the story.

Data contract implementations can prove to be absolutely transformative in modern organizations. As a bonus, they don't require the level of sacrifice and rebirth so often encountered in galaxies far, far away. But they do absolutely require our use of metrics and measurement as enabling tools to make transformations possible. This parallels how monomyth-inspired storytelling guides how we include key players related to data products as active and supportive characters in our stories.

Additionally, for our data contract adoption stories to be persuasive, the need for transformation must seem inevitable, not optional. Post-departure in the second act, the audience must feel that there is no turning back—because the way things were is no longer acceptable. Whatever short-term pain, discomfort, or sacrifices that enacting change requires are worth the benefits in the near future. While the conflict at hand may only involve a few individuals, it's the entire organization that stands to benefit. Therefore, when crafted correctly, a data contract–related story that peaks in its second act leaves its audience asking, "Why aren't we already doing this?" instead of "Why would we do this at all?"

This is the belief you're weaving: that data contract implementation will deliver on its promise for each implementation opportunity. While your storytelling efforts in the initial adoption phases may benefit from the inherent stakes of your data products being steel threads, the beauty of this approach to storytelling is that it can create urgency and inspire action regardless of the nature of the business outcomes at stake.

Return

To persuade your audience that data contract implementation must take place, you must use metrics and measurement to illustrate what the *return* phase in your story will entail. In Campbell's eyes, the return resolves and releases the psychological tension built up within the audience over the first two acts. It is where the heroes bring the knowledge, treasure, or wisdom back to where they came from, to the benefit of all.

The return is where you will outline to your audience what real, measurable, and tangible effects data contract implementation will have on a given north star metric, as well as offer evidence of the new normal, be it fewer incident rates, more reliable pipelines, or increased trust in metrics. These potential outcomes must feel as tangible as possible when using these stories to persuade.

Putting It All Together

By design, your MVMTs will clarify what matters most and how to measure it. And now you understand what and why to measure, as well as the means to push that knowledge through a persuasive and repeatable framework. With these resources, you won't end up presenting technical achievements only to be frustrated that your peers can't seem to connect to them in the way you need them to. We can summarize the needs of each of the three acts with a few key questions:

Departure
> What inefficiency, pain, issue, or risk related to this data product is most unacceptable? Who's feeling it the most?

Transformation
> What specific enabling actions can shift reality here? Will there be resistance to making a change? What will you need to do to overcome this resistance?

Return
> What will be forever changed when data contract implementation takes place? What metrics will best indicate that the transformation is having the desired effect and providing lasting benefits that stakeholders and others can feel?

To help make this all practical, Table 12-2 shows three short story frames, each built around real-world data contract scenarios. Consider these thought starters, touching on the mindset needed to structure measurement-driven stories to inspire audiences to support data contract adoption efforts in your own organization.

Table 12-2. Examples of storytelling with respect to data contracts

Act	Purpose	Metric-driven storytelling
Example 1		
1. Departure	Establish background, context, characters, and stakes. What happens if nothing changes?	*"Our north star metric—critical customer usage data—was repeatedly delayed during reporting cycles, threatening quarterly business reviews."*
2. Transformation	Show the compelling effect that data contract implementation will make possible.	*"Data contract implementation that enforces data freshness SLAs will stabilize reporting cycles within two months, restoring executive trust."*
3. Return	Post-implementation, what will immediately change for the better? How will the organization benefit as a whole moving forward?	*"Moving forward, the finance and marketing teams will treat contract violations like smoke alarms, enabling proactive fixes instead of reactive escalations."*
Example 2		
1. Departure	Establish background, context, characters, and stakes. What happens if nothing changes?	*"Despite best intentions, teams managing customer billing data have no visibility into broken pipelines until customers escalate issues."*
2. Transformation	Show the compelling effect that data contract implementation will make possible.	*"Data contracts and proactive schema validation can cut customer escalations by 35% across the next 2 quarters, reducing on-call burden by 20%."*
3. Return	Post-implementation, what will immediately change for the better? How will the organization benefit as a whole moving forward?	*"Adopting proactive enforcement will allow support teams to catch data issues before they impact customers, protecting brand trust and reducing fire drills."*
Example 3		
1. Departure	Establish background, context, characters, and stakes. What happens if nothing changes?	*"Due to undocumented schema assumptions and lack of enforceable standards, onboarding new features into products currently takes an average of three-plus months. This is costing teams momentum and trust as they constantly need to go back and fix issues."*
2. Transformation	Show the compelling effect that data contract implementation will make possible.	*"Implementing data contracts and enforcement checkpoints can reduce time to delivery by 15%, enabling faster feature releases and scaling."*
3. Return	Post-implementation, what will immediately change for the better? How will the organization benefit as a whole moving forward?	*"Embedding data contracts will allow product teams to launch new services quickly and reliably—without risking downstream integration issues."*

Leveraged together, the power of clear measurement and persuasive storytelling will elevate your efforts beyond reporting outcomes. As the tip of the data contract adoption spear, you'll shape them. This ensures your ongoing efforts are increasingly seen as a story that, when told well, builds trust, fosters ongoing adoption, and sustains lasting change over time.

Conclusion

Throughout this chapter, we've explored why metrics and measurement are fundamental not only to implementing data contracts, but to driving an organization along the data contract maturity curve.

We established why measurement matters: it reduces uncertainty, keeps progress visible, and builds organizational trust. We then reintroduced the three core phases of the adoption journey first mentioned in Chapter 11—data contract viability, repeatability, and scalability—and provided a phase-specific strategy to align measurement with each. From there, we introduced minimum viable metric trees as a practical, repeatable way to ground each implementation effort in observable outcomes.

Building on that foundation, we shifted to storytelling by adapting Joseph Campbell's storied monomyth as a strategic formula to clarify value, invite alignment, and inspire the buy-in needed for lasting cultural change.

Our emphasis on persuasion, via meaningful metrics and storytelling, is rooted in our understanding of data quality issues: that they are people and process challenges masquerading as technical problems. Furthermore, we have found that teams don't struggle at the first implementation of data contracts, but rather on scaling the solution across more teams. Solving these issues requires behavior change within the business, and thus requires 1) incentivizing our desired behaviors and 2) making it as easy as possible to do so via automation.

We touched on the following ideas:

- Why effective measurement, despite being considered sacrosanct throughout the business world, tends to be both difficult and lacking

- Why proper measurement efforts and strategies must play an essential role in data contract adoption efforts

- Why measurement over the course of the data contract adoption journey can, and should, be managed as three distinct phases

- How to create minimum viable metric trees to effectively structure and guide measurement efforts without complicating them

- Why metrics derived from measurement aren't, on their own, capable of persuading leaders and key stakeholders, and thus how clear, intentional storytelling helps bridge the gap between adoption clarity and momentum

- How to structure data contract-related stories to sustain buy-in and accelerate trust-building

This also brings us to the conclusion of the third and final section of this book. We addressed the perception gaps that you must identify before adoption efforts begin, addressed the challenges inherent in change management, discussed strategic steps needed to approach an initial steel thread POC, and covered translation of that first data contract win into greater adoption through the organization itself.

But, as with any journey, there will always be more steps to take. We'll end this book with where we think data contact adoption is heading next and what we should prepare to learn more about in the near future.

Conclusion: AI and the Future of Data Contracts

While this conclusion marks the end of this book, these final pages start the next phase of your data contract journey. One of our ultimate goals in writing this book was documenting all the hard lessons learned from researching the content, talking to hundreds of engineering teams about their data challenges, and helping multiple companies implement data contracts and grow their adoption organization-wide. Specifically, we wanted to ensure that anyone who reads this book will have a huge head start and avoid any pitfalls as they implement data contracts within their own organization. You now understand all the functional information regarding data contracts—establishing why contracts are needed (Chapters 1 to 4), how data contracts work in practice (Chapters 5 to 8), and cultural and strategic foundations for adoption (Chapters 9 to 12).

In Part I, we outlined the core problem that set the shift left data movement in motion: modern organizations increasingly struggle to scale data reliably due to implicit assumptions, poor data quality, and suboptimal accountability among professionals, teams, and departments.

Several key insights from the first three chapters extend from this assertion. First, data professionals must avoid the trap of equating data quality with data perfection. Instead, teams must keep the concept pragmatic and operative, defined by fitness for purpose and its ability to sustain business-critical workflows. Next came the need to recognize that traditional data infrastructure (i.e., OLTP versus OLAP) leads to software and data teams becoming isolated within organizations. Specifically, this is a reflection of Conway's Law, or how technical systems are reflections of an organization's communication structure. Data teams' communication typically focuses on secondary uses of the data for analytics, machine learning and AI, and driving insights (OLAP), as compared to software teams who instead leverage the data to track the statefulness of an application and CRUD operations (OLTP). While this split between OLTP and OLAP is important and widely accepted as best practice,

Dunbar's Number highlights how at scale (e.g., more than around 150 employees) communication between stakeholders starts to break down. In turn, this exacerbates translation errors and contributes to the accumulation of data debt over time. Again, to be clear, this technical design pattern is fundamental; it's just that we need to account for this challenge as software engineering and data teams increasingly need to collaborate more. At the same time, prior to any data contract adoption, data practitioners can expect any existing garbage in, garbage out dynamic to grow exponentially more problematic as the organization continues to prioritize growth despite increasing evidence that cracks in its data foundation are growing.

By extension, data leaders must embrace a set of clear priors before any data contract adoption efforts can begin. Organizations cannot scale data without also scaling accountability. The software-to-data organizational model came to formation before cloud adoption and needs to evolve. Organizational growth and data debt share an entropic relationship, as the former naturally fosters data disorder if left unchecked. Importantly, preventative alignment will, in all instances, produce better and more-lasting benefits than reactive postures that so often form the default in organizations.

Next, Part II made it possible for us to build into data contract execution—a practical exploration of how contracts themselves work in practice. This practical information included a formal breakdown of what data contracts are—formal solutions comprising modular interoperable components by which we formalize explicit expectations in an organization. We also defined how contracts function to create a clear "handshake" between data producers and consumers regarding schema, context, and accountability. We then detailed exactly how, post–CI/CD integration, data contracts provide proactive prevention and schema validation that consistently outperforms reactive firefighting and the negative-sum game of root-cause triage.

However, we also emphasized that embracing the benefits of data contracts requires accepting that related stakeholder roles and incentives must matter, making the establishment of shared contract surfaces an imperative. To bring this necessary blend of technical and nontechnical needs to life, we shared stories involving three real-world data contract implementations that, taken together, illustrate how data contracts improve visibility and reduce reactive workload while enhancing accountability.

Lastly, in Part III, we widened our aperture to focus on the contextual, cultural, and conceptual factors that successful data contract adoption efforts hinge on.

Due to data contract implementation occurring with the software development lifecycle, the effective adoption of contracts demands a bridging of the perception gaps that naturally occur between data teams, software engineers, and data consumers. The effectiveness of change management in organizations requires clear communication, explicitly defined ownership, and distributed accountability across teams. We looked at why a focus on Tier-1 data products (i.e., steel threads) is a key part of achieving initial and key wins through a proof of concept and pilots, and is is vital for generating and maintaining change-worthy inertia. And how strategic and structured approaches to both change itself and data contract measurement throughout the adoption journey are key for achieving both sustained progress and lasting results.

Altogether, as first referenced in Chapter 10, we've worked to frame data contract adoption as running an airline rather than building an airplane. By adopting and applying the information, insights, and principles outlined in this book within your organization, you're joining us in our ongoing efforts to carry forward data contract adoption and shift left thinking. More than that, you're joining a growing community of leaders, data engineers, and other data-related practitioners who, like you, understand that real progress doesn't come from better pipelines or dashboards alone—it also must come from shared ownership, clearer expectations, and a full commitment to long-term, human-centered change.

Being part of a movement like this means thinking ahead—asking not just "How do we fix what's broken?" but also "How do we responsibly shape what comes next?" As automation, machine learning, and generative AI are shaping our world while they still shape themselves, the core principles behind data contracts—shared clarity, trust, accountability, and context—will, in our estimation, become more vital in the near future of our industry, not less.

Therefore, we offer our look forward to the shifting and rapidly evolving state of AI, security, and the future of responsible data practice and how data contracts fit within this context.

Future Implications of Shift Left Data

If our vision of the future comes to pass, and we believe there is great evidence that many companies are already heading in the right direction, shift left data has several tremendous implications for the future of our industry, artificial intelligence, security, and technology management in general.

Most broadly, the way that technology-centric businesses think about code quality will change. Today, code quality is primarily concerned with what goes on within the context of a codebase. In other words, tools, techniques, and frameworks are based around the question "Will my code compile?" It is less about whether the system as a whole is functioning as expected, and more about whether the writer of code has met their own expectations of quality. The increase in popularity of data contracts has a significant implication on code quality and introduces a new question: "Will my proposed change affect the output of my code in a way that affects others?"

This question is fundamentally unanswerable today, and remains so because developers still do not understand the dataflow of their services and how that dataflow is ultimately consumed by the broader business, nor are there clearly defined expectations of what these consumers need from their data (contracts). If you are a clever reader, you may have gathered that we are using "data" here in a much broader sense than analytics and ML teams generally do. Data, under the context of data contracts, is simply information that is consumed by someone other than the person producing it. An API produces data, database writes do as well, Kafka events certainly, and simply transforming files and pushing them into cold storage is also data. In many ways, all software engineering is data engineering—you are ingesting data, doing something to it, and writing it somewhere. Therefore, the principles of data engineering certainly have their places in the SWE's toolkit. Where they differ today is that software engineers are used to handling a few pieces of data at a time in transactions, while data engineers generally deal with large quantities of data in parallel. With data becoming increasingly critical to web-based applications, we argue that more software engineers will actively learn about these data best practices. (AI has already been a massive driver of this at the time of writing.)

As the industry comes around to these ideas, you will start to see CTOs and engineering leaders looking at the world just as much through the lens of data as software. *The other day we lost $10 million because our internal payment processing pipeline went down. Why? Well, someone made a change in a different part of the system that updated the date-time column that was used to determine if a payment had been processed or not.* That's a data quality problem, and would have been prevented by applying data engineering techniques on upstream systems.

We are confident that this shift left moment is now happening with data, as we have already seen shift left take hold in DevOps with similar patterns. Specifically, the operations of IT and deployments became both more complex and increasingly important to the wider business. What was once solvable by a centralized ops team became hamstrung by the scale of changes being made across disparate software teams—resulting in the need to federate this ops work to the respective domains where changes were happening. Therefore, software engineers became more responsible for understanding operational systems and getting operations teams involved in looking at the implications of code changes. Going back to data, it is increasingly becoming more complex as well as critical to the business beyond its traditional role of reporting and analytics. Centralized data platform teams are becoming hamstrung by the scale of changes being made across disparate software teams. Today, we are at a point where software engineers must take on the responsibility of owning the data within their domains, while downstream teams need to be aware of how code impacts their data.

For example, say an outage occurred that teams have spent the better part of a month root-causing. But what exactly is being root-caused? Consider these questions:

- Who made the change?
- What was the change?

- What did the change affect?

This triage process is complex because there are no clearly defined expectations of what software systems are supposed to output and what it means for consumers. Because those definitions don't exist, the responsibility falls onto the developers who made the change to trace through the dataflow of their own code to understand what possible impacts their changes *might* have had on the broader system. The more complex the code and the older it is, the more difficult it is to do. This isn't a pure software engineering problem—it's data lineage! But instead of focusing on the lineage of data through a data warehouse, it's focused on the flow of data and interaction effects between repos and the data output flowing through them.

There are numerous problems that emerge from a lack of data engineering within the software engineering discipline. Why do migrations take years? It surely is not because net new services are so challenging to build—talented engineers can move at light speed. The challenge is tracking down who has taken a dependency on the output of the service that is being replaced, how they are transforming or manipulating the data, and helping the team understand how to ensure the switchover to the new system is seamless. This is why migrations are constant and never-ending—because there is no clearly defined expectation of the appropriate way to use an output, no understanding of what the code is doing to the ingested data, and no vehicle to map the code-level dependencies across systems.

Shifting data management left, ultimately, isn't just about adopting data contracts. The contract is the smallest, easiest, and cheapest step. It's about shifting *all* components of data management, governance, and data engineering into the hands of the developers who are doing the work. Not just to solve analytics and ML problems, but to solve the biggest data problems masquerading as code-quality problems. Once data quality is seen as being inseparable from code quality, then the adoption of the shift left mindset will be swift.

Data as Code

Every piece of data that exists in a database, or flows over the wire as an event, or is processed by any downstream system, was created, enriched, or transformed by code. The code might be written by the software developers maintaining your internal applications, the data engineers building data pipelines, or the analysts crafting metrics through SQL queries. Whatever the case, data is inseparable from the code that produces it. In the same way, a product that is the result of a factory line is simply an output of the factory. To truly understand the product, you must understand the factory itself.

Security and AppSec teams have already had their eureka moment—techniques like static code analysis allowed security engineers to infer how a program will run without running it. Their goal is not just to address the results of security issues, but to understand the various attack vectors present in software. Where *could* an attacker inject themselves into an otherwise defensible system? How bad would it be? This question of what might happen can only be answered by evaluating the code upon which applications are built.

When we consider data quality, data governance, data privacy, or any other number of issues that data teams face, we believe the question of what might happen will be far more important as we move into the next phase of data management: where *might* data quality issues be introduced? Where *might* changes break downstream systems? Where *might* a privacy leak occur? If, somehow, these questions were answered, it would transform the role of data governance from a reactive responsibility to a proactive one. Instead of putting out fires, it would be about setting standards, determining where those standards aren't being met, and creating the programs necessary to pay down tech debt.

Data as code will be the future of data management. Not reactive and after the fact, but baked directly into the day-to-day workflow of every software engineer on the planet. Concerned not simply with what *is*, but with what could be and, more importantly, why.

The Impact of AI

We wrote this book in 2025. Depending on the year you are reading this, the world might look very different—a utopian vision of artificial intelligence may have come to pass. Robot butlers in every house, and a sophisticated program interpreting our thoughts and crafting the perfect query to answer a question previously unanswerable. Even today, as we write, the impact of AI is truly undeniable. Businesses race toward adoption. Every CTO has been given the order to cut whatever budget isn't tethered down to pursue AI toward a variety of ends—saving time, saving money, making money, or all of the above. We are neither going to give you an AI doomsday prediction nor hand-wave LLMs as a technological gimmick. We believe these tools are here to stay. We also believe that AI-driven software engineering will have a large and meaningful impact on the way developers write and understand code for a boring, and altogether predictable, reason: tech debt.

The Role of Agents

We've talked about tech debt quite a bit over the course of this book, so we won't belabor the points we have already made. However, AI introduces an interesting wrinkle into the concept of tech debt. Previously tech debt was very explicitly defined as the delta between the ideal engineering implementation and what is shipped in order to solve some business problem. As AI begins writing, modifying, and deleting code, tech debt becomes the result of a probabilistic machine making errors rather than reasoned, rational decisions. You might be able to guess why this is problematic!

If we discover that our data pipeline has suddenly experienced a latency hit, we can find the author of the pipeline code to understand where they made certain decisions that could impact performance. If that person is no longer with the company (as is often the case) we need to settle for the next best thing, reading through the code ourselves to infer what decisions were made and why. But with AI, there is now the opportunity for problems to occur without a good reason. Issues where there was no true rational thought put into *why* a thing was done. This makes the inevitable errors extremely difficult to debug or, even worse, fully comprehend.

Compared to traditional software-based applications, artificial intelligence is probabilistic. This means that, unlike machines with static outcomes, you could run the same model of the codebase and produce entirely different outcomes. This introduces the possibility of error. A model with only a 1% error rate would be absolutely top of the line. While this seems fine in a vacuum, hundreds of AI engineers constantly making changes, each with a 1% error rate, will introduce multiple errors per day, which compound over time as the code gets worse and more difficult to maintain. We believe that *quality* is the most essential component of an AI engineering program. How do we:

- Understand why models are making decisions?
- Understand what systems their decisions impact?
- Trace impact analysis to ensure that these decisions are not behaving in unexpected ways?
- Identify where proper coding patterns are not being followed and correct them?
- Ensure errors don't compound over time?

As we've highlighted throughout the book, we believe that the crux of these problems is ultimately a data management issue. Data is the connective tissue between technology. Be it repos, files, or agents, data is ultimately the mechanism that allows code-based systems to communicate. By investigating and understanding how data is transformed, enriched, and processed by other systems, both internal to your own team and external to different teams or companies, we can qualify and quantify how agentic systems (and AI in general) are performing in regard to the code quality of our broader data ecosystem.

LLMs and Context

While resolving the problems mentioned so far will be challenging, there are many other areas where AI solves unprecedented problems for data management and quality teams. The true value of large language models is their capability to understand

and (this is important) translate between languages. Language in this context is simply symbols that carry with them implicit meanings. Therefore, it is equally useful to use LLMs to interpret programming languages and spoken languages and to translate between them. Many AI vendors have made the promise of "natural language to coding," that is, translating from spoken languages like English into software. But we think that an equally powerful dynamic will occur—translating from programming languages back into human-readable language.

Codebases today have a myriad of technologies, legacy software, complex chains of function calls, and arbitrary decisions sometimes made across decades. Repos can contain hundreds of thousands or even millions of lines of code. It is impossible for the full context of those past decisions to be stored in anyone's head! However, just as a reasonably intelligent software engineer could examine a few dozen lines of code from a codebase they understand, so too could a large language model, when given proper context, provide contextual information about what certain code is doing, why it's probably doing it, and how developers in the data pipeline might react to it being changed. In addition, we are already seeing the industry centering on a standard, specifically the Model Context Protocol (MCP) (*https://oreil.ly/3fGwM*), that enables applications to provide LLMs context.

We believe this is the missing promise of data catalogs. While we have talked about the challenges with data catalogs elsewhere in this book, their core value to an analyst is their metadata *about* data. It is useful to know things like who has used a table, how frequently it is accessed, and how many rows are contained within it. But these are only proxies of what people really want to know about any dataset: "What does it mean?" Data alone cannot answer that. Data, ultimately, can only be represented as rows in a table, or an event, or a log, or a file. It says nothing about *where it came from*. Meaning, therefore, *cannot* be derived by looking at the data—it can only be captured from examining the code that produced and transformed it.

> If you want to learn more about data catalogs and managing metadata, we highly recommend the two following O'Reilly books by Ole Olesen-Bagneux:
>
> - *The Enterprise Data Catalog*
> - *Fundamentals of Metadata Management*
>
> Particularly, Ole touches on the same pain points we discussed in this book with respect to managing metadata across disparate systems.

While it might be challenging for a human being to trace the full path of data through an ecosystem, identify everywhere that data is transformed, and then extract enough context from many different sources and languages to impart meaning, this is exactly the type of work that artificial intelligence is so good at. In that way, we believe that the current era of the data catalog will come to an end, replaced by systems that can understand far more information, with much more valuable human relevance, capturing and describing the source of truth, at the moment of change.

The Future of Data Contracts

If we haven't made our opinion abundantly clear, the future of data is code. Code is where changes occur (internally or externally). The code contains context about our pipeline, transformations, and ingestion. AI systems will be producing code with frightening speed, which in turn will generate massive amounts of data (again, look into the Model Context Protocol). The complex web of code will continue to spiral into tech debt, and the data teams, as usual, will be struggling to stay above water. We believe that data contracts will come to our rescue.

While we could talk at length about the way we believe data management technology will shift left toward software engineering, or even how the quality feedback loop will combine looking at data and looking at the code that generated it, versus just one or the other, this book is about data contracts. And data contracts have one of the most important roles to play: human-validated expectations of the data we expect to see coming from any producer-and-transformation-based system.

Without a data contract, it is challenging to say which data is important and which isn't. Where is it acceptable for an AI to flub an answer, and where is it not? Where do we need to pay down our tech debt tomorrow, versus what can wait one more year? The data contract lays out the requirements of data consumers. It can provide the guardrail for an autonomous agent making changes in a complex engineering environment. It can provide the stopping points for impact analysis—if a contract exists, then the system should care about what happens at the next hop down the chain.

We also believe that what enters a data contract will increasingly move toward context extracted from code versus pure data rules. Will we need to define that we should always expect to see a string or a float? Or that age should always be greater than 0? Certainly. But it's equally as important to describe what we always expect the data to mean. "Revenue" should always be the result of a certain calculation. A user transaction date should always be a non-nullable field. A new feature should never meaningfully increase or decrease the number of records flowing into our analytics database. By defining the semantic needs of our data, we can account for what will be. Quality and testing will no longer be focused solely on the schema, but on the underlying meaning of how others interpret and work with data.

Additionally, we believe that the manual definition of data contracts will be an artifact of the 2020s. With information about the code, pipeline, and downstream expectations, contracts can be auto-generated as needed. These auto-generated contracts can also dynamically produce data pipelines without data engineer involvement. Standards can be applied to any contract being created, such as ensuring a unique ID and a date-time field are always present and formatted a certain way. The possibilities for utilizing data contracts in AI-driven development are enormous and varied.

Next Steps

While this is the end of the book, we argue that this is only the beginning of your data contract adoption journey. Throughout each chapter, we aimed to provide you with practical framings of why our industry needs data contracts, clear steps (along with code) to implement them, use cases of successful implementations at enterprises you can point to, and finally, a set of frameworks to make the cultural changes needed for both buy-in and wide adoption. Furthermore, we designed this book to serve as a reference you can go back to as you face various hurdles throughout your data contract journey. Ultimately, we aimed to document all the hard lessons we learned from implementing data contracts at various companies so that you can find success quicker.

Good luck!

Additional Resources

This book has an accompanying website (*http://data-contract-book.com*) that provides additional articles from the authors, as well as corresponding videos to guide your reading throughout the chapters. There is also a GitHub repository (*https://github.com/data-contract-book*) with a sandbox environment you can run locally or within a browser to see how to implement data contracts and the data contract violation workflow.

In additon, we recommend the further readings listed here by chapter.

Chapter 1

- Will Douglas Heaven, "The Open-Source AI Boom Is Built on Big Tech's Handouts. How Long Will It Last?" *MIT Technology Review,* May 12, 2023 (*https://oreil.ly/GM0j0*).
- Matt Turck, "The State of Big Data in 2014: A Chart," mattturck.com, May 11, 2014 (*https://oreil.ly/NtQ-k*).
- Matt Turck, "The 2023 MAD (Machine Learning, Artificial Intelligence & Data) Landscape," mattturck.com, February 21, 2023 (*https://mattturck.com/mad2023*).
- "A Chat with Andrew on MLOps: From Model-centric to Data-centric AI," by DeepLearning AI, YouTube, March 24, 2021 (*https://oreil.ly/e8TFz*).

Chapter 2

- Will Douglas Heaven, "The Open-Source AI Boom Is Built on Big Tech's Handouts. How Long Will It Last?" *MIT Technology Review,* May 12, 2023 (*https://oreil.ly/e8TFz*).

- "A Chat with Andrew on MLOps: From Model-centric to Data-centric AI," by DeepLearning AI, YouTube, March 24, 2021 (*https://oreil.ly/bqVXS*).

Chapter 3

- James Ivers et al., "Industry Experiences with Large-Scale Refactoring" in *Proceedings of the 30th ACM Joint European Software Engineering Conference and Symposium on the Foundations of Software Engineering* (ESEC/FSE 2022), Association for Computing Machinery (2022): 1544–1554 (*https://oreil.ly/ohJ_9*).
- James Ivers, "Scaling Refactoring," slide deck, presentation to Software Engineering Institute, Carnegie Mellon University, October 24, 2022 (*https://oreil.ly/0I8_9*).
- Emerson Murphy-Hill and Andrew P. Black, "Refactoring Tools: Fitness for Purpose," *IEEE Software* 25, no. 5 (2008): 38–44 (*https://oreil.ly/kCVgD*).
- Hyrum Wright, "Large-Scale Changes," Abseil (*https://oreil.ly/fV2gg*).
- Jennifer Reif, "Is This the End of Data Refactoring?" *The New Stack*, November 18, 2022 (*https://oreil.ly/9jerd*).
- Scott W. Ambler, "Database Refactoring: Fix Production Data Quality Problems at the Source," *Agile Data* (*https://oreil.ly/aR2t7*).
- Scott W. Ambler and Pramod J. Sadalage, *Refactoring Databases: Evolutionary Database Design* (O'Reilly, 2006).
- Chaïmaa Kadaoui, "What We Learned from a Large Refactoring," Alan Product and Technical Blog, *Medium*, January 12, 2022 (*https://oreil.ly/nFdrX*).

Chapter 5

- Eric Brewer, "CAP Twelve Years Later: How the 'Rules' Have Changed," *InfoQ*, May 30, 2012 (*https://oreil.ly/KUj_n*)
- David Dieruf, "Event Streaming and Event Sourcing: The Key Differences," *The New Stack*, September 1, 2022 (*https://oreil.ly/Gt69L*).
- Kislay Verma, "Domain Events Versus Change Data Capture," kislayverma.com, July 21, 2020 (*https://oreil.ly/xZtRi*).
- Martin Kleppmann, *Making Sense of Stream Processing* (O'Reilly, 2016).
- Chad Sanderson and Adrian Kreuziger, "An Engineer's Guide to Data Contracts: Pt. 2," *Data Products*, October 19, 2022 (*https://oreil.ly/Cc7HK*).

Chapter 9

- Fred Brooks, *The Mythical Man-Month: Essays on Software Engineering* (Addison-Wesley, 1975).

- Martin Doyle, "Why Data Should Be a Business Asset: The 1-10-100 Rule," *DQ Global*, February 8, 2024 (*https://oreil.ly/lOOu7*).

- Lili Duan, Emily Sheeren, and Leigh M. Weiss, "Tapping the Power of Hidden Influencers," McKinsey & Company, March 1, 2014 (*https://oreil.ly/xhKHY*).

- Andy Osmani, *Software Engineering: The Soft Parts*, self-published.

Chapter 11

- Shayma Alkobaisi et al., "Steel Threads: Software Engineering Constructs for Defining, Designing and Developing Software System Architecture," *Journal of Computational Methods in Sciences and Engineering* 12, no. s1 (2012): 63–77.

- David Thomas and Andrew Hunt, *The Pragmatic Programmer*, 2nd ed. (Addison-Wesley, 2019).

- John P. Kotter, *Leading Change* (Boston: Harvard Business Review Press, 2012).

- Zhamak Dehghani, *Data Mesh: Delivering Data-Driven Value at Scale* (O'Reilly, 2022).

Chapter 12

- Douglas W. Hubbard, *How to Measure Anything: Finding the Value of "Intangibles" in Business* (Hoboken, NJ: Wiley, 2010).

- Trevor Fox and Abhi Sivasailam, "Introducing Metric Trees," Levers Labs, updated April 8, 2024 (*https://oreil.ly/UlhUk*).

- "Designing & Building Metric Trees," Data Council, video, 27:46, YouTube, May 11, 2023 (*https://oreil.ly/4TdUS*).

- Joseph Campbell, *The Hero with a Thousand Faces* (Princeton, NJ: Princeton University Press, 1949).

Index

Symbols

B

measurement
    framework, 287-288
    repeatability, 291-292
    scalability, 293-294
    strategy, 288-289
    viability, 289-291
  metrics, 284
  need for, 39
  organizational readiness, 97
  outcomes, 101-102
  perception gap issues
    assumptions, 215-216
    real-world complexity, 216-219
  pushing to remote branch, 181-182
  scaling change management, 73-74
  Schema Registry, 130-132
  security, metadata, 166
  source code flow graphs, detecting contract
    violations, 142-146
  specification file, 168-170
  specifications, 122-125
  standardization, 241
  static code analysis, error detection, 146-148
  techniques to detect violations, 141-142
  technology-first implementation, chal-
    lenges, 240-241
  version control, 93, 149
  violation monitoring and alerts, 152
    applying by stakeholder, 153-155
    components, 155
    workflow, 156
  visibility of dependencies, 102
  workflow, 90
    steps, 90-94
  workflow components, 164-165
data debt, 5-7
  compared to tech debt, 6
  database migration
    business considerations, 65
    pitfalls, 63-64
  measuring data quality, 40-41
  organizational size, 8
  trustworthiness, 6
data developers, technical data consumers, 81
data development
  change management
    challenges, 54-56
    requirements, 58-60
  compared to software development, 49-53

    pre-development, 49
    workflow, 50-53
data discovery, 51-53
data downtime, measuring data quality, 42-43
data drift, 139
data engineers, 17, 81
  impacted by data quality, 45
data industry timeline, 32
data lakes, disadvantages, 16
data layer, change management challenges,
  84-86
data lifecycle
  data consumers, 82
  data contracts, implementation, 95-97
data lineage, 84
  data contracts, detecting violations, 142-146
data loss, database migration, 63
data management
  challenges, 4-5
  data debt, 5-7
data migration files
  reverting, 183
  updating, 178-180
data models, 12
data observability, compared to data contracts,
  102-104
data platform engineers, 82
data platform team, data contract implementation, 236
data producers
  data contracts, confirmation of viability, 92
  role, 79-80, 83
data product managers, data contract implementation, 236
data products, 98
  defining, selecting for contract proof of con-
    cept, 254-255
  steel threads, selecting for contract proof of
    concept, 255-257
  weighted decision matrix, contract proof of
    concept, 257-261
data profiling, 87
data quality
  ACID, 114
  analytics databases, 112
  change detection
    methods, 136-137
    quality issues, 137-138
  change management, 66

DuPont analysis, 284

E

early-stage startups, change management, 56
ELT (Extract, Load, and Transform), Fivetran, 18
end-to-end lineage, data contracts, detecting violations, 144-146
engagement plan, contract proof of concept, 262
entities
    cardinality, 12
    dimensions, 10
ERDs (entity relationship diagrams), data warehouses, 10-12
ETL (Extract, Transform, Load), data quarantining, 141
EVA (event-driven architecture), data contracts, 117-120
event sourcing, compared to event streams, 117-120
example data contract
    application architecture, 162
    contract definition, 168-170
    contract implementation, 164
    data assets, 166-167
    dataset, 160-162
    detection, 171-173
    prevention, 173-175
    project directory tree, 162-164
    scenario, 160
    violation scenario, 178-189
    violation workflow, 176-177
    workflow components, 164-165
executive leadership sponsorship, contract proof of concept, 267-269
expectations, measuring data quality, 43
Extract, Load, and Transform (ELT), Fivetran, 18
Extract, Transform, Load (ETL), data quarantining, 141

F

federated collaboration, 77
feedback, data contracts, 255
first-principles thinking, data contract adoption, 212
Fivetran, 18
floss refactoring, 60

foreign keys, ERDs (entity relationship diagrams), 11
forward-looking problems, data contract implementation, 239
friction, user experience, 240-241

G

garbage in, garbage out (GIGO) (see GIGO (garbage in, garbage out))
GDPR (General Data Protection Regulation), 65
    compliance, Adevinta Spain case study, 206
generative AI, data science workflows, commoditization, 27
GIGO (garbage in, garbage out), 4
    causes, 9
    data model complexity issues, 193
Git, version control, 150
GitHub, 232
    collaboration, 77
Glassdoor case study, shift left data practices, 196-200
gradual data drift, 68

H

historical detection, 137
hypothesis-led approach, data contract buy-in, 244
    issue analysis work plan, 248-249
    issue prioritization, 247-248
    problem statements, 245-246
    problem structure, 246-247

I

implementation, example data contract, 164
    contract definition, 168-170
    data assets, 166-167
    detection, 171-173
    prevention, 173-175
    violation scenario, 178-189
    violation workflow, 176-177
    workflow components, 164-165
incremental data drift, 68
institutional knowledge, loss of, 84
integrity, data quality, 138
invariants, transactions, 114-115
issue trees, change management, 246

S

SCA (static code analysis)
    error detection, 146-148
    Glassdoor case study, 197
scalability
    data, 239
    data contract measurements, 293
Schema Registry, 130-132
schema-based contracts, challenges, 240
SCQA framework, data contract buy-in, developing recommendations, 250-251
security
    DevSecOps, 226
    metadata, 166
shift left data
    future outlook, 305-307
    Glassdoor case study, 196-200
    importance of, 28
    maximizing benefits from, 227-228
    perception gaps
        between key parties, 215-216
        real-world complexity issues, 216-219
    preconditions to adoption, 212-214
    software engineers, measuring quality-of-life improvements, 224-225
    software-data gap, 220
        building trust, 220-222
        evidence-based approach, 222-223
        technology-forward approach, 223
shift left movement, xi
    DevSecOps, 225-227
single source of truth
    data warehouses, 10
    effect of microservices, 20
slide deck, gaining executive leadership approval, 268
small companies, change management need, 233
Snowflake, cloud-based database, 18
software development, compared to data development, 49-53
software engineering
    architectural specifications, 50
    change management, pull requests, 53-55
    data engineering, need for, 307
    pre-development, 49
    processes, 50
    requirements documents, 50
    technical specifications, 50

software engineers
    communication overhead, effect on efficiency, 214
    impacted by data quality, 46
    shift left data
        adoption considerations, 212-214
        measuring quality-of-life improvements, 224-225
software lifecycle, refactors
    assessing need, 60
    large scale, 60
    use case, 61-63
software teams, compared to data teams, 213
software, functionality compared to data functionality, 39
software-data gap, 220
    building trust, 220-222
    evidence-based approach, 222-223
    technology-forward approach, 223
source code flow graphs, detecting violations, 142-146
source data, 83
    data contract placement on, 236
staffing, issues with database migration, 64
stakeholders
    communication, data quality issues, 89
    consulting on data quality issues, 89
    contract proof of concept, identifying, 264-267
    data consumers, 81-83
    data producers, 79-80
    data quality issues, surfacing, 86
    role in change management, 59
standardization, data contracts, 241
static code analysis (SCA) (see SCA (static code analysis))
steel threads, identifying for contract proof of concept, 255-257
storytelling
    data contract adoption, 295-296
    and MVMT, data contract adoption, 298-300
stream processing, detecting violations, 141-142
streaming data, 117
    dead letter queues, 140
sudden data drift, 68
supply chains
    change management, 234

as data, 233-236

T

teams
    metrics, data contract impact, 281
    perception gap issues, 217-219
tech debt, compared to data debt, 6
technical data consumers, 81
technical metrics, data contract impact, 281
technical specifications, software engineering, 50
technical viability, 238
technology-first implementations, challenges, 240-241
third-normalized form (3NF), 35
ticket volume, measuring improvements, 224
timeliness, data quality, 138
timing, role in change management, 59
tracer bullets, 255
trailing indicators, 40
transactional databases, 113-116
transactional events, 79-80
transactions
    invariants, 114-115
    OLTP databases, 34-36
transformation, storytelling for data contract adoption, 296, 297-298
transformations, 7
    (see also data transformations)
    analytics databases, 113
trustworthiness
    data debt, 6
    measuring data quality, 41-42
    obstacles to, 21

U

uniqueness, data quality, 138
unit testing, 180-181, 186-189
use cases
    data warehouses, 12
    discussing with downstream team, 183-184
    refactoring code, 61-63
user experience, friction, 240-241

V

validity, data quality, 137
venture capitalists, funding model, 19-20
version control, 76
    change management, 53
    data contract code, 93
    data contract error prevention, 149
    GitHub, 77
viability, data contract measurements, 289-291
violation monitoring and alerts, data contract error prevention, 152
    applying by stakeholder, 153-155
    components, 155
    workflow, 156
visibility, data contracts, 242-243

W

WAP (write-audit-publish) pattern
    detecting data contract violations, 141
    Glassdoor case study, 197
weighted decision matrix, contract proof of concept, 257-261
workflows
    components, example data contract, 164-165
    data contract violations, 176-177
    data contracts, 90
        first-party data on third-party platforms, 121-122
        steps, 90-94
    data development, 50-53
    data science, trend of commoditization, 26-27
    data, compared to supply chains, 234
    software engineering, 50
    technical data consumers, 83
write-audit-publish (WAP) pattern (see WAP (write-audit-publish) pattern)

Y

YAML (Yet Another Markup Language), 18

About the Authors

Chad Sanderson is one of the most well-known and prolific writers and speakers on data contracts. He is passionate about data quality and fixing the muddy relationship between data producers and consumers. He is a former head of data at Convoy, a LinkedIn writer, and a published author. Chad created the first implementation of data contracts at scale during his time at Convoy, and also created the first engineering guide to deploying contracts in streaming, batch, and even oriented environments. He lives in Seattle, Washington, and operates the Data Quality Camp Slack group and the *Data Products* newsletter, both of which focus on data contracts and their technical implementation.

Mark Freeman is a community health advocate turned data engineer interested in the intersection of social impact, business, and technology. His life's mission is to improve the well-being of as many people as possible through data. Mark received his M.S. from the Stanford School of Medicine and is also certified in entrepreneurship and innovation from the Stanford Graduate School of Business. In addition, Mark has worked within numerous startups where he has put machine learning models into production, integrated data analytics into products, and led migrations to improve data infrastructure.

B.E. Schmidt is a lifelong Midwesterner, a former creative director, and a writer with nearly two decades of experience in advertising, content marketing, and digital strategy.

Colophon

The animal on the cover of *Data Contracts* is an Algerian keeled sand racer lizard (*Psammodromus algirus*). It is native to North Africa, as you might have guessed, as well as Southwestern Europe—it's the most common lizard on the Iberian Peninsula. Psammodromus (pronounced sam-uh-DROM-us) algirus inhabits a wide variety of environments, from coastal shoreland to temperate mountain forests.

Psammodromus algirus has yellowish lateral stripes, a long tail, and overlapping *keeled* scales, meaning ridged down the center. Males exhibit color differentiation during mating seasons—reddish heads or yellow throats, depending on the subspecies (there's debate about the taxonomy). Females and adolescents often display orange on their tails and hind legs. When threatened, these sand racers burrow in the ground.

Psammodromus algirus faces habitat loss, but still rates an IUCN conservation status of Least Concern. Many of the animals on O'Reilly covers are endangered; all of them are important to the world.

The cover illustration is by Karen Montgomery, based on antique line engraving from *Lydekker's Royal Natural History*. The series design is by Edie Freedman, Ellie Volckhausen, and Karen Montgomery. The cover fonts are Gilroy Semibold and Guardian Sans. The text font is Adobe Minion Pro; the heading font is Adobe Myriad Condensed; and the code font is Dalton Maag's Ubuntu Mono.

O'REILLY®

Learn from experts.
Become one yourself.

60,000+ titles | Live events with experts | Role-based courses
Interactive learning | Certification preparation

**Try the O'Reilly learning platform
free for 10 days.**

www.ingramcontent.com/pod-product-compliance
Lightning Source LLC
Chambersburg PA
CBHW080913220326
41598CB00034B/5558